More Praise for *Power Failure*

"After all the news coverage, the books, even a clumsy TV movie, what's left to say about Enron? [*Power Failure*] provides the one thing that has been missing: in-the-room insights into the cynicism, backstabbing, and moral rot of the key players . . . Illuminate(s) the personalities that drove the company to ruin." —*Houston Chronicle*

"A frank, behind-the-scenes look at Enron . . . Captures something most previous books haven't: the female perspective." —*Rocky Mountain News*

"Filled with fascinating miniprofiles of top executives . . . Delivers just enough tidbits about the strip clubs, fast cars, and office romances that marked Enron's 'best and brightest corporate culture.'" —*Dallas Morning News*

"Thorough reporting and brisk writing." —*People* magazine

"Should be required reading in college business ethics classes." —*Albany Times Union*

"Ex-Enron accountant throws the book at 'em." —*Charlotte Observer*

"Eminently readable." —*Long Island Newsday*

"Quite touching and real." —*Independent on Sunday* (London)

"A stunning job of chronicling the power games within Enron." —*Publishers Weekly*

POWER FAILURE

The Inside Story of the Collapse of ENRON

Mimi Swartz

with

Sherron Watkins

CURRENCY

DOUBLEDAY

New York London Toronto Sydney Auckland

A CURRENCY BOOK
PUBLISHED BY DOUBLEDAY
a division of Random House, Inc.

CURRENCY is a trademark of Random House, Inc., and
DOUBLEDAY is a registered trademark of Random House, Inc.

POWER FAILURE was originally published by Doubleday in March 2003.

All photographs, unless otherwise credited, are from Sherron Watkins's collection.

Book design by Tina Thompson

The Library of Congress has cataloged the hardcover edition as follows:

Swartz, Mimi.
Power failure : the inside story of the collapse of Enron / Mimi Swartz with Sherron Watkins. — 1st ed
p. cm.
Includes index.
1. Enron Corp. 2. Energy industries—Corrupt practices—United States. 3. Arthur Andersen & Co.
4. Accounting firms—Corrupt practices—United States. 5. Business failures—United States—
Case studies. I. Title. Inside story of the collapse of Enron. II. Watkins, Sherron. III. Title.

ISBN 0-7679-1368-X
PRINTED IN THE UNITED STATES OF AMERICA

First Edition: March 2003
First Currency Paperback Edition: April 2004

SPECIAL SALES
Currency Books are available at special discounts for bulk purchases for sales promotions or
premiums. Special editions, including personalized covers, excerpts of existing books, and
corporate imprints can be created in large quantities for special needs. For more information,
write to Special Markets, Currency Books, specialmarkets@randomhouse.com

1 3 5 7 9 10 8 6 4 2

To my mother and father, husband and son.
—Mimi Swartz

*To the memory of Arthur Andersen, the man, who established
a firm and a culture that taught me in the formative years of my career
that public accountants owe their allegiance to the investors in
corporate America, not the companies themselves.*

*Second, To the smart, hard-working employees at Enron who for
so many years made Enron fun, and for me, a great place to work.*
—Sherron Watkins

Contents

Contents

Timeline: The
Changing Faces of Enron

1985   InterNorth Inc. and Houston Natural Gas Corp. (HNG) merge to form the largest natural-gas pipeline company in America.

1986   CEO Ken Lay christens the new company the Enron Corporation. *Enron's vision:* To become the premier natural-gas pipeline in North America.

1989   Enron forms a new trading division known as the Gas Bank, run by CEO Jeff Skilling.

1990   The Gas Bank becomes Enron Finance Corp. and Enron Gas Services.
        Enron's vision: To become the world's first natural-gas major.

1991   Rebecca Mark becomes Chairman and CEO of Enron Development Corp., a unit formed to pursue international markets.

1995   Skilling's division is renamed Enron Capital & Trade Resources.
        Enron's vision: To become the world's leading energy company.

1997   Skilling becomes the COO of Enron Corp. Enron Capital & Trade Resources becomes Enron Wholesale Services.
        Enron Energy Services is created to focus on retail energy business.
        Enron Development Corp. becomes Enron International.

1998   Enron Corp. creates Azurix, a water company. Rebecca Mark leaves Enron International to be its CEO.

1999   Enron creates a new broadband unit, Enron Broadband Services.
        Enron Online is launched and becomes the largest e-commerce site in the world.
        Jeff Skilling disbands Enron International.

2001   Jeff Skilling becomes CEO of Enron Corp.

Enron's vision: To become the World's Leading Company.

Note: Enron Oil & Gas and Enron's pipeline companies never changed their names throughout the history of the company.

Preface

Put Me in Enron!

FOR as far back as anyone could remember—since 1958, when he'd started his firm—the old-money families in Houston had referred to Fayez Sarofim by his first name only, as if he were a secret they all shared. These were the families whose wealth dated back to cattle and cotton and timber, but more important, they were the families who had made their money in oil early, in the first twenty years of the twentieth century. To them, the enigmatic Egyptian with the flawless manners, the impeccably tailored suits, and the modern art collection—Robert Motherwell, Willem de Kooning, Christo—was someone to be respected and revered. They admired his taste in general—Sarofim always seemed to know what was new and best before they did—but mostly they admired his taste in money. Families who had made their fortunes in oil knew just how volatile the business was—how quickly prosperity could vanish through carelessness, capriciousness, and arrogance—and so depended on Sarofim and his investment firm, which managed more than $40 billion in assets, for stability.

He was a man for whom consistency was a daily practice. Throughout 2001, for instance, Sarofim ate his workday lunch with the same woman (his secretary, Mrs. White), at the same club (the Coronado, inside the old Bank of the Southwest building), at the same table (adjacent to the giant television screen tuned routinely to CNBC's market reports). He was neither handsome nor particularly unhandsome—in late middle age, he was balding and portly, his eyes and lips were narrow, and he wore glasses with heavy, square frames. Like many prominent Houstonians, Sarofim had endured some volatility in his personal portfolio: His $250 million divorce from Louisa

Stude, an heiress to one of Houston's great fortunes, had made news; so had the revelation of his semisecret life, the requisite parallel Texas family that included mistress, child, and so on. But Sarofim rarely spoke to the press—his lawyers advised against it—and the stories faded and he returned soon enough to his life of carefully crafted obscurity. "Nervous energy is a great destroyer of wealth," Sarofim liked to say, and he lived by those words.

He detested risky investments. His firm's philosophy, the one that enabled it to outperform the Standard and Poor's Index in eleven of the past fourteen years, was as follows: "We believe that long-term stock price appreciation is based on long-term earnings growth. Sustainable earnings growth is predicated on dominance in an attractive industry. Dominant businesses usually reside in large companies that can produce superior earnings growth and market leadership over long periods of time." In 1993, *The New York Times* called Sarofim "A Top Financier with a Passion for Brand Names." In 1997, *Barron's* called him a "Brand-Name Champion." He liked Johnson & Johnson. He liked Procter & Gamble. He liked General Electric and Coca-Cola.

But in the late 1990s, something happened to Sarofim's loyal clientele. The bull market was raging, and they wanted him to invest their money in a company called Enron. Enron was then the World's Leading Energy Company, by its own account and everyone else's. Its glossy annual reports showed earnings in the hundreds of millions, and those earnings grew by almost 20 percent every year. From 1998 to 2000, the stock price bounded from around $20 a share to close to $90 a share. And better yet, it was a Houston company. The old-money crowd was very taken with Enron's CEO, Ken Lay—they worked with him to raise money for the United Way and the Houston Museum of Fine Arts; they drew up Houston's future alongside him at the Greater Houston Partnership and the River Oaks Country Club. Ken Lay was a good man, they insisted; he knew what he was doing.

Buy Enron! Put me in Enron! It was like a fever that, if Sarofim had been in Houston in the oil-crazed 1920s, might have seemed familiar. But Sarofim was immune to such entreaties—*Nervous energy is a great destroyer of wealth!*—and he would refuse. His explanation was very simple: "I can't understand their balance sheets," he said.

Grumbling, his clients would listen, nod their heads, and retreat. But they were sure they were losing out on the deal of the century, and so would call again and demand the stock—*Buy Enron! Put me in Enron!*—and again Sarofim, in that soft, calm, resolute voice, would refuse. He didn't put his clients in anything he didn't invest in himself, and he wasn't investing in Enron.

He made them mad. Fayez was getting old, the children and grandchildren and great-grandchildren of the wildcatters complained. Fayez couldn't see the future when it was staring him in the face. He was mired in the past, too damned old-fashioned. Fayez, they said, just doesn't get it.

POWER FAILURE

1

Winners and Losers

S HERRON Watkins went to the Enron Corporation's November management conference for the year 2000 determined she wouldn't be taken for a loser. The year before, at her first such meeting after being promoted to vice president, she had blown it. Booked into the Hill Country Hyatt and Resort for three days of corporate team building, she had opted, in the recreational hours, for the company-sponsored salsa-making class. At affairs such as these, where Enron took over the entire hotel and offered an array of afternoon networking and socializing activities, it was important to pick one that advanced your career. A smart, ambitious employee would never sign up for the afternoon of fly-fishing, for instance, because you couldn't lose the smell of fish in time for the evening cocktail party, and because you could wind up wasting your afternoon with guys who worked in the once crucial but now irrelevant pipeline division. That left, as career-building activities, skeet shooting, the Road Rally, tennis, golf, facials, pedicures, outlet shopping, and antiquing in a nearby Hill Country town.

To understand the loaded nature of the choices, you had to understand the loaded nature of life at Enron. Salsa making, for instance, had turned out to be a disaster. One of the small hotel conference rooms had been converted into a kitchen for the occasion; Sherron had entered straight from her facial, without makeup, without combing her hair, and she was chopping jalapeños with three pipeline guys—middle-aged men shaped like bumpy Bosc pears—when the then COO, soon to be CEO, Jeff Skilling, had walked in. Or, rather, he'd poked his head into the room, narrowed his eyes, and raised his peaked nose, as if to test the air. It had not pleased him. At just that moment, he'd caught sight of her. "Uh, hi, Sherron," Skilling had said, and then, *whoosh*, he was gone. In his wake, Sherron found herself enveloped in that uniquely Enronian sense of dread: She knew she'd been caught with a bunch of losers, far, far away from Skilling's winning team.

Once, the pipeline guys had mattered, but that was long ago. In the 1980s, Enron was one of the largest pipeline companies in North America, moving natural gas from the Gulf Coast to the East Coast, the West Coast, the Midwest, and beyond. But as Jeff Skilling's influence over CEO Ken Lay grew, Enron changed identities several times. It always positioned itself as the company of Vision, but it supplemented its base. In the late eighties and early nineties, Enron revolutionized the way natural gas was bought and sold by operating more like a finance company than a gas company. In the mid-nineties, Enron started selling and trading power, battling across the country to deregulate entrenched electric utilities.

Lately, with the boom in dot-com and high-tech companies, Enron was vigorously morphing into an Internet/telecommunications conglomerate. Enron Online, the company's online trading platform, was already the largest e-commerce site in the world, and now "Broadband" was the new buzzword inside the company. Enron was gearing up to trade space available on high-speed telephone lines in order to deliver movies and more into private homes over its Enron Intelligent Network, a new and improved Internet. It was poised to dominate AT&T and all the other behemoths. This corporate shape shifting made Enron seem, to Wall Street, less like an IBM or an Exxon and more like the poster child for the New Economy, a business so fast-paced, so protean, and so forward-looking that it could change its stripes, virtually overnight, to suit the zeitgeist. So if you wanted to get ahead at Enron, you had to be able to change, too.

Sherron, for instance, had successfully engineered herself into the hottest sector of the company, Broadband. Broadband was the reason Wall Street analysts were deliriously touting Enron—after the company rolled out its telecom plans at an analysts' meeting in January, Enron's stock moved thirteen points in one day. Broadband proved yet again that Enron's employees were the smartest, the shrewdest, the most dedicated and ambitious on the planet.

They were purveyors not of products but of ideas, of what Jeff Skilling called "intellectual capital." A company didn't need bricks and mortar to triumph in the new age. It needed smarts—smarts that, as Skilling liked to claim, would propel Enron from its old role as the World's Leading Energy company to its destiny as the World's Leading Company. So far, Enron's numbers were on track to do just that: to land Enron in the top ten of the Fortune 500. Third-quarter revenues had grown over 150 percent from the prior year's corresponding quarter to $30 billion, bringing total revenues for the first nine months of 2000 to $60 billion—up $20 billion from 1999. The company's stock had quadrupled in value since January 1998 to almost $90 a share. In just five years, Enron grew to rival 1990s tech giants like Cisco and Microsoft, and behemoths like GE. It was a media darling: *Fortune* magazine hailed Enron as the country's most innovative company for five years in a row, and included Enron in the top quarter of its list of the "Best 100 Companies to Work for in America." Skilling was widely regarded as the most brilliant corporate leader in the country, a Jack Welch for the new millennium. CEO Ken Lay had laid the groundwork for Enron's global reach: He could get virtually any world leader from China to Costa Rica to return his phone calls in an instant; he counted among his closest friends powerful state legislators, entrenched members of the U.S. Congress, current and former presidents. Everywhere Sherron Watkins looked, there were bright young people who had made revolutionary changes and made incomprehensible fortunes in return—and all before getting close to their fortieth birthdays.

Enron was, in short, a company of winners. At the dawn of the twenty-first century, those who were bright, young, and fiscally ambitious were reassessing their career choices. They could slave away in some fusty commercial bank or corporation for years at a salary in the high five figures. Or they could join a Wall Street investment bank, where they could make a lot of money but never really create anything of value. Silicon Valley was great, but it was overrun. And then there was Enron. Those who packed their bags and raced to Houston were the ones who wanted to run their own show right away—by the time they were twenty-five, salary commensurate with their genius.

Certainly Enron had worked for Sherron Watkins. She grew up northwest of Houston, in the small town of Tomball, which had its moment in the sun during the oil boom of the 1920s. There were drilling rigs inside the city limits when Sherron was a girl, sharing a small two-bedroom house with her divorced mother and younger sister. Her mother, Shirley, taught business at a nearby high school, and encouraged Sherron to go into accounting. It was secure, something she could build a career on. Sherron took her advice, graduating from the University of Texas with honors, and getting a master's in accounting in 1982. Arthur Andersen had recruited her, promoted her to audit manager within five years, and, at her request, shipped her off to the New York office in 1987. From Andersen, Sherron worked briefly in a Manhattan commodity finance boutique, then in 1993 followed the well-trod path from the offices of Andersen to those of its biggest client, Enron.

She could hardly believe her luck when she was hired—the trips on the corporate jet to schmooze California investors, ski jaunts with bankers in Colorado, sales trips to the UK, South Africa, Chile, Peru, Panama, the Philippines, and Korea, helping to expand Enron's energy markets—or, as she imagined, bringing cheaper, cleaner power to people who desperately needed it. For her efforts, Sherron, whose mother pinched pennies, had been richly rewarded by any standards other than Enron's own: From a starting salary of $95,000, she was now clearing $150,000, along with stock options and bonuses that more than doubled her income. She owned a home in one of Houston's best neighborhoods, and never had to ask for the right tools to get the job done: Enron gave her the laptop, the Palm Pilot, the cell phone, the business-class tickets, the ergonomic desk and office chair, and the assistant who did not have to be told where to book dinner or hotel reservations in London.

Even though she had been at Enron since 1993, she was still amazed by the high-end toys parked in the company garage, the dizzying array of BMW sedans, Porsche convertibles, Ferraris, Mercedeses, Range Rovers, and customized SUVs. She loved Enron's oval-shaped tower of mirrored glass, with its twin tower rising across the street; the purposeful people from all over the world scurrying across the lobby's glossy granite floor to get to their desks *faster*; the brightly colored ceiling banners heralding employees' commitment to Enron's "Vision and Values": Respect! Integrity! Communication! Excellence! The lobby's twelve-foot, multiscreen television reported perpetual NYSE, NYMEX, and Enron Online updates, as did the miniscreens in the elevators. The company café featured spring rolls and gourmet wraps. The coffee bar featured custom lattes and mochas; mini-massages were available in the company gym. It was almost, but not quite, too much: If you deserved all this, you knew you were very, very important.

Of course, there was a downside. It wasn't easy being the company of the future; Enron was constantly reorganizing to stay ahead of the pack, and a lot of people just couldn't cut it. Maybe employee X couldn't close a multi-million-dollar deal within the requisite six months. Or maybe Employee Y got crosswise with a higher-up—he wouldn't give up credit to his boss. Or maybe Employee Z, for some reason—parenthood, a change in circumstances at home, et cetera—resisted the sixteen-hour workdays, the eighty-hour workweeks, or the trips to places like Clifton, Kansas, or Calcutta. He would lose faith that he was creating the future through his association with Enron. And then he would stumble, and soon enough, he'd be branded a *loser*. Too lazy, or too obstructive, or worse, just not smart enough. And then, almost as ephemerally as it had begun, the employee's career at Enron would draw to a close. No more lunches of gently poached sea bass at Houston's best seafood trattoria, no sirloins at Houston's hippest steakhouse, no more top-of-the-line Cuban cigars; goodbye to the silver Porsche Boxster, the 5,000-square-foot mini-mansion, and the summer house in Santa Fe. Employee X, Y, or Z would pack up his dreams like he packed up his desk, while former colleagues froze him out and a guard waited to escort him from the building.

All this Sherron had sidestepped for seven careful years, maneuvering herself into four different jobs, the descriptions of which would have stumped most Ph.D.'s. In Broadband she "developed the critical processes, systems, and procedures for the global network services group to enable complex network element asset management and pricing." At Enron International, the company's foreign development arm, she expanded "Enron's international metals and mining strategy aimed at bringing Enron's core competencies of power asset development, energy price risk management, physical trading, and merchant finance to the energy-intensive mining sector." Before that, working in the finance group at Enron Capital & Trade Resources, she was "responsible for the off-balance-sheet investment vehicles of Enron." In English, this all meant that Sherron had parlayed her background in accounting into one job as a portfolio manager for various multimillion-dollar funds, another job where she wined and dined bankers to keep loans flowing, and another job where she traveled the world to drum up new clients for Enron's international energy division. But every time she got comfortable, mastering the position and the attendant politics, she'd get word that a reorganization was in the works and she'd have to start all over again. She knew from office gossip, in fact, that her boss at Broadband was on the way out. If Sherron wasn't careful, she would be too.

B y the time the sun set on the Hill Country Hyatt, Enron's executives had secured the hotel and set up central command in the bar. The occupying army was mostly young—average age at Enron was around thirty—mostly male, and dressed in weathered-but-not-too-weathered khakis and tired-but-not-too-tired golf shirts, the studiedly casual uniform favored by young, upwardly mobile rich guys. Crammed against each other in the bar, they were well on their way to getting extravagantly drunk, stoking themselves up on free drinks and their own spectacular accomplishments. Charley's Long Bar was outfitted as a Wild West saloon, and the guests, who usually had little use for history, seemed very comfortable in gunslinger mode. Some were Texans, but many were not; lots had come from small towns in the Midwest and appeared, from a distance, eager, apple-cheeked, almost boyish. Others came from India or Pakistan, England or South America. But wherever they were from, they were all obviously hungry, restless, and tightly wound. You could see it in the way they slugged back their

6

drinks or geared up for the poker game later that evening, the one with $1,000 stakes.

The mood had been more somber the year before, because Enron had not been doing quite so well. The stock price had split near $80 a share, in hopes that a $40 price would attract more investors. It hadn't. Instead the stock dipped to $39—and then parked itself there. Wall Street's analysts had grown restive, and so, in turn, had Jeff Skilling. He turned the 1999 management conference into a grim tutorial on "growing earnings" or, in layman's terms, boosting profits. Despite the free food and the glistening chandeliers, the Hyatt's ballroom felt like a reeducation camp, as every speaker stressed the new corporate dogma, which was that Enron's hard assets could no longer be depended upon to keep the stock price rising at Skilling's desired rate of 20 percent a year, an expectation that, before the days of the raging bull market, would have seemed, well, nuts. Enron's mandate was to become more nimble, more flexible, more innovative—or else. The speakers, one from the oracle-of-the-moment consulting firm of McKinsey & Co. (Skilling had been its youngest partner ever), as well as a few investment bankers, had droned on about that mission for hours, stressing the need for "return on invested capital," meaning, simply, that money spent by the company should return ever-larger profits. Most of that day, Skilling prowled the perimeter of the ballroom, making sure his acolytes were, in his words, "getting it": accepting the fact that pipelines and power plants, once Enron's bread and butter, would no longer keep the company where it deserved to be, rated with the Microsofts, Ciscos, and Intels of the world. Enron needed new ideas. Now.

The only break in the tedium that year came from Samuel J. Palmisano, then IBM's COO. Palmisano was a touchy-feely guy: a big, burly Italian who paced the stage as he spoke. But his message had been somber too: Palmisano confessed that IBM, mired in its old identity, missed the boat on computer software. The company had to come up with a new idea almost overnight, and though it did so—reemerging as an Internet solutions consulting firm—Palmisano admitted that IBM's stock price had not yet recovered. IBM was going to miss earnings targets that quarter, he confessed. Suddenly, it was all too much for Palmisano. His eyes began to fill, and then his voice quavered. And then he had to stop talking. Everyone could see that he was trying not to cry.

The guys in khakis and golf shirts began to stare at the floor and shift uneasily in their upholstered dining chairs. When they looked at one another, they could see, reflected, a sharp, embarrassed panic. So, naturally, when Palmisano finished and apologized for his emotional display—he'd been through so much with IBM, he explained, he loved it like his family— they leapt to their feet and gave him a long, lusty ovation. They waited until the evening cocktail party to stick it to him: "Did you see that?" they asked, elbowing each other in the ribs. "The guy cried! He *cried!*" Behind Palmisano's back, they were cracking up; he was just another . . . *loser!* If Sherron Watkins or anyone else wondered that day why Enron never seemed to miss *its* earnings targets, they didn't have the time or inclination to pursue the question. Introspection, on a personal or professional level, was not an activity highly valued at Enron.

Now, a year later, Sherron Watkins had other things on her mind, like keeping her job, which at that moment meant navigating the perils of the November 2000 Management Conference. She wasn't good enough at tennis or golf to sign up for those events—she could cost the team a victory, which could, in turn, cost her. Skeet shooting: Growing up in Tomball, Sherron had learned how to fire a shotgun; she knew it beat the hell out of your shoulder. No thanks. There was the Road Rally through the nearby Hill Country: Ken Rice, at forty an old hand with the company, had brought a few of his Ferraris to compete. Since Rice was the head of Broadband, the race was probably Sherron's smartest political move. But the idea of getting in a fast car with a testosterone-crazed trader—some guy with questionable judgment and a perpetual hard-on—did not appeal to her either. Outlet shopping was too cheesy. That left antique shopping, dull but safe. Sherron could burnish her prospects by going with a group from Broadband.

She never used to care about such things. When Sherron worked in Manhattan in her twenties, she was one of those strapping, blond, good-humored Texas girls whose laugh could fill a room and who could drink her dates under the table. Guys fought to give her rides back to the city on their private planes after weekends in the Hamptons. But now she was forty-one, married to a fellow Texan who was not a Wall Street financier, and they had a one-year-old daughter. Sherron was still a blonde, but not the kind of sultry, Enron blonde who got ahead. She was carrying some twenty postpregnancy pounds and had a reputation as a bull in a china shop—The Buzzsaw, they called her, because she was stubborn, didn't suffer fools, and after six years in Manhattan, used terms like "circle jerk" and "dickweed" reflexively. Worse, in a company that made no secret of its preference for Ivy Leaguers, Sherron had a degree from the University of Texas. She was, in short, a practical, pragmatic, middle-aged woman at a novelty-worshiping, image-conscious company that revered youth. Sherron was feeling pretty vulnerable, especially after she stepped out onto a balcony to get some air and almost collided with Kevin Hannon, the dour chief operating officer of Broadband, who was deep in conversation with two other executives, neither of whom was smiling. Hannon looked peeved. "Not now, Sherron," he said, as if scolding a puppy.

She wandered inside, toward the Mexican buffet. Filling her plate, Sherron felt someone at her elbow. "Want to sit together?" It was Andy Fastow, Enron's CFO, who had been her boss at Enron's Capital and Trade Division, where she had managed funds for various companies in partnership with Enron. On the subject of Fastow, Sherron was ambivalent. He had made her laugh, but he'd also asked her do some things that had made her uncomfortable. After a few years she'd had enough, and transferred to Enron International. But in her current situation Fastow looked pretty good. He wasn't exactly popular at Enron—he had evolved into a brat and a bully, famous for his tantrums—but he was a Skilling favorite, and therefore untouchable. Tonight, he was beaming like a Buddha. It took Fastow eight years to land the CFO's job, one he had coveted with single-minded intensity. He was now almost forty and his once dark hair was prematurely streaked with silver, but like so many people at Enron, he seemed perpetually young. His step was bouncy, his eyes twinkled, and his grin was wide, though whether it promised something benign or malignant was anybody's guess.

Unlike many other Enron executives, Sherron had never been afraid of Fastow, and in her vulnerable state, sitting with him boosted her value, as the heads swiveling in their direction indicated. The two of them took seats at a round table of Enron blondes, tall, striking women with sharp suits, glittering jewelry, and big hair swept off their faces, the contingent from Human Resources and Public Relations. Fastow ignored them and nudged

Sherron. "When are you going to come back and work for me?" he asked. Before she could conjure an answer, they were distracted.

The evening's entertainment was an auction for the navigator's seat in Ken Rice's Ferrari during the Road Rally the next day. The proceeds would go to charity. Rice stood and took a bow, introducing himself to a crowd that knew him well. He had joined Enron before it was Enron; Rice had worked at the Omaha pipeline company that merged with the Houston pipeline company to create it. He was farm-boy handsome, with blue eyes and a sly smile. He could afford to be carefree: Rice was running the hippest unit at the company and vacationed with Skilling. Rice was also a ladies' man, so riding with him afforded unique opportunities for professional advancement, which, in Enron terms, made him a perfect fund-raising tool.

A few people threw out some joke bids—$100 here, $150 there. The head of Human Resources, Cindy Olson, bid once. Louise Kitchen, the creator of Enron Online, upped the ante in her British accent. Then, from the back of the room, came a familiar, distinctly southern drawl: "One thousand dollars."

Necks craned and heads bobbed until the high bidder was located: It was the guy in charge of Broadband's NOCC—Network Operations Control Center; he was known around Enron as the NOCC—pronounced "Knock"—Doc. When something went wrong with video feeds or downloads, for example, the NOCC Doc was supposed to fix the problem. But that never seemed to happen. It was assumed that the problems weren't getting fixed because the NOCC Doc was in over his head. The standing joke at Enron Broadband was "Knock, NOCC. Who's there? No one!" The NOCC Doc was bearded, laconic, and overweight—he didn't really fit in. So everyone figured his $1,000 bid was a ploy to save his job. Ditto the $500 he added. And the next $500 used to knock some Enron babe, anxious for a few hours of personal time with the Broadband chief, out of the bidding.

"Sold—at $2,000!" Ken Rice, arms folded, looked irked.

At 7:40 the next morning, Ken Lay, founder and longtime CEO of Enron, gave the formal welcome. Even though he, too, was dressed casually, his casual—pressed jeans and a crisp white button-down shirt—

was still a little starchy, an ensemble from another time. He was fifty-eight, which was nearly elderly at Enron, and his audience treated him that way — respectfully, but just a little restively. Lay had been playing the gentle sage to Skilling's samurai for years; a balding, somewhat jowly man of average build, he spoke with a sharp midwestern twang and lately had sometimes seemed too folksy for the sleek, sharklike company he had created. Maybe he knew that, because for the last few months Lay had been orchestrating his exit. Clinton was leaving the White House, and Lay's enormous, long-term investment in the Bush family was about to pay off again. (Lay didn't wonder, in November 2000, who really won the deeply contested presidential election. He was an indefatigable optimist, and a major donor to the Republican party.)

Lay had succeeded beyond his wildest dreams. He was worshiped in Houston both as a political kingmaker and for his philanthropy. His was the classic American success story: He had triumphed over childhood poverty, a bad stutter, an antiquated, regulated business, and enough financial setbacks to kill most companies. And now, in late middle age, he was ready to let go. He had already anointed Skilling as his successor. If he didn't join the Bush administration, maybe he would run for mayor of Houston. Whatever he did, it would be big. But on this particular morning Lay was focused solely on Enron. "Our future has never looked rosier," he told his many heirs. Enron was in businesses today it had not been in just five years earlier; he hoped that in ten years Enron would find more new business worlds to invent and dominate. At Enron it was always the future that mattered: inventing it, shaping it, ruling it.

The ashen, hung-over executives applauded politely. They'd heard this before.

And so it went for the next several hours. The editor of the hip *Red Herring* magazine extolled the glories of the Internet, followed by a pep talk from Gary Hamel, a stylishly shabby Harvard professor and the author of the best-selling *Leading the Revolution*, in which he championed the corporate innovators of the late nineties, especially Enron. "It pays to hire the best," Hamel said of the company. "You can't build a forever restless, opportunity-seeking company unless you're willing to hire forever restless, opportunity-seeking individuals." That Hamel was also a paid adviser to Enron didn't seem to bother anyone in the crowd. He was a Harvard professor, after all, and behavior that would once have been characterized as a conflict of interest was, by the late nineties, simply viewed as synergistic.

Finally, Skilling took the podium, and the enthusiasm in the room contracted noticeably. Skilling, like Lay, was small in stature. (In fact, almost everyone who got ahead at Enron was short.) But where Lay was soft and self-assuredly self-deprecating—almost Sunday schoolish—Skilling was sharp and cool. He was dressed casually, almost carelessly, like his troops, and he wore his hair combed off his face in the style of Hollywood producers and Wall Street financiers. He was assiduously fit; his eyes were ice blue and his gaze was steady, and he spoke in clipped, flat, supremely confident tones. Everyone at Enron knew that Jeff was twice as smart as they were—twice as smart as they could ever hope to be—and they hung on every word. It was Skilling who had made the revenues grow from $4 billion to more than $60 billion, an increase of nearly 2,000 percent. It was Skilling who had made the stock price ascend to the heavens. So it was Skilling who made Enron's troops frantic to live in fast-forward mode, who made them anxious to prove that they could deliver any concept he could dream up, who made them desperate to tag along on his extreme adventures—rock climbing, bungee jumping—around the globe. Because if Jeff Skilling thought you "got it," you really did.

Skilling's appearance onstage signaled the arrival of an annual event: his stock-price prediction. In years past he had been on the money—Enron had gone from $40 to $60 a share in 1998, and soared to $80 in 1999. Now he stood before his faithful and bowed his head, as if he had to think about what he had to say. When he looked at the crowd again, he was beaming. Enron stock, he told them, would hit $126 a share in 2001. There was just a second of stunned silence before the crowd burst into applause. No one quite knew how the stock was going to increase another 30 percent, even with the success of Broadband, which was not exactly a sure thing. Neither was Enron Energy Services, the company's foray into the management of power needs for large corporations. And a few people in the crowd had heard of problems in Fastow's finance group. But no one was that worried. They reminded themselves that they worked for Enron and, no matter what, Jeff would find a way. Because he always did.

There was, in fact, only one cautionary note sounded that morning. Skilling introduced the crowd to Tom Peters, the author of the best-selling business bible *In Search of Excellence*. Before abandoning the stage to Peters, Skilling wanted to boost morale a little higher. Enron, he reminded the crowd, had found the one successful business model that could be applied to any market.

Peters strode to the stage, abandoned his prepared speech, and started pacing back and forth. He was even sweating slightly, which made some in the audience think he might be another loser. "That's the scariest thing I've ever heard," Peters said to Skilling, his former colleague at McKinsey. What, exactly, had Enron done that was so novel? he asked. What accounted for such self-congratulation? The company had taken a model and replicated it in other fields—Enron had created markets where none had existed before, in gas, in power, probably in telecom. But everyone knew that now. Other businesses were already copying Enron, and the novelty would soon wear off. And then where would Enron be? Where were the company's new new ideas? "An excess of self-confidence kills companies," Peters warned.

In the audience, Sherron Watkins scribbled notes furiously on a pad, listing Peter's signs of a company in trouble:

1. denial of problems
2. nostalgia
3. arrogance

Listening, Skilling and Lay sat frozen in their seats, smiles locked on their faces. When Peters stopped speaking, Skilling jumped up to the dais, thanked him, and repeated himself: Remember, he said, *Enron had found the one successful business model that could be applied to any market.*

Enron liked to close its meetings with humor, and this year was no exception. A videotaped skit began to roll, purporting to show how Enron innovated.

It opened with a tired cleaning woman emptying a trash can in the office of an overworked young associate. "Gee," she tells him, "you guys should find something to do with all this paper you throw away." The junior associate, slumped over his desk from the rigors of his eighty-hour workweek, suddenly sits bolt upright. Cut to the next morning. He dashes to the head of Enron's trading group and breathlessly shares his idea: Enron should create a market for trading recycled paper and pulp. "It's huge!" he promises, spreading his arms wide.

As soon as the associate leaves, the head trader, who was cool to the idea, leaps from his chair and speeds to the office of the head of the Wholesale trading group, played by Greg Whalley, the real head of Wholesale trading. The head trader starts to sell Whalley on *his* idea of creating a paper trading business. "It's a very inefficient market," he stresses. "We can make a killing!" Whalley, a man well known for his aggressive style, grabs the trader by the lapels, puts a finger to his lips, and pulls him into a restroom, the only place, everyone in the audience knows, that Enron's hidden cameras and listening devices can't go. Whalley peeks under every stall. Then he listens, intently, to the pitch again. "We should develop the business plan and go to Skilling," he says. "Get cracking!"

But Whalley and the trader have not been careful enough. A low-level employee has overheard their conversation through an air-conditioning vent. While the executives dither, he races back to his desk and makes a phone call. Jeff Skilling's secretary answers and gives him an appointment to discuss *his* idea—for creating a market in paper and pulp. The low-level employee is played by David Cox, who in real life went from a minor job running Enron's graphics department to creating the company's paper and pulp trading division. He was now, true to form, another Enron multimillionaire.

The audience applauded wildly when the skit ended—sure, the culture at Enron was treacherous, but that was the point. Enron hired the best and the brightest, so fighting your way to the top was tougher. But once you got there, you knew—it was incontestable, incontrovertible—that you were a winner.

That was how Sherron Watkins felt by the end of the conference. She had secured face time with Skilling. Yes, she'd prattled anxiously about her favorite Web sites and he'd passed her on like a pol at a crowded fund-raiser; he was a busy man. But Kevin Hannon, the executive who had snubbed her the first day, had later thanked her for her hard work. "Come February," he said, "we'll talk about your long-term goals." So Sherron figured Broadband looked secure, and, if things got rough, she could go to work for Fastow again. Like Enron, she was in a win-win position.

What didn't occur to Sherron, or virtually anyone else at the conference, was that very little of substance had been discussed. No future goals had been outlined, no business plans debated.

What few knew was that, even as Enron executives were trumpeting their success, their company was already doomed. Within months, Enron's finances would be in shambles. Instead of being praised as the world's leading company, Enron would be vilified as one of the world's most callous and corrupt. Its name would become shorthand for the excesses of American business and American culture at the end of the twentieth century. And in the months to come, the people who had won and the people who had lost through their associations with Enron would ask themselves the same question: Had it ever been a real company? Or had Enron been, from the very beginning, just a brilliant illusion?

2

Mythology

FROM the beginning, Enron was a story with a mystery at its center, for Ken Lay was a mystery to many people. Just about everyone who met Lay for the first time liked him, from world leaders to the ministers from Houston's poorest neighborhoods. A very rich man as early as the mid-eighties, he was always able to convey, at least from a distance, that he was a man of simple tastes and good works. His dark eyes were unusually soulful, though they could turn as hard as onyx, and he had the oversized, enveloping hands of a farm boy, which he had been. He also possessed the politician's gift—or the habit of the minister's son, which he also was—for remembering not just your name but the name of your sister, and the ability to recollect when she had recovered from her last heart surgery. He knew when your son had graduated from high school, which classes he excelled in, and what college he wanted to go to, and that it was a good school. In short, Ken Lay made it easy to believe that he had not forgotten where he came from. This talent, when coupled with the great success of his company, meant that he was able to walk into a room of international power brokers in Washington or New York or into a Houston church social, and the effect was the same. The crowds parted for him with something like awe, and he, in return, shook every hand and knew every name, and business could proceed with a feeling of the very best intentions.

Later, when Enron began to teeter, and then tumble into chaos, people would be forced to reconsider their idea of Lay, an activity that was particularly painful in Houston. It would be easy for East Coast reporters and midwestern senators to paint him as another imperial CEO, representative of the narcissistic greed of the times, a man who lived large at the expense of his shareholders. But in Houston, Lay's fall would cause the kind of soulsearching, teeth-gnashing, and rending of garments alien to this inherently optimistic city. Lay had been one of them, and maybe better than them; he brokered countless peace agreements between warring political factions, donated untold millions to the arts and various charities, built a state-of-the-art baseball field, promised a future that guaranteed the greatness Houston lusted after. Seeing all that in shambles made people wonder whether they had ever really known him at all.

In fact, Ken Lay belonged to Houston as much as Houston belonged to him. Enron's rise and fall had much to do with the pressures of Wall Street and the malleability of Washington, but no one could understand Ken Lay or the company he built without understanding Houston.

People who visit Houston for the first time are often surprised by how green it is. They come expecting the classic Texas of cactus and tumbleweeds, and find instead a messy collision of tropics, coastal plain, and piney woods—a thick, overgrown semiswamp, riven by bayous, that in summer exudes a humidity that is, literally, breathtaking. It was and still is an environment that speaks to a particular kind of person: Houston has never been conventionally pretty; but, hot, shady, and overgrown, it's always been alluring to those who saw, or more likely sensed, opportunity in its overwhelming, almost overweening, fecundity.

Geography was destiny. In most of Texas—western, central, southern, the Panhandle—the mythological load fell on the cowboy. That land was suitable for ranching—that's about all it was suitable for—the spaces immense, attracting the independent, expansive, and irascible. But Houston was different. It took a certain kind of person to study the swampy, wooded topography, and the distance from other thriving urban centers like New Orleans, and see opportunity. That's what happened in 1836, when two brothers from New York, Augustus and John Allen, placed an ad in papers around the United States for the sale of lots in what they called "The Town of Houston."

As Houston historian Marguerite Johnston wrote—admiringly—in *Houston, the Unknown City, 1836–1946*, "No twentieth century marketing expert could have promoted a city more shrewdly." The Allens' ad promised that there was "no place in Texas more healthy." Houston was "handsome and beautifully elevated." It "had an abundance of excellent spring water" and a "sea breeze in all its freshness." Situated near the sea and just northeast of Mexico, not far from New Orleans, this new city, they promised, would "warrant the employment of at least ONE MILLION DOLLARS [caps theirs] of capital, and when the rich lands of the country shall be settled, a trade will flow to it, making it, beyond all doubt, the great internal commercial emporium of Texas."

There is an old gambling expression that has always been popular in Texas, the phrase "betting on the come." It pretty well describes what the Allen brothers were up to. They discovered a natural turning basin upstream on Buffalo Bayou, an as-yet-unnavigable waterway that flowed into Galveston Bay. From that, the brothers envisioned a major inland port. "Envisioned" is, of course, the operative word: In reality, their hilly, breezy utopia was flat and maddeningly hot, and the bayou was so choked with flora that the brothers had to hire a steamer to prove its navigability. (It barely made the trip.) Their Town of Houston consisted of twelve ragged squatters and one log cabin. But none of that mattered: Four months after publication of the ad, by November 1836, Houston had a population of 1,500 hopeful, ambitious souls.

This creation story marks the moment when the local distinction between optimism and hucksterism would forevermore depend on the outcome of a given proposition. From then on, Houstonians would tell themselves that here anything was possible, and that they could make "anything" happen—preferably without interference from anyone else. As the city grew, this passion evolved into a generalized love of "progress." Houstonians have always told themselves, and still tell themselves, that vision and determination are the only things that matter here; pedigree, formal education, and history do not.

That notion became an article of faith after 1901, when oil was discovered in east Texas at a place called Spindletop. The well gushed 800,000 barrels of oil into the air for nine days—more oil than any single field had ever produced in history—and flooded the surrounding countryside with gooey black muck. It would subsequently produce 142,000,000 barrels of oil, as well as Houston's fervor for the energy business and all its attendant metaphors.

Almost overnight, the young city became the capital of the oil business. (Beaumont, closer to the oil play, was too mean and scrubby to fit the bill.) Houston had the rail lines and a nice gloss of culture—it had the ambition and the kinds of places where you could show off your money—and it was all too happy to abandon a constricting cloak of southern gentility to make the new oil-rich feel at home. No one cared when the town was overrun with speculators, because Houston was growing, and it was growing very, very rich. By 1906, following another massive find in nearby Sour Lake, the city could boast thirty oil companies, seven banks, and twenty-five newspapers, and the installation of the wildcatter as the central figure of myth.

The wildcatter was a different sort of heroic figure from the cowboy, though both characters liked to see themselves as solitary and shrewd, more comfortable outside than inside. But the wildcatter was bolder: He took bigger risks, seemed a lot more comfortable around women (in general, he liked them), and had the courage—or so he said—to fail. He was flexible: In contrast to the South's land-bound gentry, he leased his acreage and moved on if things didn't work out. When they did, he made a lot more money than his archetypal cowboy cousin, and was therefore a lot more fun. The classic example is Jett Rink, the wildcatter of Edna Ferber's *Giant*, whose character was based on a real wildcatter, Glenn McCarthy. (It was McCarthy who built the Shamrock Hotel for $21 million in 1949, and entertained guests by throwing a weighted $100 bill across the enormous swimming pool, which was, of course, the world's largest.)

This was the kind of Texan just about everyone could like: rich, funny, a bit of a rogue, and, outsiders could tell themselves, kind of a hick. Eventually, as Houston became known for its hospitable business climate, wildcatter worship turned into entrepreneur worship. Houston became a haven for developers who were just a little more inventive than the norm—guys who hired world-class architects for their skyscrapers, mansions, and malls; guys who put an ice-skating rink in the middle of an upscale shopping center (in a city that rarely sees a thirty-two-degree day), even guys who built a ski slope at the intersection of two freeways. Like Las Vegas, everyone was welcome to come to Houston and try their luck.

Houston's entrepreneurial role model was a man named John Henry Kirby. Born five years before the Civil War, he was Houston's first tycoon, the so-called Father of Industrial Texas, and the state's first multimillionaire, and as such, the man who instantly changed Texas's opinion of itself and its possibilities. Kirby had the speculator's passion for risk, the oilman's optimism, and a grandiosity that was all his own. He had the requisite childhood of great American financiers: Poor and self-educated, he left home first to become a lawyer and then to create a corporate empire. According to the *Houston Chronicle*, "Those who knew him were well aware of a burning ambition on his part to organize a timberland company of monumental size—one which would provide a vehicle for consolidation of his own holdings together with those land properties which he already controlled and managed for others." Soon enough, Kirby owned more timberland than anyone else in the world. Soon after that, he created an oil/lumber conglomerate worth $40 million. He hobnobbed with President Woodrow Wilson too.

Anyone familiar with the lives of many prominent Houstonians can probably predict what happened next: By 1904, Kirby fell out with his Boston partners and was missing loan payments. His backers sued, and then his situation got worse. ("How about my allowance this month?" his daughter, Bessie Mae, cabled in 1909. "Can't send it. Haven't got it" was Kirby's answer.) Even so, Kirby had the money to build a $300,000 shingled, gabled, and onion-domed mansion that covered an entire city block, and accessorized the place with faux rustic gardens, a sprawling greenhouse, and an indoor pool with a ballroom upstairs. When asked, he blamed his problems on Wall Street, launching another great local tradition.

Of course, Kirby died nearly bankrupt at age eighty. He remained loyal to Houston to the end. "I don't think there is any limit to Houston's future growth," Kirby told a reporter on his seventy-ninth birthday.

Houston, however, soon forgot John Henry Kirby, as it would forget all but the most glorious shapers of its past. It became a city without memory, hell-bent on the future, which was always going to be bigger and better than what had gone before. Allen's Landing, the site of Houston's founding, would become a barely locatable marker in a forgotten corner of downtown. The Astrodome, which for decades called itself the Eighth Wonder of the World, was abandoned. Freeways flourished in a constant state of rebuilding and repair; there would be no historic districts to speak of. Houston's passion was always for the new.

Most locals now know only the boulevard that carries Kirby's name—fittingly, it's the major thoroughfare through River Oaks, the city's wealthiest neighborhood. But several of Kirby's businesses remain, as well. The most famous is the Kirby Oil Company, which endured a series of sales and mergers to emerge more famous at the beginning of the twenty-first century than it was at the start of the twentieth. By then, of course, it had a new name.

It was called Enron.

K en Lay seemed like the polar opposite of a risk-obsessed wildcatter who might drive a company and, maybe, the local economy off a cliff. Born into a deeply religious family in the Midwest, he had a Ph.D. in economics. He served in the Navy and worked as a policy wonk in Washington. He came up through the ranks of a series of colorless pipeline companies. In short, he had very low embarrassment potential in a city that was still trying to throw off its image as a place populated by free-spending oil zillionaires who, just a few years back, were barefoot and ignorant. Houston wanted to stand alongside New York and Los Angeles as a major international center. Ken Lay was smart and sophisticated, and he wanted to help Houston be modern just like him. From the beginning, they were made for each other.

Lay's early years are deeply, almost elegiacally, American. He was born in the town of Tyrone, Missouri (population: 100), in 1942. Opportunities were few. Lay grew up a restless, imaginative child who would have sensed that the pervasive moderation of the Midwest had little to offer him in the face of a dying farm economy. But the way out wasn't entirely clear: His parents, Ruth and Omer Lay, were decent and hardworking, but they couldn't make a go of it. Omer tried his hand at business—he worked in a feed store and sold farm equipment—but success eluded him. The final straw came when a truck carrying a load of his chickens crashed, forcing him into bankruptcy. Sometimes the family, down on their luck, moved in with relatives; one Christmas dinner consisted of baloney sandwiches. Either because of or in spite of his father's failures, Ken Lay, the second of three children and the only boy, became a determined, almost frenetic worker. By the time he was twelve, he was painting houses and delivering three different newspapers, covering his own expenses; later, baling hay for another summer job, he plotted his exit strategy from the back of a tractor. He dreamed of J. P. Morgan and John D. Rockefeller, men who knew that success lay in getting to the future before anyone else.

Omer Lay's real passion was for God. He was a Southern Baptist, which meant that his God was judgmental and unforgiving; humans were conceived in sin and spent their lives trying to escape the bitter, ineluctable pull of evil. After preaching on an itinerant circuit for several years, he eventually found a permanent position as a minister at the Baptist church in the tiny town of Rush Hill, Missouri. It is not hard to imagine that, in this small, claustrophobic world, Ken Lay would have learned not just the lessons of faith but the lessons of the church, the most important being that it was just as important to look good as to be good. Lay was the preacher's son, with all the social pressures that role demanded; he would strive to be flawless in the eyes of God and, not incidentally, in the eyes of the public, too.

Rush Hill's Baptist church also provided a perfect introduction to the world of politics that would so entrance Lay later in life; there's no place better than the church to observe and hone the twin leadership skills of influence and inspiration. Ken Lay, dressed by his mother in homemade clothes of cheap fabric, would master it all. In high school, he was president of his sophomore class, sang in the choir, played slide trombone in the marching band, and, of course, made straight A's. But he was just getting started. He had a natural optimism he had inherited from his parents, and the road ahead looked limitless.

Neither his mother nor father went to college, and both parents were determined that their children would have that opportunity. But they spent all their savings—and all of Ken's savings—on educating their oldest daughter, Bonnie. Soon after, Omer and Ruth moved Ken and his younger sister, Sharon, to Missouri's capital, Columbia, so that they could go to the state university too. At the University of Missouri, Lay excelled effortlessly. He was serious and intense, a top student, president of his fraternity by his junior year. He graduated Phi Beta Kappa in 1965. Lay also formed two crucial relationships: he became close friends with another sharp, ambitious student, Rich Kinder, and he became the protégé of Pinkney Walker, a tall, wry, popular economics professor. In Walker's classes, Lay found a discipline that gave form to his ambition. He became fascinated with markets and how they worked; success, he believed, went to the man who could predict evolutionary changes, take advantage of the resulting chaos, and emerge the dominant player. Lay intended to go into business right after graduation—"I've got to make some money," he told Walker—but let Walker talk him into staying on for another year to get his master's degree while he worked as Walker's assistant.

When Lay did leave a year later, it was for Houston. He had a job lined up as a senior economist at Humble Oil and Refining Company, the predecessor of Exxon. Whatever Lay was supposed to do at Humble, he wound up, almost instantly, as a trusted speechwriter for chairman Mike Wright. For the second time in his life, Lay affixed himself to a powerful man who could advance his prospects: At twenty-three, he was representing Humble in speeches at the Wharton School of Business, and might be chairman of Exxon today except for the Vietnam War. Lay enlisted in the Navy, where once again he advanced quickly. The Assistant Secretary of the Navy for Financial Management needed an economist on his staff, and Lay got the job. In 1968 he was Pentagon bound, and supervised an economic study to determine the effect of a Vietnam pullout on the U.S. economy. (The topic eventually became the subject of Lay's doctoral thesis at the University of Houston, which he finished by attending night classes.) It wasn't long before young Ken Lay was working happily alongside retired Navy admirals.

He was learning a lesson common to many smart, small-town boys who come to the big city: that they are just as smart as, if not smarter than, the people who are already entrenched there. Lay was polite, but sure of himself and his ideas, and his confidence had the usual effect on the older men. They were charmed by the smiling, tireless young officer from the Midwest with the prematurely receding hairline and polished manners. Lay seemed older than his years, at home in the halls of power. When his committee's work was eventually adopted by the Council of Economic Advisers, Lay seemed poised for the cozy life of a Beltway insider.

That future looked assured when, in 1971, President Nixon appointed Pinkney Walker to the Federal Energy Commission, a precursor to the Federal Energy Regulatory Commission. Lay was supposed to go back to Humble when his military tour was up, but Walker intervened on his behalf—he wasn't about to give up a protégé who showed up at six A.M. and had the work done before he made it into the office by eight. Walker called Wright and, in a lesson in politics that would serve Lay well, reminded the CEO that it was better to have a friend in Washington than a speechwriter in Houston. Lay stayed on, giving impassioned speeches in favor of deregulation and the benefits of a free market. Lay was toeing the Republican party line, and he won for himself the chance to serve as Undersecretary of Energy under Rogers Morton.

But Lay was restless. The life of a policy maker had plenty of intellectual prestige, but it lacked the comforts and the exposure he longed for. In 1973, he wrote to Jack Bowen, a tall, rangy Texan who was then chairman of Florida Gas, a business Lay had regulated while at the FEC. "I feel it is now time I begin thinking about returning to the private sector and resuming my career in business," he stated in the letter. "The natural gas industry obviously faces some difficult challenges in the news and in the years ahead. I would like to be in a position in the industry to help meet those challenges."

The gas business was once a stepchild of the oil business—oilmen initially saw natural gas as waste they had to dispose of to get to the good stuff.

It was only in the years between the world wars that it became an increasingly valuable product. The federal government viewed the development of the natural gas industry as a common good; it would provide a clean-burning fuel for businesses and homes, and reduce the country's growing dependence on imported oil. In the beginning, the gas business operated like any regulated public utility: Producers sold their natural gas at just and reasonable rates to interstate pipeline companies that, in turn, transported that gas for sale to local distribution companies at just and reasonable rates. Gas went from wellhead to end user in one simple, bundled transaction that included the cost of the supply and its distribution. It was a steady, lucrative monopoly for the pipelines. Everyone knew, year in and year out, how much money they'd be taking in.

But while transporting gas was easy to price, finding gas was not. Exploration was and is prohibitively expensive, with high failure rates for which companies were never adequately compensated. Over time, they stopped looking for gas, and the market stagnated, causing shortages across the country in politically treacherous sites like schools and hospitals. By the 1970s, policy makers were scrambling to find a way to unbundle gas so that competitive market forces could jump-start the industry. Essentially, this meant starting from scratch in the way gas was found, bought, and sold. Enter Ken Lay, who believed that the opportunity to let the market set the price of gas, instead of the government, promised enormous benefits to everyone. In the coming years, the fight to deregulate would become his mission, and he would preach for it with a passion he had learned at home. Rules were made to be broken, and success went to the businessman who was ready to embrace change—someone who was a "visionary," a word that would be increasingly associated with Lay in the coming years.

Jack Bowen had come from the old school—he'd built pipelines with his own hands—but he saw in Lay just the kind of resourceful, wonkish protégé who could help his business survive the coming chaos. He checked out Lay's references, which were all glowing ("May be too ambitious," a sole reference cautioned), and hired him in 1974 as vice president of New Energy Ventures. The package wasn't lavish: $38,000 a year and no company car.

Even so, Lay quickly adapted to corporate life at Florida Gas's headquarters in bucolic Winter Park, Florida. He traded his Washington blazers for madras and lime-green sport coats, left the rearing of his two children to his wife, Judy—they were college sweethearts who married in 1971—and by 1981 was president of the company, returning triumphantly to Washington to continue his push for deregulation of natural gas. The government wasn't moving fast enough to suit Lay; a truly competitive gas market, he believed, would come only when buyers and sellers of gas had open access to all pipelines.

Just a year later, Lay was on the move again. Bowen had left Winter Park a few years before to head a Houston pipeline company called Transco, which owned an enviable 10,000-mile system stretching from the Gulf Coast to the Northeast. Lay called him, and told him he was getting a divorce and wanted to come back to Texas. The timing was fortuitous— Bowen wanted to retire and hadn't yet found a successor. Lay had all the right ideas, and he was a seasoned executive. Soon enough, Ken Lay was installed as Transco's president and chief operating officer.

Just as Walker showed Lay the ropes in Washington, Bowen became his guide to Houston. Lay first came to town in the late 1960s, when the city was just beginning to feel its possibilities. Houston wasn't quite a big city, though it would appear that way to someone from a small town in the Midwest. There were no skyscrapers, but there were tall buildings. It was home to several major oil companies, and it was also Space City. NASA was gearing up just south of town, and the city was full of people who were, like Lay, seduced by the call of the future. In the intervening decade and a half, while Lay was in Washington and Florida, Houston entered its golden period, that brief time in the late seventies and early eighties when the city seemed to be the center of the universe, the subject of newsmagazine cover stories, the epicenter of Texas Chic, and America's fastest-growing city. Houston then seemed within sight of fulfilling its grand ambition: Philip Johnson dotted the city with rigorously trendy skyscrapers; the most elegant local department store opened a St. Laurent boutique; it was possible to buy an Italian meal that was not spaghetti and meatballs, but pasta, a dish that seemed much more exotic, especially when it was tossed with caviar at Tony's, the Houston equivalent of Manhattan's "21." New York City bankers and Middle Eastern potentates rushed to town, eager to deposit a seemingly endless supply of money in Houston's coffers.

It was during this time that Lynn Wyatt, the wife of oilman Oscar Wyatt, feted Princess Grace and Mick Jagger in her mansion at the end of River Oaks Boulevard, and Joanne Herring, the wife of Houston Natural Gas mogul Robert Herring, was accessorizing the parties in her Inwood mansion—the one she liked to convert into a casbah for her Middle Eastern guests—with Boy Scouts dressed as Nubian slaves. Houston was drunk on itself, and on $40-a-barrel oil, which was never, ever going to decline in price.

Of course, it did, hitting $29 in 1982 and heading south. It was the year Ken Lay came back to town. What he found was a city going into shock—a place that could not believe that its moment in the sun had been so fleeting. ("Lord, please send me another oil boom," the bumper sticker of choice read when oil hit $9 a barrel. "I promise not to fuck it up next time.") Bowen took Lay in hand and introduced him to other comers, like Robert Mosbacher and James Baker, respectable men, not the crazy wildcatter types. Slowly, Lay eased his way into the clubby cadre of vastly rich men who liked to decorate their offices with pictures of themselves beside President Reagan and Vice President Bush. These men liked Lay; the Houston economy was going down the tubes, the eastern press was scoffing at the city's hubris, but he seemed to be a man of ideas, someone eager to help rebuild.

Lay would have seen that the people who made up Houston's old guard—the heirs to the East Texas and Spindletop fortunes—and its new guard came from backgrounds a lot like his. Without benefit of family money or school ties, they'd amassed sprawling mansions, vast south Texas ranches, private planes, and the allegiance of governors, congressmen, and presidents—seemingly infinite wealth along with seemingly infinite power. There was plenty of room in Houston, he saw, for a man like him.

Lay became a bachelor about town, still somewhat military in his bearing. He kept himself assiduously fit by jogging at Memorial Park and playing racquetball with other senior executives. He had custody of his young son and daughter, while Judy remained behind in Florida. "She didn't finish things," was the way he described his former wife. She had trouble keeping up the pace. Lay could be charming, but he was always driven; the preacher's son told one date that the businessman he admired most was takeover king T. Boone Pickens.

By 1984, the deregulated gas business had become a free-for-all. Oscar Wyatt, then head of an oil and gas conglomerate called Coastal Corporation, made a $1.3 billion bid for Houston Natural Gas, a company in turmoil after the death of its beloved leader, Robert Herring. The move scandalized Houston. Wyatt was perceived as a coarse, barrel-chested bully, nothing better than oil field trash, despite Coastal's $5 billion in annual revenues. Bob Herring, despite his wife's propensity for eccentric galas, was seen as a straight shooter, a community leader whose word was his bond, and his company retained that image of integrity after his death. Houston Natural Gas was also the third-most-profitable company in town behind Shell and Tenneco.

HNG fended off Wyatt's takeover attempt by paying him $42 million to go away, but the board was unhappy with its then president, an older man who nearly lost the company. In the new deregulated climate, the board knew that other takeovers were likely, and they wanted young, aggressive leadership to protect themselves. The person who came to mind was Ken Lay, the executive who was so helpful when Transco served as a white knight in the face of Wyatt's onslaught.

Bowen had been grooming Lay as his successor, but when the HNG board asked Lay to meet with them on a Saturday morning, he went. The following Monday, Lay met with Bowen, who told him he would not stand in Lay's way. Within a few weeks, HNG's new CEO greeted his staff in a crisp ivory suit, his balding head shining under the hot lights of the company auditorium. "I'm here to have fun," he told the uneasy crowd in his sharp Missouri twang. "Every career decision I've made was where I could have the most fun." He introduced the crowd to his new wife, Linda. The pert blonde had been his secretary in Florida; he had found a job for her in Houston, and the two had married almost immediately after Lay's divorce was final. He was stepping out of the shadows, coming into his own.

Despite Lay's promises of fun at HNG, a stream of firings and departures followed his ascension. Ken Lay liked men like himself—men with college degrees and impressive credentials. HNG was built by men who in many cases had worked their way up from digging pipeline ditches. Lay also began an expansion plan, partly because he had dreamed of creating a gas major since working at Humble, and also because taking on debt made the company less vulnerable to takeover attempts.

At the time, HNG was competing with an Omaha company called Inter-North to be the country's largest pipeline company. InterNorth had also been the subject of a recent takeover attempt by corporate raider Irwin Jacobs. The CEO of InterNorth, Sam Segnar, offered to end the madness by buying out HNG, and promised $71 a share. HNG executives were stunned; their stock was then selling for $25. The merger would make them richer than they could ever imagine.

But the deal that was considered a purchase in Omaha was being viewed in Houston as a merger. Segnar was impressed with Lay and thought he should take over the combined company. Lay wasn't afraid of deregulation; in fact, he had aggressively positioned Transco to take advantage of the new world. At Transco, he'd started buying and selling gas on the spot market long before the regulators got around to implementing market-priced gas. Lay was always out front, one step ahead in the new free-market economy for natural gas. The old way of thinking required companies to get approval from regulators for every move; now, if the regulators didn't expressly prohibit a transaction, Lay saw it through. If a novel combination of regulations got the results he wanted, he cobbled them together and wait-ed for the regulators to complain. Segnar couldn't help but be impressed. All he wanted was time, eighteen months, to get his employees accustomed to the transition. InterNorth had always been run as an old-fashioned com-pany; no one was ever really fired—people signed on after college and left at retirement.

As the sale/merger progressed, Lay got busy. He began lobbying for higher salaries for the board members, and he began cultivating the big-gest stockholders. He promised he would move to Omaha; the company headquarters, he swore, would not be shifted to Houston. The board threw its support behind Lay; within six months, despite Lay's assurances, the sale of Houston Natural Gas to InterNorth gave birth to a new, Houston-based company called Enron, with Ken Lay as its new CEO. As a longtime lobbyist for Enron would note at the time, "Ken Lay plays offense, not defense."

For the first time in his life, Lay was a rich man—he had made $4 million on the sale of his HNG stock and was suddenly the fifth-highest-paid CEO in America. Enron bought the new house Lay would share with Linda in River Oaks, the contemporary brick mansion that once belonged to Robert Herring.

Enron's birth in 1985 had not been an easy one, and neither was its childhood. From the beginning, the company's strengths were its weaknesses—the impassioned embrace of deregulation, the constant risk taking, the incessant reorganizations, the instant adoption of the hottest new energy/business ideas. At its best, Enron epitomized entrepreneurial success, and at its worst, it spent with a carelessness that shocked its competitors. Lay's first attempt to name his new company turned out to be an embarassment. He hired a New York consulting firm to come up with the right name, and after four months he was presented with the word Enteron. The *En* was supposed to evoke energy and the environment; the *on* was meant to link the company with other oil and gas powerhouses like Exxon and Chevron. The letters in the middle were chosen at random. Unfortunately, after a flashy rollout of the new name, it turned out that Enteron did mean something—it was a medical term for the small intestine. Lay quickly changed the name to Enron.

Other mistakes were not as easy to fix. Enron came into the world loaded with debt, thanks to the premium InterNorth had paid for its Houston competitor and Lay's prior expansion efforts on behalf of HNG. A worker pension plan was raided to the tune of $230 million to get rid of Irwin Jacobs, who owned enough stock in the new company to make Enron's executives nervous. Soon Lay was going to junk-bond king Michael Milken at Drexel Burnham to keep the company afloat.

And there were still more problems. In 1984, the FERC had issued a series of orders that basically drop-kicked pipeline companies into competition with one another. Pipeline customers, typically large local gas-distribution companies, were freed from their old contracts; with open access, they could buy gas from anyone and insist it be shipped through the very pipes owned by the company they'd just dumped as a supplier. Soon after, all the major pipeline companies—which had posted profits of between 10 and 20 percent in 1982—were facing single-digit returns on equity or, worse, were going into the red. Their debt ratings dropped to junk-bond status.

Searching for cash, Lay tried to sell off a piece of a successful oil and gas subsidiary, but he was stymied by the stock market crash of 1987. At almost the same time, he learned that something was wrong in Enron's crude oil trading operation based in Valhalla, New York.

The Valhalla trading group had been inherited from InterNorth; its offices were lavish, and because it produced enormous profits for the company, it was left largely alone after the merger. Earlier signs of trouble had been ignored: Arthur Andersen warned of problems as early as 1985, and so had Enron's own internal auditors. Then, in January 1987, a New York bank called Enron's Houston headquarters, concerned about unusually high-dollar transactions flowing through a small local branch. As one auditor would later note, "The whole Valhalla operation was fictitious. There were a lot of expensive people working there, and it was impressive looking, but it wasn't legitimate work," he said. "It was pretend. It was a playhouse."

Ken Lay, his COO and former college chum Rich Kinder, and a handful of experienced internal auditors made a visit to the New York trading shop to investigate the matter. Within the first hour of the investigation it was obvious that foul play had occurred. First, the explanations about the bank account given by the head trader and his finance executive, Louis Borget and Thomas Mastroeni, made no sense and did not match the bank statement activity. The trades looked falsified—Borget and Mastroeni had made up absurd customer names, like M. Yass (for "My ass," the auditors surmised).

Then there were the collect telexes. Back in the late eighties, trades were confirmed via telex—faxes and e-mail didn't yet exist. Each trading company paid for its end of the telex confirmation. Enron would send a telex confirming a buy or sell and the customer would telex the reply confirming the matching sell or buy. The trading shop had collect telex replies from the customers with questionable names—more evidence that a real company had never been on the other side of the trade.

In truth, the traders were keeping two sets of books, one for legitimate purposes—to show Enron and auditors from Arthur Andersen—and another in which to record their ill-gotten gains.

One of the internal auditors thought the company's next move was obvious. Kinder agreed. "If it were my decision I'd shut it down," he told the auditor. "I'd fire them all." But Lay's new company was facing bankruptcy, and his reputation as a CEO, so freshly minted, was heading for oblivion. When the group reconvened to discuss strategy, he shocked his colleagues with his decision: The traders would not be fired. Enron would simply institute and enforce strict controls. Whether Lay did so out of his own natural benevolence or to save his company will never be known. Either way, he obtained promises of reform from the traders, and, more important, an unstated guarantee that the past trading profits would continue.

But Borget and Mastroeni did not reform. In fact, they ignored the company-imposed trading limits and made a big bet on the price of oil. When that position began to erode, Valhalla's head trader began acting like a Vegas gambler on the ropes, doubling down on a losing bet over and over again. By the time Houston was alerted, the position had the potential to wipe out almost all of Enron's 1987 earnings. A seasoned trader was sent in to trade the gaping loss back to a manageable loss of just under $150 million. Thanks to him, Enron was able to announce a loss of only $85 million in the third quarter, and Lay declared the incident an expensive embarrassment. What should have been a turnaround year for the company was one in which it almost lost its life.

Borget served a year and a day in prison and paid a $6 million fine. Mastroeni served two years' probation. Ken Lay promised that his company would never enter into the trading business on a grand scale again. It was a promise he would not keep.

3

Star Search

I N February 1993, Enron's stock split. To mark the occasion, each of Enron's 7,800 employees was to receive a crisp new $50 bill. Scheduled to announce the giveaway and thank the staff, Ken Lay wasn't there. Instead, he was in Davos, Switzerland, at the World Economic Forum, acting as roving ambassador for one of the world's greatest new companies. Enron was only eight years old by then, but the clamor for Lay's services had already reached a crescendo—his public relations staff was scrupulously rationing his time, as if he were the president of a small but influential nation. He was an august member of the Republican establishment, having been a very generous supporter of George Herbert Walker Bush's 1988 presidential campaign. Lay now counted among his friends not just the Bushes (portraits of whom casually adorned his home) but the John Sununus and Brent Scowcrofts of the world. But it wasn't just the Republicans who sought Lay's counsel: Texas governor Ann Richards put him in charge of a blue-ribbon commission.

Lay's résumé shimmered with increasingly impressive credentials: President Bush had tapped him to run the Economic Summit of Nations in 1990, when the leaders of the free world had convened in Houston. (Cool and collected throughout a Houston August, Lay put street cleaners in spiffy yellow uniforms and tamed the international press by offering free gourmet meals around the clock.) He also headed the Host Committee for the 1992 Republican Convention, held in the Astrodome, and though that confab would be remembered for its bitterness—the Bush contingent had vastly underestimated the fury of the religious right, as evidenced by Pat Buchanan's hate-laced keynote speech—Lay cemented his position as someone Washington could count on to get the job done, and Houston could count on to raise the city's profile. Enron contributed $250,000 to the convention alone to ensure its success.

But there was more to Lay's triumph than hard work and the right connections: If the late eighties and early nineties saw the rise of the cult of celebrity in America—Nancy Reagan's imperial, star-studded White House; the latest Hollywood confessions on the cover of Tina Brown's *Vanity Fair*—it wasn't long before those values seeped into corporate culture as well. Lee Iaccoca's jaunty autobiography; the irreverent reverence of *Manhattan, Inc.* magazine; the walking hyperbole that was Donald Trump—none of this business hype would have been lost on Ken Lay, who fashioned for himself a more subdued, more serious image. He was a Ph.D.—he liked being addressed as Dr. Lay—and so he became the progressive, professorial CEO, one who was not afraid to fold morality and ethics into his corporate persona. After the *Exxon Valdez* tanker spilled nearly 11 million gallons of crude oil in Alaska's Prince William Sound in the spring of 1989, Enron wanted the world to know that it was wedded to natural gas, the friendly fuel. On Earth Day, Lay even went on Houston's drive-time radio, talking up the benefits of his product.

By the early nineties, Enron was much more than a gas company; in fact, it had completely surpassed its initial mission statement—"to become the premier natural-gas pipeline company in North America." Enron had the largest natural-gas transmission network in the United States and the most extensive physical assets, a 38,000-mile integrated pipeline system that stretched from Florida to California and from the Mexican border to

Canada. Enron had also evolved into a power plant developer and operator, a finance company, a risk-management company, and more. As early as 1989, more than 60 percent of the company's earnings had come from the pipeline business, but Enron then promised stockholders that within six years that number would drop to 25 percent. That year Enron's stock was already returning 57 percent to its shareholders. The company was out-performing its peers' returns of 36 percent and was trouncing the S&P 500's overall market return of 27 percent. And because Lay was available and quotable—critics in a *Chronicle* story described him as "a cocky show-boater, a publicity hound who will say anything if he thinks it will win him some ink"—the financial press couldn't get enough of him. In 1987— the year Enron started to dismiss its worst problems in the press—Toni Mack, a reporter for *Forbes*, wrote a glowing profile of Lay titled "Orderly Mind in a Disorderly Market." Enron, she predicted, would thrive in the world of deregulation ("Here's a man to watch and a company to watch"). It wasn't long before Wall Street analysts followed suit, urging investors to buy, buy, buy.

The company unveiled a new vision in 1990, having fulfilled its old one so quickly. In the coming decade, Enron would strive to embody Lay's lifelong dream, "To be the first natural gas major" as well as "the most innovative and reliable provider of clean energy worldwide for a better environment." If that mission would seem wildly ambitious for most companies, Lay had an ace up his sleeve. As he would tell the *Washington Post*, "My goal when I came into this business was to try to get a superstar in every key position. You must have the very best talent, and then let them develop a good strategy." It was the gospel of Ken Lay: A company staffed with the best and the brightest, who were allowed to develop to their fullest potential, couldn't be beat.

M aybe it was his propensity to take people at face value, maybe it was that he hated to be the bad guy, but Ken Lay was a man who did not like to say no, and his employees soon learned to exploit his weakness. His people performed, but they also extracted their pound of flesh—most often in the form of large cash rewards.

Lay must have known that he was not a disciplinarian, which was why, in self-defense, he had hired Rich Kinder, the college classmate he'd brought in during the Florida Gas days and subsequently made chief operating officer of Enron. Kinder, a cigar-chomping, agate-eyed former attorney, was known for his toughness—he didn't need to be liked—and for his caution. Unlike Lay, Kinder had a passion for actually running the business—he had a near-photographic memory for figures, recalled the intricacy of each transaction, loved the orderliness of the balance sheet. And Kinder had been bankrupt once; the experience made him circumspect where Lay was inclined toward profligacy. "Let's get all the alligators out on the table," he'd say of any potential problems; "Let's not be smoking our own dope" or "Let's not be drinking our own whiskey," he'd tell overeager executives. He'd also look the other way when Lay gently but firmly insisted the company use his sister Sharon's travel agency, and put his son Mark on the payroll. Lay's were the sins of a small-timer, but Enron was big enough and rich enough that no one seemed to mind.

If Lay would always need a Kinder in his life, he needed him very badly in those early days, largely because the other people Lay hired were, to say the least, difficult. "Volatile" was a word frequently applied to the gas business after deregulation. It was also a word often used to describe John Wing, who in the early days of Enron was charged with bringing in business, from originating deals to negotiating contracts. A short, stocky, ruddy-complected executive who sometimes came to the office in his workout clothes, Wing had the kind of credentials Lay wanted for his modern, forward-looking company. He was a West Point graduate and had served with distinction in Vietnam; he went to Harvard, and worked at GE under Jack Welch, corporate America's most admired guru. Lay had hired Wing as an executive at Florida Gas, then used his services on the HNG/InterNorth merger. (Wing was one of those who saw the deal as a merger and not a sale, and he was both shrewder and more aggressive than the naive Omaha group, who never stood a chance.)

Wing was a brilliant strategist, with the poker ace's ability to read his opponents, but his most useful attribute, for himself and the company, was his talent for theatrics. If Wing couldn't seduce or cajole his way to success, he threw tantrums. He once threatened to blow up the car of an accountant slow to cut him an expense check. In a new company bent on accomplishing big things, this behavior was not always viewed as a negative.

It was Wing, for instance, who got Enron's first big power plant on line, in Texas City, Texas, and it was Wing who then executed a far bolder plan: the construction of a massive power project in Teesside, England. In the late eighties, Margaret Thatcher was trying to deregulate her country's utilities; Wing had the moxie to convince a group of British power companies to go with a young, relatively unknown, thoroughly unproven Houston firm for a project that would be both bigger and more modern than anything constructed before—the world's largest natural gas–fired power plant. Generating both steam and electricity, it would add a full 4 percent to the United Kingdom's power generating capacity. Teesside was, for Enron, a bet-the-company deal: If Enron failed, the size of the plant—1,875 megawatts— would doom Enron's global reputation. On the other hand, success would make Enron an international player overnight.

To make Teesside happen, the company had to contract for vast amounts of North Sea gas to fuel the plant, but at the time that seemed a small price to pay. And maybe it was—Teesside, at a cost of $1 billion, opened to broad acclaim, brought in more than $200 million in profits to Enron, and solidified for the company a reputation for boldness and innovation on a global scale. Not the least of Wing's innovations was an adaptation from the construction industry of "construction while in progress" earnings, which allowed profits to be booked when contracts were executed—not, as was standard, when plants went on line.

Wing also got Lay to approve a new way of compensating Enron executives on project development deals. Based on the net present value of Teesside, he demanded, and got, a stake amounting to about $11 million; more important, he got the money at the closing of the deal, not before the plant went into operation. What this change did for the quality of Enron's work remained to be seen, but in the short term it made Wing and a few others impossibly rich and, not coincidentally, beyond reproach at the company. From then on, he was a little like the star athlete on a pro team, or the above-the-title actor in a Hollywood blockbuster—indispensable. His tantrums increased. His passion for the ladies—Wing was married—was boundless. He was forever renegotiating his contract—was he a consultant this month, or an employee? No one could remember. Sometimes Wing would quit in a huff, only to have Lay hire him back; sometimes Wing was fired and then rehired some months later, at a new title and an even higher salary. This lesson was not lost on others at Enron: If you made big money for the company, you could do no wrong.

Ultimately, Wing may have been most important as the mentor to his protégé, Rebecca Mark, who came into the company at a crucial time in Enron's history and in the history of American business. Margaret Thatcher was not the only world leader in the late 1980s who wanted to privatize and modernize her country's infrastructure; there was then an almost global desire to transfer the work of growth from governments to private industry. This created enormous opportunities for American companies willing to take on enormous risks. At Enron, the person who had an almost religious fervor to change the face of power around the world was a young woman named Rebecca Mark.

Rebecca Mark woke up each morning, stared herself down in the mirror, and insisted that she would prevail. She possessed an indomitable will, a quality she could not have survived without, considering her sex, her career choices, and the size of her ambition. Her hardscrabble history was strikingly similar to Ken Lay's. Like him, she was born poor, in a forlorn corner of Missouri, on a farm, to devout Baptists. In the great American narrative she would later shape for reporters, Mark worked alongside her brother, mucking out pig stalls, baling hay, and handling heavy machinery (read: as well as any man). "Sometimes it was so cold in our farmhouse that frost was on the quilt," she liked to say to reporters. She was a 4-H star, showing hogs and cattle, and aced home economics, balancing the family checkbook and making her own dresses by the age of seven. She excelled at languages—she mastered Spanish in grade school—and was a voracious reader, everything from Zane Grey to Tolstoy, anything that took her to faraway worlds and scenes of high drama.

Mark saved enough money to transfer from a small religious junior college to Baylor University, in Waco, Texas, a much larger school, and one that was very influential in Texas. She had never seen the kind of wealth she found there—girls in matching sweater sets from Neiman-Marcus, boys with their own shiny new cars. Mark was small, broad-faced, and, except for her freckles, plain; she had not had the benefit of the dental work that was the birthright of the upper middle class; she didn't have time for the football rituals that were the building blocks of social life in Texas. Mark had, instead, a forty-hour workweek to pay her school bills and the outsider's vantage point, nose pressed perpetually against the glass.

She got her degree in international management and minored in psychology, and in 1978, at the age of twenty-four, found a job for herself at First City Bank, lending money to energy companies.

To say that a twenty-four-year-old woman worked at First City in the late seventies is, for those Texans who recall the period, a kind of shorthand for a fantasy world that is now long gone. It was that time in Houston when the perpetual rise in the price of oil was taken as a given, and First City was at the center of it all. Based in a sparkling white Skidmore, Owings & Merrill tower downtown, it was the city's most politically connected bank. The silver-haired and silver-tongued John Connally, former Texas governor and U.S. Treasury secretary, sat on the board for years. First City was also the wildcatters' bank—guys with names like Rattlesnake Bill flew into town in helicopters, cash stashed in briefcases, hoping to lunch in the city's plush new strip joints. The bank was a great place to get an education in the folkways of power in Texas, and in the energy business in general, but women bankers were just expected to fetch the coffee. One of Mark's contemporaries was given a pair of knee pads on her first day.

Mark persevered. She worked in regional and international banking as a junior loan officer, wore boxy Brooks Brothers suits with little string ties, got her first taste of London, and had a ringside seat for the collapse of the Penn Square Bank in Oklahoma. (Later, at Enron, there would be moments when it would come to mind.) She left in April of 1982, just as First City was beginning to have problems of its own. Mark saw it coming—the spending without concern for available cash, the enormous overhead—but by the time the bank imploded, she had landed safely as an assistant treasurer at Continental Resources, which was bought by Houston Natural Gas. There she met up with Wing.

Whatever did or did not happen between the two—they have always denied publicly that they were lovers, and few have ever believed them—it was during this time that Mark survived a trial by fire and emerged transformed. Wing treated her much like he treated everyone, piling on the abuse—browbeating her in front of customers and colleagues, demanding she fetch him coffee, and labeling her a failure—but he also brought her into the biggest deals, like Teesside, which made her, overnight, a multimillionaire. So Mark put up with all of it, learned to protect herself, learned the business, and, in her downtime, got a Harvard MBA. As Wing faltered, she stepped in, burnishing her relationship with Lay and other executives. She listened, pressed the flesh, and remade herself, understanding the value of short skirts, straight teeth, and a mane of blond hair. "It's amazing," Mark would later say, "how men will open up and tell you their deepest secrets if you just show a little sympathy and compassion."

When Wing finally wore out his welcome and left Enron for good, Mark asked for—and got—a promotion. Ken Lay made her the CEO of her own company, Enron Development Corporation. Her mandate was to open energy markets for Enron around the world, and soon enough she commandeered a company jet and was flying around the world, launching projects in China, Central America, the Middle East, and India— there was no place she would not go to make a deal. She was one of the richest, most powerful women in the world, and Enron had her all to itself.

If Rebecca Mark reflected Ken Lay's international ambitions, Jeff Skilling embodied his adulation of intellectual firepower and blue-chip credentials. Like Lay and Mark, Skilling was obsessed with the new, but in a more academic, almost abstract, way. Where Mark and Lay dreamed of a globe dominated by Enron's physical presence, Jeff Skilling dreamed of creating a new business model that could change American capitalism forever. He didn't really care about technical innovation—building a better turbine, say. His passion was for commercial innovation in services, that branch of the United States economy that was heralded as the future in the late seventies and early eighties. In some ways, Mark and Lay were forever farm kids, in love with heavy equipment and extracting wealth from the earth. Skilling was a city kid who understood, from personal experience, the perpetual change that defined urban (and, maybe more important, suburban) life and, intuitively if not expressly, the emptiness that often lay at the center of it.

He had lived it. Skilling's father was a sales representative for a valve company, and he spent his childhood, with his mother and three siblings, waiting for a promise to be fulfilled. Skilling's father had been told that if he stayed on, he'd end up running the company, but the company was sold and the job went to someone else. The effect on the family was devastating. Skilling's mother had grown up poor and fatherless and had never shed the fear that she would wind up poverty-stricken again. When the best job prospect forced the family to move from the East Coast to a blue-collar suburb of Chicago, she never quite recovered from the disappointment. She pushed her kids, but, fearing failure, tended to look on the dark side. As a result, her son Jeff would grow up with an ambivalence toward risk. He was rebellious, yet sure he knew where the line was.

It was Jeff who held the family together, with his energy and his enthusiasms. He taught his younger brother Mark to play chess and locate the planets in the night sky; planned outings in the woods to build tree forts and intricate, working dams; and rewired the family's stereo system inside the house, creating a radio station in the basement. He was the kind of kid other boys followed without question, and he was absolutely fearless. He played to win, so much so that he was often in a cast.

Skilling did well in school, but by the time he was fourteen, he had already found himself a job, following his older brother Tom, a budding meteorologist, to a local TV station. The place was not unlike the *Saturday Night Live* parodies of local access TV—Skilling was allowed to do most anything, and he did it, waxing the floors until they glowed, producing programs when an employee walked off the job unexpectedly. He learned, early on, the importance of presentation, of making the most innocuous things look like so much more.

When it came time for college, Skilling intended to follow in his father's footsteps and study engineering. When he got to Lehigh University, in Bethlehem, Pennsylvania, it was 1970, a recession year, and he was facing college in the center of the Rust Belt. Jeff Skilling looked down the Appalachian valley, saw the skeletons of abandoned steel mills, and felt the promise of his life seeping away. Luckily, he returned home to find that his National Merit Scholarship status had attracted the attention of a school in Dallas, Texas. Southern Methodist University was offering him a full scholarship. Skilling left Chicago on a day the temperature was twenty-five degrees and arrived in Dallas, on the same day, to seventy-six degrees and sunbathing coeds. He toured SMU and never looked back: Dallas was then one of the few cities in the country that was thriving—Texas Instruments had made the city a high-tech center, and the healthy Texas economy made the city a big financial capital. The spanking new skyscrapers outlined in neon at night made the place look like Oz, a capital of new ideas.

It wasn't long before Skilling abandoned his engineering major and began to study finance. He devoured the two-volume, 1933 biography of John D. Rockefeller, and felt his life change after discovering a tome called *Beat the Market!* He threw himself into the world of hedges, warrants, options—a whole new way of making money while avoiding risk. He dreamed of creating a new currency. By junior year, Skilling was counting the days before he could make his mark on the business world. Alone in the evenings, he would drive up the city's Central Expressway to a spot where, night after night, he could see one light burning on the eighteenth floor of a darkened office building. That's who I want to be, he told himself. That guy up there.

From SMU, Skilling, like Mark, moved to First City, though he worked mostly in corporate planning, with little customer contact. Soon enough he rose to become the youngest officer at the bank. When his mentor found errors on his spreadsheets, Skilling was mortified. Look, there can't be any mistakes, the older man told him, and Skilling worked at them, night after night, until they were perfect.

He wanted an MBA, and gave himself a choice: He'd make it to Harvard, or he'd go to night school at the University of Houston. Interviewing with a Harvard admissions officer at the Hyatt Hotel in downtown Houston, he thought he was blowing it. Skilling was trying to sell his myriad accomplishments but his interviewer had heard it all before. Abruptly, the man cut him off.

"Are you smart?" he asked.

Skilling paused, weighing for just a minute how to answer the question. "I'm fucking smart," he said finally.

"Are you ambitious?" he asked.

"I'm fucking ambitious," he answered, this time without hesitation.

At first, he was intimidated by Harvard. It was a school full of rich guys—guys who'd been to Choate, guys returning to school with big careers already under their belts, guys related to guys who ran major corporations or Third World countries. But like Ken Lay, Jeff Skilling found out soon enough that he could hold his own. He aced the first round of exams—known around the business school as The Screen, because it eliminated those who couldn't keep up—and he won an award for making the highest grade in a famously tough marketing class. If there was one thing Jeff Skilling knew how to do, it was sell. Focused on any idea that excited him, his voice grew flat but accelerated, and his blue eyes seemed to grow both wider and more intense, meeting and holding the gaze of any doubter. *I'm right—you know I'm right—so why argue?* Politically, he was a conservative; faced with hypothetical corporate dilemmas, "his allegiance was to the shareholders of a company versus public service or mankind," according to a former classmate. Jeff Skilling had built a life for himself out of nothing, and others could do the same. By the end of the second year, he was a Baker Scholar, an honor awarded for landing in the top 5 percent of his class. By the time he left Harvard, he was afraid of no one.

Skilling joined the Houston office of McKinsey & Co., the consulting firm that was, by the early eighties, considered the natural next step for business-oriented overachievers. During this period, American business appeared on the verge of collapse, losing ground, hourly it seemed, to the Japanese. CEOs had to learn to navigate the world of leveraged buyouts and corporate takeovers—to make their companies leaner and meaner—and they turned to consultants for help. Ostensibly, consultants had the latest thinking and could help plot strategy, or value new acquisitions. CEOs who wanted the best hired McKinsey, "a SWAT team of business philosopher kings," in the words of *New Yorker* journalist Nicholas Lemann. For a young, ambitious person like Jeff Skilling, McKinsey offered the chance to put some of his ideas into practice—it was a risk-free way to see whether his theories could actually hold water. Once again Skilling worked around the clock, and after a few years he was the youngest partner in the firm's history.

He was also a somewhat paunchy, balding, pasty-faced man whose shirts never stayed tucked in and whose oversized wire-rimmed glasses were hopelessly out of date. He was ill at ease with small talk, most dynamic when he was selling strategy, happiest alone, with his work. Skilling had married before heading for Harvard, and by the mid-eighties had two young children with a third on the way. But his real love was for the business that so far existed only in his imagination.

It was no wonder that Ken Lay was drawn to McKinsey, and it was no wonder that, in turn, he was drawn to Jeff Skilling. Skilling had a way of talking that could be almost messianic; in the turmoil that was enveloping the gas business in the mid-eighties, this would have been very reassuring. Things had not turned out exactly as Lay had envisioned: The deregulated gas market had created an industry subject to unreliable prices and an unreliable supply. Initially, gas distribution companies had jumped at the chance to cancel "take or pay" contracts that required them to do just that—buy gas whether they used it or not. They turned instead to the spot market, which, in the beginning, offered relief from high prices. In fact, proponents of the free market could claim victory: The price of gas had dropped from $4 per million British thermal units (mmbtu's) in the mid-1980s to $3 by the end of the decade. The cumulative gas savings was in excess of $50 billion. But as the overall market settled down, the spot market revved up. Prices rose, supply fell, and no one seemed able to get what they needed when they needed it—and that included Enron, which was still struggling under its merger-induced debt load. Lay had to find a new way to do business if his business was to survive at all. His blue-chip tastes drew him to McKinsey; it wasn't long, in fact, before the halls of Enron were thick with bustling young McKinsey consultants, who became almost indistinguishable from their Enron counterparts.

Jeff Skilling was different from many because he had a background in finance, not gas. As the U.S. economy had changed, so had the rules of finance—hard times had encouraged businesses to find novel ways to increase profits and, more important, to simultaneously strip out risk. Technology had changed business, too—high-powered computers made it possible to create mathematical models that could analyze the pros and cons of financial transactions in ways that had been unimaginable just years before.

While these tools were common in New York investment banks, they were unknown in the gas business. Skilling sometimes joked about the Texas Hedge, which meant, simply, that Texans looking for gas simply assumed the price would go up once they had it to sell. The Texas Hedge was predicated on the energy business's natural optimism—being broke was just part of the game, and things would get better. But Skilling wasn't an optimist, and he wondered why some of the newest financial tools couldn't be applied to the foundering gas business.

He came up with a very simple idea that he called the Gas Bank. Because of its newfound volatility, the deregulated world of finding, selling, and buying natural gas was no longer creditworthy, a status that threatened to strap the industry even further. Skilling had a plan to reverse that course. Enron would create a pool of gas suppliers, in much the same way a bank puts together a pool of depositors. Then the company would sell their gas to purchasers, in much the same way banks lend money. Enron would take its profit on the spread between those two transactions. It was a good idea, but it was also fraught with risk: To create a dependable business, Enron couldn't be just a broker—it had to own the supply, and contractually guarantee that and the price of its gas to its network of buyers. Its knowledge and control of the market would have to be absolute.

Skilling thought it was possible. Enron already had a successful oil and gas unit to furnish the initial supply. Then, too, he didn't have any competition: Gas was not a glamour business like oil. It was populated by smart enough people, but people accustomed to the security of regulation. So Skilling began to tinker with a mathematical model of his plan, and, in his own words, found the results "absolutely compelling." Then he took the idea to his client, Enron. He stood before a room of twenty-five executives at Enron's headquarters, his idea distilled to one page—and flopped. "They thought it was stupid," Skilling would later recall.

At the end of the meeting, Skilling walked with Lay to the bank of elevators outside the conference room, apologizing profusely. Lay punched the button and then turned to Skilling. "Let's go," he said.

The Gas Bank was not an overnight success. There were many nights

Skilling awoke in a cold sweat, sure that he was going to deal a death blow to Enron. But on other days he knew, without a doubt, that he could change the way business was done, maybe forever.

And then Enron sold $800 million worth of gas in a week. From then on, the contracts rolled in. Skilling could tell when a deal was going to work: If the customer was under fifty, he would go for it. Young guys wanted to be in on the future Enron was creating.

He did too. In 1990, Kinder and Lay convinced Skilling to come to Enron and run his own unit, which would be called Enron Gas Services. Thanks to a quasi-ownership interest, he would soon become a very wealthy man. And, over the next few years, Enron did in fact transform the gas business—and increase its own profits. In a state reeling from the energy bust, Enron became the bank of choice—it was the only bank, really, to support the growth of the industry. People started exploring again: Enron backed two unknown Louisiana landmen named Jim Flores and Billy Rucks in a deal that made them big players overnight. Flores eventually bought Oscar Wyatt's River Oaks mansion, and Enron made about $20 million in profit. A transaction with a power company called Sithe brought in another $11 million. Other gas deals with independent gas producers like Forest Oil and Zilkha Energy brought in billions of cubic feet of gas that Enron then sold to its customers at a hefty profit.

As the U.S. economy improved, business became more customized. *Have It Your Way!*—Burger King's motto—could just as easily be applied to toothpaste companies that tried to develop a product to appeal to twelve-year-old boys who liked to skateboard, or dog food companies that developed myriad products for puppies, older dogs, overweight dogs, active dogs, etc. Enron followed suit, developing customized products for its ever-growing customer base. Some wanted a guaranteed gas supply long into the future— so they could finance a big gas-fired power plant, for example—but they didn't want to be locked into a given price. Enron gave them an option to pay a fee to buy the gas at a specified price on a future date. By combining a finance business with Enron's almost limitless physical supply, there was always a way to make a deal. In 1989, representatives of a Louisiana aluminum producer walked away from the table when they thought Enron's gas transportation fee was too high. The deal was saved when someone suggested Enron write a financial contract in which the customer paid Enron a fixed price for the gas, while Enron, in turn, supplied the gas by paying the floating prices of a gas producer that was located nearby. That way, the Louisiana company held down its energy cost with just the kind of contract it wanted, and Enron eliminated its vulnerability with another customer with an opposing need. This transaction would soon be known as the first natural gas "swap." Soon enough, Enron was back in the trading business in a big way—as the major player in the gas market.

There were two more changes that assured Enron great success in the years to come: By 1990, gas trading had become so popular that the New York Mercantile Exchange established a new market for gas futures—a contract to buy or sell gas at a later date at a specified price. Because Enron had become so dominant in the business, it was the dominant company when it came to setting prices as well. The NYMEX's first gas contracts went forward only eighteen months, while Enron offered much longer contracts at long-term prices. And you didn't have to actually buy the gas to participate—financial traders jumped in and out of the market to take advantage of fluctuations in the price. In the process, they made the market even bigger. Because many of those traders were Enron's, the company could effectively grow the market, set the prices, and control it at the same time.

Then, in 1991, Enron Gas Services' recently hired assistant controller Rick Causey convinced the Securities and Exchange Commission to allow Enron to account for its trading profits by using a method called "mark to market accounting." This method was common in the financial industry, where so much money was going in and out the door—to be paid and collected a few years hence—that old-fashioned accrual accounting was useless. Trading houses, for instance, set the value of future deals on current market prices, thus the term "mark to market." No energy firm had ever asked to use this method before. But Enron asserted that the value of its product fluctuated just as wildly as any trading company. It, too, had to know its credit risks at all times. The SEC agreed, and from then on, Enron could, for example, buy gas from a supplier at $2mmbtu ten years into the future and sell gas to a power plant at $3 per mmbtu for the same period, and recognize all the profits right away. Enron convinced the SEC that it should treat each contract separately, to accurately measure its credit risk for its shareholders. But the technique that measured Enron's credit risk from day one also measured its long-term profits from day one. Of course, this wasn't real money.

The agreement was a little like a grocery wholesaler who might sign a ten-year contract with a farmer for gourmet tomatoes at 25 cents a pound, and sell the tomatoes, for the same period, to a gourmet restaurant for $1. All goes well if the farmer and the restaurant stay in business. But what happens if the farmer has a bad year or the restaurant closes?

This was the cautionary note sounded by *Forbes*'s Toni Mack when she reconsidered Enron in May 1993 in a story called "Hidden Risks." "On Wall Street and in the oil patch, Ken Lay's Enron Corp has been a smashing success," the headline read. "Here are some things that could go wrong." Mack noted the company's enormous success—revenues of $6.4 billion in 1992, the 20 percent surge in earnings from 1992 to 1993, its stock price trading at three times its book value and eighteen times its expected 1993 earnings. Enron sold or transported a fifth of the nation's natural gas.

But Mack also noted that according to the rules of mark to market, if Enron's contracts lost value, the company would be forced to book losses, and Enron had plenty of customers, financial partners, and suppliers who were historically not dependable. Mack also pointed out that booking mark-to-market profits set the company on a constant search for growth—Enron would have to book ever more deals every year to show that their income was rising. Skilling's reassurances that the company had $49 million in reserve left Mack unconvinced. "Is that enough for a $2.7 billion (revenues) gas marketing operation?" she asked.

Enron's response to Mack's piece was swift and sure. Lay sent her an angry letter, insisting that Enron's accountants, Arthur Andersen, had supported the move to mark to market—who was she to question them? Within days of the story's publication, Enron's PR department rounded up a cabal of Wall Street analysts to support their position. From Donaldson, Lufkin & Jenrette: "We regard the 'Forbes' recitation of risks as an inaccurate portrayal of the business and as showing a lack of understanding of the operations of the EGS unit and the industry." The Donaldson, Lufkin & Jenrette report noted that the company still rated Enron "very attractive." So did Lehman

Brothers, which insisted that Mack's story was "misleading and demonstrates a considerable lack of understanding." ("1-M buy reconfirmed!") Goldman Sachs raved: "Enron is an even better company than investors believe."

The final shot was heard almost a year later, with the publication of a glowing Harvard Business School case study on Skilling and his inspiring pursuit of innovation at Enron Gas Services. It cited the *Forbes* story as "one Jeff Skilling could dismiss."

4

Enron Smart

IN 1993, Sherron Watkins* was working in Manhattan as a vice president for MG Trade Finance Corporation, a small commodity-lending boutique that was a subsidiary of a fine old German industrial firm called Metallgesellschaft. She spent her days managing their oil and gas loan portfolio, the contents of which were worth close to $1 billion, but she had the sense, common to many people who are not born and raised in New York City, that it was time to go home. She had enjoyed the New York experience—she lived in the right part of town (the Upper East Side), and dated master-of-the-universe types. Now Sherron's closest friends were married and starting families. Their next step would be the move to the suburbs, which meant she'd be spending more and more of her weekends alone. Being a single woman in Manhattan in your thirties, she knew, was very different from being

*Sherron Watkins joined Enron in 1993 under her maiden name, Sherron Smith. In 1997, she married an energy consultant, Richard Watkins. For simplicity's sake, she is referred to throughout the book as Sherron Watkins.

a single woman in Manhattan in your twenties, and she was ready to move on.

There was really only one place to go: Houston. It was just thirty or so miles from her hometown of Tomball, and her mother and stepfather, and it was a big city, with plenty of opportunity in her field of expertise. Her father was in Houston too. There was really only one place Sherron wanted to work in Houston: Enron. If you were in the world of finance or the world of energy, you heard about the kinds of things they were doing and wanted to be a part of reinventing the future. There was no place hotter or hipper— even in New York—and Sherron was determined to land a job there.

In her mind, she was perfect for the place. She had graduated from college with honors in accounting, and she had worked at Arthur Andersen, the accounting firm that was practically joined at the hip with Enron, for eight years. As an auditor, she'd worked with big-name clients—she'd been part of the Andersen team hired in 1988 to help defend Leona Helmsley for tax evasion. (A U.S. attorney had bragged that prosecuting Helmsley was one of his easiest jobs, because Helmsley made so many enemies happy to kick her when she was down. Sherron would never forget that observation.) She'd also worked briefly for Enron, or, more specifically, Internorth, though she wasn't sure she'd want to go into the details with an Enron interviewer: In 1985, the company had been concerned about a crude oil trading division run by two guys named Borget and Mastroeni, and Internorth had asked Andersen's Houston office to investigate. Andersen had in turn asked Sherron, a twenty-five-year-old auditor with barely two years' experience, to go to New York to check them out. Her partner was a young man who looked fresh out of a UT frat house.

Sherron stayed at the New York Hilton, and could hardly focus on her work, because she was so excited to be in Manhattan for the first time. The Internorth traders took her to lunch at a chic Japanese restaurant. Not to be outdone, Sherron ate sushi with chopsticks and enjoyed the infamous two-martini lunch—the traders urged the Andersen team to try a new variation, a sake martini with a cucumber slice. Back at the trading office, she'd scarcely combed through the spreadsheets, which didn't matter because she didn't really know what she was looking for anyway. Then she flew home to Houston, wrote up a short report, and, following standard operating procedure, billed the client $10,000 plus expenses.

It was the Helmsley experience that inspired her to find another job, however—Sherron didn't want to work for another client she'd just as soon see in jail. Her next employer, Metallgesellschaft, had a great reputation and gave her many opportunities to learn more about financing oil and gas deals, and about trading in oil, gas, and metals—all of which should impress Enron, with whom MG competed.

But the headhunters were not encouraging. Enron wanted Ivy Leaguers and Stanford graduates—and she had gone to UT. Besides, Sherron was competing with people from Merrill Lynch, Goldman Sachs, and other big investment banks, too; that's who Enron wanted. Her Andersen contacts might help, but she still might not make the cut. Undaunted, Sherron sent her résumé to two former Andersen colleagues who worked at Enron, and they came through—at least, they arranged for her to have a few interviews. She took vacation time to fly to Houston, arrived at the fifty-story skyscraper, and was ready to close the deal. She was wowed by the high-end décor, the way the oval shape of the building was echoed by the granite inlays in the lobby floors and the granite tables in executive offices. Enron did things right, she could tell.

But the first interview did not go well. A vice president who financed oil and gas drilling quizzed her about how she took care of her energy clients at MG. "Who takes 'em hunting?" he asked. "Who takes 'em fishing?" Maybe Enron wasn't as modern as Sherron had heard—this guy didn't think a woman could cut deals in the oil patch.

The next day, however, she interviewed with Andy Fastow and knew she'd been right all along. He was young and energetic—dark-haired, bright-eyed, with a Jersey accent that she found oddly comforting—and he was married to another Enron executive, so he couldn't have a problem working with women. Sherron had done her homework—Fastow was the creator of a new investment group, a partnership between Enron and CalPERS, the California Public Employees' Retirement System, the largest public-sector pension fund in the country. Sherron thought she would be perfect to manage the portfolio, and told Fastow so. He agreed.

There was just one problem, he told her when he called her in New York a few weeks later to offer her the job. Fastow couldn't match her MG salary or her title. She'd have to come to Enron as a director instead of a vice president. That was just the way things were done at Enron—everyone had to prove that they were worthy of being Enron VPs. He knew she'd work her way back up the ladder quickly. Sherron weighed her options. It was fall in New York, a beautiful season, but winter was coming. She also knew her money would go further in Houston, where the cost of living was so much lower. And she wanted to go home. "Okay," she told Fastow. "You've got a deal."

She started at Enron Gas Services in mid-October 1993. Not more than six weeks later, MG imploded. From her office on the twenty-ninth floor, she devoured news accounts of her old firm's collapse. "In a mixture of greed, stupidity, and arrogance, this U.S. subsidiary of Metallgesellschaft . . . tried to outrun the market and got caught," *Futures* magazine asserted. Their traders had bet wrong on the price of oil, and they'd bet big. "MG wanted too much too fast," the story continued. "Giddy from their initial trading profits and eager to expand, MG executives were slow to recognize the flip side of the market—fortunes are made in a day but are lost even quicker."

Sherron felt as though she had escaped a burning building, only to land in a cushy office at Enron. It was certainly cushier than anything she'd had at MG: She had a large black leather chair, that oval-shaped worktable of chrome and black granite (*desks were for dinosaurs!*), a credenza and bookcase made of richly stained wood, and the requisite whiteboard for all those spontaneous Enron brainstorming sessions. She had beautiful prints on her wall, courtesy of Enron's archive. She also had a Mont Blanc pen that Fastow gave her, a welcome gift with the acronym JEDI—short for Joint Energy Development Investments, the portfolio she was running—emblazoned on the side.

She had plenty of work, even though the fund was new. Fastow had promptly handed over all the JEDI management responsibilities to her. JEDI's mission was "to invest in a diversified portfolio of natural gas related investments strategically linked to Enron Gas Services' core businesses." The fund could lend money to energy companies, form partnerships with other energy companies, or buy equity in other energy companies; the only requirements were that the investments be natural gas related and increase Enron Gas Services' core trading business—and thus continue to boost Enron's stock price. Because Enron had $250 million in Enron shares invested in JEDI, when Enron's stock went up, JEDI's value increased. It was a circular investment chain that helped both partners.

Sherron soon found that much of her job involved instilling discipline

in the young men charged with developing deals JEDI might fund—
"originators" in Enron-speak. She wasn't going to allow money to be spent
on any old project, and that was sometimes what they brought her—half-
baked ideas written up in half-baked ways. It wasn't long before she was
using salty language to convince the originators to use a proposal form she
had swiftly invented. Listening to her, one young associate confessed he had
never heard the term "buttfuck" used in a business meeting before. Go visit
the trading floor, she retorted, meaning, "I belong here—what about you?"

In early December, as press reports of MG's collapse were gathering
steam, Sherron's phone rang. It was Jeff Skilling's secretary, asking her to
come to his office. Sherron stood up and smoothed her short purple skirt,
relieved that she had worn something bright and attention-grabbing for this,
her first real meeting with The Boss. Oh, she had seen Skilling in the halls
and exchanged pleasantries, and he had dropped in on meetings, wowing
everyone in the room with his quick solutions to problems that stymied everyone else. Once, for instance, Sherron had been in a conference with Fastow
and another executive, fretting over the pitch for a new fund, named YODA
after yet another Star Wars character. No one could come up with the right
language to show the synergies Enron Gas Services could provide; everything
seemed too convoluted and self-serving. Then Skilling popped in, listened
briefly, walked up to the floor-to-ceiling whiteboard, and grabbed a marker.
Instead of words, he drew three circles, which he described as a three-legged
stool, his graphic representation of EGS's business model. Each leg represented a different service provided by the company—the physical delivery of
the gas, the financing of the gas, and the risk management—yet all were interdependent and, when combined, all-encompassing for the customer. (*It's that
simple! A three-legged stool! Each leg equally important!*) Then he walked out.
The three of them quickly scribbled a copy of the drawing, to be replicated in
their pitch books. That was the Skilling effect: He moved so fast that when he
left the room, you felt invigorated and stupid at the same time.

His office was on the thirty-third floor and was similar to Sherron's, only
it was three times bigger. The furniture was sleek and contemporary, with
that same dark, authoritative Enronian stain. His bookcase was stocked
with deal toys—souvenirs of successful ventures—and framed press clips.

Skilling, Sherron noted, had his own granite and chrome, oval-shaped conference table.

She walked in to find him behind his desk and Cliff Baxter facing Skilling in a chair that gave him a floor-to-ceiling view of Houston's flat, almost primordial landscape. From this height, the city was a sea of green stretching to the horizon. The lush treetops and overgrown vines seemed ready at any minute to reclaim the skyscrapers and shopping centers, returning Houston to the wild.

Skilling and Baxter looked solemn. Sherron took a chair next to Baxter and waited. She liked Baxter. He was a big man with a florid ego who loved nothing more than the high-pressure, theatrical world of mergers and acquisitions. He was also a member of Skilling's inner circle, a group Sherron had begun to study with intense interest.

Skilling explained: They were worried about the effect MG's collapse would have on Enron's stock price. Enron Gas Services was a new company, and its gas-trading business was even newer. Trading was going well at Enron, but Skilling was concerned that MG's fall would cause a loss of confidence in other, similar companies. If Enron's stock dropped, its leadership might withdraw support for his fledgling trading operation before it really showed what it could do. Memories of the Valhalla fiasco were still fresh, after all. What Skilling and Baxter wanted to know was this: What really happened at MG and what safeguards could they put in place to assure people—the Enron board, Enron executives, the analysts and investors— that such a thing could never happen in Enron's house?

Sherron was nonplussed. In her mind, Enron and MG had nothing in common. She told Skilling that MG's collapse was not exactly as reported in the press. Trading had been a problem, but the deeper issue had been on the balance sheet. The traders placed huge bets to try to gamble the company out of trouble. The problems at MG, she said, were caused by "desperate moves by desperate people."

Skilling grimaced impatiently. "That's not a good answer," he said, his eyes locking on Sherron's. "We could become desperate one day." The words hung in the air: Enron? Desperate? It was as if Skilling knew something she didn't, about the company, or, maybe, about himself.

Baxter came to Sherron's rescue by suggesting that Enron Gas Services probably needed an internal control system along with a PR plan, which would explain those controls to the market. Skilling agreed; EGS had to have bulletproof controls in place, procedures that would stop anyone from taking big chances on the trading floor. The public had to know that Enron was a company of risk managers, he said, not a company of speculators.

Skilling consulted an Arthur Andersen partner and came up with a plan. First, the controls and trading position limits had to be approved by the board of directors, who would write the trading rules. Second, a formal independent risk-evaluation group was needed. And last, EGS needed a zero-tolerance policy—traders who hid a position would be summarily fired.

It didn't occur to anyone then that similar bulletproof controls might be needed on the funding side of EGS. Someone like Andy Fastow, for instance, would never have seemed like a risk; he was raising money, not making it.

Jeff Skilling had come to Enron with nothing more than an idea—The Gas Bank—and in an incomprehensibly short time built one of the most successful businesses in the country. As the 1994 Harvard case study pointed out, Enron by 1992 was "the largest non-regulated gas merchant in North America, manager of the largest portfolio of fixed price gas and natural gas derivative contracts in the world, the largest supplier of gas to the electricity generating industry in North America." EGS was the second-largest contributor to Enron's net income in 1992, reporting earnings before interest and taxes of $122 million, more than double its 1991 earnings and more than four times its 1990 earnings. But along with financial success, Skilling had built a culture that was edgy, willing to shuck tradition and go out on a limb.

He had come to Enron as an outsider, and in the beginning was content to build a world within a world for himself. That his division existed within a stolid, steady, rather unimaginative pipeline company didn't matter. Ken Lay gave him his head—*Let's go!*—and Skilling spent his early years hiring the kind of people he needed to build the kind of business he wanted. What he wanted, most of all, were smart people, and a lot of time and effort went into convincing people like Sherron Watkins that Enron had the top business school graduates and investment banking emigrés. But Enron found that it was pretty hard to entice people to move to Houston from Harvard and Manhattan; it was easier, as it turned out, to find ambitious self-starters from the Midwest and Texas. You did have to be smart to work at Enron, and it helped to have a degree from a prestigious university, especially when you were negotiating your salary and perks. But Skilling didn't really want eggheads. He wanted people like himself—ambitious, driven, self-made, with something of an edge. You had to be glib, you had to be aggressive, and, most of all, you had to be able to sell. You also had to have a healthy disrespect for the established order—how else could you keep innovating? When Skilling found such people, he didn't care where they had come from—he hired a gifted trader named Jeff Shankman when he was selling jewelry at Tiffany's in Manhattan.

In turn, Skilling engendered a kind of loyalty that, even in the early years, was almost cultlike. "He took a chance on me," Shankman liked to say, which meant *Jeff saw how smart I was when no one else did*. Skilling had an instinct for misfits—Cliff Baxter, for instance, was the rough-edged son of a policeman from Amityville, New York. He was moody and cantankerous, but an incomparable negotiator. Skilling was untroubled by eccentricity when a person produced, and his small group—Andy Fastow, in charge of funding; a shy, taciturn former banker named Gene Humphrey; a sly, secretive head trader named Lou Pai—seemed to have an idea a minute. Why rein them in?

Once Skilling had a small team in place, however, he began to chafe at his surroundings. He wanted Enron Gas Services to be more like a fast-paced New York investment bank and less like a sluggish, regulated utility. Finance, in the late eighties and early nineties, was hip—people could make gobs of money at it in a very short period of time, if they knew what they were doing. Enron had to focus more on taking risks and creatively managing them instead of selling something that had, until recently, been a waste product for the oil industry.

It was risk taking and creativity—and the promise of instant wealth—that also appealed to the generation that was exiting American business schools at the time Enron was coming into its own. The smartest, most ambitious MBAs weren't about to work at a corporation for the rest of their lives, as their parents and grandparents had done. That was for plodders. Twenty-something business school graduates in the early 1990s witnessed the stock market crash of 1987, but what was burned indelibly into their brains was its roaring recovery. They read voraciously about the junk-bond and takeover kings of the go-go eighties, but came to a different conclusion than did readers a generation or so older; James Stewart's *Den of Thieves*, about the rise and fall of Michael Milken and Drexel Burnham, was to them not a cautionary tale but a road map. Business was being reinvented, and as they saw it, more money could be made than ever before. These were young men and women to whom $1 million a year did not seem like an outrageous benefits package. They didn't wish for luxuries, they expected them—flashy cars, cutting-edge art, trekking trips to exotic locales. But more important was one particular intangible: freedom, which they believed could be bought like anything else.

Their thinking went like this: If you devoted sixty, maybe eighty hours a week to the right company you could, conceivably, cash out by the time you were forty and never have to work again. You would have total free-dom—live in a psychological and social free market without rules or regu-lations—for the rest of your life, which, if you were only in your twenties, sounded like a very long time. It happened to people who worked on Wall Street; it happened to people who worked at Microsoft. That the single-minded pursuit of money might be self-limiting in other, psychic ways was not really considered. This was a speeded-up world; introspection was for retirees.

And so, consciously or unconsciously, Enron Gas Services was built to suit the times. Skilling hired people who were very young, because very young people did not insist on coming in at nine and leaving at five, or on keeping things as they had always been, or, for that matter, on questioning authority once they had signed on with him. He tore down walls so that everyone could work together in a creative hive. He installed television monitors that constantly broadcast NYMEX reports, to keep the kids pumped. He blasted through floors, to build interior staircases to eliminate the pesky wait at the elevator. He let them bring toys to the office—foosball games, dart boards—and made fun of the dowdy administrators who chased after him with forms, traditions, rules. If the rest of Enron resented him—and they did—Jeff Skilling didn't care. He wanted to deregulate himself and his people from the rest of the company.

Enron Gas Services was also a meritocracy—no special dispensation for the deadwood, no sentimental attachments to people who didn't "add value," in company parlance. Skilling had brought along a lot of concepts from McKinsey—"loose/tight" for free thinking and strict controls, for instance—but the Performance Review Committee, or PRC, was the most crucial import for building the kind of organization he wanted.

In theory, the PRC was a 360-degree process that allowed workers to get feedback from everyone around them—their bosses, their peers, their staff. But it could also be used to dispatch the people who couldn't measure up. Early in Skilling's tenure, a classic pipeline guy named John Esslinger, who headed Enron's traditional gas marketing arm (it bought and sold gas off Enron's North American regulated pipeline system), went to Skilling and proposed a merger. By combining the businesses, he reasoned, they could offer much more to their customers. Better yet, Esslinger offered Skilling the chance to run the show. Skilling hastily accepted; Esslinger had offered him a blueprint for expanding his domain and, simultaneously, eliminating any competition for a spot in the executive suite.

He developed a very clever M.O.: He would suggest that a successful division head join forces with him, and then the two would combine their organizations. Within a matter of months, however, that division head would somehow be gone, with Skilling alone atop a much larger business unit. His bottom line—and his own income, as stipulated in his contract— would be fattened from every takeover. Skilling dispatched a few much-beloved leaders in the process, but he hadn't come to Enron to make friends. One popular executive knew the name of everyone in the company, but what did he know about taking Enron into the future? Pipeline guys weren't headed in that direction. They liked to go home at five to be with their families; they didn't "get" that they were part of a titanic struggle to make Enron the World's First Natural Gas Major. The only downside to these internal mergers was the excess staff—the deadwood—Skilling picked up in the process. That's where the PRC came in.

It worked like a star chamber crossed with fraternity rush. Each level of the Enron Gas Services organization, from clerks to executives, was evaluated on the basis of its performance on a curve that allowed for 5 percent to be judged outstanding—"water walkers," in company parlance—25 percent excellent, 25 percent strong, 30 percent satisfactory, and 15 percent needing improvement. This bottom 15 percent were in jeopardy, with at least 5 to 8 percent of the workforce targeted for elimination. In theory, people were judged by how much value they contributed to the company—how much money they brought in, or how their contributions helped to bring in money—but the fix was in. People who worked in trading or finance almost always had the opportunity to make much more for the company than people who worked, say, in a conventional pipeline or gas-storage unit that Skilling may have absorbed.

Judgment Day took place at a Houston luxury hotel in a conference room outfitted with a large table in the center and a U-shaped table skimming its perimeter. In the middle stood representatives of Enron's Human Resources Department, who, much like game show hostesses, advanced or demoted employees according to their rankings by moving placards with their names toward the front or the back of the table. Committee members sat around the perimeter and watched, Politburo style, to keep them from grabbing and moving the placards themselves. In the PRC's earliest incarnations, committee members routinely grabbed a placard from the top of the table—*"There is no way in hell this guy is a water walker!"*—and shove the card of some hapless youth down to the end of the table with the rest of the losers. His champion would then snatch it back, and slam the card back down at the top of the table. This went on for hours. Now unhappy committee members could only scream at their HR stand-in until they moved the cards.

To maintain order, strict rules of play were instituted: No "old tapes" were permitted (i.e., if an employee did something great or awful the year before, it no longer counted). Evaluations were limited to a person's current accomplishments or lack thereof. Rankings were based on direct experience. No one was supposed to say—though they did—"I don't know the fucker, but I've seen him in the halls and he just can't be good."

After about eight hours of this jockeying, the room would grow quiet—mostly from exhaustion—and it would appear the task was done. Then HR would count the cards and announce that too many people were in the top group, and at least five people had to move down. Then the process would start all over again, dragging on until three or four in the morning, until committee members reached the required consensus. This moment was called "Voting the Table."

Meals and snacks—a cornucopia of popcorn, M&Ms, sodas, and cookies—were provided, but even so, goodwill did not prevail. It was one thing to use the PRC to get rid of people who were not cool—the pocket protector, pipeline set. But once they were weeded out, managers had to choose between people who were cool and people who might be just marginally cooler. This situation produced hairsplitting debates, as committee members began running down employees they hardly knew just to save their own. Executives started horse trading in advance of the committee meetings—they sacrificed good people just to go home and get some sleep.

Eventually, it became clear that the PRC was hurting more than it was helping. Enron Gas Services was developing a reputation as a predatory place where people would sell each other out to survive. People outside the company got the word, too, and blue-chip recruits became leery of signing on—a death knell for Skilling's plan to attract the best and the brightest. The PRC process would continue, but by 1995 the forced bell curve ceased—it became a goal but not a requirement.

By then Skilling had his team in place anyway. These people knew how smart they were—they'd beaten their college honors programs and Enron's PRC, and if they had occasion to doubt, generous bonuses well into six figures served as proof of their superiority. Everyone who worked at Enron was smart, but people who worked for Enron Gas Services were *smarter*. By October of that year, EGS had grown from 300 to 1,400 employees and changed its name to Enron Capital & Trade Resources, which had as its mission "worldwide energy solutions." At the celebration, Skilling, wearing a grass skirt complete with lei and a Hawaiian shirt, pumped up the crowd with praise for their many accomplishments, and then asked everyone who had been at Enron for one year to stand up. Almost everyone stood. Then he asked that everyone who had been at Enron for over two years to remain standing. Many people sat down. "How about those who have been at Enron over three years?" Another large group took their seats. "Now those who have been at Enron over four years?" he asked. In the large ballroom, it was hard to find anyone still on their feet. This, to Skilling, was a source of great pride. His team was young and fresh, and he intended to keep it that way.

In private moments, the speed at which Skilling had achieved his success surprised even him. Riding in one of the corporate jets, he'd peer out over the clouds and say to no one in particular, "Who would have believed it?"—that in four short years he had built a financial powerhouse. "Do you think Ken understands what we do at all?" he'd ask. "Do you think he gets it?" No one would answer, but everyone would smile encouragingly, so Skilling would answer the question himself.

"Naaaaah," he'd say. "I don't think he gets it."

Four months into her tenure at Enron, in February 1994, Sherron Watkins went on a business trip to Aspen, Colorado, with Jeff Skilling, Andy Fastow, and several other members of Skilling's fund-raising team. They were headed for a conference called Pensions 2000/Alternative Investments—Reaching New Peaks, an event created to encourage relations between large public pension funds (for firemen, teachers, police officers, and other public employees) and big-money managers like Aetna Capital Management, Alex Brown Kleinwort Benson Realty Advisors, Bear Stearns & Co., and Kohlberg, Kravis, Roberts & Co. The idea was to help pensioners grow their money. In early 1994, investing in the stock market was still a little dicey. Savvy players wanted diversified portfolios—the goal was to spread investment risk around by combining funds that provided steady returns with speculative deals that boosted growth.

Hence the pension fund advisors' interest in Enron. Skilling's group was there as a guest of Pacific Corporate Group, Inc., a La Jolla–based boutique firm that recommended alternative investments—the kind that returned 25 percent instead of the average 12 percent—to large public pension funds like CalPERS, the Oregon Public Employees Retirement Fund, and the Pennsylvania Public School Employees' Retirement System. PCG was headed by a man named Chris Bower, who had been attracted to Enron's

reputation for innovation. He thought the company would be a great partner for CalPERS, which had, at its disposal, more than $80 billion. Bower's
enthusiasm—and the financial opportunity he represented—seemed to
Enron almost too good to be true.

Enron Gas Services was not able to grow as quickly as Skilling would
have liked, because of the companywide prohibition against increasing
debt, a hangover from the HNG/Internorth merger. Enron's high debt load
kept it from improving its credit rating, which in turn limited its ability to
borrow, grow, and improve its stock price. Specifically, the low credit rating
limited the growth of Enron's trading business. Highly rated companies—
those with A to AAA ratings—did not trade with companies like Enron,
whose rating was below BBB.

So Enron had to find a way to grow without growing its debt. The company turned to something called Special Purpose Entities, or SPEs, which
were then popular financial products that allowed businesses to expand
without increasing debt. In these new vehicles, a company could group specific assets, borrow money against them, and treat the transaction as a sale.
Meanwhile, the debt in the new SPE wouldn't show up on its balance sheet.
SPEs were quickly embraced in the marketplace.

Enron had come up with an innovative product for the gas business
called a volumetric production payment, or VPP. Oil and gas producers
received a large up-front payment from Enron Gas Services in exchange for
a long-term interest in the producers' oil and gas reserves. The customer
could use Enron's VPP as both a financing tool and as a hedge—as cash to
buy and develop fields, and as money that covered operating costs. Enron
then took the balance of the gas or oil production at a fixed price as payment
for its "loan." In a cash-strapped industry, VPPs were a godsend.

They were also a godsend for Enron. Not only did they ensure the company a reliable gas supply for its customers, but, thanks to successful lobbying on the part of Enron, they changed the nature of production payments
in the oil patch. Traditionally, the oil in the ground stayed with its owner,
even in hard times. But VPPs were created to be bankruptcy proof. Once a
producer made a deal with Enron, Enron had possession of the oil or gas
reserves forevermore, bankruptcy or no. This, in turn, allowed Enron to use

the value of these VPP assets as collateral to fund its own low-interest, off-balance-sheet SPEs.

The first of these Enron-sponsored off-balance-sheet SPEs was called Cactus, and it made its creator, Andy Fastow, one of the first five people Skilling had hired at Enron Gas Services, a star. (A protracted lawsuit brought by a New York businessman claimed that Fastow had stolen the concept from him. The case, filed in 1995, is still following a torturous route through the courts.) Fastow combined the energy assets in complicated vehicles that he then sold to large institutional investors. The Cactus SPEs funded Enron's volumetric production payment business, jump starting its trading operation.

But once the Houston banks began to recover from the 1980's oil bust, producers had no need of VPPs; the banks would cut them better deals and didn't demand their gas. Enron was back where it started from—scrounging again for deal flow.

Enter CalPERS, which was offering Enron real money instead of money it would have to borrow. Better yet, that money could be used for a host of Enron deals, not just VPPs. CalPERS presence was so fortuitous that when its investment advisor Chris Bower made a cold call to Skilling to talk over a possible partnership, Skilling thought the call was a prank. Even after the first meetings in La Jolla, the Enron team half expected to discover Bower was a fraud. They couldn't believe that a somewhat disheveled, touchy-feely Californian controlled so much money—and had offered it to them.

But Bower was for real. He dropped $250 million in Enron Gas Services's lap in the summer of 1993, allowing Skilling and Fastow to look like heroes and their unit to expand exponentially almost overnight. CalPERS required Enron to add $250 million of its own stock to the pot, but who cared? Suddenly Enron had an off-balance-sheet fund that was an enormous player; Fastow put together $500 million in loans for the new partnership, giving it three quarters of a billion dollars to invest in energy-related ventures.

Fastow chose the name Joint Energy Development Investments to evoke the brave Jedi knights of the Star Wars series. The Enron board objected to

the name—it was too flashy, not serious enough—but Fastow had persevered, and it stuck.

Now, eight months into the deal, Enron Gas Services was putting in a
mutually beneficial appearance in Aspen at what was, essentially, one
long sales pitch to the pensioners. Bower talked up Enron's record of innovation. Skilling reminded the crowd that Enron was, as he never tired of
saying, "on the side of the angels." Thanks to Enron, heavy industry had
been freed from the fuel shortages that had previously brought business to a
halt. Thanks to Enron, schools were no longer closing and the elderly were
not freezing, because there was enough gas at a fixed, reasonable price for
everyone.

Totally snowed, the pension fund managers treated Enron's executives
like heroes. They put them up at the best hotel, invited them to the best
cocktail parties, treated them to the best gourmet meals at the exclusive
Caribou Club. There were plenty of free lift tickets, too. (While Skilling was
comfortable on the slopes, Fastow, true to his temperament, was a daredev-
il; he once had his pass revoked after skiing in an avalanche-prone no-ski
zone.) For Sherron Watkins, another benefit was that she got some face time
with Skilling in the bar at night. The man never seemed to relax. How could
they make Enron better? he wanted to know. Whom should they hire? What
else did they need to be truly great? Even in a plush armchair, Skilling was
overtaken by his own velocity. Talking to his team, he leaned forward on the
edge of his chair, his eyes shining, his voice racing ahead in a modulated,
seductive, almost hypnotic drone. Sometimes he asked for advice, but mostly he answered his own questions.

Skilling flew out the next day, leaving Sherron and the others to enjoy
another day of skiing and dinner set up by Chris Bower. Bower was coy
about the plan, saying only that he'd wanted to share a very special place
with them, and that they should wear something that would "work in the
snow." Sherron put on some après-ski wear she had brought for the trip; it
was pretty, and she didn't anticipate being outside for long. She left her
down mittens in the hotel room, too, and brought only lightweight gloves.

A van met the small group of seven—Bower and his wife, the conference
organizer, and the remaining Enron gang, Fastow, Gene Humphrey,

Sherron, and another executive named Mitch Taylor, a former banker Fastow had recruited—and ferried them to a rustic outpost, where a man associated with Bower's chosen restaurant, the Pine Creek Cookhouse, handed Sherron a pair of cross-country skis. They were skiing to the restaurant, he explained, which was situated "around the mountain from Aspen."

As it turned out, no one in the group really knew how to cross-country ski—Texans who skied tended to go for the more thrill-inducing downhill version of the sport, which also demanded a flashier wardrobe.

Sherron put her purse in a locker provided by the restaurant and started suiting up. How bad could this be? she wondered. It was just a gimmick, most likely a short hop across a snowy field. It would help her work up an appetite.

Once the group was dressed, the man from Pine Creek handed them some headgear. Sherron studied hers carefully. It looked an awful lot like a miner's hat, except that instead of a helmet with an attached light it was an elastic band with an attached light. She was supposed to position it over her forehead so it could illuminate her way to the restaurant.

Sherron put it on, struggling to stretch the elastic over her nice velvet headband. She thought wistfully of the ski hat and mittens she'd left in her hotel room.

She overheard the conference planner ask a pointed question: Was there any other way to get to the restaurant, besides on skis? Yes, there was, the man from Pine Creek said—a sleigh ride. The conference planner promptly returned his skis. But the Enron team did not. Enronians took risks. They opted for adventure. No one ever rode into the future on a sleigh.

The cross-country track was narrow and well-packed, and as long as Sherron stayed on it, she noticed she was safe from the high drifts along the side. The first group to suit up—Fastow, Taylor, and Watkins—took off, chatting; no one minded that they lacked a guide, nor did anyone ask for directions. They were satisfied with the Pine Creek employee's instructions: "Just through the field."

Sherron was keeping up pretty well until she heard a sound like *zzzzllli-iiippp*. It was the elastic band that, until that moment, held her headlight in place. She stopped, bent over, and searched the snow for her light. The stars were not yet out, and there were no city lights to help her along. It took a few minutes to locate and reposition the thing.

By then, Fastow and Taylor were long gone, without so much as a backward glance. It then occurred to Sherron that she was very cold. It was February, it was pitch dark, and she was in the mountains of Colorado, insufficiently clothed and alone.

As she trudged on, the wind picked up, biting her nose and ears. The gusts of snow made it harder to see, and Sherron could tell from the pain in her calves that she was traveling uphill. Where were Andy and Mitch? No mining lights ahead, and none behind. Had she made a wrong turn? What kind of glamorous boondoggle was this? She was going to die here, the first person in Enron history to succumb to perk death.

The trip "around the mountain" and "across the field" amounted to a thirty-minute, one-and-a-half-mile trek. By the time Sherron arrived at the restaurant, she had just enough feeling in her hands to strip off her gloves and fling them angrily to the floor of the restaurant. She found Fastow and Taylor nonchalantly warming themselves by the fire. They'd decided to race ahead to see who could get there first, assuming that Sherron could take care of herself. Lagging behind the others in his group, Gene Humphrey had fallen into a snowdrift. The hosts were just about to send out a search party when he arrived, shivering and unhappy, forty-five minutes later.

Sherron got the message: If she was going to make it at Enron, she was going to have to pick up her pace.

Ken Lay may or may not have understood Jeff Skilling's plans in intricate detail, but he knew that greatness is rarely achieved without government assistance. Lay had worked in Washington and saw how the wheels of progress were greased with the right contacts and the right contributions.

If George H. W. Bush had won reelection in 1992, Lay's story, and Enron's story, might have been different. Lay was rumored to have been a choice for a cabinet post, and Rich Kinder might have taken over the company then. But Bill Clinton was elected president, and Lay continued to conduct business as usual. He started networking with his old friend and Clinton aide Mack McLarty, who arranged a golf game for Lay with Clinton, while, at the same time, Lay continued to cultivate his powerful congressional sources and his friends at the myriad federal agencies. Power had a price, Lay knew; just as he was willing to pay enormous salaries to staff his company with people he considered the best, Lay believed he'd have to buy Enron's way into Washington. Only a naïf thought otherwise.

In 1992, Lay chaired Texas senator Phil Gramm's reelection campaign, charming, cajoling, and strong-arming on behalf of the powerful chairman of the Senate Finance Committee. The two were natural allies—both had been whiz kids, both had doctorates in economics, both left academics for politics (Dr. Gramm was an economics professor at Texas A&M), and both were free-market zealots. But the relationship paid off far beyond the bounds of ordinary friendship: In January of the following year, Phil Gramm's wife, Wendy, the chairman of the Commodity Futures Trading Commission, moved to exempt energy derivatives and related swaps from government oversight. This meant that the kind of highly lucrative trading Enron was most passionate about—making financial trades based on the movement of the gas market, as opposed to simply trading gas—could now proceed without any regulation. Wendy Gramm had scheduled the vote hastily, before Clinton took office, and Enron got what it wanted. Five weeks later, she joined Enron's board, earning a $50,000-a-year salary along with stock options and other cash benefits.

Overall, Enron contributed nearly $300,000 to members of Congress during the 1992 election cycle. By 1994, that number had climbed, to $500,000, with results that would aid Enron tremendously as it moved toward the future.

Lay also understood that major players in business had to play Wall Street's game as well. As the economy began to recover under Clinton and the Bull Market took off once again, companies were expected to show annual growth of 15 percent. The drive for ever larger growth, like so many of the factors that drove Enron, had its roots in the buyouts and takeovers of the mid-eighties, when the term "shareholder value" was added to the lexicon. The stock price became the indicator of corporate health; senior managers became, in a weird way, more focused on their shareholders than, say, their customers. Quarterly earnings reports, once ignored by all but the most compulsive auditors and investors, suddenly became crucial to a company's public image: This was where a business could prove that its growth was on the proper, speedy trajectory. So, like everyone else, Enron began project-ing, and then miraculously meeting, earnings targets four times a year, to glowing reviews from analysts and the business press. A company that missed its numbers got the same treatment in reverse: Wall Street analysts would hammer the company and the stock price plummeted.

It was Rich Kinder's job to make sure Enron made its quarterly numbers. In the beginning, he cut fat to increase them—Enron "outsourced" ("laid off" or "paid an outside firm to do the work, saving the cost of overhead") various divisions that had once been considered crucial, like internal audit-ing, which routinely reviewed the company's projects and expenditures. (That this occurred after the Valhalla fiasco would be remembered with bit-terness and paranoia by many of Enron's oldest internal auditors.) Another quarter, Enron made earnings by selling and leasing back its building. But eventually Kinder outsourced all he could, and the pressure was on to con-solidate divisions or close more deals. This created what became known around Enron as "a sense of urgency."

People who stood in the way of progress eventually found themselves on the outside looking in. James Alexander, for instance, was no novice; he had worked at Drexel Burnham before joining Enron, where, supported by Rebecca Mark, he rose to become president of a division called Enron Global Power, which was created and spun off from the parent company in 1994. Enron Global Power was a publicly traded company that bought power plants and pipelines in the Third World; Enron owned 52 percent of the stock but considered it an independent business.

For that reason, Alexander felt that he should defend his shareholders' interests when they conflicted with those of Enron, something he found himself doing more and more often as time went on. Global Power often found itself pressured into buying poorly performing plants from Enron, for the full amount Enron had spent to develop the project rather than at a market value, which was sometimes far less. Alexander complained, and Kinder browbeat him for doing so. Other top executives at Global Power treated him as if he were disloyal—too often, they said, he was wearing his Global Power hat when he should be wearing his Enron hat. A lot more people owned stock in Enron than in Global Power—where were his priorities?

In 1995, Alexander took his concerns to Ken Lay, a man he considered a friend, someone who had sponsored his membership in the River Oaks Country Club. He also mentioned some rumors he'd heard—that some Enron executives boosted the price of power projects to increase their compensation, that some accounting methods were used incorrectly to keep the costs of lost bids on the books. Lay listened to Alexander's recounting of the conflicts of interest and suspicious accounting practices for about fifteen minutes. Then he grew distant. He wouldn't meet Alexander's eyes, and he stopped responding. Finally, he said, "I'll take it up with Rich." Then the meeting was over.

Even so, Alexander left the meeting relieved, sure that changes would be made. And changes were made: Within a very short time, key members of his staff, including his accountants, were placed under Jeff Skilling. In turn, Alexander's controller resigned, refusing to sign off on documents based on calculations that his staff had not performed. The message was clear— Enron would do nothing about his concerns. Soon after losing his staff, Alexander resigned too. In his wake, people at Enron began referring to him as a flake, someone who was not a team player, someone who could not move forward with the times.

And times were very good at Enron then. During the spring of James Alexander's travails, Ken Lay and Rich Kinder issued a memo to the staff as a preview of the good news to be contained in the upcoming 1995 annual report. "As you are all aware," it began, "we have declared victory on Enron's vision of becoming the world's first natural gas major." The memo thanked employees for their hard work. Enron had become the largest natural gas company in the largest natural gas market in the world. The most creative force, with the best people in energy worldwide, they said. The operator of the largest natural gas pipeline system in the world outside Russia. The developer of more natural gas–fired independent power plants than any company in the world, and the owner and operator of energy facilities in fifteen foreign countries. Better yet, it had provided shareholders a compound annual growth rate in earnings per share of 20 percent since 1990.

Now, the memo continued, it was time to reach higher by changing the company's vision. Now it would strive to become "The World's Leading Energy Company," creating innovative and efficient energy solutions for growing economies and a better environment worldwide. "In today's competitive environment," the memo continued, "we cannot rest on our laurels."

5

The Monkey House

B y the end of her second year at Enron, Sherron Watkins was having
some trouble navigating the politics at Enron. Sometimes she thought
back to a conversation that followed one of her first meetings at the
company. Gene Humphrey, the preternaturally reserved former banker, had
asked her about her impressions. "Enron seems incredibly slick," she told him.

Humphrey, one of Skilling's true believers, was taken aback. "Is that
good or bad?" he'd asked. "Slick can have negative connotations."

Realizing she'd been too frank too soon, Sherron backpedaled. "It's just
that everyone is so energetic and optimistic," she replied, smiling like a girl.

In truth, there were lots of things Sherron did like about Enron. The
people she worked with *were* usually energetic and optimistic. Then, too,
there was a lot of prestige associated with working for Enron. By the mid-
nineties, it seemed that almost every smart person in Houston left their
accounting firm or law firm or PR firm or investment firm — or their bank —
to work there. So you were surrounded, every day, by smart people. Given

her own predilections, Sherron certainly couldn't complain about the foul language that was ubiquitous there, and she relished the black humor that thrived around it. (One memo, falsely attributed to Humphrey, suggested acceptable replacements for obscene, if commonplace, phrases. "I'll have to think about that" replaced the intolerable "Fuck off"; "That's a creative approach!" replaced "You are out of your fucking mind!" "That's quite an accomplishment" replaced "Big fucking deal." And "I will consider it" should be substituted for "Fuck that.")

Even so, as time passed, Sherron realized that her initial response to Humphrey's question had been the right one, even if it hadn't been Humphrey she was referring to when she had used the word "slick." He was a nice, well-meaning man who was horrified when an unskilled client accidentally shot a young Mexican boy helping out on a bird-hunting trip; forevermore he substituted golf outings to prevent future shotgun strafings.

The problem, really, was Andy Fastow, Sherron's boss. In a lot of ways, he was an okay guy. He was funny and smart. He loved his wife; they were planning a family. He gave generously to good causes. He liked practical jokes—calling friends and colleagues to tell them their new Lexus or Porsche had just been towed—and, especially, toys. In the mornings, he drove a small, remote-controlled car up the legs of female employees on their way to the restroom. *The cops are after you—nyaaa-nyaaa-nyaaaaa!!* He was entranced with a greasy substance called Slime that he threw at the glass partitions in the Enron Capital & Trade offices. It hit with a *thwack!* and then slid down the sides, staining the walls. No one minded but the cleaning crew. At a business retreat, he gave away counterfeit money—$5, $10, and $20 bills emblazoned with his picture. "Come to me—I can finance your deals!" he promised. In a lot of ways he was like an overgrown kid, which, at Enron, just helped him to blend in.

But his childishness was a problem, because, like many a two-year-old, he had a terrible temper. You could see the tantrums coming on like one of Houston's sudden summer thunderstorms. One minute he wore his pleasant smile and his dark eyes shone. Then something would set him off. He'd twist his head, stretch his neck, and jut his chin, like a boxer warming up in the ring. The torrent of curses followed. Fortunately, he usually unleashed his fury on Enron's bankers, not his own employees. Fastow's job at Enron was to raise capital, but he didn't think charm was, necessarily, the way to go. He screamed at a slow-moving banker, "I've got attorneys and accountants here. And I'm sitting here with my dick in my HAND because YOU . . . WON'T . . ." Sherron would hear him scream at bankers from Chase, Citicorp—the largest banks in the world, it didn't matter. Fuck this, goddamnit that, the decibel rising each time the person on the other end of the line tried to respond. "You're not going to fucking get it, and further-more, you won't ever do another fucking deal with Enron again if you don't close this deal!" When the tirades became interminable, Sherron or a col-league would get up and close Fastow's door. Everyone knew he'd make it up to the bankers later, with ski trips or golf outings. And, of course, deals.

She wasn't fond of the 7:15 A.M. meetings Fastow called every morning, either. But what bothered her most was that Andy didn't keep his promises. He was forever telling her that her work was exemplary, but the big raises she was promised when she'd signed on never materialized. Worse, Sherron discovered that Fastow made, and broke, such promises routinely. On the day of her PRC review, he was out of the office, probably taking flying les-sons. The person he delegated the job to approached Sherron in the hall: "I need to find Andy," he said frantically. "I need some more meat on what y'all have done."

Sure enough, Andy abandoned her at review time, just as he had in the mountains of Colorado. Without the "meat," she was summarily dismissed by the PRC. Her bonus came to $14,000, about 12 percent of her salary; Sherron's twenty-three-year-old analyst, who was making a quarter of her income, received the same amount. Her bonus at MG the year she'd left— at a higher salary than she was making now—was over four times as much. That was why people got into finance, for God's sake. It was the bonus, not the salary, that people worked hard for every year.

When Sherron confronted Fastow about his absence, he stammered and sputtered about the difficulty of peer review. But he really had no excuse; in fact, he hung several other employees out to dry in similar fashion. Two sen-ior people even left Andy's group, disappointed with either their bonus or their lack of advancement.

The truth was, Fastow was self-centered, but he also didn't have the power to get what he needed for his people. And that was his biggest problem. To become more powerful within Enron, Fastow was forever trying to convert his division, which raised money for Enron Capital & Trade, into one that made money for ECT—a "profit center," in Enronspeak. The only people who had power at Enron were those who made money—lots of it—for Enron, and until he did so, Fastow was never going to have the respect and influence he craved.

So he spent his time coming up with harebrained schemes to get a piece of other people's deals. Fastow didn't really understand—or didn't think he needed to understand—the fact that businesses were created. Someone had the idea to use the natural gas that came out of the ground to heat homes and schools, for instance. Or someone thought they could make a better shoe—just for running. Or someone thought a handheld calculator might be more efficient than an abacus or an adding machine. Fastow didn't have those kinds of ideas. His creativity was heavily influenced by the LBO kings of the eighties—stripping out profits, selling off excess, making financial structures that gave him pieces of transactions just for figuring them out. To the originators, who prided themselves on coming up with new products (even if they were financial products, or deals), he was seen as a fly at a picnic. Fastow, in turn, complained to Skilling. His structures were in Enron's best interest—he was trying to help the originators get better prices for their deals, to keep Enron Capital & Trade's portfolio liquid. The originators didn't "get it."

At the same time, he went to the originators, promising to help them get cash to fund their deals. He knew bankers and how they worked. His operating motto was "Never say 'no' to a deal," no matter how flimsy or how questionable. To be seen as a naysayer at Enron was the kiss of death, and he knew it. Consequently, Fastow started hiring more bankers, because bankers had the contacts to close more deals.

Hence Sherron's problems: She didn't have the contacts the bankers had, and she didn't like the pressure Fastow was putting on her to fund deals with CalPERS' money, whether they fit the criteria or not. The pressure at the close of every quarter—to close deals and get the bonuses—was immense, and Fastow was on the side of the originators.

Then, suddenly, in September of 1995, Andy was gone. Skilling decided on one of his frequent reorganizations—the joke at the company was that everyone wrote their organization charts in pencil. Enron, with lots of advice from McKinsey, was going to start a retail electricity effort—competing with the big utilities to provide power to homes and businesses—and Fastow won the honor of leading the new division. Sherron's new boss was a man named Rick Causey, the former Andersen accountant who engineered SEC approval for Enron's right to use mark-to-market accounting. His first act was to declare that the division would no longer try to turn itself into a profit center.

With relief, Sherron Watkins put her résumé back in a drawer. She would stay at Enron Capital & Trade.

It was around this time that Enron's employees were given the results of an Enron job-satisfaction survey. Overall, they were confident in management and its ability to lead the company, but many were uncomfortable about openly voicing their opinions and, as the survey noted, "telling it like it is at Enron."

Lay and Skilling, who signed off on the survey, deemed these results "unacceptable." "Steps are now underway in each operating company," they wrote, "to develop and implement corrective actions which you will hear more about very soon."

What was rarely stated aloud, but what most people in the company knew, was that the trouble spot was located in Enron Capital & Trade, Jeff Skilling's creation. Specifically, people complained about the behavior of Skilling's traders. In theory, the traders, who were almost always male, spent their days buying natural gas and crude oil from suppliers and then selling it to their customers. Enron made money on the difference—"the spread" between the "bid" and the "ask" price, in trader parlance. But the job description did not tell the whole story.

Part of the problem lay in the past. Despite Ken Lay's promises in the wake of the 1987 Valhalla fiasco to keep trading to a minimum, he saw the future—and the profits—through Jeff Skilling's eyes. Trading was essential to the Enron Capital & Trade business model. The idea was to replicate the makeover of the gas business in as many new markets as possible: First, buy a few key assets, like a major gas pipeline (in the future the company might buy an electric utility, or, further into the future, nothing more than the option to use an asset). Then set up a trading business to expand the new market. In step three, market dominance is achieved—superior knowledge of and contacts in the market you created make that inevitable. Finally, when the market is crowded with imitators and gross margins shrink, you sell all the assets, and emerge as a pure trading company, smart enough to take advantage of market fluctuations because your company was smart enough to see them coming—or because you've been able to move the market yourself through the size and quantity of your trades. This blueprint gave Enron several advantages: First, its markets never really achieved "transparency"—since Enron created and then dominated the market, Enron also made the rules, and everyone else had to play by them. And more often than not, the people who made those rules were the traders.

That was not true in the beginning. Originally, power within Enron Capital & Trade (and Enron in general) resided with those who brought in business, the originators—those who found and, more important, made deals. Deals to supply gas long term to power plants, deals to buy gas-storage facilities, deals to build power plants, deals to finance oilfield exploration. The skill set required was not very complicated and not very different from what it had always been: You had to be outgoing, you had to be clever, you had to have good contacts, you had to keep an ear to the ground. In other words, you had to know how to sell. Traders had no market then. They were the people who simply set the value of deals according to a price curve—they looked at who else was trading and at what price, and evaluated the risks, which meant balancing buys and sells in a trading book and hedging vulnerable positions with the New York Mercantile Exchange or other large institutional trading houses.

The trader had nothing to do with physical delivery of the product—getting the gas to or from the customer. That was the deal guy's job. For that, he got 80 percent of any commodity-trading value brought to the company. That is, the originator got the bulk of the money for the gas trades associated with his deal. After all, he put it together.

But traders like to trade. As the commodity market grew larger, Enron's traders were able to make financial trades on top of old-fashioned trades. They could trade futures on the value of gas contracts written to mature at different times—maybe you needed to sell your ten-year contract immediately to get cash up front for a new venture, for instance. Or they could trade derivatives, which were basically side bets that served as protection against price volatility in a given commodity. (You could buy a "put," for instance, which would pay the difference if the price of gas in a futures contract went lower than a contract specified.) The traders lobbied Skilling to increase limits on speculative trading positions imposed by the Enron board, and they argued and won the right to manage the physical trading books instead of the originators. This gave the traders the ability to take advantage of market anomalies and make still more money. For example, if gas prices spiked in Chicago, traders would move gas meant for the Gulf Coast and sell it there instead to capitalize on the higher prices. (One Enron trader was constantly starting rumors that offshore gas production facilities were being shut down because of Gulf Coast hurricanes, sending business into a frenzy over imagined shortages.)

If this sounds like betting, it was. Skilling made a name for himself by promising to reduce risk, but it wasn't long before Enron Capital & Trade was making the bulk of its money from very shrewd trading. As his lieutenant, Lou Pai, would explain to a recruit one night in front of Skilling at Café Annie, one of Houston's best restaurants, "We're bookies. We're making bets." Only the risks were lowered—because of Enron's controls, and because the company had market dominance.

As the traders became more successful, they began to claim that their work was riskier, more time-consuming, more complicated, and more creative than the originators'. And—crucial within Enron Capital & Trade— they could show that they were generating enormous income for the company. Soon enough, with Skilling's blessing, the traders were getting 80 percent of every deal, and the originators had to settle for the remaining 20 percent. This switch caused fistfights in the office, but bonuses flowed accordingly: Some traders made more money in a given year than Lay or Skilling. The fact that they made so much money—in a company that valued making money above all—meant that the traders became increasingly exempt from the rules at Enron.

Soon, the host of modifiers that were once applied to the deal originators were transferred to the traders. The words all seemed to begin with "a": aggressive, abrasive, arrogant, abusive. Other employees would go out of their way to avoid the trading floors. The people who worked there were young—few were over thirty—and relatively inexperienced. A new associate hired into a yearlong training program could find himself, within a matter of months, promoted to making actual trades. Enron needed the bodies to keep up with the growing market that they were, in turn, making even larger.

Given the level of wealth and the levels of postadolescent testosterone, the floors had the feel of a locker room crossed with the court of the Sun King. The traders got whatever they wanted: catered gourmet meals around the clock during bid week, the period when they locked in their positions for the month. In violation of all sorts of sexual harassment laws, photos of female employees were posted on a "Hottie Board." Women who complained found threatening notes on their cars that could have been written by Gambino family muscle. ("Keep your mouth shut or else. . . .")

Language was routinely and impressively foul. "Fuck" was used as a noun ("What the fuck?" or "You fat fuck"), a verb ("Don't try to fuck me on this" or "Fuck me? What about fuck you?"), and as a modifier ("That fucking asshole" or "That fucking fuck"), sometimes all in the same sentence. Complaints to Human Resources resulted in a finger-wagging memo from Skilling and, finally, a floor meeting in which Skilling pleaded with the traders to seriously watch their language, though everyone assumed he couldn't be fucking serious. The traders set up a glass bowl on the trading floor and dropped in a dollar every time they used a bad word. Soon they started prepaying, effectively creating a futures market in cursing.

But mostly, the traders bet—on anything. When the stock split in 1993 and every Enron employee was given a $50 bill, the sentimental types framed the reward. The traders pooled the money and placed a huge bet, so that the money would at least come to something respectable in their eyes, like a happy-hour party. Enron also had the usual football and basketball pools, but the traders added so many complicated financial instruments on top of the standard bets—swaps, derivatives, costless collars, and other semi-comprehensible financial structures—that only the shrewdest people really knew what they were betting on (a game or a series of games?) and how much they were actually in for ($20 or $500 or much, much more?). They knew how to maneuver themselves into a winning position no matter what. As one trader described his bets on the January 1996 Super Bowl, "If Pittsburgh wins I make $1,500, but if Dallas wins I make $1,300."

Winnings could range in the tens of thousands of dollars—one executive supposedly won enough to buy a Porsche. Someone had to lose, though, and the youngest traders were sometimes unable to pay debts that could surpass a month's salary. Eventually, the individual losses got so high that management, afraid of a raid by the Houston Police Department, shut the gambling pool down. Within a few months, it was back in business.

During Enron Capital & Trade's best years, the gambling book was controlled by Greg Whalley, a hot-tempered West Point graduate who was the head trader for crude oil stocks. Whalley was a hero to his troops. His favorite fictional characters were James Bond and Jack Ryan. His favorite novel was *Atlas Shrugged*, Ayn Rand's celebration of selfishness. (Rand was a favorite of many traders, though they ignored her semons on moral responsibility while trumpeting her paeans to selfishness. Rand knew that unchecked egotism might lead to market dominance, but that it would also lead to market ruin, as the "egoists" exploited every customer down to their last dollar.) Whalley had a finger-to-the-chest management style but got away with it because of an almost savantlike recall for numbers; he was, like many Enron traders, someone who could not have fit in elsewhere but who burrowed in at Enron. "You'd see him on the trading floor and think you could never dress that guy up," said one colleague. When Whalley retired as chief bookie, after management's first "raid," responsibility passed into the hands of a young associate who managed the book right into the ground. By acclamation, Whalley was forced to return, and in an interesting parallel to the Valhalla trading scandal, he gambled the book back to life.

If the traders saw themselves as being better—smarter, tougher, meaner—than the rest of the company, they did not have much team spirit within ECT. The person in charge of all trading was Lou Pai, the son of Chinese immigrants (he was born in Nanking but educated at the University of Maryland after his parents moved the family to the United States). Pai, hired away from Conoco Oil, demonstrated a gift for trading that caught Skilling's eye early. Broad-faced, perpetually assessing, and not unhandsome, Pai nevertheless lacked social skills—he wasn't warm or particularly friendly, and he had a reputation around the company for being solely out for himself, which was really saying something in a culture that was evolving along Enron's intensely narcissistic lines.

Pai's management style was unique. His idea of bonding was to take young traders to Houston's best "gentlemen's clubs," which were strip joints on steroids. The oil boom of the seventies brought an air of sophistication to this lowly branch of the entertainment industry. With upgrades—wing chairs, VIP rooms, all-you-can-eat buffets, big-screen TVs constantly tuned to ESPN, and "lap dancing" (dancers left the stage and performed just for you)—the clubs became one of the few bankruptcy-proof businesses in town. They also mirrored the growing social stratification that greater wealth was creating in American society at the time: The Men's Club, Houston's most exclusive, looked sort of like the Harvard Club and was supposed to have dancers who, in their off hours, were coeds at SMU, the school with the reputation for having the prettiest girls in Texas. Its chief competitor, Rick's, was sleek and modern, and professed to have more *Penthouse* centerfolds than any other club in town. Though Enron employees were treated like rock stars in both places, and despite a companywide tendency to claim conoisseurship in all fields, Pai frequented Treasures, a somewhat more downscale club in the same neighborhood. He liked to brag that after visiting Treasures he would stop at a gas station to douse himself with petrol before heading home, so that his (soon-to-be-ex-) wife would not detect the smell of the club on his clothes.

Eventually, that activity became too demanding and/or time-consuming and Pai was caught by security cameras (and various employees) bringing dancers into the office. He subsequently married a dancer, which probably solved a lot of problems for him and probably saved Enron a lot of money. (For many years, the company picked up the tab at the bars, which easily ran into five figures with large groups.)

When Pai was not acting as a mentor, he was scheming. Enron once handed out free to its employees copies of the best-selling business-motivation tome *The 7 Habits of Highly Effective People*, by Stephen R. Covey. Pai ordered his traders to throw the books away and study Sun Tzu's *The Art of War* instead. Or they could just watch him in action. An early nemesis was a trader named Joe Pokalsky, the man who was the real star behind the gas-trading business, the one Skilling relied on. Pokalsky joined Enron after Skilling showed him one simple equation—the difference between the razor-thin margins he could make trading in New York's established equity and commodity markets, and the mammoth margins in the fledgling gas-trading business in Houston. In 1991, the year Pokalsky arrived, a gifted trader could extract a premium from both ends of a transaction, because producers and purchasers were so desperate to make a deal. But he was a little too talented in Pai's eyes.

Pokalsky probably brought some of the ensuing hell on himself. He fit in on Enron's trading floor because he had a robust personality, shorthand at Enron for "extremely difficult." "Beyond the bounds of what you'd expect even from a New Yorker" was the way one Gulf Coast originator described Pokalsky's behavior. "I never met anybody who could get along with him" was the opinion of many. Pokalsky took what was his and more, and seldom deigned to help originators with their deals. Worse, he made everyone feel stupid. In fact, he told them they were stupid on a regular basis. But he was a great trader, and that was what mattered.

However, Pokalsky often disagreed with Pai over the calculation, upward, of the company's math—the setting of price and profit curves that was the traders' domain for Enron Capital & Trade, and eventually for the whole company. When Pokalsky became too recalcitrant, his days were numbered. Pai instructed Pokalsky's staff to set erroneous prices for the originators' deals, blamed Joe, then complained that he had to clean up Pokalsky's mess.

It was a clever ploy, but only one of many. Pai knew that while Skilling liked eccentrics, he hated troublemakers. He expected people to work out their differences among themselves. So Pai never complained about Pokalsky himself. He simply repeated to others what Pokalsky said about them and let them take their complaints to Skilling.

When the anti-Pokalsky faction became too large to ignore, Skilling was forced to act. He spent $30,000 to send him to management training sessions ("charm school" in company vernacular), in hopes that he would learn to be nicer. Meanwhile, Pai took Pokalsky's soon-to-be ex-wife to lunch, trawling for more information.

In the end Pokalsky resigned, faxing in his resignation from Georgia, where he found a job with a competitor, and where noncompete clauses in out-of-state contracts were rarely enforced. Pai, in turn, expanded his power base, becoming president and COO of Enron Capital & Trade. He had made his peers look like whiners, and he had driven off one of the few people who posed a threat to his position with Skilling.

He remained, in the words of one politically incorrect trader, Skilling's Ninja.

In the fall of 1995, Sherron Watkins had one outstanding obligation from Andy Fastow's reign: the Paint Ball War. It was Andy's idea. The bankers for JEDI were scheduled to come to town in November, and rather than bore them with the usual golf outings, Fastow wanted entertainment that was novel and edgy—worthy of Enron. He found it in the form of a small business north of Houston that arranged for people to conduct corporate warfare with automatic weapons that fired marble-sized paint pellets. Andy had pushed the bankers around for years with Enron's deals. Now they were jetting in from New York and Los Angeles, from Chase, First Boston, Royal Bank of Canada, and Credit Lyonnaise, and could hardly wait to take him down.

The planning took weeks—Fastow's staff sent the invitations out early. A trophy shop prepared appropriate awards for the best shot, the worst shot, the most Rambo-like warrior, etc. The buses to the war games were equipped with kegs of beer to keep the guests well-lubricated. The only problem was that Andy was no longer around to be nailed by his former victims. But Sherron was.

She arrived at the location—a scrubby, pine-shaded lot covering several acres—where an attendant directed her to a small cabin in which camouflage jumpsuits, made of thick canvas, were strewn about the floor. She found her size, and also accepted a helmet with a clear plastic visor that covered her entire face. A thick pair of gloves completed the ensemble.

Houston in November can still be very hot, as it was on this day. In two layers of clothing, Sherron began to sweat. The suit smelled like the inside of a damp horse barn.

The bankers were given fresh outfits, courtesy of Enron: camouflage shirts, coveralls, and hats emblazoned with the Enron Capital & Trade logo. They suited up, grinning like jackals.

The first activity was "Capture the Flag," which seemed harmless enough. Sherron walked into the "War Zone" and someone opened fire from fifteen feet away, hitting her with a paint pellet. "Damn! That hurt!" she cried. In the next round, she was hit on the cheek, despite her protective gear. She put her hand to her face and found her own blood flowing into the blue paint. "Jeez Mareez," she thought. These guys were serious.

Sherron got some "kills" of her own, but was soon covered with enough paint to be pronounced dead and exiled from the combat zone. Walking toward freedom, she encountered some of her teammates and started to warn them about the enemy bankers up ahead. Unfortunately, some of them were already hiding in the bushes nearby and opened fire. Sherron was caught in the cross fire. "I'm already dead!" she yelled. "Stop shooting me!"

"Get out of the way!" someone yelled back. Then bullets peppered the back of her legs.

Finally, a bullhorn sounded, signaling break time. Most of the weekend warriors took the opportunity to chug another beer and check their wounds. One guy who lost or forgot his gloves bled profusely from his knuckles. Another stone-faced banker used his downtime for more target practice.

The next game was more elaborate. The paintball referees divided the group into two teams, mixing Enron employees and bankers, sensing it was easier to keep aggressions in check. Each group was told to pick a President and two bodyguards. Sherron was elected President and Commander in Chief of her group. A referee escorted them to a rusted-out car and told them the goal was to get from the car to a fort constructed of rubber tires. As the enemy approached, her teammates were supposed to supply cover, protecting her from assassination.

But Sherron wasn't about to sit in the car and wait to be rescued. "We're sitting ducks here," she said. "Let's go hide in a ditch." But her bodyguards wanted to wait for reinforcements. Finally, one of the referees approached, tossing a smoke bomb under their car.

"You're supposed to get out of the car!" he yelled.

They jumped out and sprinted for their lives—only to be plastered with hundreds of paint pellets.

When it was all over, Sherron received a trophy of a dog barking at a squirrel in a tree, engraved with the words "Treed Squirrel Award."

It was not the way she liked to think of herself, but at least Andy's reign was officially over.

6

Fair Value

WITH former controller Rick Causey installed as Fastow's replacement, Sherron's days were blissfully free of tantrums and nutty schemes to raise her boss's profile. Causey was Enron's Pillsbury Doughboy; he liked to go along to get along. His idea of excitement was a trip to Austin for a University of Texas football game.

Life at Enron Capital & Trade remained volatile, however. Enron's success in gas trading encouraged competitors to join the fray. The traders began to worry; their market was maturing and growing ever more efficient. ECT still had the largest market position, but traders were looking at margins of five cents or less, which meant smaller profits and smaller bonuses.

Then an unexpected cold snap hit Chicago and the Northeast in late November and continued through December. Gas prices, which had been trading well below $2 per mmbtu, soared to $4. The traders jumped into action, shifting gas between customers, pulling gas from storage—whatever it took to exploit the higher prices. The banner month even brought a smile to the face of Joe Pokalsky's replacement, a tall, sepulchral man named Kevin Hannon.

Then, for some reason, in December, just as everyone was anticipating their bonus checks, Enron's stock price dropped nearly $3 a share to $34. The cause was a rumor that Enron had actually lost money in the recent run-up.

The story started in New York and was fueled by cash margin calls Enron Capital & Trade had to pay under its NYMEX contracts. ECT had thousands of customers who had signed long-term deals for gas, and Enron had plenty of physical gas supply to meet their needs. Some of the supply positions had been hedged on the NYMEX with shorts, which meant that Enron had essentially purchased insurance policies to protect itself from sudden price decreases. When gas prices spiked, the NYMEX positions were underwater and ECT had to pay up. It could easily cover the margin calls, but the market players, who had only the NYMEX positions to go on, assumed the worst. So the patently false rumor grew until the word was that Skilling had been removed from the building in handcuffs, the future of Enron's trading business in doubt.

In response, Enron's PR machine went into high gear. Lay spoke to the *Wall Street Journal* in December. "Rumors of losses, an inability to meet margin calls, and reprimands or termination of our trading personnel are totally without merit, unfounded and untrue," he declared. A hastily assembled stock-repurchase plan mollified investors. Enron's auditors, Arthur Andersen, prepared a letter reaffirming Enron Capital & Trade's compliance with strict limits on the amount of exposure the traders could subject the company to. Lay told *Gas Daily* in December 1995, "Arthur Andersen's validation occurred after the firm conducted a thorough internal review of ECT's sophisticated systems and controls, including the accuracy and completeness of the company's commodity position reports, examining the daily broker's statements, and other procedures and activities as considered appropriate." In no time, the rumors were defused, Enron's health was reaffirmed, and the stock rebounded to $37.50 a share. (Very few people paid attention to a Merrill Lynch analyst named John Olson. "It intrigues me that when the rumors in the gas business get out of hand, Enron always seems to be the focus," he told *Gas Daily.* "I would think the company also would be curious about this.")

Then, one day, just before the end of the year and the close of accounting, the young associate who oversaw the interest rate books on the trading desk came rushing into Sherron Watkins's office, his face ashen. His job was to hedge the interest rate risk so that ECT's overall trading position was balanced between gains and losses every day. Usually, the net cash flow amounts varied little, if at all.

But not on this particular day. "Seventy million dollars just fell out of my book," he told Sherron, looking as though he needed CPR. Inexplicably, $70 million was missing from his account.

Sherron, who prided herself on her Enron intelligence network, put in a call to accounting, and got an explanation. The young associate shouldn't worry. Enron was just "correcting and fine-tuning" some of the forward gas price curves. In other words, Enron had made more money during the fiscal year than needed and was moving earnings into the next year. The money would likely flow back into the associate's book in early 1996, an accountant told Sherron. In other words, Enron was manipulating its earnings, a questionable practice that was not illegal but was unethical in the business world. It was also becoming increasingly common in the frenzy of the Bull Market, as executives tried to manage the expectations of Wall Street and keep their stock prices rising. Sure enough, the associate appeared in Sherron's office in January, just as troubled as he had been in December, to say that the $70 million had come back into his book.

A s infallible as the traders felt themselves to be, they made a very large mistake in the summer of 1996: They bet wrong on the price of gas and found themselves in the hole by $90 million. With a quarterly goal of $100 million, Enron Capital & Trade was suddenly $190 million behind in its earnings targets. Since Enron had never missed its earnings targets, this was cause for near panic within the unit. There were weekly and then daily meetings in ECT's conference room, the one with the sprawling, twenty-foot mural of Enron's triumphs in the energy world.

All the big Enron Capital & Trade stars gathered there: Lou Pai and

Kevin Hannon from trading, Andy Fastow, Rick Causey, Jeff Skilling, and a very concerned COO, Rich Kinder. Midlevel executives were brought in, too: guys from Canada and London, even directors like Sherron Watkins. Who knew who could come up with a fresh idea? Over and over, the group asked one another the same questions: Could they trade their way out of the loss? Or was there an innovative way to make it up? In their search, they cast a cold eye on the company's equity investments—the companies in which Enron had an ownership stake.

This portfolio had been a source of great ambivalence at Enron. Its history dated back two years, to the recovery of Houston banks from the eighties oil bust. Once the banks began lending again, Enron's customers, or "counterparties," wondered why they should be forced to give up nearly all of their production for several years to Enron in exchange for Skilling's beloved volumetric production payment, when they could get plain-vanilla, low-interest loans from banks now. In recent years, Enron had become the lender of last resort, and they had learned to act like it, demanding tough terms and conditions in exchange for keeping businesses afloat. But now, with the return of better times, customers could get loans from banks, pay down their bank loans with cash, and hold on to their precious production. Prices had gone up—as oil and gas optimists knew they would—and Enron was losing a lot of business to bankers they'd not so recently viewed as dummies. Worse, the company could not borrow money to grow, because Kinder was still refusing to increase Enron's debt load.

On the other hand, Enron Gas Services, as Skilling's company was then known, was flush with money from JEDI to fund new ventures. If lending opportunities were fading away, why not move into owning? Maybe the risk was greater, but Skilling had borrowed and refined risk-management tools from Wall Street to protect the company from overreaching. So it was soon decided that EGS would begin to fund mergers, acquisitions, and management-led buyouts; they would purchase equity in small and large amounts, and in return, these new clients would have to sell *their* gas to EGS, or financially hedge their production with EGS, or minimize gas price risk with complex options and swaps from EGS. The opportunities looked endless. All the company needed was a high-profile deal to put itself on the map.

They found one in an Australian company, Bridge Oil Limited, that had a subsidiary in the United States. Specifically, it had large gas reserves in South Texas. The company's total assets were worth around $515 million. In May 1994, Bridge was trying to fend off a hostile takeover by a Midland, Texas, company called Parker & Parsley that publicly announced its intention to spin off the Australian properties and consolidate the Texas reserves with its own. (Read: Bye-bye Bridge Management.)

Enter Enron Gas Services as a white knight for a management-led buyout. Using funds from JEDI, Enron offered a $263 million high bid for Bridge—63 cents a share, four cents more than Parker & Parsley. Because the fight looked to be protracted and nasty, Skilling dispatched Cliff Baxter, the resident M&A expert, to ride herd on the deal.

In the halls of Enron, Baxter's reputation was somewhat mixed. He was a large man with blue eyes that could go from morose to steely in seconds; usually he moved through the company's halls with an elaborate, Enronian swagger, chain-smoking. After helping Skilling acquire a gas marketing company, Access Energy, Baxter acquired the lead M&A role at EGS. He quickly announced to the financial team that any and all future deals—if they were big—belonged to him. "So you're the Big Dog around here?" one of his colleagues retorted. The sarcasm went over Baxter's head, and he soon began referring to himself that way. "I'm the Big Dog, and I get the Big Deals," he liked to say, puffing his chest.

One of six children, Baxter graduated from New York University and went on to become a captain in the Air Force in the early 1980s. After receiving his MBA from Columbia, he headed for Wall Street, where he joined PaineWebber. He signed on at Enron Gas Services in 1991, after convincing Skilling his talents were wasted in other divisions. Soon, Baxter became his friend and confidant, as well as a brutal but intuitive negotiator. Baxter knew just how far to push a deal to get the terms he wanted. But he was also high maintenance. At the end of almost every deal, he collapsed from emotional exhaustion and threatened to quit because he was not appreciated. Everyone knew that the best way to keep Baxter's rampant insecurities in check was to stroke him—and stroke him often.

Enron and Baxter moved into the Bridge deal with typical confidence. Gene Humphrey, who was in charge of the entire operation, dispatched Baxter to Australia with an Enron team, which then proceeded to spend vast amounts hiring local lawyers, a local investment bank, and Hill and Knowlton, the American public relations firm, at a cost of $200,000. The team shuttled back and forth between Sydney and Houston, determined to win.

In late June of 1994, Parker & Parsley increased its bid to 66 cents a share. Enron Gas Services, in response, did so too. Then Parker & Parsley raised their bid again. The stakes rose until Bridge's stock price hit 90 cents a share near the end of the month. Enron debated going to 95 cents—it needed the deal—but then learned that Parker & Parsley had quietly bought 21 percent of Bridge's stock. In other words, it was almost impossible for EGS to win controlling interest in the company. Enron Gas Services had been seduced into a very expensive game of chicken, and now it blinked. Having spent millions, the team headed home empty-handed.

EGS extracted two lessons from the disaster. The first was to overpay for all future acquisitions to come out a winner, and to avoid embarrassment in the public eye. The second was to sell the Enron board on new concepts up front, to avoid the kind of Monday-morning quarterbacking that followed the Bridge failure.

In the ensuing years, Enron successfully bought a few oil and gas companies, however. Using JEDI funds, it paid $197 million in February 1996 for Coda Energy, for instance, a purchase price that was effectively seven to eight times the company's current earnings, high for oil and gas companies. At the time, Sherron Watkins received a call from her old boss at MG; he didn't understand what Enron was doing. It didn't make sense to Enron's board either, which required the team to make a detailed presentation to support their purchase. Board member Bob Belfer asked, for instance, why Enron was trying to sell its top-of-the-line company, Enron Oil and Gas, and purchasing second-rate companies like Coda. He didn't get it. Enron Capital & Trade intended to use the contents of its merchant portfolio not just as freestanding businesses but also as a kind of portfolio hedge for *other* Enron Capital & Trade businesses. It was a way to balance Enron Capital & Trade's entire business just as an investor might balance his portfolio: An equity position in an oil and gas company might decrease with declines in energy prices, while an equity position in a steel company might increase based on lower energy costs. An equity interest in an oil and gas company might also offset a trading loss. Eventually, the skeptical Enron board went along with his idea.

The board's concern did made Skilling nervous, however. He asked Rick Causey to form a Portfolio Management Advisory Committee to assess and manage the risk of the company's new equity portfolio. Causey, in turn, put Sherron Watkins in charge. The new committee ran some analytical models and came up with bad news: It wasn't possible to hedge these equity deals with any degree of accuracy. Simply put, buying—and overpaying—for companies like Coda was a long-term strategy with a lot of short-term hiccups. It was impossible, they told Skilling, to try to predict the peaks and valleys in the value of these entities. Skilling was unconvinced. Be more creative, he told Watkins' committee. "You're looking for your lost car keys under the street-light," he said, quoting an old joke that cautioned against exploring only the simplest solutions (". . .because the light's better there"). Causey's advice was a little bit clearer: He told Sherron to hire a headhunter who could find the company a true equity expert—someone who could do what Skilling wanted.

But in the summer of 1996, with a $190 million earnings hole to fill, squeezing earnings from the JEDI equity investments became the focus of the rescue efforts. Enron's transaction accountants, an elite group hired in the early nineties by Rick Causey to develop Enron Capital & Trade's cutting-edge techniques, came up with the idea of revaluing those assets. It could be the salvation Enron was looking for. Just as Enron had used mark-to-market accounting to recognize the full value of long-term oil and gas trading contracts immediately, the *future* value of the companies ECT had acquired could now be used to resuscitate the company's current bottom line. It was a matter of redefining the nature of ownership. If Enron could prove, according to generally accepted accounting principles—GAAP for short—that these assets were being held for *resale* instead of as part of the company's core investments, and that a market existed for them, Enron could include unrealized gains in the "fair value" of those assets immediately. In fact, the accountants reported, there were enough assets now in the JEDI portfolio to solve the problems for the quarter.

The whole idea struck Sherron Watkins—the manager of the JEDI portfolio—as cuckoo. A company called Mariner, that JEDI had purchased in May of 1996 for $95 million, was now, a few months later, valued at $140 million? JEDI had purchased a company called CGas in early September for just over $30 million. Now Skilling's unit was saying it was worth $45 million—a 50 percent increase in little more than twenty-seven days. This was like buying a house for $100,000, making no improvements, but claiming, a few weeks later, that it was worth $150,000.

Nonetheless, everyone else seemed enthusiastic about the idea, particularly Andy Fastow, who had recently returned to the fold as Sherron's boss, having failed at retail electricity after only nine months on the job. Fastow returned to the Treasury group of ECT a chastened man, worried about his future. He immediately set about building a new power base for himself. The "fair value" concept fit the bill perfectly, because he was in charge of the people who came up with the models for the numbers.

The Risk Assessment and Control group, or RAC, was part of Skilling's vaunted risk-management plan. RAC was charged with developing mathematical models that analyzed the risk of every Enron Capital & Trade deal, via computations of what was called the Risk Adjusted Return on Capital, or RAROC (pronounced "ray-rock"). Like the trading division, RAC was populated largely by very young associates and analysts who worked under enormous pressure. They were usually told on Friday that deal originators needed valuations for presentations to Jeff Skilling the following Monday. This required them to spend the next forty-eight hours poring over spreadsheets and calculations, trying to come up with any number that would allow a given deal to close. But their numbers were unreliable because the deal originators had long ago learned that they could control the outcomes by limiting the information they gave to RAC. Hence, the work tended to be incomprehensible, and anyone who tried to point that out was seen as obstructive. The essential skill for working at RAC was the ability to remain calm in the face of many angry people intent on getting their way. A lot of recruits simply weren't up to that: Once a supervisor went to the apartment of a young analyst who didn't show up for work and found her paralyzed by a work-induced anxiety attack. She could not leave her apartment.

But the advent of fair value also meant a dramatic increase in power for the RAC group, because their models would be the ones used for creating the actual "fair value" of each asset involved. This group could now help Enron Capital & Trade generate income by setting (ostensibly higher) values for assets instead of limiting income by pointing out the risks of various deals. In other words, it could spend more time saying yes than saying no, always a plus at Enron. Eventually, the operative phrase at Enron became not "mark to market" but "mark to the model," which meant that mathematical formulas could be adjusted to come up with virtually *any* desired calculation. These valuations, created by half-crazed twenty-somethings desperate for advancement, would become ever more crucial to Enron Capital & Trade's income stream. But, in 1996, they just looked like a way to erase the trading loss, and RAC was for it.

All that was needed now was Arthur Andersen's approval. Sherron Watkins was sure they would never go for it.

A rthur Andersen founded his auditing firm in 1914 with the motto "Think straight, talk straight." During the Depression he made a name for himself by providing auditing that was answerable to companies' shareholders, not their executives. The Arthur Andersen audit came to be synonymous with a balance sheet that was beyond reproach. But as Andersen moved into the future, the firm changed in ways that would alter its reputation considerably. In the 1950s, for instance, an Andersen engineer made a crucial discovery: He could use computers to automate bookkeeping and show clients how to do it too. This discovery would lead, eventually, to an explosion in consulting for the company. With increased competition in the mid-eighties, accounting fees began to drop, and Andersen was looking for a new way to keep itself profitable. The audit partners were pressured to graft consulting projects onto the firm's auditing functions.

In the 1990s, that looked like a very good idea. Consulting exploded, in fact, while auditing remained flat. The only problem was that, eventually, the consultants at Andersen were making most of the money and resented sharing their bounty with the company's auditors. At the same time, the merger trend that hit the accounting industry a few decades ago left Andersen standing alone—it could find no partners to live up to its tough standards. Andersen, riven by internal strife, was unattractive to others and could not merge with any other Big 8 firm. Where it had once vied for the number-one spot, it now sank to number 5 of the remaining big firms.

As the consulting business surged, more and more pressure was put on auditors to bring in business, and to hold on to the clients they had at all costs—Andersen couldn't afford to slip any further in the rankings. To save money, the company began enforcing its early-retirement age of fifty-six. This meant that, on the auditing side, the company was staffed with younger and younger people who were brash and aggressive but knew less and less about actually investigating their clients' accounting practices. The people who made partner, in turn, were great salespeople but not as technically proficient. Those who made partner, it was said around the office, were the ones who could replace all their business within one year if all their clients were taken away today.

In the early 1990s, a self-made, street-smart auditor named Steve Samek came to prominence within the firm, despite the collapse of one of his major clients, Boston Chicken. Samek was a man of his time: In 1996, the year fair value would be presented by Enron, he was preaching the power of marketing by giving inspirational speeches accompanied by a violinist (so the auditors would think of themselves as maestros). The subtext, if not the stated message to the Andersen troops, was this: Marketing is a lot more fun and a lot more lucrative than old-fashioned accounting, which was boring and didn't bring in enough money anyway. The new, unstated motto became "Make it Work." Give the client what he wanted.

These changes in corporate identity had their effect on Enron. Andersen was the auditor for Internorth, Enron's predecessor, and Ken Lay, drawn as he was to companies with blue-chip reputations, saw no reason to change. Andersen gave the fledgling company legitimacy. It was then, in the mid-eighties, the biggest accounting firm in town, and had most of the prestigious clients, including Pennzoil and Tenneco. Andersen was the oil patch accounting firm of choice—strict, by the book, but also, when the economic bust hit, creative when they had to be, to keep their clients afloat.

As Enron grew in size and prestige, the balance of power shifted. The relationship became more symbiotic. Andersen took on Enron's internal audit staff when they were outsourced, for instance, and had an office in Enron's Houston headquarters that was soon as big as some of Andersen's other regional offices. In psychiatric terms, the two firms became enmeshed—there came to be a well-traveled career path between Andersen and Enron, as more and more people left the pressured, lower-paying confines of Andersen for the more pressured but more lucrative freedom of Enron. (Rick Causey and Sherron Watkins were just a few of the hundreds who made the journey.) Enron and its executives—Ken Lay, Jeff Skilling, Rebecca Mark—became the stars of Arthur Andersen's annual oil and gas symposium. The joke was that the symposium should be renamed the Andersen-Enron Energy Conference.

Throughout this period, Andersen was giving more and more power to their local managing partners, who at the same time had to make numbers for their region. Hence, for a man like David Duncan, lead Enron audit partner, it paid, as it did for Rick Causey, to get along and go along. By the mid-nineties it was clear that Andersen needed Enron more than Enron needed Andersen, both for the prestige and for the billings, which were closing in on $1 million a week. Consequently, as Enron pushed Andersen to approve ever more aggressive accounting techniques, Andersen had more trouble pushing back. Cynicism set in, to the extent that a partner in Andersen's energy division wrote a song about the company's most high-risk client, the one that hated to record losses. Set to the tune of the Eagles song "Hotel California," it was called "Hotel Can't Afford Ya."

The accountant sang about busting his butt and then busting rocks, and how, when the "suits" arrived everyone should bring their alibis. At the end of the song, the client—Enron—says, "Relax." They are set up to succeed.

You can audit anytime you like
But we will never bleed.

Given that, it was not surprising, notwithstanding Sherron's concerns and the subtle objections of Andersen's non-Enron partners, that Andersen's Enron team signed off on the plan to use fair value accounting to help cover the $190 million loss.

Walking down the hall soon after, Sherron spied two of her old Andersen colleagues, Tom Bauer and Carl Bass, heading toward her. "When are you guys gonna grow some balls?" she called out by way of greeting. "Are you really going to let us get away with this fair value stuff?" The men could only grin sheepishly in response.

The next day, Andy Fastow called her to his office. He looked at Sherron coldly as she took a seat. The champion of fair value now told her that she had used very bad judgment in joking with her friends. It was a serious mistake to make fun of this new accounting technique. The company had to present a united front, with no dissension about its appropriateness. Sherron should stick to funding, and stop butting in where she wasn't needed. She left Fastow's office with the feeling that she had made a very bad career move.

There were others who felt as she did. Vince Kaminski, a vice president and head of ECT's research group, thought the company was dooming itself. He compared the attempt to write up the merchant portfolio to asking a stockbroker to sell a $50 stock for $80 now, because it might reach that in three years. "The broker would hang up on me," he said. The same opinion came from a candidate Sherron was still trying to hire as an equity expert for the Portfolio Management Advisory Committee. Sherron had found a candidate from Harvard Trust, but, after meeting with Skilling in a second round of interviews, he turned down the job offer. "Skilling thinks there's a way to hedge away the majority of equity risk in your portfolio," he told her. "It can't be done. It's called equity risk for a reason. I'm not about to take a job that's doomed to fail." He wished Sherron good luck and caught his cab to the airport.

It may have been this failure that inspired Sherron, at Andersen's December Oil and Gas Symposium, to bring up fair value again when she ran into Tom Bauer, Carl Bass, and David Duncan, whom she also knew from her Andersen days. They dismissed her. Enron made its bed, Bass said. "You live by the sword, you die by the sword." What Enron was writing up in value today, Enron would simply have to write down when the assets' worth fell, as they inevitably would.

Sherron had no intention of waiting for that to happen, especially on her watch at JEDI. She told Rick Buy, the company's chief risk officer, that she was going to look for a new job outside of Fastow's funding area. She was worried, she said. Her name was all over the JEDI portfolio, and she wouldn't be associated with this risky accounting method. It would hurt the reputation of anyone who touched it, she predicted. Buy just shook his head.

Sherron had another reason for wanting to leave Andy Fastow's department. Fastow was annoyed that CalPERS and its advisor, Pacific Corporate Group, Inc., were reluctant to invest in a power fund he wanted to launch. The issue, for CalPERS, was the lack of a business plan. The fund managers wanted to know just how Enron intended to develop a wholesale and retail electricity-trading business. They wanted to know how the company was going to gain market share when the residential arena was still tightly regulated. Enron didn't really have a response other than to say that no business plan was needed—it would develop one after it found the right market opportunity to invest in. That was too risky an answer for CalPERS, which politely bowed out of Fastow's plans.

He now called CalPERS's advisor, Pacific Corporate Group, and insisted to their lead contact, a man named David Graus, that his client missed a major opportunity. As Sherron stood beside his desk waiting to brief Fastow on a JEDI matter, she heard him tell Graus that he had just closed a deal for Enron's first power fund, called Alpine Investors. CalPERS dragged their feet, he said, so he cut them out. "You've lost your preferred-investor status, David," Fastow continued. "We did our first power deal without you."

Sherron could discern that on the other end of the line Graus was begging for a second chance; he asked for the information memorandum and said he'd try to convince CalPERS to go along next time.

The only problem was that Alpine was actually a financing—it wasn't a power fund. Fastow hung up the phone, turned to Sherron, and told her to meet with his new protégé, Michael Kopper, and dummy up the Alpine bankbook to make it look like an equity investor power fund. Then, Fastow said, she should send it to Pacific Corporate Group.

Sherron argued against it—PCGI was well-connected and would surely realize the deception—but Fastow cut her off. Get with Kopper and do it, he said.

Instead, Sherron met with Fastow's in-house attorney, Kristina Mordaunt, and Kopper, both of whom opposed the idea. "We can't dummy up information memorandums—that's ludicrous," Kopper told her. They agreed to stall, hoping that Fastow would forget about the idea. Fortunately, he did, as did PCGI—but it was a close call.

It was another departure that shook Enron at the end of 1996. For five years, Rich Kinder had waited for Ken Lay to step down from the CEO's job and hand the title to him. Kinder had effectively been running the company for quite a number of years, urging it forward but also imposing discipline, while Lay had served, increasingly, as its public face. Kinder had expected that the CEO's job would be his in 1992, when Lay had hoped to land a cabinet position after George H. W. Bush's reelection. But Clinton had won, and so Lay stayed on for another contract term. Then Lay was going to leave in 1996; he had hoped for the job of CEO at AT&T. But he did not get the job, and he decided to stay on again.

Lay and Kinder had been close in college, but their interests had diverged over the years. Kinder had remained enamored of business, while Lay had explored the wider stage. But the differences were also personal. Kinder had fallen in love with Nancy McNeil, who had been Lay's longtime executive assistant. The affair (Kinder was married at the time) caused discord in the company and in the executive suite. Whether or not the two were undermining Lay's power, as water cooler gossip had it, Lay clearly resented the relationship, which may have been another factor in his refusal to give his job to the man who had supported him for well over a decade. Considering, too, that Lay's second wife, Linda, had been his secretary at Florida Gas, his response was hypocritical. But Lay was not bothered by such contradictions. Neither, as it turned out, was Kinder. When Lay refused to leave in 1992, Kinder renegotiated his contract so that if Lay wanted to stay on again in 1996, Enron would pay him $25 million. Now he walked with his cash, leaving Lay to sort out the chaos. Lay in turn appointed Jeff Skilling to replace Kinder as president and COO of Enron. "Appointed" may not be the right word. Skilling went to the Enron hangar, where Lay was leaving on a trip, and gave him an ultimatum: the COO job, or he was gone. Lay was in a tough spot. He couldn't lose two top executives in the same month. So Skilling was in.

There was a lot of melancholy joking within Enron at Kinder's departure. One employee, Keith Power, penned a clever list, à la David Letterman, of Rich Kinder's Top Ten Reasons for Leaving Enron. They included "Profanity became unbearable when walking through [trading] floors 30 and 31"; "Would have been necessary to obtain a double PhD in accounting theory and statistical probability to understand ECT's fair valuation methodology"; and "Got tired of Ken Lay greeting me every morning with 'Hey Stupid, you still working here?'"

As a going-away gift, those closest to Kinder made a video for him. Both George Bushes wished him well; Lay, in a flawless bit of theater, closed his office door and then asked Kinder whether he'd really done "all those ugly things to people to have them make their numbers." Rick Causey joked that, in his new job as chief accountant, managing earnings had turned out to be "easier than I thought it would be." Jeff Skilling, in a meeting with the corporate secretary pretending to be Kinder, promised even greater profits in the coming year. Trading would go from $10 million to $64 million; finance would go from $15 to $92; retail would go from "nothing" to $42 million. All told, he promised to raise profits from $60 million last year to $423 million. "We're going to move from mark-to-market accounting to something I call HFV, or hypothetical future value accounting," he said. "If we do that, we can add a kazillion dollars to the bottom line."

Everyone thought he was kidding.

7

Vision and Values

I N early 1997, it didn't seem to matter that Rich Kinder was gone—publicly, at least. Enron still had its stars in Rebecca Mark and Jeff Skilling, and with Lay signed on for five more years as chairman and CEO, the company projected a sense of continuity and glamour. *Business Week* named Lay one of its Top 25 Managers of the Year in January, alongside the great corporate gods of his time: Bill Gates of Microsoft, Sandy Warner of J. P. Morgan, Cisco's John Chambers, Dell's Michael Dell, and GE's Jack Welch. The story praised Lay for turning a domestic gas pipeline company into an integrated global natural gas major—"from a stodgy pipeline company into a corporate colossus" was the cliché of choice for Enron's transformation—and for his zealous push into the $200 billion domestic electricity market. But good notices in the business press were not enough for Enron. Wall Street knew the company well, but Main Street did not. For a company with Enron's stratospheric ambitions, this was a problem.

And so, in the early part of 1997, Ken Lay decided it was time for a New

Enron. As the World's Leading Energy Company, Enron was no longer a gas company but one venturing into the world of electricity, attempting to supply power to businesses and homes. At the same time, Enron was expanding its trading—along with gas, and the financial trades it was making off its gas trades, it was also gearing up to trade electricity, paper and pulp, and even weather derivatives (i.e., it created a desk to help businesses hedge against the damage bad weather might inflict on their profits). Enron wanted to grow, of course, but Enron also had to grow to keep up with Wall Street's demands for ever-increasing earnings. Because Enron's expansion had been so spectacular in the past, however, keeping up was going to get harder and harder. Hence, every year—almost every quarter, in fact—was dominated by the search for more profits from existing businesses, as well as for some new idea, like the Gas Bank or electricity trading, that would make an enormous financial difference in a very short time.

During the same period, it became an article of faith to Lay and his marketing team that another way to make more money was to raise Enron's profile. The late 1990s was an era when the concept of "branding" became popular again. A brand could be a person or a business; either way, marketing experts from Hollywood to Madison Avenue believed that the better a person or business was known, the better it was for business. It didn't matter whether everyone actually went to a particular star's movie or bought a particular product; the goal was to generate "buzz," because customers felt more secure patronizing a business that everyone else seemed to know and like. They were reassured that they had picked a winner. Their taste and judgment were affirmed. Part of Enron's grand plan, then, was simply to become popular, in the way of an ambitious high school freshman. To become a major force in retail electricity, for instance, it had to be the kind of company people would want in their homes. To wrangle that invitation, Enron had to become better known and better liked—as familiar as GE, Sony, or Coke.

Marketing at Enron was then headed by a tall, svelte, exceedingly well-turned-out blonde named Beth Tilney. She was a southerner, and her manner and her accent reflected powerful belle-like proclivities—she wore very expensive jewelry, and she liked to advise her staff on the proper way to extract diamonds from their husbands at holiday time. Despite, or because of, her persona, Tilney was perfect for Enron's upwardly mobile milieu. Her husband, Schuyler, handled the Enron account at the Merrill Lynch office in Houston, and, she liked to brag, acted as Ken Lay's personal investment advisor. Her detractors wondered why Tilney deserved $800,000 a year for what was essentially a cheerleading job. To some her role seemed typical of Lay's tendency to blur the lines, or grease the wheels, between Enron and the investment banks. On the other hand, Tilney had the breeding and style Lay found irresistible.

And she loved her work. Tilney had an almost religious faith in Enron and was determined to make it a household name. She also knew how difficult the task would be. Enron ran some name-recognition tests in the United States and overseas, and the results were disappointing. People thought Enron was a weapon the Klingons used on Star Trek, or the name of a fruit importer, a cosmetics company, a hiking shoe company, or a golf ball manufacturer— and many of these responses came from Houston, where the company had its headquarters.

In order to shape Enron's new identity—to figure out what it should be—a team from Enron's ad agency, Ogilvy & Mather, arrived from Manhattan to interview its employees and find out what mattered to them. Ogilvy found Enron to be a company of "believers." Employees believed in Ken Lay and Jeff Skilling; they believed Enronians were the best and the brightest, and they believed they were doing good in the world by opening new markets and creating new products and services.

As a result, Enron and Ogilvy decided to hone its vision, and its new ad campaign, around a concept called "What We Believe." Those beliefs included "the wisdom of open markets" and "being a laboratory for innovation." Creativity was crucial: "Enron is all about energy; we want leaders here who create our own brand of energy." "Everything we do is about change," the literature put out by Enron's new Vision and Values team stated. "Change a goal. Change a habit. Change a mind." Lush photographs of flowers and children illustrated a small booklet that laid out Enron's values: Respect, Integrity, Communication, and Excellence. The whole campaign was not unlike a religious tract from a New Age megachurch, but instead of directing disciples to God, Enron hoped its congregation would be inspired to join its mission to make itself The World's Leading Energy Company.

The crusade began with an Enron television commercial that premiered during halftime at the Super Bowl. In conjunction, the company hired legendary graphic designer Paul Rand to redesign the Enron logo, transforming it from something that looked very mechanical (the O in Enron looked like the head of a screw) to the brilliantly hued, jaunty E. The campaign rollout was staged as a mock Hollywood premier, starring Elizabeth Taylor and Whoopi Goldberg look-alikes. (The E had to be redone after the yellow hue Rand selected didn't reproduce.) Tilney redecorated the Enron building with inspirational banners so that it resembled the capital of an emerging nation (or, as one cynic noted, a high-school gym at homecoming). "Attempt the impossible in order to improve your work," one banner proclaimed, quoting Bette Davis. "Opportunities multiply as they are seized," said another, quoting Sun Tzu. Ogilvy also added inspirational messages it collected from Enron personnel. "If you're not in the box, you don't have to think outside it," ran one message. Another advised, "We are bound to make mistakes. We are not bound to repeat them."

The ad campaign spoke directly to Ken Lay's missionary instincts. But it did not appeal to Jeff Skilling, who carped about phrases like "Arrogance does not belong here" (*Why bring up the word at all?*) and who resented a PR campaign that cost millions and seemed to add no value to the company.

But Tilney persisted, as only a determined southern woman can. If Skilling wouldn't sign on for the whole campaign, she convinced him to perform with Lay in a Vision and Values video that went out to all employees. The two men narrated the film from two wing chairs, wearing identical white shirts and narrow ties, as they shared what was great about Enron with each other and, presumably, their audience. They talked about Respect and Integrity, Communication and Excellence.

"A lot of organizations like to stamp out the nonconformist, the nonconventional thinker," Lay said, "but a lot of times they're the people who really are the future, because they're thinking about things differently, they're coming up with new ideas." "Yes," Skilling chorused. "You know when you work for Enron you're going to see the newest thing, the newest products, the newest services, the newest ways of thinking about things."

As they spoke, the video cut to scenes of bright young Enron employees hammering out their differences on whiteboards, and weathered men inspecting pipelines at dusty, remote locales. A smiling Asian woman draped a lei over a beaming Ken Lay, while her countrymen in business suits nodded and bowed gratefully. "If there's one thing I hope we can achieve," Lay said, his face thoughtful and earnest, "it's to create an environment where our employees can come in here and realize their potential."

Skilling waited just a beat before agreeing. "It's a wild ride," he said, and then both men laughed. They laughed the way people do when they've pulled off something they never thought they could.

R ebecca Mark understood the power of signs and symbols, too. Circling the globe on Enron's behalf, she became a devotee of mystical priests and shamans, who all told her, in one way or another, that her destiny was to bring light into the world. Studying the *Tibetan Book of Living and Dying*, experimenting with the I Ching, she reincarnated herself into a New Age corporate diva the likes of which had never been seen before. But, true to her roots in Western capitalism, Mark was also determined to do whatever had to be done to close a deal.

Mark's timing was fortuitous: There were not many senior female executives in the mid-nineties, much less attractive female CEOs who worked in the energy field. Mark had found her niche, and consciously or not, her role models were Hollywood's female stars, the ones who understood that the uses of theater extended far beyond the screening room. It was a tribute to her skills that the attractive Mark was almost universally described by staffers and global leaders as a knockout. The press saw her that way too. By the late 1990s, editors were hungry for inspirational stories of women executives, and Mark's was perfect. She was featured prominently in a 1996 *Fortune* cover story titled "Women, Sex & Power." (The subtitle read: "A politically incorrect story about seven remarkable women—each better than all the men.") For a company that never missed a marketing opportunity, Mark offered what is known in Texas as a twofer, as in two-for-one: Outside Enron, she was a great rainmaker and provided exceptional brand extension; inside the company, she was a perfect recruiting tool. When Mark sped through

River Oaks in her ruby-red Jaguar XK8, entertained in her 8,000-square-foot home, or jetted to her ranch in Taos or her Manhattan pied á terre on the company plane, she was a living, breathing billboard for Houston's flamboyance and Enron's cocky aggressiveness.

But there was another reason people were drawn to Mark: Like so many men at Enron, she was a gambler. Most companies were afraid to build massive power projects in emerging nations, believing the problems—ignorance, corruption, poverty, etc.—were insurmountable. But Mark was hooked on the thrill of just that kind of deal. She believed in the Enron business model: The biggest rewards, she knew from John Wing, went to the company that took the biggest risks. And so, sometimes with her twin sons in tow (like many people at Enron, Mark was divorced), she started jetting around the world, churning up business on Enron's behalf, determined that her energy company would be the first to make inroads into Brazil, China, Puerto Rico, the Philippines, Qatar. Her boldest prospect was India, where she intended to build the largest power plant ever.

When she found a likely counterparty, Mark drove bargains that were typically Enronian: If Shell Oil wouldn't let Enron into a joint venture to build a pipeline from Boliva to Brazil, Mark went to the Bolivians and convinced them they needed Enron on their side. When the World Bank opposed the India project—they didn't think the country needed a project of the size Enron was pushing, nor did they think the government could afford it—she found other financing. Governments changed and opposed her. Mark was undaunted. She fought the lawsuits—twenty-four of them—added a few of her own, and kept the India project going. In the Middle East, Ken Lay dispatched her to Qatar to negotiate with sheiks married to women prohibited from appearing in public. She came back with a signed deal for a power plant. "If you'd been here earlier," one government official complimented her, "we'd have finished this deal months ago."

She bullied, befuddled, and seduced. She insulted: "Apparently RM [Rebecca Mark] told the PM [Prime Minister] her jet was waiting and she didn't have much time," reported one concerned Enron executive in a confidential memo. "Prime Minister also did not appreciate RM's remarks to the press telling how PM should do job." She played hardball: Government officials who didn't go along might find themselves the subject of negative stories by reporters, who were, more often than not, in Mark's thrall. She could make her face as open as a child's, her brown eyes warm and liquid, her expression searching; a touch to the forearm, a cross of the leg—and they were hers.

It was this package that made her a star at Enron. That and the fact that Mark was closing deals left and right. By early 1997, Mark had operating assets in Argentina, Colombia, Guatemala, the Dominican Republic, the U.K., and the Philippines. She had more than $19 billion in projects under construction or in negotiations and without notes could recite the specifics of each. More important, she could show growth, which Enron desperately needed to impress Wall Street. The price-to-earnings ratios for stocks of stagnant pipeline companies or risky trading houses were much lower than they were for international construction giants that were expanding exponentially. If Mark took enormous bonuses in return—following Wing's lead, she and her team made 10 percent of the net present value of projects when the deal was signed, rather than when operations commenced—no one seemed to mind.

No one, that is, but Jeff Skilling.

Like John Wing, Rebecca Mark kept Enron International physically separated from the rest of the company. Most of Enron was located in the bright, gleaming headquarters at 1400 Smith; Enron International, however, was located in a separate building nearby, Three Allen Center. Mark also spent much of her time far from Houston, trawling for business around the globe. This absence may explain why she was oblivious to growing threats to her power and autonomy at home. Then, too, Mark knew that Ken Lay's passion was not for finance but for global renown. As long as she remained his one-woman international advance team, her job was secure.

But Mark's work began to bother Rich Kinder as early as 1994—he was concerned about the quality, not the quantity of her deals. Skilling seconded his concerns and took advantage of every opportunity to weaken her position.

Skilling and Mark were natural opposites—she loved the coaxing, prodding, and seducing that was part of deal making. Skilling liked to say that he didn't want to be in any business where the customer had to like him. He opposed Mark's massive construction projects on principle—they generated a rate of return that was far too low for Wall Street's, and therefore his, tastes. Mark was also the last conceivable competitor to Kinder's job if and when Lay finally decided to step down. Skilling had dispatched every other adversary.

As CEO of what was originally called Enron Development, Mark had a mandate to develop power plants in the industrialized world—in Texas, the Northeast, and, internationally, in the United Kingdom. But almost immediately, she moved beyond those borders, building or buying pipelines and power plants in developing countries, promising to bring clean-burning, gas-fired electricity to those who, in her eyes, needed it most. That didn't mean Mark was an easy mark; her core development teams scoured the Third World for deals that fit very specific criteria. First, they found a foreign government, as opposed to a business, that would buy the power. Second, they nailed down a few equity partners to share the risk and keep the project off Enron's balance sheet. Third, they sought and got nonrecourse financing, which meant that in the event of a financial (or any other) meltdown, all claims ended with that specific project—Enron Development, or Enron Corp., could not be drawn in. In exchange, Mark's team developed the project for a fee, financed the project for another fee, operated the project for yet another fee, and, best of all, managed the joint venture between Enron Development and its equity partners for still one more fee. And all this money was collected before Enron moved a molecule of gas or electricity, though Mark promised greater profits, of course, once the project was on line in two to three years.

But problems occurred when deals didn't go according to plan, and Mark's solutions could be expensive for the company. A failed deal, for instance, would be "saved" by folding it into a newer, bigger deal—the development costs for a small power plant that never got built would be applied to the development costs of a larger power project in the same area, which, if that faltered, would become part of a still-larger power and pipeline system considered for the entire region. In a few countries—Vietnam and Mozambique in particular—these capitalized costs were nicknamed "The Snowball," because they got bigger and bigger without generating revenue for the company. Mark, on the other hand, labeled such expenditures "strategic." Sometimes the company had to spend money to make money, she claimed; it had to invest in the future. What bothered Skilling was that Mark got her bonuses, future or no.

In 1994, he found an ally in a young Enron attorney named Amanda Martin, who was anxious to leave law behind and move into commercial endeavors. With Kinder's blessing, Skilling put her in charge of investigating Mark's projects. Martin was South African by birth; she came to Enron via Vinson & Elkins, the company's outside law firm. Her background was consistent with that of the most powerful Enron executives: She grew up poor and somewhat plain, but was inordinately bright and had an instinct for the most direct path to success. Over the years Martin emerged, like Mark, into a bombshell, a witty, shrewd, deeply ambitious blonde whose South African accent rendered most of her male colleagues dithering fools. In other words, she was another Enron star in the making. Martin headed a newly formed Joint Venture Management Group, responsible for studying all the joint venture contracts and supervising the staff to ensure that Enron was living up to its contractual obligations. Her staff just happened to include all the accountants who worked for Mark. Mark, in turn, saw no harm in contract reviews and welcomed Martin to her world.

It was a colossal mistake. Mark was, above all, a deal maker, and the best thing that could be said was that once she made her deals, she lacked follow-through. Martin made it her business to visit every foreign investment, and in too many cases found disaster. A power plant floating on barges in the Dominican Republic ("dead on arrival," in the words of one auditor) was permanently docked without any attention to the prevailing winds; as a result, debris from the bay in which it was situated washed into turbines that powered the plants, stopping them dead. Enron had to hire workmen to stand in boats all day, physically pushing trash away from the turbines with oars specially designed for that purpose. In addition, soot from the plant's smokestacks curled up a nearby mountainside, coating guests at a luxury hotel and spawning a nasty lawsuit. In China, the Enron ship that was supposed to bring diesel fuel upriver to the Enron plant was too heavy to navigate the shallow waters; the river had to be dredged to get the boat through until a new, smaller ship could be built. In San Juan, Puerto Rico, tons of gas designated for a particular pipeline was simply lost—inspectors eventually discovered at least seven leaks for every mile of pipe.

Not surprisingly, many of Mark's plants were not operating as she had forecast in her models. Expenses were sometimes higher, fuel costs weren't always locked in, and as a result varied considerably—always dangerous in a volatile energy market. Armed with the information from Martin, Skilling reran the models on most of Mark's earlier projects, and his numbers showed that every project was riskier and would produce a lower return than Mark claimed. He subsequently insisted that all of her future deals should be approved by the Risk Assessment and Control group, which he controlled. After that, Mark understood who she was up against.

Mark went to Lay and Kinder, and won the next round. They formed a new company, Enron Global Power and Pipelines, and gave her control of her own books again. Skilling was neutralized.

But only temporarily. Mark's new group's shortcomings were the very sins that James Alexander complained about to Ken Lay, most notably that the plants never lived up to her projections. Alexander had been rebuffed—Skilling was one of the people who marginalized him. But now Skilling himself took up the cause. He knew how to gripe—and whom to gripe to.

He complained to anyone who would listen—employees, executives, board members—sometimes behind Mark's back, sometimes when she was in the room. It was bad enough that her projects generated such a low, slow rate of return, he claimed. But you couldn't trust her calculations either. She didn't know how to analyze a deal; she didn't know how to use risk analytics to protect the company from loss. By then her very presence offended him. He refused to ride with Mark on a company jet when both of them were attending the same meeting at Harvard. He made fun of the C's on the back of her Chanel jacket. He would not be stopped.

One reason Mark may have denied the tenuousness of her position at Enron was that, in private, Skilling sometimes treated her as a friend and confidante. She found this behavior confusing but, given her ambition and her almost preternatural desire for connection, irresistible. Skilling could be abrasive and intimidating, but he also had a Hamlet-like side, a doubting and confessional aspect to his personality that so appealed to women and, for that matter, anyone who wanted to bask in the reflected glory that came from being close to power at Enron. Mark was one of the few people who knew what holding power at Enron was like, and so when Skilling's marriage collapsed in 1995, he confided in her. (He explained the dissolution of his marriage in his 1999 Harvard Business School alumni notes: "Sue and I ended 21 years of marriage in a swirl of pain and recrimination. Years of airplanes, late nights, consulting challenges, heady exhilarations, equity markets that rise and fall, and general personal exhaustion make for a bad relationship partner. So there it is.") He said things—to Mark and others—that didn't sound like a typical CEO candidate. Skilling talked about chucking it all and running off to a deserted Caribbean island, for instance. He talked about taking time off to get his head together. (In a move uncommon for a CEO, he quietly took a sabbatical from Enron Gas Services.) But his concerns about his legacy in the business world always trumped those desires. Would he ever be as influential as G.E.'s Jack Welch? he wondered. Would he ever accomplish as much?

After he divorced, however, Skilling chose a new path. Before, he seemed like a man who had bypassed adolescence—he preferred to work. Now he explored life's pleasures with the intensity he'd once reserved for his spread sheets at First City. He got rid of the rumpled, button-down shirts and the middle-aged paunch. He dispatched his glasses with Lasix surgery.

He adopted the aggressively understated uniform of Hollywood producers and Microsoft multimillionaires—T-shirts and jeans, and on special occasions (like industry speeches), a designer sports jacket. He had lived modestly for years, but now he bought a large, oak-shaded tract in River Oaks that once belonged to a Humble Oil heir, and commenced construction on an 8,000-square-foot Mediterranean-style mansion. (His interior designer chose a color scheme of black and white, either as a tribute or a capitulation to Skilling's penchant for absolutes.) He trimmed down, pumped up, and started hosting extreme adventures as corporate retreats— bungee jumping, rock climbing, Jeep races through the desert—Ken Rice, Cliff Baxter, and Andy Fastow joined in, a merry band of corporate boys.

He floated passes at female employees. In the parlance of the times, Jeff Skilling began living large. In a few years, he would supplement his hairline too.

During this period, he was also laser-focused on Enron. Skilling's strategy was twofold: to discover the next new thing that would dramatically enhance the company's numbers, and to get rid of anything or anyone he believed was a drag on the balance sheet. Rebecca Mark, and what he saw as her antiquated business philosophy, fell into the latter category.

With encouragement from McKinsey, Enron had been eyeing a move into electricity—buying it, selling it, trading it—since 1994. It was a chance to replicate the Enron business model, a chance, once more, to be on The Side of the Angels. Electricity was dominated by entrenched utilities that were not consumer friendly; Skilling began barnstorming the country to spread Enron's gospel of cheaper power. The market was distorted, he said. Consumers paid from three to eight times the cost of wholesale electricity. Savings in the $200-billion-a-year market could amount to $60 to $80 billion a year.

In Skilling's mind, Enron could break up the monopolies and make a bundle for itself in the process. Better yet, electricity tied into Enron's grand convergence plan to make itself The World's Leading Energy Company.

As it had done with gas, Enron looked to Washington to ease the way. It didn't hurt that Ken Lay chaired the 1992 Republican Convention; President Bush signed the Enron benefiting Energy Policy Act into law before he left office in 1993. Among other things, it allowed new producers to scour the country for the cheapest sources of power for the market. Meanwhile, older utilities were stuck, locked into high-priced contracts with local generators. The new law also allowed open and equal access along transmission lines, mirroring the freedom that deregulated gas pipelines a few years back. In 1994 (a year in which Enron was the sixth-largest political contributor in the energy sector, with gifts totaling close to $500,000), the company won from the SEC an exemption from the Public Utility Holding Company Act of 1935, which prevented electric companies from monopolizing their geographic regions. Enron claimed the rules did not apply to them because they would not be owning plants, just trading electricity.

But even with Washington in its corner, Enron had some challenging flaws in its business model. Electricity was not, as the company insisted, like gas. It didn't flow steadily through pipes but flitted through a complicated grid that was easily disrupted by things like thunderstorms. For this reason, businesspeople wanted providers they could depend on, and once they found them, were loathe to switch. Second, the electricity business wasn't like the gas business, either. It didn't deregulate from Washington, as gas did. Instead, the political action was in the individual states, where entrenched utilities were masters of the local turf. Finally, Enron believed it could make money in electricity without actually owning power plants—its intent was simply to bundle and sell services, the first test of Jeff Skilling's "asset lite" strategy. But as it turned out, there was no real way to make money without owning a physical source of power. For one thing, in many states it was against the law to trade power without actually owning it. Much of this news should not have come as a surprise to Enron's electricity zealots, but in fact it did.

There were naysayers within the company when Enron forged into electricity in the mid-1990s, but they were gradually overcome by what came to be known as the McKinsey Gestapo, the young recruits who swept through the offices, interviewed everyone involved on a given strategy, and then constructed plans that had less to do with marketable ideas than with silencing the opposition. No one wanted to be told "No," least of all Jeff Skilling: When one executive told him that Enron could not legally trade power without owning it, Skilling's response was to urge him to be more creative. Find a way in which Enron could, he said. When the regulatory law firms in Washington and New York told Skilling the same thing, he and one of his lieutenants, Ken Rice, scoffed. These were just the kind of arguments they heard when they were fighting gas regulation. This was a fight for the future—didn't they get it? If you weren't moving forward, you were moving backward, every day.

While these arguments continued internally, Enron spent millions externally, lobbying state legislators and a few struggling utilities, and producing clever television commercials that stressed the consumers' right to choose their electric provider. (One depicted a stubborn New Englander demanding freedom from electrical tyranny.)

Since no one wanted to tell Skilling that his ideas were flawed, they kept re-doing models instead, and bringing in McKinsey to try to come up with a workable solution. "Every other day, Jeff would sit down with everyone and pontificate," one executive recalled. "He was very convincing right up to the point where he would start to describe how it was going to happen."

But it didn't happen. Enron wasn't evolving into a player in the world of electricity. Skilling had grossly underestimated the importance of physical assets: Enron had enormous gas reserves when it pushed its ideas on the business, so customers knew it could back up any deal with its own reserves. But when it came to electricity, Enron had nothing more than a few small independent power plants and wind farms scattered around the country. Literally and metaphorically, it lacked power.

Eventually, Skilling bowed to the inevitable. In 1996, Enron negotiated a merger with Portland General, a large utility in Oregon. It looked like a good choice of partners: The New York Mercantile Exchange, the world's largest commodity futures exchange for energy products, had decided that one of its primary delivery points for new electricity contracts would be the California-Oregon border, near Portland General's location. The company could also serve as a point of departure for Enron's residential electricity efforts in California.

Buying Portland General was difficult and expensive. The local public utility commission claimed Enron's rates would be too high (so much for being on the side of the angels). Enron brought in former Trailblazer Clyde Drexler (later a Houston Rocket) as a pitchman, but even so, the deal barely went through. The deal was finalized on July 1, 1997, only after Portland General's customers were guaranteed cost reductions of $141 million. But in the end, Wall Street scoffed: The collective wisdom was that Enron, which shelled out $3 billion for Portland General—a 48 percent premium to shareholders—overpaid. As Chuck Watson, the head of Natural Gas Clearinghouse and one of Enron's competitors, noted, "I've had several calls from utility guys saying 'You want to pay a 40 percent to 50 percent premium? We're yours.'"

The person who did best by the merger was Cliff Baxter, who negotiated the deal over a period of months, in total secrecy, from a resort hotel in Phoenix, Arizona. Closing Portland General proved, once again, that he was the Big Dog.

Baxter had left the company in a huff a year or so before, and moved his

Above: Ken Lay. Lay was as much of a mystery as the company he founded. (© *Wyatt McSpadden*)

Right: From left, Andy Fastow, Jeffrey Skilling, and Sherron Watkins, skiing in the Rocky Mountains during a 1994 pensions conference in Aspen.

Above: Former Enron COO Rich Kinder. Kinder was the nuts-and-bolts guy behind Enron's early success. (© *Houston Chronicle*)

Below: Andy Fastow handed out dollar bills with his picture on them at an internal Enron meeting to emphasize his motto—"Come to me, I'll fund all your deals."

Above: Enron International's 1997 *Wizard of Oz* skit, spoofing Enron's funding process. (Kneeling) Rodney Faldyn (playing Andy Fastow); Brett Wiggs and Adil Jaffrey as Munchkins. (Standing) another Munchkin; Mike Brown as the Cowardly Lion of Enron Construction; the Tin Man representing the "heartless" Joe Sutton; Ellen Fowler (playing Good Witch Rebecca Mark); Mitch Taylor and Scott Porter (before donning Dorothy and Toto costumes); Sherron Watkins (partially dressed as the Wicked Witch of RAC); and Jere Overdyke (playing himself as the brainless Scarecrow).

Below: Andy Fastow (center), with Ben Glisan (left) and friends, celebrating their financial acumen during a bank funding trip in South Beach, Miami.

Above: Enron's famous logo outside the company's world headquarters. It would later be auctioned off for nearly $50,000.

Below: Sherron Watkins, with John Vorberger and Curly Baca, evaluating a bauxite mine in Guinea, in western Africa, in 1997.

Left: Lou Pai, Jeff Skilling's right-hand man at Enron Gas Services, and later the head of Enron's much-vaunted electricity retail effort, Enron Energy Services. (© *Wyatt McSpadden*)

Below: Enron COO, and later CEO, Jeff Skilling. Skilling transformed himself from a paunchy, bespectacled nerd into the epitome of corporate hipness. (© *Wyatt McSpadden*)

Right: Ken Rice, a longtime Skilling favorite, who briefly headed up Enron's quixotic Broadband division. (© *Wyatt McSpadden*)

Below: Wooing potential customers with lavish trips on Enron's private jet was a way of life at Enron. Here Sherron Watkins takes clients to a 1998 Masters practice round.

Above: Enron executive Amanda Martin gave Jeff Skilling the ammunition he needed to undermine his chief rival, Rebecca Mark. (© *Houston Chronicle*)

Below: Expensive "deal toys" commemorated Enron executives' biggest triumphs.

Above: Enron's high-tech trading floor, where the epithets rang out and the revenues rolled in.

Right: Ken Lay and Jeffrey Skilling at the height of their power. (© *Wyatt McSpadden*)

family to Kansas, where he took a job at Koch Industries. It did not work out. At Enron, Baxter was able to call Jeff Skilling at all hours, keeping him on the phone as the sun rose, turning over the intricacies of a given deal. Baxter quit often, but he always came back in a few days or a week, acting as if nothing ever happened.

But then he got into a turf war with another executive and quit Enron for good, even though Skilling begged him to stay. In return, Baxter called him an asshole and accused him of never giving him the support he needed. He said he was going to a place where he would get the respect he deserved. Fine, Skilling told him, but you'll always have a home at Enron. Two months later, Baxter was on the phone. Before Skilling could draw breath, he launched into a Koch critique, complaining that the company was populated by dinosaurs. Baxter said he'd been thinking about Skilling's offer. I'm just not sure these guys up here get it, he said.

Skilling offered him a job in Corporate Development. Baxter agreed, as long as he could be Senior Vice President. And he had one more request: He wanted to be sure that no one gave him any grief about leaving and coming back.

Skilling spent the next few days journeying from duchy to duchy within Enron, making sure his troops supported Baxter's return. He got it, though there was some dissention. *Cliff, we're all thrilled to have you back!* Baxter was told. Baxter, in turn, told everyone that Skilling begged him to come home to Enron.

The people at Koch were not sorry to see him go. They were midwesterners to the core, soft-spoken, considerate, uninterested in living on the edge every minute of every day. They could live quite nicely without the Big Dog's volatility. In the wake of Baxter's departure, those who misbehaved at Koch sometimes found squares of chocolate on their chairs—Baxter Bars, the locally made candy—a not-so-subtle hint that they had stepped over the line.

Almost immediately after Jeff Skilling took over from Rich Kinder, he targeted Rebecca Mark for annihilation. As a consolation prize for losing out on the COO's job, Lay gave her virtually all of the international businesses outside of Europe and North America, even those that had previously been part of Skilling's Enron Capital & Trade. But what looked like a plum—Mark loved emerging nations, after all—was actually another carefully laid Skilling trap. Enron International was now infiltrated with Skilling loyalists from ECT who previously chased businesses in those countries. They, in turn, fed intelligence back to The Boss or they turned up in foreign locales, introducing themselves as the *real* Enron representatives. Mark was trapped in a Marx brothers movie: she got calls from bureaucrats asking who they should work with—her team, or the twenty-year-old who just left. Mark's team proposed infrastructure deals—roads, bridges, the twentieth century—while the Enron Capital & Trade caller pushed high finance—derivatives, costless collars, the twenty-first century (the one they hadn't entered yet). She started ordering her ex–Enron Capital & Trade employees to stay away—not just from particular meetings but from entire countries.

Skilling opened another front in the North Sea. Enron had a massive problem there that came to be known as "J-Block," the name of a sizeable oil and gas field that had been developed by the majors. Nearly all the field's natural gas was committed to Enron to fuel Teesside, the British power plant that made the company an international player. But, as part of the deal, Enron agreed to take or pay for the gas for years at a fixed price. Enron roped itself into the kind of lose/lose contract it had vilified during the fight for deregulation. Even worse, Enron agreed to take or pay for transmission as well.

By the time J-Block was ready to produce gas, prices had declined significantly. If Enron took the gas at the contracted price, it would have to pay twice the price of gas on the open market. Skilling pushed hard for a settlement against many of the major oil companies that had sued, demanding payment—from Phillips, Amoco, British Gas, and more. Finally, in June of 1997, Enron gave $440 million in cash to the owners of the J-Block field to renegotiate the price. That was the good news. The bad news was that Enron had to take a loss in the second quarter of $1.40 per share while the stock price dropped 3/4 of a point, to $40 a share.

Skilling went on the warpath. The fault for J-Block was laid at Mark's doorstep, even though she was just a junior member of Wing's team when Enron cut the original deal. This time, he was powerful enough to require her to submit deals to the Risk Assessment and Control group for approval. RAC was headed by Rick Buy, who reported directly to Skilling.

When he was the head of Enron Capital & Trade, Skilling lobbied to keep all of Enron's business units separate, so that his numbers were exclusively his own. He liked to use the metaphor of silos—separate and sealed to the outside world. But as COO, Skilling wanted to consolidate, which enabled him to buttress trading losses and exploit Enron International at will. "One curve, one book, one Enron" was his new mantra. In other words, he wanted control of everything—price curves, trading books, and the analytics that gave him veto power over whatever Enron bought or sold.

He drew Mark into a bitter battle of accountants. Skilling would claim a deal was a money loser; Mark would say she recouped Enron's investment and then some. Her accountants brandished reports showing profits; Skilling's accountants insisted she wasn't making any money. To avoid paying foreign taxes, Mark's experts had the international bookkeepers "loan" project dividends to Enron each year until the end of the project's life, when the "loans" would be repaid and a massive dividend passed on to Enron. But this meant Mark's returns were never visible to shareholders—earnings and cash flow drove the stock price. In Skilling's eyes, she was nothing but a generator of massive debt.

There were attempts to make peace—at a retreat in Cabo San Lucas, Skilling and Mark jumped into the pool together in a show of solidarity. But it was clear that Skilling intended to take no prisoners. There was room for only one person at the top, and he intended to be that person. It didn't help that Lay was still sending mixed signals about his successor. "Just don't know," he told *Forbes* on that subject in 1998, in a lengthy profile of Mark. "Jeff is the number-two officer in the company, but Rebecca is a very, very talented individual."

One day, an Enron executive was being driven through a small village in China, she spied some gaily decorated banners and asked her driver to translate. "Market Day," he said, and then he chuckled and a glint came into his eyes. "When Dr. Lay was here, the sign said 'Welcome Dr. Lay.'"

The U.S. economy was improving, and corporate titans were making a comeback. Lay, a short, balding, fifty-five-year-old man was suddenly a star.

In March 1997, *Fortune* anointed Enron the country's most innovative company. (The runner-up was Mirage Resorts, "a dazzling collection of Las Vegas gambling casinos.") The magazine was besotted with Enron. "Companies that know how to innovate don't necessarily throw money into R&D," the magazine said. "Instead, they cultivate a new style of corporate behavior that's comfortable with new ideas, change, risk and even failure." A glowing profile of Lay followed in *Business Week* a few months later. "The Quiet Man Who Is Jolting Utilities" was illustrated with a picture of Lay in jogging clothes that prominently displayed the Enron logo. The story noted some potential risks in Enron's foray into electricity and international projects, but mainly it made Lay out to be a visionary. He was "the most visible and feared advocate of opening the nation's $215 billion retail electricity market to competition. . . . A master strategist" whom Senator Phil Gramm praised as a Renaissance man, "as comfortable talking about the ancient Greeks as he is the competitive selling of electric power." The story also admired Lay's houses in Aspen and Galveston, as well as his twenty-one-foot Boston Whaler. Skilling was mentioned glancingly, Mark not at all.

It is hard to know whether Enron or the business press came up with the concept of Lay as The Innovative CEO, but it stuck. By 1998, he was polishing that image with his contribution to a best-selling book, *Straight from the CEO*, subtitled "The World's Top Business Leaders Reveal Ideas That Every Manager Can Use." Lay's contribution was a chapter called "The New Energy Majors" in the "Innovation and Creativity" section. His major theme was "rule breakers get to the future first." "While many of the winners and losers in the new energy industry have yet to be determined," he wrote, "it is clear that some firms are well ahead of others. And Wall Street knows who they are."

Lay went on to reveal his theories about rule breakers. Successful ones had a clearly defined vision that promoted change (i.e., Vision and Values) and a campaign of corporate giving. In fact, Enron dumped millions on the Museum of Fine Arts, the Holocaust Museum, various Bush-blessed literacy campaigns, the United Way and more. Every executive had a special charity—Skilling supported a grueling bike race to raise money for multiple sclerosis. Lay also became deeply involved in the construction of a new baseball park in downtown Houston that was eventually christened Enron Field. ("The new energy majors will be able to tap into a wealth of marketing expertise. . . . Major sporting events are proving to be one of the best vehicles for reaching a mass audience.")

Rule breakers also create their own "competitive environment by leading industry-wide change." Lay did so by attacking his competition at every turn. Enron competed with the local utility, Houston Lighting and Power (soon to be Reliant) not only in business—he called them dinosaurs in his speeches—but in society. HL&P sponsored the rodeo; Enron sponsored theatrical premieres. Don Jordan, the head of HL&P, had a thick Texas accent and a weathered face, and he liked to go hunting. Ken Lay wore impeccably cut suits and served world leaders on Spode in his office. Who did a futuristic city prefer? Lay inserted himself into Houston's power structure—the influential Greater Houston Partnership, the membership of the River Oaks Country Club—just as Enron had inserted itself into the center of the gas market.

What Lay did not say in his chapter was that his kind of rule breakers always cultivate the rich and powerful. He sent a company jet to retrieve General Colin Powell for a tête-à-tête about a possible presidential run. When Powell demurred, he moved on to Bob Dole, supporting his 1996 candidacy.

When George W. Bush was gearing up in 1997 for his 2000 presidential run, his longtime consiglieri, Karl Rove, contacted Lay about a possible spot at Enron for right-wing spokesperson Ralph Reed. The Bush team didn't want Reed to stray to another candidate, but didn't want him publicly linked to their inner circle, either. Lay obliged, putting Reed on the Enron payroll at $20,000 a month in a job lobbying for electricity deregulation in Pennsylvania. At around the same time, Bush contacted Pennsylvania governor Tom Ridge on Enron's behalf. ("I am certain," a grateful Lay wrote the future president, "that will have a positive impact on the way he and others in Pennsylvania view our proposal to provide cheaper electricity to the consumers in Philadelphia.")

When Lay met with the president of Uzbekistan on behalf of Enron, he also arranged for a meeting for a future U.S. presidential candidate. "I know you and Ambassador Safev will have a productive meeting," he wrote Governor George W. Bush, "which will result in a friendship between Texas and Uzbekistan." Bush may not have liked Lay as much as his father had—he once called him "the turd in the punchbowl" when Lay pushed too hard for electricity deregulation in Texas—but he was more than happy to accept his largesse.

At the prestigious World Economic Forum at Davos, Lay preached the virtues of Third World development, hobnobbed with prime ministers, and thought globally alongside the likes of Jack Welch and J. P. Morgan Chase's vice chairman, Jimmy Lee. It was all good for business. In 1997, for instance, Lay was an honored guest at the opening of Rice University's James A. Baker III Institute for Public Policy, where he made sure that the Enron photographer caught him with former Secretary of State James Baker (an Enron consultant), former Secretary of Commerce Robert Mosbacher (another Enron consultant), and former Secretary of State Henry Kissinger (ditto); he took breaks only to pay his respects to old friends George and Barbara Bush. The following day, Lay awarded the institute's Enron Prize for Distinguished Public Service to Mikhail Gorbachev.

In January 1997, Sherron Watkins started working for a man named Jere Overdyke in a newly formed group created to find deals in the metals and mining industry. This move coincided with the reorganization of parts of Enron Capital & Trade into Enron International after Skilling's appointment as COO. Sherron was now responsible to Rebecca Mark and her lieutenant, Joe Sutton. She wasn't happy about the change: As a loyal member of ECT, for years she'd heard the stories of Mark's supposed profligacy and incompetence. Sherron was surprised to find, however, that working for Mark was not as Skilling had advertised; there were controls, there was cohesion, and there was supervision. And she felt imbued with purpose: Sherron wasn't a fund manager anymore. She was bringing cheap, clean energy to parts of the world that needed it. She also felt she had valuable knowledge to share with her new team: Sherron knew how to navigate the Risk Assessment and Control group.

Sherron spent the next year circling the globe, looking for deals in places like the Philippines and Hong Kong. She attended a conference in South Beach in Miami. She barely had time to squeeze in a June wedding and honeymoon with Rick Watkins, an oil and gas consultant whom she met through a friend at Enron. Then she was off again in July to Guinea, in western Africa, to inspect a hydro plant that could be used to support an aluminum smelter. In late August, she traveled to South America, to check out copper and zinc mines.

On her way from Chile to Peru one day, she checked her voice mails and found frantic messages from her colleague Mitch Taylor. The two hadn't worked together since Taylor left Fastow's group in 1995. Now he, too, had been shuffled to Enron International. He needed Sherron's help on something really important: a skit for the unit's upcoming annual meeting at the Del Lago resort, north of Houston. They both had intuited, fairly quickly, that skits were crucial to succeeding at Enron International. People even hired professional writers and costume designers for the occasion. The rule was: The more elaborate, the better. A Middle East team once dressed up like Egyptian slaves and carried a colleague, outfitted like a sheik, on a litter. Last year, the theme was "The Culture of Your Region," and the African team aced the competition by entering the party astride a real elephant. Mark, being more familial, included all Enron International employees in this yearly get-together. The teams from India, Brazil, China, Bolivia, and Colombia flew into Houston, as did those in Mozambique, Vietnam, and Indonesia. The three-day event also featured motivational speakers, rock-and-roll bands, and open bars. In other words, expectations ran high.

This year's theme was mental toughness, as in "Are you mentally tough enough to get an international deal done?" Mitch told Sherron that Overdyke was determined to win. First prize was a trip for the whole team, and their spouses, to San Francisco for two nights, all expenses paid. (In typical Enron fashion, second prize was a visit to an earthworm festival in East Texas. In other words, there was no second prize.) And so, while Sherron finished up in Peru, her colleagues hastily hired acting coaches from the University of Houston's drama department. Taylor and a few friends wrote the script, based on *The Wizard of Oz*. Sherron was the Wicked Witch of the West.

When she grumbled at the news, Taylor cut her off. If he could play Dorothy in a dress, he told her, she could be the Wicked Witch.

Sherron flew home and got to the resort just in time for some last-minute rehearsals. Then they were on—unwanted transplants from Enron Capital & Trade, performing in front of a demanding Enron International audience.

The show opened with Taylor trying to teach a colleague how to get a deal approved by the RAC group. These folks, were an ill-tempered breed who didn't get out much, he said as he led his coworker through some imaginary dungeons in an imaginary Enron building. This scene went over well: The Enron International crowd saw the RAC group just that way in real life.

Taylor's deal was a plan to convert the company's Rio apartment into a gentlemen's club. This was a great idea, he said, because the property would need so few capital improvements. The Enron apartment already had a built-in dance floor, sound system, and floor-to-ceiling mirrors.

While Taylor was explaining his plan, Sherron entered as the Wicked Witch of the West. In a deep, sultry voice, she told them she could help them get their deal approved. The men turned to her, all ears. To succeed, she explained, they had to clear the Risk-Adjusted Discount Rate (pronounced "Radar"), a magical number imposed by RAC. "You gotta do it the Enron way—you just need a little smoke and mirrors!" she said. Then she disappeared in a puff of smoke and glitter.

When the smoke cleared, Taylor was in a dress, transformed into Dorothy. His sidekick was in a dog suit as Toto. They ran into a group of Munchkins with grim faces, who sang, as they marched, that they represented the Risk Committee, and that Taylor's deal "sucked."

Taylor was distraught. Why? The Munchkins replied that the return on the deal was below the Risk-Adjusted Discount Rate—*below the Radar*. "Your return has to be ABOVE the Radar!" they chirped, making for the exit. As the Munchkins left, the lights dimmed and Taylor gazed into the night sky, knelt on one knee, and mournfully sang:

Somewhere over the Radar
Deals fly high
Deals fly over the Radar
Why, then, oh why can't mine?

As Dorothy and Toto wondered what to do next, a scarecrow entered—Jere Overdyke, playing himself, on the way to see the Wizard of RAC. But because he didn't have a brain, he couldn't decide which way to go. The audience thought this was pretty funny too—Overdyke was well-known for his reluctance to pull the trigger on his deals. For his Scarecrow number, he sang:

> *I could be Rebecca's cohort,*
> *Move the offices to Shreveport,*
> *Be a player in the game.*
> *If my team were only willing,*
> *I could be another Skilling,*
> *If I only had a brain.*

Then the trio headed down the Yellow Brick Road. Along the way, they met the Tin Man, supposedly Joe Sutton, who growled at his employees and wished he had a heart, and the Cowardly Lion, playing an executive with Enron's construction unit who padded contracts because he lacked the courage to find earnings on his own. It was a real crowd pleaser.

Once in Oz, the group looked for the Wizard of RAC, but all they found was a large black box that screeched "Go away" and "Too busy" and "Put it in writing." Finally, someone stripped away the front of the box to reveal Rodney Faldyn, Overdyke's head accountant, dressed in a scarlet satin pimp suit.

"I'm Andy Fastow," he said, "the Wizard of RAC."

"Where are the computers?" Dorothy and her team asked. "We thought RAC used computer models."

"Naw, dude," the pimp said. "I make all the funding decisions around here." He told Overdyke, the Scarecrow, he didn't need a brain to do deals at Enron. Sutton, the Tin Man, didn't need a heart, either; Fastow said he had gotten by just fine without one. And the earnings-stealing Lion was offered a job in his funding department—"You're my kind of guy," the Fastow character told him.

As for Dorothy and Toto's desire for Mental Toughness, well, Fastow said they were out of luck. He offered to reject their deal now and save time.

Just when all seemed lost, the Good Witch of the East, supposedly

Rebecca Mark, appeared. "You've had the power to fund your deals all along," she told them. "You just have to call them . . . 'strategic.'"

The Enron Capital & Trade émigrés won handily. Soon enough, Sherron, a newlywed, found herself ordering room service with her husband at the Mandarin Oriental Hotel in San Francisco.

8

Living Large

A S 1997 drew to a close, Enron had no happier employee than Sherron Watkins. She loved working for Enron International. She had hoped that her metals and mining experience from her years at MG Trade Finance Corp. would give her a leg up, and it had. She helped evaluate a major acquisition of a London-based metals-trading unit—refreshingly, she was treated like a real executive instead of a glorified bean counter—and she loved circling the globe, trawling for deals. But after more than three years at Enron, she still lacked the vice president's title after her name, and the big bonuses that went along with that promotion. To achieve those goals at Enron, Sherron knew, she had to close a big deal of her own.

Doing so was harder than it sounded. She heard of a proposed copper mine in Panama that needed power and financing, but that project wouldn't close for years. She found another promising mine in New Mexico, but the prospect there was hesitant to take on more debt to expand. Also, a group from Enron Capital & Trade tried to move in on the deal and claim it for themselves.

It was this kind of intrusion that Sherron tried to ignore, but she knew it contained, for her, the seeds of future frustration. The truth was, Enron International was changing as management shipped in more and more people from Enron Capital & Trade. Even though Rebecca Mark and her number two, Joe Sutton, were nominally in charge, working there was a little like working under an Enron Capital & Trade army of occupation, with the resultant collision in culture and values. ECT people saw the Enron International types as global moonies. Like Sherron, most of the former came to EI with preconceived notions about the competence, or lack thereof, of the international deal makers. Day in and day out, they'd heard from Jeff Skilling that Mark's group had no concept of effective risk management and didn't know how to analyze deals (although they certainly learned how to boost the value of their projects to boost their own compensation). Enron Capital & Trade refugees were also highly skeptical of the missionary zeal that permeated Enron International—they just didn't buy all those fuzzy-headed notions about changing society with clean-burning liquefied natural gas.

In turn, the Enron International contingent thought the Enron Capital & Trade people were selfish, cynical short-termers who wouldn't know Qatar from Djakarta—they got paid too much for creating little of social value. Moreover, the novel finance and accounting solutions brought over by Enron Capital & Trade's "innovators" scared EI to death. The ECT newcomers were constantly pushing for faster growth from International so they could get lucrative gas and power trading going, while Enron International kept pushing for business plans. How, exactly, would Enron Capital & Trade develop and capture their share of this new market?

The situation with Promigas, a publicly traded Colombian gas pipeline company in which Enron owned about a 40 percent stake, was a case in point. Enron Capital & Trade bought into the company in 1996 when the Colombian gas market was deregulating; Enron wanted to be a player there in future gas trading. The company opened an office and staffed it with gas marketers who waited for business to roll in. When Skilling succeeded Kinder, Promigas became part of Mark's jurisdiction as part of her Third World consolation prize.

Gradually, as the market grew, Promigas's stock price increased. Any experienced employee of Enron Capitol & Trade knew what to do next: The investment should be recast from its role as a core, or long-term strategic property, to a merchant investment, one that Enron might sell at any time. As a merchant investment, Enron could book the stock price jumps as earnings right away, using "fair-value" or mark-to-market accounting, which it did. But then Promigas stock began to flatten in late 1997, and again in 1998. Then it started to drop, and Enron was faced with reporting a loss, which it definitely did not want to do.

The solution dreamed up by someone from ECT was to open a brokerage account and send Enron employees out, near the end of every quarter, to buy shares of Promigas. Colombia had a very small stock exchange then, and Promigas had an even smaller public float (the amount of stock available to be bought and sold by the public), so Enron's small purchases could make a huge difference. In fact, at the end of every quarter, Promigas shares rose like clockwork to match the older, higher values Enron used to write up the investment. Then, once the quarter end passed, the stock was allowed to dip until the next quarterly reporting date. This went on for several quarters, until the stock price eventually fell so low that Enron could not continue the charade. At that point, Enron went back to the drawing board, adding a "control premium" for any potential buyer for its 40 percent stake in the company and, in the process, making up for the shortfall between Promigas's currently traded stock price and Enron's now inflated book value for the investment. (Surprisingly, Andersen went along with this.)

But Sherron wasn't in the core gas and power business; she was in a new arena, metals and mining, which seemed blissfully free of such highjinks. At a conference in Miami in the spring of 1997, she met an investment adviser who gave her a tip about a U.S. mining company that wanted backers to expand. He offered to provide her with an introduction. As a result, Sherron met Jeff Ward and Rich McNeely, partners in a New Mexican copper venture named Cobre Mining Company. Soon after their first meeting, they invited her to tour the mine they wanted to upgrade. Sherron liked both men right away. Ward was fortyish and polished, with degrees from the University of Arizona and London's Royal School of Mines, along with an MBA from the University of Chicago. He was the son of a well-known mining executive, Milt Ward, the chairman and CEO of Cyprus Amax Minerals, a large global mining company. Jeff Ward's business partner, Rich McNeely, had a hard hat background, with a degree from the Mackay School of Mines at the University of Nevada–Reno. McNeely had more than twenty-five years of expertise working on older mines.

Both men, Sherron noted, were emotionally attached to their mine — they choked up when they talked about its history and the close calls they'd had trying to keep it going over the years. Nevertheless, they successfully took the company public in Canada, where the local stock exchanges act like an incubator for small mining start-ups in much the same way the Nasdaq does for tech start-ups in the United States. Now, however, the mining sector was depressed, and the additional money the two hoped to raise in new equity offerings simply wasn't there. They were excited about expanding the mine's production capacity, but nervous about risking foreclosure if the company took on too much debt. These men were not interested in improving and then flipping a business; they were in for the long haul.

Sherron knew she had found her deal. Enron could loan Cobre money to expand and improve the mine, sell the company power to run the mine more efficiently, and then buy the copper (presumably at a big, friendly discount) to jump-start Enron's fledgling metals- and mining-trading operation. She got a nonbinding proposal to the partners as soon as possible. Then, nothing: Ward and McNeely told her they wanted to take their time and study their options.

Sherron had all but given up on Cobre when, about eight months later, she got a frantic call from Ward. His company was threatened with a hostile takeover by a much more powerful global metals firm, Phelps-Dodge, which owned a large copper mine adjacent to Ward and McNeely's. Phelps-Dodge had made offers to buy the Cobre mine in the past, but Ward and McNeely had always turned them down. They never imagined they'd be the subject of a hostile takeover because they owned such a large block of Cobre's outstanding stock. But now Phelps-Dodge offered a nice premium to the currently traded stock price. Soon the other shareholders pressured Ward and McNeely to take the deal or come up with a better plan — a higher price, in other words. Ward and McNeely wanted Enron International to serve as a white knight.

Hearing of their plight, Sherron realized that her good deal was now a great deal. She took the request to her boss, Jere Overdyke, who, in turn, took it to Skilling, who gave a tentative go-ahead within a few days. More meetings followed. Cobre had a shareholders' rights plan that meant that any tender offer had to be held open for sixty days. Phelps-Dodge could not execute its hostile-takeover attempt until February 3, 1998. Skilling and his corporate development team (Enron's version of a mergers-and-acquisitions group) wanted assurances that Cobre would not try to "better deal" Enron and seek another white knight during that time. Ward and McNeely were reluctant to comply—they didn't want to sign an exclusive agreement that was binding to them but not to Enron, because they had been stiffed by partners in the past. Finally, however, they relented when Sherron said that Enron was unlikely to back out of the deal. With the exclusivity guaranteed, Skilling seemed appeased and the deal was struck.

Enron International would be Cobre's white knight under an arrangement that provided Enron with a fee and expense reimbursement if they were not successful. If they won, Enron got a ten-year copper marketing agreement from Cobre, giving it enough copper volume to easily fund a start-up copper-trading unit. The management buyout was structured as a 50/50 deal: Enron put up approximately $55 million in equity funds, as did Ward and McNeely, who used their equity position in the company to contribute the same amount. Enron also threw in a bridge loan of $40 million, to be refinanced after the takeover was complete. Sherron believed that Enron's $150 million offer to Cobre's shareholders left Phelps-Dodge's deal in the dust.

Everything had to be in place for a January 30 launch. Sherron stayed up around the clock to oversee the drafting of shareholder and management agreements. Salomon Brothers flew in to work out the debt financing to replace Enron's bridge loan. Term sheets were executed with everyone involved. Ward and McNeely shuttled between New Mexico, Canada, and Houston, negotiating final terms with Enron and strategizing with their board of directors and Canadian investment advisers. Everyone was excited: Thwarting Phelps-Dodge would be a major coup.

Then, in mid-January, Jere Overdyke called Sherron. Skilling was waffling, he said. "What do you mean?" Sherron asked, her voice climbing into the higher octaves. "We've negotiated an exclusive deal with these guys!"

"That was then" was essentially Overdyke's answer. He told Sherron that

Skilling came back nervous from a management meeting focused on Enron's stock. For the first time since 1991, Enron's stock price ended the year lower than it started. Shareholders incurred a loss of 1.5 percent for 1997. The stock was now stalled at around $39 a share, where it had been for most of the year. Everyone was panicked; why wasn't Wall Street happy with the company? Maybe the Portland General merger was still costing them; maybe it was the $440 million J-Block settlement. But Skilling was not ending his first year as COO in triumph. He expected to see at least a $3 to $5 share increase by the end of 1997, and that just didn't happen.

Hence the January summit to address the stock price crisis. Upper management concluded that Enron had a perception problem; Wall Street thought the company had too many irons in the fire. They agreed that Enron would focus on its core businesses. Now was not the time to announce experiments with novelties like weather derivatives, coal, and metals and mining.

Unfortunately for Sherron Watkins, that decision coincided with the Cobre deal's closing.

Sherron and her team met with Skilling to go over the final numbers. In his capacious, two-story office, he studied the paperwork and winced. He asked Sherron why her first big metal deal had to involve such a nasty, public battle, an indication to Sherron that he was still haunted by the Bridge Oil spectacle that had left Enron humiliated in the marketplace. She explained that this deal was different—in Cobre, for example, Enron had two shareholders who together held more than 27 percent of the company, and that had not been the case with Bridge. This time, the competing bidder was requiring a 90 percent tender—they would be stymied when Ward and McNeely refused to hand over their shares. He seemed appeased, again.

But that afternoon Cliff Baxter, then head of corporate development, called Sherron and her team into an Enron International conference room. "We're not gonna do it," he said. Skilling, he explained, did not want Enron's first foray into the world of metals and mining to end in any sort of public mess. Sherron tried, briefly, to save the deal—was there another way? could Enron get a frontman, someone to hide behind until success was virtually assured?—but the answer was no.

With her small and beleaguered metals and mining team, she trudged the ten or so blocks across downtown to the Four Seasons Hotel, where

Cobre's unsuspecting partners were waiting in their suite to sign the final papers. When she gave Ward the news, he was livid. Cobre had signed an exclusive with Enron, and now his company was out of time, with no other protectors in sight. "You just tell Ken Lay and Jeff Skilling they are the most unethical people I've ever met," he said. Then he turned to Sherron. "I don't see how you can stay here and work at this company."

Sherron was embarrassed and angry. One member of her team quit soon after, and an industry consultant they had been trying to hire permanently turned them down. Ward lost his company, though in the end he triumphed—Phelps-Dodge eventually closed the mine and Ward took an early payday, which turned out better than having Enron as a long-term partner.

Overdyke offered Sherron a consolation package to stay: a bonus of more than $60,000—though only a third of what she would have gotten if the deal had gone through—and with the end of the metals and mining unit looming, a transfer to Enron International's mergers and acquisitions group under a man named Frank Stabler. It was not what she wanted—now she'd be competing for standard energy deals against at least two dozen world beaters who had a head start on her. At the same time, Sherron knew she'd never get a good job anywhere else unless she got promoted from director to vice president—on paper, she'd look like someone who'd been running in place for four years.

So Sherron made a decision: She would devote herself to finding a deal that got her promoted. Then she'd rethink her options.

In the meantime, working for Enron wasn't so bad. Despite the transfer and the death of her division, Enron sent her on a previously arranged trip to a major metals and mining conference in South Africa. The conference was already paid for; Enron *could* still sell power to the mining companies. Sherron spent a splendid week at the conference in Capetown, then another in Johannesburg. She managed to tour both Table Mountain and the Cape of Good Hope, and take a Sunday safari to view rhinoceroses. It was the kind of trip an Enron executive came to expect.

By the late 1990s, there were others inside Enron who, like Sherron Watkins, were ambivalent about the company, people who might have seen or heard about things that seemed strange, or silly, or improper. But, like Sherron, they were also aware of the benefits and the prestige of working at a hot company that was not only famous for innovation—*Fortune*, *Business Week*, and *The Wall Street Journal* all said so—but that paid well. Why focus on the negatives?

This form of denial was perfectly in tune with the times: The mid to late 1990s promised to be the era of the New Paradigm, when people were convinced that the rules of business, and even American life, were being rewritten. Bill Clinton, himself a master of denial, preached the New Paradigm in his election campaigns, styling himself as the youthful president of new ideas, presiding over the booming economy that proved the new ideas were paying off. The tech fever that fueled the New Economy was the inarguable case in point—it was going to make life and work faster and better, cheaper and smarter, as it made investors multimillionaires seemingly overnight. Federal Reserve chairman Alan Greenspan warned of "irrational exuberance" in the stock market as early as 1996, but no one listened to him. The New Paradigm—with its new technology, its new forms of finance, its new ways of accounting, and its new ways of thinking—was going to make everyone rich. And soon Greenspan, too, changed his tune.

The Millionaire Next Door was a best-seller: "Who are the rich in this country?" the cover asked. "What do they do? Where do they shop? What do they drive? Can I ever become one of them?" Those who weren't millionaires yet—or worse, weren't even close—experienced the nagging sense of falling behind. As the Dow Jones soared from 4000 to nearly 9000 from 1995 to 1998 and the Nasdaq climbed from 800 to 1800, getting very rich seemed less and less irrational as a goal; people who weren't millionaires, in fact, started to look like drones with no ambition, or worse, chumps. The growing gap between rich and poor troubled ambitious types only in the sense that they might, somehow, land on the wrong side of the divide. The ends justified the means; shaving a moral corner here and there didn't really amount to much as long as everything came out well in the end (i.e., Monica Lewinsky didn't matter—it was the bull market, stupid).

Just as Houston always seemed to embrace and then exaggerate American enthusiasms—capitalism, free markets, free will—so, too, did Enron emerge as the city's uncontested ambassador to the New Economy. This required a paradigm shift in the attitude of the local citizenry: In the past, for instance, Texans had scorned Ivy Leaguers—Houstonians didn't particularly value book smarts or academic credentials, largely because getting rich in this part of the world hadn't historically required a fancy degree. Instead, it demanded long hours in the hot sun, or the wiles to eavesdrop on Petroleum Club gossip and *then* spend long hours in the hot sun. Who needed a Harvard education for that? But getting rich in the New Economy demanded—or seemed to demand—mastery of new and complex technology and constantly shifting financial rules. Suddenly, a chichi degree looked pretty helpful.

The attitude toward risk changed too. Taking huge risks—like drilling for oil at great expense when you didn't really know whether it was there or not—was long central to Houston's identity. Risk made the oilman a figure of romance and a role model of sturdy optimism. But the oil bust changed that. In the early 1980s in Houston, everything failed—the oil business, the banks, real estate—and as associated and interdependent businesses went down, so too did the city's collective nerve. People lost their fortunes and their homes and their good names, and it took a long time to crawl out of that financial hole. In the aftermath of that bloodbath, taking big risks—depending on that nonexistent "Texas Hedge" Skilling liked to joke about—started to seem foolhardy, especially when there were so many new financial instruments to alleviate economic dangers. Consciously or unconsciously, Enron knew how to freshen Houston's mythology for the next century—to return it to the city cleaned, pressed, and retrofitted for the future.

The city and the company were a good match from the start. Just as Houston was passionate about the new, so, too, was Enron. But Enron's culture claimed that you couldn't go forward without stepping into the modern age—without superior brainpower and without knowing how to hedge risk. Since the company was one of the great American success stories of the 1990s, it spoke to Houston with authority. You could blend the ethos of the wildcatter—*the independence, the guts, the creativity!*—with the best corporate values (*security, team spirit, stock options!*). Enron could become a new kind of company that seemed, on its face, a contradiction in terms: the entrepreneurial corporation.

You could have it all: You could take risks (but they were hedged risks,

under a huge corporate umbrella), you could be—in fact, you were supposed to be—an intellectual (and no one called you a nerd!), and of course,
you could get really, really rich, maybe even overnight—the way it had
always been in Houston.

In short, if you worked at Enron, you could embrace the old myths in a
new way: You became a brilliant risk taker who was backed by a multibillion-
dollar corporation—and the rewards were the same as they'd always been.

So, people flocked to Enron to embrace the conundrum. There was
pressure, there was abuse, there were near-psychotic levels of competition,
but everyone knew they were just a deal away from making it really, really
big. You just had to hang in there; leaving Enron would be like a star
reporter quitting *The New York Times* or an honor student walking away
from Harvard or a bound-for-glory baseball player abandoning the Yan-
kees—anything else was going to feel like a step down. Did you want to work
with average people who made average incomes and had average ideas?
Leaving Enron meant admitting that you, too, were average—instead of
being the smartest, the fastest, and the best in the business.

As the millennium approached, the company's growing success in fact
bred two Enrons. The first was the idealized Enron—the Enron that the
New York Times called "a model for the new American workplace—every bit
as much as the Silicon Valley start-ups that usually come to mind when the
subject is entrepreneurship or innovation"—the company that routinely
landed on *Fortune's* lists of the most innovative and best companies to work
for in America. The survey Enron submitted to *Fortune's* "100 Best Companies to Work for in America" poll made Enron sound like corporate heaven:
"On many of our floors the offices have glass walls or no walls at all, even for
management," the scribes in the PR department wrote. "Nothing is hidden,
secrecy is passé." Enron was benevolent: "If employees fail, there is no time
for recrimination because they are already in hot pursuit of the next opportunity." Enron's leaders were the kind of guys you'd want for your best
friends: "Ken, [and] Jeff, . . . clearly set the tone for how the rest of the company operates. They are friendly, approachable and ready to listen. They say
hi in the elevator and ask how you are doing . . . they personally read and
reply to all employees' suggestions and comments and they hold open
forums for discussion at floor meetings. . . . [T]heir passion for new ideas and

ways of doing things has sparked the creativity among employees that is building brand-new markets around the country and the world."

But Enron insiders knew hype when they saw it. Contributors to *Fortune's* "100 Best Companies to Work for in America" survey were supposed to be selected at random from within their companies. But at Enron, the same executives in Human Resources and Public Relations filled out the forms every year, creating out of thin air the corporate oasis that annually ranked higher and higher on the business press's laudatory lists.

Eventually, Enron employees came up with a different name for their company: The Bizarre Social Experiment. This company was forever reorganizing, so no one ever really knew for whom they were working or what, exactly, they were supposed to be doing. This company put ever-younger and less-experienced people in charge of business units. This company threw ungodly amounts of money at new business concepts. This company devoted itself to perpetual and monumental change: As Ken Lay liked to say, "In ten years we expect the majority of our profits to come from businesses that we aren't even in today." Unless, of course, the market suggested you were unfocused, and then it was time to backtrack.

In other words, despite the great press, Enron was a company enveloped in chaos.

Sherron Watkins' attempt to close the Cobre deal coincided with both the turmoil and the values then prevailing at Enron. The cover of Enron's 1997 annual report was a lush tropical scene, with one giant green leaf situated front and center. Around the company it was known as The Fig Leaf, the one used to obscure Enron's financial statements for the year. Gas trading margins were shrinking, and Enron Capital & Trade had not found a rabbit to pull out of its financial hat. Sometimes profits could be generated by reorganizing, "resegmenting" Enron's business lines into new success stories. Losing businesses were grouped into a pro forma "nonrecurring" or "noncore" reporting group; winners stayed in the core "recurring" category. The power plants and gas pipelines could be used to freshen Enron Capital & Trade numbers; international assets that generated hefty "wholesale" profits sometimes obscured less than stellar trading.

In those days, any good idea—particularly one that generated income—made its creator a hero overnight. Jeff McMahon, an old friend of Sherron's from Andersen, came to Enron as a business unit coordinator—a glorified accountant—in early 1994, but a year later he transferred to the London office and found himself the effective treasurer of British operations. In 1996 and 1997, McMahon and his staff devised a series of innovative structured finance deals for Enron's power plants in Britain—Teesside and a new project called Sutton Bridge. For Sutton Bridge, McMahon molded an accounting rule, called FAS 125, that was meant solely for financial assets into an application for power plants. Most such FAS 125 financings allowed entities to "securitize," or sell off financial contracts, in much the same way banks bundled and sold home mortgages. This process allowed the issuing company to recognize a gain on sales and cash flow from operations, yet it remained the manager of its projects. McMahon improved on the concept: He wrapped financial contracts around the cash flows expected from the British power plant, which allowed Enron to use the FAS 125 accounting rule to effectively book all the profit streams expected over the next several years into one.

FAS 125, issued in June 1996, stood for "Statement of Financial Accounting Standards No. 125, Accounting for Transfers and Servicing of Financial Assets and Extinguishments of Liabilities." The accounting rule and its accompanying implementation guide was more than 30,000 words long and superseded or amended over twenty older rules. Needless to say, it was subject to interpretation, something Enron was very good at. In no time, the company got what it wanted—a way to apply an accounting rule devised for financial assets to front-load anywhere from five to twenty years' of anticipated profit streams on large power plants into *one* year. Essentially McMahon came up with a system like mark-to-market accounting that could be applied to Enron's hard assets. When the company ran into a few assets that the banks were less than thrilled to lend against, Enron had a solution: the Total Return Swap. Banks would loan against the power plants' future cash flow streams, get the up-front fees and a back-door guarantee, while Enron got the cash up front that it could book as revenues and cash flow from operations. Everyone thought this was a great idea, too. McMahon took his place among Enron's annointed.

But while FAS 125s in particular and structured finance in general were wonderful tools, they did nothing to advance Enron's much-touted business model. Electricity was supposed to do that—prove that Enron's invention and domination of the gas market was not a fluke. Electricity was, in Skilling's words, the Big Kahuna.

Enron got into the business on McKinsey's advice—the company believed it could capture about 5%–8% of the $290 billion electricity market, make a 1%–3 % gross margin—adding $300 million per year to the bottom line for Enron sometime . . . soon. But while Enron was great on atmospherics—it spent megamillions on advertising and marketing—it stumbled when it came to execution. Organizing the business seemed beyond the powers of Enron's chieftains.

Skilling never found the right leader for Enron Energy Services. He replaced Andy Fastow with Rick Causey, who was replaced by an outsider from a long-distance telephone company, one who, Skilling hoped, would use his experience challenging AT&T to help Enron win market share from the electric utility monopolies. When that didn't work, Skilling turned to Lou Pai, the former head of trading and a trusted lieutenant who tried to put Enron on the map by boldly charging into states that were deregulating the fastest. Skilling actually bragged to Wall Street about how much money Enron Energy Services was spending each quarter, suggesting that big rewards would soon follow.

Meanwhile, they couldn't figure out how to make and send a bill to customers for less than $1. This might have mattered more if Enron had actually *had* customers. One reason Enron didn't have customers is that its increasingly elitist culture prohibited the creation of a standard sales force to push power over the phone. Enron's boiler room, for instance, had to be an Enronian boiler room. Instead of hiring the usual phone-bank types— bored housewives, high school dropouts, people on the fringes—Enron was trying to get their $30,000-a-year analysts to find customers. Needless to say, they clashed with their boss, a man nicknamed Polyester Dan, who insulted their intelligence and sophistication by suggesting they jump up and ring a cowbell whenever they made a sale. Enron did not have time for old-fashioned motivational techniques.

Lou Pai tried to establish a beachhead in California's retail markets for about six months, then gave up but not before spending an average of $50,000 per customer in California (whether that spoke to the advertising budget or the lack of customers or both is anyone's guess). In 1997, Skilling announced to Wall Street his intention to sell 10 percent of Enron Energy Services to at least five investors, partly to demonstrate the inherent value of the new venture. On January 6, 1998, Enron did that, selling 7 percent of the new business to two investors, CalPERS and the Ontario Teachers Pension Fund. The press release accompanying the sale stressed that since the investors had paid $130 million for their 7 percent stake, Enron Energy Services now had an implied value of nearly $2 billion, or $5.50 per share.

But that didn't impress anyone. Skilling's earlier pronouncement led Wall Street to expect a better showing—more buyers and a higher stake. CalPERS was already an Enron loyalist through JEDI; Wall Street didn't see anything new there. That left Ontario Teachers as Enron's only new investor. So what? When Enron announced the deal, its stock price didn't budge. Skilling was deflated.

Then Pai had a new idea. Enron Energy Services would stop trying to be a plain vanilla electricity provider. Instead, he added a new service line— Enron Facilities Management Services—and offered customers just what the name suggested: Enron would monitor air conditioning systems, replace lightbulbs, and do all the things that go into maintaining energy efficiency and holding down costs for large electricity consumers. If this new focus smacked of defeat—it sounded much smaller than total domination of the electricity market—it did allow Enron to get into management of sports facilities, something that appealed deeply to Enron Energy Services's twenty-something, overwhelmingly male workforce.

And, best of all, Pai wouldn't lose any money. Like Skilling, he had a cut of EES from its inception; he maintained a phantom equity interest in Enron Energy Services that would eventually convert into a mega-stock position in Enron itself.

As was Enron's way, the new EES had to look and sound more innovative and exciting than its predecessor, more exciting than plain old retail energy sales. "Enron Energy Services announced today that it has signed a four-year agreement to provide an innovative combination of energy and energy services," an early press release declared. "Enron will finance, construct, operate, and maintain new energy infrastructure for Lockheed-Martin Missiles In Space, lower Lockheed-Martin's energy costs, and improve reliability in delivery of its energy supply," said another. One more press release declared: "Enron Energy Services announced it would form strategic alliances with CB Richard Ellis Commercial Real Estate to provide a full range of energy services to [its] office and industrial property clients." Each release contained mind-boggling figures intended to convey to the casual reader that the contract was worth vast amounts to Enron—but no one could discern quite how much. "Enron Energy Services announced today a $116 million long-term agreement for total energy management services" or "through a $60 million ten-year energy commodity agreement, Enron Energy Services will provide electricity as well as services . . ." And the customers were very impressive: Along with Lockheed-Martin and CB Richard Ellis, the San Francisco Giants' Pacific Bell Park, the Archdiocese of Chicago, and Ocean Spray signed on with Enron too.

The press was pumped. In April 1998, an article from Bloomberg News noted that "Enron's first-quarter earnings report sold analysts on what Enron executives have been saying for a long time: their electricity business is hot." Enron told the press in first-quarter earnings announcements that its core business groups had achieved a 46 percent overall increase in income before interest and taxes, and declared that virtually all of this increase came from Enron Wholesale Energy Operations and Services (which by then was both the traditional trading outfit and all the international operations as well). The analysts were thrilled: One raised his twelve-month target on Enron from $50 a share to $63; another expected Enron to earn at least $50 million from retail power by the year 2000. A third was cautious, saying growth might not be seen in profits for three or four more years, but he still rated the stock an "outperform."

And the stock price went up. From the dismal performance of 1997—the whole year's flatline of $39 a share—Enron started trading at $51 a share, a 30 percent increase in its stock price in just under four months.

Even so, no one at Enron could quite figure out how this business was going to make money anytime soon. Enron Energy Services signed ten-year management deals with its customers, contracts that guaranteed lower energy costs over the period. Just to be sure their customers were happy, EES also paid cash back to its customers to make sure the promised 10 percent savings in energy costs was achieved right away. EES figured it would make up this difference . . . later. ("Another example of EES paying money for the right to do something" was the explanation given for two deals on a chart listing the who's and why's of the various ventures.) The present, however, remained grim: EES reported an operating loss each quarter in 1998. And the company had no way of predicting when it might venture into the black.

An Enron executive pushed Andersen's professional standards group to allow the company to mark to market the electricity expected to be sold under EES's long-term energy management contracts. That helped EES's income statement, but it didn't bring in cash. Even the best outside accountants could not discern what many in Enron's upper reaches knew. Almost all of the company's boost in earnings in the first quarter of 1998 came from FAS 125 deals or fair-value accounting—from booking future profits or inflating the value of Enron's assets. Some young analyst in the RAC group took a few positive investment-specific factors or a run-up in the general equity markets and—*voila! Instant profits!* Enron wouldn't file its 10Q until May, and by then few would bother to compare that information with Enron's earlier, far more optimistic press releases and analysts meetings about power. To Enron's credit, the 10Q clearly stated that nearly all of Enron's first-quarter gains came not from electricity marketing but from "finance and investing"—over 80 percent, in fact. Only 20 percent of the earnings increase came from physical trading and marketing. (In 1997, "finance and investing" provided 90 percent of the gains for the whole year.) Enron mentioned but never stressed "finance and investing" in analysts' calls or earnings releases, and few people paid attention to the numbers in the SEC filings.

In truth, the only hope of future earnings in Enron's electrical miasma was electricity trading. The traders and marketers managed to insert themselves between enough buyers and sellers of physical power so that electricity-trading revenues were climbing, even if gross margins were still negligible. This was a period that Skilling stopped talking so much about being on the side of the angels. In the first quarter of 1998, as the traders experimented in different power markets around the country, they sensed they could make big money if they could make some bigger trades. Skilling agreed, and allowed the traders to raise their position limits, the amounts of money they could risk. Then, with sufficient power under contract and control of certain pivotal points on the electric grid, they had only to wait for their chance to bet big.

That happened in June 1998. Several midwestern power plants were taken off line for repairs in order to prepare them for high usage during the traditionally hotter months of July and August. But this year turned out to be different—a severe heat wave hit the region early. Simultaneously, storms knocked plants out of commission that might furnish backup power. Immediately, supplies of electricity tightened and prices climbed. Several small utilities were caught short—they couldn't afford the rising prices and defaulted on supply agreements. Power that normally sold at $20 to $40 per megawatt-hour under long-term contracts suddenly hit $500 per megawatt-hour.

Once the small power marketers started defaulting, real panic set in. With the fear of blackouts, prices jumped as high as $7,500 per megawatt hour in a matter of minutes. In the old world, utilities bought and sold electricity to one another at reasonable prices when such regional shortages appeared. But in the summer of 1998, good manners were gone, and so were the rules. The power landscape was instead dotted with fly-by-night companies—five guys in an office with a phone bank—who hoped to take advantage of the new rules. These companies had, as the traders say, gone short. Trying to adhere to the maxim of "buy low, sell high," they first sold to one or two customers and thought they were ready for action. But before they could buy low they got caught in a classic short seller's squeeze. When prices spiked, they could not afford to buy the electricity they promised to sell, and defaulted on contracts with some of the biggest utilities in the country. This meant the big utilities, in turn, had to buy power on the spot market—where prices were well over ten times the usual amount.

For Enron, it was Christmas in July. They had the power, ready, in just the right location. One trader made $60 million for the company in one day. Though the midwestern power emergency ended within days, Enron continued to profit long after. Small power companies went bankrupt—LG&E Energy Corporation, the state of Kentucky's largest electric utility, announced that it incurred a $225 million loss from the weeklong crisis and was getting out of the electricity trading business. Coastal Corporation, Oscar Wyatt's company, took a one-time loss of $14.6 million on its power-trading venture. Dynegy and other companies begged federal regulators to consider price controls. There was some suggestion in the press of market manipulation.

But Enron had no such complaints. It used the crisis to push even harder for deregulation, claiming that a market that was only partially deregulated was partly to blame for the summer's high prices. And, at the same time, Enron's internal electricity crisis washed away in a sea of cash. Traders were promoted into management, and Jeff Skilling looked like an even bigger genius than before.

Sherron landed in the traditional energy Mergers and Acquisitions group earlier that year, only to find, in her words, that all the best countries were taken. She was assigned to Africa, the continent no one else wanted because no one else could figure out a way to make decent money there.

But then things started looking up. She took five executives from two Houston-based clients interested in a West African oil and gas transaction to the Masters golf tournament in March 1998. Because clients were involved, she got the big jet, the one with armchairs, sofas, and plenty of headroom. She boarded to find wine chilling in ice buckets, trays of boiled shrimp, finger sandwiches, and hors d'oeuvres. A van met the group at the airport and escorted them to the house rented for the event. The house, like the plane, featured a well-stocked bar and waitstaff, including a chef. The next day the van took the group to the practice round, where Sherron got an autograph from Tiger Woods's caddie, Fluff. Maybe, Sherron thought on the way home, she should forgive and forget about Cobre.

Then a major deal fell right into her lap. Enron's Asia Pacific team had been chasing opportunities in the region for quite some time. Enron operated power plants in the Philippines and Guam; developed projects in China, Indonesia, and Vietnam; and opened a trading office in Singapore, with another one under way in Sydney, Australia. But despite a McKinsey report that highlighted the countries in the region that embraced deregulation—and therefore looked ripe for Enron-style exploitation—no one in M&A

focused on Korea. That was why, when one of Enron's executives in the region got wind of a particular deal there and passed it on, as required, to Sherron's boss in M&A, he in turn lobbed it her way. No one griped when he gave it to Sherron, because no one thought this deal would be worth much.

But Korea was showing signs of an early recovery from the recent Asian economic crisis and, more important, reacted to that crisis by embracing deregulation. The Korean government encouraged its large *chaebols* (Korean for "conglomerate") to welcome Western partners, and planned to privatize the government-owned power and gas monopolies. One of the largest chaebols in the country, SK Corp., was looking for Western capital for a joint venture to distribute gas throughout the country. SK owned six such companies, and wanted a Western investor to value them in a bidding process. The winning bidder would become SK's partner in the new joint venture, with SK contributing the gas-distribution companies and the new partner contributing the winning bid in cash, setting the stage for a grand expansion that would acquire still more gas businesses in Korea. In other words, this deal had "Bonus and Promotion" written all over it.

Sherron met with the Asia Pacific guys to go over the basics of the deal and, following Enron procedure, prepared to take over as the M&A representative. Her boss, Frank Stabler, still thought it was a long shot. The deal had been put out for bid, making it even less desirable, given the likely competition of major energy companies from England, Belgium, France, and Japan, none of which had to adhere to the U.S. Foreign Corrupt Practices Act. Even so, Sherron thought she had a chance, largely because of the personal relationships already forged by Enron's team in Korea.

In April 1998, Sherron got the preliminary go-ahead from Enron International's executive committee to start working on the deal full-time. The next month was spent putting together the due diligence team. Along with the regional group and Sherron from M&A, the team needed a tax specialist, an in-house attorney, in-house engineers, accountants, and the usual cadre of associates and analysts to run numbers, chase down market research, and prepare the innumerable PowerPoint presentations that were a dreaded part of deal closure at Enron. U.S. and Korean law firms were identified and cleared for use, and Andersen's Seoul office agreed to look over the materials SK made available in the data room.

Some days Sherron thought she would not be able to withstand the pressure. In May she was called out of an SK meeting to learn that she had to race to the hospital—her eighty-year-old grandmother suffered a blood clot and was not expected to live. She missed the chance to say goodbye. That same month, she had a miscarriage. With her husband working in Calgary and her obligations in Korea mounting, Sherron realized they might never be in the same place at the right time again—the SK deal might cost her the chance to have a child.

But she pushed on, devoting June to selling the deal internally at Enron. Just chasing a deal worth $300–$500 million was costly. There would be lots of international travel, not to mention the cost of the outside attorneys and accountants. The deal had to look good, and the prospects for victory even better. Sherron and her team flooded EI's high-ranking executives with memos and PowerPoint presentations that explained the advantages of the deal—why this region, why this country, why this company. Finally, they got the go-ahead to fly the team over to Korea and go through the data, but there was one condition: At the end of two weeks, if the team didn't believe the deal could be converted from a bid deal to one that was closer to a negotiated deal—eliminating or at least weakening the international competition— it was over. Enron would cut its losses and walk away.

They headed for Korea in July. The basic flight plan included a four- to five-hour trip west to Los Angeles, San Francisco, Portland, or Vancouver, and ten to fifteen hours across the Pacific to Seoul. The work was brutal, with long days studying the financial data, followed by even longer nights updating Houston. Because of the fourteen-hour time difference, calls to Enron in Houston started at 10 P.M., then continued all night until 6 or 7 A.M. Back in Houston it was the end of the business day.

All went well until a special operations guy Enron had used on a deal in Mozambique tried to muscle his way into the Korea deal, offering to investigate SK's principals on Enron's behalf. Sherron had seen the guy's sleazy techniques in Africa and put in frantic calls to her superiors to get him taken out of the picture. But it was too late. J. J. Yu, the lead deal maker for SK, got wind of his inquiries and politely asked Sherron why Enron was investigating his company's top guys. Then he asked to meet some of Enron's other business partners. He wanted a few references before making a final decision.

This request threw Houston into a tizzy. Sherron's superior explained that Enron was like a bad ex-husband; it didn't *have* a lot of partners who would say nice things. Enron couldn't contact Shell, for instance, because of problems on a Bolivia-to-Brazil pipeline. Singapore Power wasn't happy with Enron on their joint project in China, the Hainan Island power plant. After more than a few frantic phone calls, Enron finally located a grateful partner in the Philippines who would vouch for them.

After that, Sherron and her team had just a few weeks to finish their due diligence and negotiate with SK and their advisor, Merrill Lynch, to revise the bidding process. SK would make their decision based not just on the dollar amount of the bid but also on the joint-venture structure proposed by each bidder. A closer relationship was forged over myriad business dinners at which Sherron's team barely mastered crispy jellyfish and marinated sea cucumber. The continuous rice wine toasts left more than one of her perpetually jet-lagged team members bolting for the rest room.

Back in Houston, Enron International's executive management was warming to the SK deal. The engineers had good reports on the facilities they'd visited and SK had a good reputation as a partner. But Joe Sutton, Enron International's number two, now warned the Korea team that they were facing tough internal competition. He knew that the South American M&A team wanted to bid on a Brazilian electricity-distribution company that might go as high as $1 billion, and Rebecca Mark had her eye on Wessex, a British water company with a market capitalization of more than $2 billion. For a few years, Mark had been considering a move into the water business, and she finally found a company that looked good. Either one of those acquisitions could eat up all of Enron's available investment capital, and Sherron and SK would be left out in the cold.

But Sherron was nothing if not dogged. She plowed ahead, working with the attorneys on the joint-venture term sheets, the documents that laid out all the requirements for the deal. It was during this time, in July 1998, that she heard office gossip about the killing the traders had made on the midwestern heat wave. Not only were the 1998 earnings in the bag, one trader told her, but Enron had at least the first quarter of 1999 sewn up as well. Moving earnings from one year to the next, she thought, was becoming a habit.

Skilling was riding high. His model worked in gas, and now it appeared to be working in electricity. So he began to loosen the purse strings. First, he let the South American team bid $1.3 billion for Elektro, a São Paulo electricity-distribution company, on July 16, 1998. (Enron was the winning bidder by $300 million, a margin that was not exactly cause for celebration.)

Just a few days later, Enron announced the $2.2 billion, all-cash offer for Wessex water company in the U.K.

Meanwhile, Sherron held her breath. SK agreed to preliminary terms in September. Enron and SK would be 50/50 partners, but SK would staff the CEO spot, while Enron would choose the COO. From there they would alternate, with SK picking the CFO, Enron the lead accountant, and so on. SK hinted that if the bid number was right, the deal just might be Enron's.

There was just one problem. SK wanted the deal closed by year end. Sherron's team kicked into hyperdrive. She raced between Houston and Seoul, forgetting to sleep. On top of everything else, she found out in early October that she was pregnant. Every morning, she had to dab perfume under her nose to fight the nausea that now arose from the aroma of garlic that permeated the Seoul streets. She had no intention of letting anyone at Enron know about her condition—it might signal the end of any chances for promotion. She hoped no one would notice she was no longer participating in the rice wine toasts.

The collective wisdom of the team, with associates weighing in just as strenuously as the senior members, was that the SK gas companies were worth at least $250 million. The tax and legal departments fully vetted the specifics and found just one hitch, a Korean double-taxation issue that would prohibit cash dividends to the newly formed parent joint venture. Enron's lobbyists jumped right in, working to change Korean law so that Enron would not be taxed twice on its investment.

Finally, in December, Sherron prepared the summary of the deal for the Enron board. Deadlines loomed. But Joe Sutton, the new head of Enron International following Mark's departure for the water business, was out of town. Sherron e-mailed him the summary, but she had to attend a meeting with Skilling before Sutton could weigh in.

When Sutton returned and went over her work, he was particularly keen on one PowerPoint slide that explained the rationale for the deal, the one she intended to show the board as part of her sales pitch—until Skilling told her to throw it out. Worse, Sutton hated another slide that Skilling thought was the most useful for summarizing the deal. The months of work had come down to a war over two slides between two men who did not get along. "What should I do?" Sherron frantically asked Frank Stabler.

Her boss paused for just a second before he answered. "You've got to listen to the guy who's deciding your bonus."

Sutton's slide went in, and Skilling's came out. At the board presentation, Skilling didn't notice. Cash was pouring in from Enron's power trading, and he was feeling expansive. When the board asked, Is this our best partner? Skilling nodded in agreement, while Sutton answered, "We think so," and, like that—*We think so!*—the deal was approved.

There was only one last thing to do: pick out and distribute the deal toy. In the early days of Enron, Gene Humphrey's oil and gas financiers gave their partners Lucite cubes to commemorate deals, and everyone was happy. But over time, such gifts started to look, well, cheap and uncool. Michael Kopper, in Andy Fastow's division, substantially raised the bar in 1995 and 1996. Kopper got his deal toys from Neiman-Marcus; he handed out mahogany bookends topped with antiqued globes, engraved Nambé trays, and kaleidoscopes set on pedestals. He was the father of the sophisticated deal toy; in her JEDI days, Sherron received a kaleidoscope, a Kosta Boda crystal sculpture, and a mariner's telescope, all courtesy of Kopper's influence. Fastow followed his lead, handing out life-sized Chewbaca heads for a deal called Chewco.

Sherron had her secretary call Neiman's gift department, which came up with the perfect thing: a $700 Steuben crystal arch perched atop a black granite base. The top guy on the deal, the Asia Pacific managing director, loved the idea. Then they had to figure out how many toys to buy.

Koreans, like Japanese, are big on gift giving. To ensure that no one was insulted, they needed at least a dozen for the Korean SK team alone. Then there was the Enron International team: Of course, they had to buy one sculpture for Joe Sutton and one for Sherron's boss, Frank Stabler; the three top regional team members would each get one; and certainly the in-house attorney deserved one too. Sherron ordered twenty of them in all, including one for herself. Fifteen thousand dollars and some impressive engraving later, her stunning deal toys were ready for distribution. The granite base supporting the crystal expanse read:

SK–Enron Company, Ltd.
January 1999
a bridge between cultures
a bridge between companies
a bridge to the future

Everyone else who worked on the deal—about 110 people in all—got smaller Lucite replicas that added another couple thousand to the tab.

The formal closing occurred in January 1999. It was Sherron's last trip to Seoul. She had come to love the city of ten million, the world's fifth largest. It was hilly and green in spots, with a wonderful mixture of skyscrapers, Las Vegas–style neon, and gorgeous three-thousand-year-old Oriental palaces. The bridges that spanned the Hangag River made her think of Seoul as a pretty Pittsburgh. But now she had to keep herself busy in the Houston office. Her pregnancy was advancing, but she still had no intention of telling anyone about her condition until promotions and bonuses were doled out in February. Finally, that time came. Stabler was traveling, and so had Sherron meet with Mitch Taylor, her longtime colleague who had just been promoted from vice president to managing director. She sat across from him while he offered congratulations; she was being promoted to VP and would receive a bonus of $175,000.

One hundred seventy-five thousand dollars was more than her whole year's salary. Even so, Sherron remained outwardly calm. Only losers at Enron looked thrilled when they got their bonuses—you were supposed to act like you deserved it two years ago.

A few months later, an executive from Enron Global Finance and a transaction accountant called on her to see whether the SK deal fit the FAS 125 criteria. Since the SK deal looked fairly profitable (all those gas-distribution companies were throwing off decent earnings), maybe SK could give the company a big earnings boost in 1999, the accountants said, and it might be great for Sherron, too—if her deal met the FAS 125 criteria, she'd probably get another big bonus.

When they met, the accountants drew a lot of boxes and arrows on a white board to see if the SK deal conformed. After a few hours, they shook their heads. Enron couldn't have any significant management in the deal, and despite the fact that SK controlled the CEO spot, Enron had too many people in other executive positions. Sherron was flummoxed. Other deals that weren't so different from hers worked just fine. Can we try this, she'd pressed. Why can't we do that? But the answer was still no. Disappointed, she let it go.

She took her real bonus and every in-the-money stock option she owned and started house hunting with Rick. The baby wasn't due until June, but Sherron couldn't wait to get out of their two-bedroom apartment. She put in a call to Kathy Wetmore, Enron executives' Realtor of choice—she had sold houses to Jeff Skilling, Andy Fastow, Michael Kopper, and Mitch Taylor, among others. Wetmore drove Sherron past a pretty colonial in Southampton, a tony, tree-shaded neighborhood near Rice University. At first Sherron balked—the idea of living so close to Fastow, Kopper, et al., made her feel like she had joined a cult. But Southampton was so pretty, and the house was perfect—except that it was priced at just above half a million dollars. Sherron would have to stretch, but, she reminded herself, her job at Enron was secure. Within a few weeks, she even told her colleagues that she was expecting.

It seemed to Sherron that, finally, she had made it. She was happily married, living in a dream house, with a healthy baby on the way, and she was only thirty-nine. Enron's stock price had closed at $56 at the end of 1998 and was still rising. Enron was also very proud of her deal: During the summer of 1999, Ken Lay and Enron consultant Henry Kissinger attended a black-tie event in its honor, with SK and other dignitaries, in Seoul. Sherron missed the evening because she was in Houston giving birth to her daughter, Marion. Still, she read Lay's prepared remarks with optimism: "We at Enron are proud to have been the largest direct energy investor in Korea in 1998, and look forward to expanding our business here."

Later, Sherron would wonder whether Lay actually spoke those words aloud. If he did, then what happened next must have certainly appeared odd to the Koreans, not to mention many at Enron. Management decided that not another dime was to be spent in developing countries. There would be no expansion in Korea, no more projects in Brazil, Panama, or China. Sherron was barely home from the hospital when Frank Stabler and Mitch Taylor called her. "Are you sitting down?" they asked. Skilling was reorganizing the company—again. Enron International was gone. They would all have to find new jobs. "You could probably stay on maternity leave until next February and no one would notice," Taylor joked.

One week after Mark's new water company, Azurix, went public, Enron International was dead. Each region was to form a new company with a separate CEO and COO, reporting directly to Skilling. Joe Sutton was promoted to vice chairman of Enron Corp., a position known around Enron as The Ejection Seat. Sherron's international M&A group was no more; each employee would have to scramble to be "hired" in a new region.

Over the next few weeks, Sherron considered her options. Normally, she'd use her success in Korea to build a power base for herself in Asia. But if she went to work for the Asia Pacific region, her hours would be a mess because of the time difference, and the international travel demands would be impossible with a new baby. She could ask Rebecca Mark for a job at Azurix, but it bothered Sherron that Frank Stabler had turned Mark down when she offered him the chance to be her second in command. He told Sherron he didn't want to leave the energy business, but she suspected that something about the business model made him nervous, which, in turn, had made her uneasy.

Besides, Sherron was much more interested in a new division of the company she had been hearing a lot about. It sounded very innovative and very hip. Enron Broadband Services.

9

Andy's World

IN his early days with Enron, Andy Fastow was a relatively innocuous presence. He had a well-deserved reputation as a serial prankster, but his pranks were for the most part amusing and harmless. Even his friend Beth Tilney forgave him when he made fun of her Vision and Values cube—Fastow spent more than $600 to make one of his own, parodying Enron's promise to act with integrity ("When we say we will do something, we will do it") with "When Enron says it will rip your face off, it will rip your face off." Initially, Fastow got along well with his colleagues and was reasonably good to his staff, inviting them to his house for holiday parties at Christmastime, organizing impromptu happy hours and group lunches. Even as his hair turned prematurely gray, his eyes retained their twinkle; he was eternally boyish, the corporate whiz kid. He romped with his dogs at nearby parks, he pursued high-risk hobbies like skydiving. He went glacier hiking and gorilla watching.

But as Fastow rose within the ranks of Enron, the pranks and the good humor faded while his need for power and control intensified, as did his violent tantrums, focused on anyone who stood in his way. Once, colleagues saw Fastow as childlike; now they saw that his childlike desperation to fit in—to close the deals, to be seen as a major player—concealed a drive to succeed at any cost.

Inordinately proud to have been a member of Skilling's first hand-picked team, he named his first son Jeffrey in 1995. After rock climbing became Skilling's favorite pastime, Fastow talked it up, too. He became more socially acute, introducing Ivy League recruits, but not his own clerks, to colleagues he encountered on the streets at lunchtime. He started culling the guest list of his annual holiday party, inviting only the Enron comers. ("We had a problem this year—several invitations were lost in the mail," his wife, Lea, an Enron assistant treasurer, apologized afterward to those left off the list.) The couple started collecting art.

In Fastow's history it is possible to discern the same sort of ambition that drove Skilling, and Lay—if possible, he may have been even more driven. Born in Washington, D.C., in 1961, he was raised in New Providence, New Jersey, a tiny, self-contained town that, because of urban sprawl, evolved as a suburb of Newark. His father was a buyer for a grocery and drugstore chain, and his mother sold real estate. In many ways, Fastow had a typical 1970s suburban upbringing, heavy on popular culture. (He decorated his room with *Star Wars* characters, a passion he would draw on later to name many of the financial vehicles he created.)

He grew up, like Skilling, the middle child in a house full of boys; but unlike his boss, Fastow came of age in the shadow of an older brother whose brilliance was an accepted fact of family life. What Fastow lacked in intelligence—and he didn't lack for much—he made up in nerve. He had to win, and he almost always did. His fierce competitiveness revealed itself in elementary school when he joined the debate team. By the time Fastow got to New Providence High School, he was a star: His grades were outstanding, he played tennis and soccer, and, in band, he mastered the trombone. But he still had plenty of drive left over for politics: The school was socially and economically stratified—"A snob school," in the words of one classmate—and Fastow was devastated when he lost the race for class president in his sophomore year. He came back, however, as a junior to win election to the presidency of the student council. (An editorial in the paper that year complained that he did not make good on his campaign promises.) As a senior, Fastow talked his way into an emeritus role and pushed for a liberal agenda that included teaching students family planning.

Classmates and teachers considered him a kid to whom the word "no" was a minor impediment. When he got a B, he nagged and negotiated with a teacher to get the grade raised. Although he wasn't first in his class, Fastow still managed to secure the role of class valedictorian. He knew how to work people; for that reason, his classmates assumed he would wind up in politics.

But at Tufts, which he attended on a financial aid package, he turned toward business. Fastow successfully pushed the school to adopt a major in Chinese, because he thought it would help him stand out—he was already résumé building—and he spent a year in Taiwan. In the end, he majored in both Chinese and economics.

It was the beginning of the Reagan era, and over the next few years people like Michael Milken and Ivan Boesky, Saul Steinberg and Henry Kravis, would redefine what it meant to be really rich; they made their spectacular fortunes on their own, and to a young man with a flair for the esoteric and a gift for sales—and the belief that money was the only measure of success—the path was clear. Fastow, in tune with his times, affected the ironic pose that none of it mattered, "it" being wealth, position, and power. "It" was really just a game, a great cosmic joke. No one needed to know how badly he needed to succeed. But he was ambitious and fearless when it came to satisfying his ambition. At Tufts, he helped a coed drag a huge trunk into her dorm on the first day of school; soon enough, he was engaged to Lea Weingarten, the daughter of one of Houston's wealthiest families.

The Weingarten name was synonymous with a local grocery chain—by the late 1960s, there were more than a hundred Weingarten stores across the South and Southwest—and, later, a real estate empire and numerous good works in the city. Lea grew up in a sprawling, magnolia-shaded mansion in a neighborhood known as "The Jewish River Oaks," but her life was not circumscribed by the Jewish community. She went to one of the city's best private schools and had friends among Houston's oldest guard. Her mother, Miriam, had been a Miss Israel. Plump and sweet, Lea was the kind of person people wished the best for.

Overnight, Fastow moved from a comfortable middle-class existence to European jaunts with the in-laws and invitations to the homes of Houston's most prominent people. The possibilities of infinite wealth were now positioned at eye level; all Andy Fastow had to do was prove himself.

After college, the couple moved to Chicago, where both worked on MBAs from the Kellogg School of Business at Northwestern University. Fastow was almost broke by graduation, anxiously awaiting an offer from Continental Bank's training program; to support himself he worked as a host at the International House of Pancakes on Lakeshore Drive. He was so dynamic that management tried to recruit him for *their* executive training program. Fortuitously, the Continental offer came through—for both Andy and Lea. Once there, Fastow shunned the new hire milieu; he kept to himself. But his competitive edginess got him into trouble; during his first year, he was reprimanded by a supervisor for talking to coworkers about using inside information to make a profit trading stock in Coastal Corporation. Maybe Fastow was just talking big, but Coastal was one of Continental's major clients.

It was also at Continental that Fastow worked on some of the first contract securitization deals, or as they were known more commonly, structured finance. These transactions became very popular in the 1980s as a way for banks and their customers to grow, and Continental pursued them aggressively. They involved the bundling and resale of financial assets like home mortgages or car loans to hundreds, if not thousands, of investors who, in return for their money, got an indirect ownership interest in a pool of financial contracts. The home mortgage securitizations developed into such a big business that they became part of the financial lingo of the time; people talked about the CMO market (Collateralized Mortgage Obligations) at Wall Street cocktail parties just as often as the equity market.

From CMOs, businesses moved on to something called asset-backed securities. In an ABS deal, a heavy-equipment company would pool its fleet of dump trucks, for instance, into a special-purpose entity and then "sell" the SPE to investors. Since the SPE was "leasing" the trucks back to the company, the lease payments provided the investors with their return, while the company used the cash to expand. Such deals depended on homogeneity—an investor couldn't review hundreds of home mortgages or kick thousands of tires, but he had legal assurances that the contents of his investment were consistent and secure—hence the term "securitizations."

At Continental, Fastow worked on a new kind of securitization deal that was more creative and more risky. Contract securitizations involved a pool of less homogeneous loans or assets that were pooled in a special-purpose entity that *contractually* balanced the risks. Investors took the risk of the new entity's performance, while the accounting rules allowed the issuing company to treat the transaction like an asset sale. They didn't have to consolidate the special-purpose entity on their balance sheet as an increase in debt, or explain the deal in annual report footnotes. All these structured financings—CMOs, ABS deals, contract securitizations—were called "monetizations" by the issuing company. By following a few simple accounting rules and by creating a few simple (and not so simple) special-purpose entities, a company could "monetize"—literally turn its assets into money and generate revenue. The cash wasn't debt, it wasn't disclosed, but it was there when you needed it. Fastow worked almost exclusively on these types of transactions during his five years at Continental, making a name for himself in the process.

SPEs could do a lot of good at a cash-starved/debt-averse/growth-craving company, and as it happened, Jeff Skilling at Enron Gas Services needed a well-connected banker type who could help him fund his natural gas volumetric production payments in just such a manner—off balance sheet, so the company could grow without growing more debt. At the time, Enron was having difficulty attracting talent from the East Coast—not everyone wanted to leave Wall Street for the wilds of Houston. Fastow was young and eager, and he had mastered structured finance. "He was available," a colleague would remark dryly.

Enron was "available" to Fastow, too. Lea wanted to go home to Houston, and, once Fastow had an offer, he pushed to include his wife in the deal. Within a very short time, the couple was Houston bound.

By December 1990, Fastow was a director at Enron Gas Services, devoting virtually all his time to raising off-balance-sheet money. He was also an excellent billboard for future recruits: He was young and nice-looking, and only a few found him too slick when, raving about Houston's climate, he bragged that he took his wife's fur coat to the dump.

Fastow understood, intuitively, that he was home. He worked tirelessly—

on vacations he remained in obsessive contact with the office—and could think the way Skilling wanted: outside the proverbial box. But what Fastow did best was sell. In the eyes of Enron, bankers were basically dim bulbs. They had to be led—and sometimes coerced—into the complex financial future Enron was inventing. Over the next few years, faced with a blank whiteboard and a crowd of eager customers, Fastow would begin drawing furiously, connecting boxes to other boxes with a series of arrows, all the while jabbering about Enron's ability to carve up any deal or grouping of deals into just the right, risk-specific chunks for his customers. (High-risk portions went to those eager for high returns or hefty tax deductions, for instance, while the investment-grade, lower-risk portion went to the cautious.) Fastow had a favorite slide that showed how Enron could subdivide at least twenty different kinds of risk in a given portfolio. If he sometimes didn't make sense, well, the bankers told themselves, they could figure it out later. If his Enron colleagues in the room knew that Fastow couldn't always deliver on what he was promising—if he was sometimes just writing gobbledygook on that whiteboard—well, they figured they'd work that out later, too.

Fastow's motto—"Never say no to a deal"—came to mean pushing for any transaction, no matter how complex or how irrational. One Enron division wanted to expand its natural gas liquids refinery operation but was hamstrung because of Enron's prohibition on increasing debt. Fastow wanted to use money from the JEDI fund for the expansion project, even though it didn't make sense—JEDI didn't need a partial interest in some refinery parts. It would be like buying a transmission in someone else's car—what use would that be? Another customer wanted JEDI to finance his house as well as his business venture. Those were the kinds of propositions that made Sherron Watkins nervous. But when those working for him balked at his schemes, Fastow complained that they weren't creative enough. "You're thinking like an accountant," he'd say to Sherron Watkins. "You're thinking like a lawyer," he'd tell attorney Kristina Mordaunt. "You have to learn to think outside the box."

As Enron's need for off–balance sheet debt grew, so did Fastow's bullying: Anyone who slowed down a deal moving toward a successful closing—an obstreperous in-house lawyer, a cautious banker, a plodding accountant—found himself a target of Fastow's anger. Potential recruits from the banking industry worried about working with him: "Does he bully his staff like he does the banks?" they asked. After one banker finished a particularly scary phone call with Fastow, he was visibly shaken. No one had ever used such obscene language with him before. "That's just how Andy does things," he was told.

And then, after being promoted out of Enron Capital & Trade's funding group to run his own division, Fastow failed. His salesmanship skills indicated he was the right man to head Enron's 1995 retail electricity effort. Fastow went into the venture with high hopes; he would be managing his own business within the company, something that traditionally brought huge rewards at Enron, both politically and financially. But Fastow had no idea how to create or run a business—as opposed to packaging its pieces—and he spent his days in something of a swivet, chatting aimlessly with his few employees, or in terror as Skilling rejected proposal after proposal and became increasingly impatient with him. Enron was not a mentoring environment—executives were expected to come up with ideas on their own and execute them on their own. People who failed, failed on their own, too. In just nine short months, Skilling replaced Fastow and brought him back to Enron Capital & Trade—promoting him to managing director with the move.

Fastow returned to ECT determined to get back into Skilling's good graces—to work longer hours and be even more creative. He knew what the stakes were. "Who knows how long I'll be here," he told Sherron Watkins worriedly. He knew, too, that deals and more deals would be his only salvation.

He got his big chance when Enron announced its plans to purchase Portland General, the Oregon electric utility. The minute the merger was approved by Oregon regulators, Enron would be considered a power utility by both federal and state regulators. No one noticed until after the fact that this situation could have a disastrous effect on Enron's balance sheet.

Enron owned four power plants in the United States that operated as nonregulated power generators. The status of those plants was set by various federal and state laws. Texas, for instance, classified them as Qualifying Facilities, meaning that Enron, a nonutility, had been given special permission by local regulators to operate power plants in another utility's regulated market area. But once Enron became a power utility itself—as it would with ownership of Portland General—the plants would immediately lose their Qualifying Facility status. If that happened, debt covenants would be violated and the outstanding debt on each power plant—many millions' worth—was due immediately. Fastow's mission, then, was to find a way to replace Enron as the plants' owner of record.

An outright sale of the projects was not feasible, given the time constraints, particularly since Enron had third-party equity partners that would have to approve any sale. The only viable alternative was to employ an SPE, one that would leave Enron as a de facto owner from the perspective of its third-party partners, but not the owner as far as the regulators were concerned.

Fastow threw himself into the project with his protégé, Michael Kopper. Kopper had come to Enron from Toronto Dominion Bank and had a reputation as a banker's banker, someone who understood the needs of his colleagues and worked creatively to satisfy them. Like Fastow, Kopper was young, just thirty years old, and attractive—tall and thin, dark-haired, with penetrating black eyes and hollow cheeks. Kopper's background was less like the average Enronian's, which meant that he came from wealth. His father was a prominent publisher; the family lived in comfort in Woodmere, Long Island. Kopper graduated from Duke University, then earned an advanced degree from the London School of Economics.

Kopper was also gay, and though he neither advertised nor hid the fact, it set him apart at Enron, as it had set him apart in life. He wasn't a natural for Enron's macho culture—he had a wry cynicism that matched Fastow's, and he was quick and glib, with the gift, like Fastow, of making the incomprehensible seem almost but not quite fathomable. ("What did you just say in there?" an Enron colleague asked Kopper after a virtuoso sales pitch. He shook his head, as if dazed. "I don't know," he replied.)

And he was funny. Attending a meeting of Merrill Lynch bankers and Enron strategists who introduced themselves as Schuyler, Grant, and Dwight, Kopper leaned toward Sherron Watkins and whispered, "What is this? *Days of Our Lives?*" There was a particular group that loved gathering at his home to watch the British sitcom *Absolutely Fabulous*, and people sought him out for style tips because of his discerning taste. Kopper spent exquisitely—on the requisite Armani armor, on his trainer, on his tan, on international travel with his partner, Bill Dodson, and on their home, which had the sort of inventive touches that were the envy of Enron wives. (He remodeled his one-story Southampton bungalow into an austere, Japanese-style jewel.) That Kopper was Jewish helped to make him one of Fastow's favorites—he introduced the young ex-banker to prominent members of the community and helped him find a temple to join. It wasn't long before Kopper was a regular at the Fastow home and on family trips; he became "Uncle Michael" to Andy's kids. He was also inordinately beholden to his mentor.

Kopper and Fastow rescued Enron from potentially life-threatening debt acceleration with a deal christened Alpine Investors Limited—the very Alpine fund that Fastow tried to force on Pacific Corporate Group, claiming it was a power fund when it was a financing. The two men closed the deal by year-end 1996, to ovations within Enron Capital & Trade. They somehow managed to do the impossible; Enron could buy the big Oregon utility and became a "utility" itself in the process, but against all odds, still hold on to its four smaller nonregulated power plants through a series of deals within deals.

It was during this rescue effort that Fastow may have noticed that no one at Enron seemed to care *how* he had financed Alpine. All they cared about was that the structure worked. In the past, Fastow pushed to get the cheapest deals possible for Enron. But in Alpine, Enron gave up more fees and interest rate points than usual to close before year-end 1996, just in case the Oregon regulators approved the Portland General acquisition by then. No one complained. Avoiding the massive debt payment was the priority, and Fastow avoided that handily.

When Skilling ascended to COO at the end of 1996, he rewarded Fastow with a job as head of a newly formed unit, Enron Capital Management, a companywide treasury function. Fastow took the title but made clear his profound lack of interest in the day-to-day requirements of the job—cash management and commercial paper funding, for instance. He just used the position to solidify his power base with Skilling, to whom he was now a direct report. His passion remained with his SPEs.

In 1997, Fastow got a chance to be even more creative with his financing. He formed a special-purpose entity to buy some California wind farms for Enron—part of the company's bigger, cleaner energy push—that, because of the Portland General purchase, were also in danger of losing their Qualifying Facility status. The Oregon regulators were incredibly difficult to appease and the Portland General acquisition did not close until mid-1997. The delay was lucky for Enron, because just as the company was late to recognize its problems with its nonregulated power plants, it overlooked the same issue on its California wind farms. Fastow and Kopper named this rescue effort RADR (not to be confused with RADAR, the risk-adjusted discount rate calculated by RAC, the Risk Assessment and Control Group).

To qualify for off-balance-sheet treatment, Andersen instructed Enron that its special-purpose entities must have at least 3 percent outside equity at risk, which meant there had to be some real money, as opposed to debt, in the deal. That 97 percent of an SPE could be debt financed was a tribute to Enron and Andersen's ability to select the FASB interpretation that suited their needs. Enron's SPEs were popular, offering, as they did, something for everyone: The minority three-percent investor got controlling interest in the SPE and the healthier returns that go with higher risk, while avoiding the hassle of ownership; the actual management of the underlying assets and theSPE itself stayed with Enron. At the same time, Enron usually kept some infinitesimal ownership slice that happened to confer management rights, but it also got to keep virtually all the deal debt off its balance sheet. If structured correctly, what was in reality a huge loan wouldn't even have to be disclosed in the *footnotes* of the company's balance sheet. In other words, it was free money. Large borrowings stayed secret, and it was all perfectly legitimate.

With RADR, Fastow focused on the third-party three-percenters. It would be more convenient if these were passive or, better yet, friendly investors, people who wouldn't ask a lot of questions. So he brought close friends into the deal. Thus was born the FOE—the Friend of Enron. He pulled in a Houston heiress, and his real estate broker, Kathy Wetmore. Somehow they were able to come up with the necessary 3 percent, and RADR closed to great acclaim inside the company. Again, Fastow worked it out so Enron retained most of the rewards of ownership without actually *being* the owner, while only a small amount of money went to the RADR investors. Small was, of course, a relative term—over time, that tiny amount would climb into the millions and would not escape Fastow's notice.

But again, no one at Enron seemed to care how the deal was structured or how much it cost, just as long as it closed quickly, stayed off the balance sheet, and caused no perceptible drag on Enron's quarterly numbers—and everyone got their bonuses. Soon, Fastow and Kopper, with help from a new transaction accountant, Ben Glisan, were seen as a team of financial super-heroes. And if anyone at Enron tried to cross Kopper or slow him down, he would go to Fastow, or threaten to; if anyone tried to cross Fastow or slow him down, he would go to Skilling, or threaten to.

They always got their way—or almost always, that is.

In the last half of 1997, when Skilling wanted to sell a piece of Enron Eneregy Services to demonstrate its value in the marketplace, Fastow was part of the team designated to find investors. CalPERS signed on, but it imposed one big condition: They'd invest in Enron Energy Services only if Enron bought them out of their current position in JEDI, which was then worth about $383 million. Enron had to go for it: If other investors found out that one of the company's oldest partners wasn't on the EES bandwag-on, they'd smell failure and stay away in droves.

To make the sale of Enron Energy Services a sure thing, Enron had three choices: It could buy out CalPERS directly, which would be disastrous for Enron's balance sheet, because all the JEDI debt would then be consol-idated with Enron's. If that amount was added to the $383 million purchase price (which would also have to be borrowed), Enron would end up increas-ing its debt by nearly $1 billion. Enron might also find a real third-party investor to buy CalPERS's interest in JEDI, but that looked improbable, given Skilling's rush to announce investors in Enron Energy Services by the close of the year. Finally, Enron could create a special-purpose entity, like Alpine and RADR, that would borrow the money to buy out CalPERS, keeping both the JEDI debt and the $383 million purchase-price debt off the balance sheet. Clearly, the SPE was the best choice to get CalPERS out of JEDI and into Enron Energy Services. All Enron had to do was find a third party to risk 3 percent of the deal, $11 million of equity money. The other 97 percent of the SPE could come from one of Enron's many willing bankers, who would collect a hefty fee for their participation as lender.

Eleven million dollars was chicken feed by Enron standards. In fact, the amount was so small that Andy Fastow offered to invest that amount personally, with some help from his in-laws. He went to Skilling and suggested that he manage this new entity, which he had named Chewco investments—after Chewbacca, the furry *Star Wars* wookie. This would be a great deal for Andy: He would get a piece of the pie, equivalent to the phantom equity Skilling got at Enron Capital & Trade, and Lou Pai got at Enron Energy Services.

But it wasn't a good deal for Enron. Skilling nixed the idea, and so did Enron's attorneys at the law firm of Vinson & Elkins, who pointed out the obvious: An Enron senior executive purporting to be the third party in a special-purpose entity was not really an outside third party, as the accounting rules required. Plus, it was a clear conflict of interest, and as such would require approval of the board and disclosure in the company's proxy statement. In other words, it would create more problems than it solved. Fastow retreated—but only temporarily. His next suggestion was to make Michael Kopper Chewco's managing partner. Kopper was not a senior executive, so his role in the creation of the SPE would not have to be disclosed in the proxy. *No one was going to outsmart the SPE king!*

Michael Kopper, in fact, was perfect to manage a fund that, as it turned out, no one was supposed to ask any questions about. He could shut down any meddler with a quip or a sneer.

As Chewco was forming, in fact, it seemed veiled in secrecy to many who worked in Fastow's group. There was some question, for instance, as to who, exactly, was providing the third-party equity funding for the deal. Paperwork that had once been the responsibility of clerks was now overseen by only one director-level employee, who also oversaw the sending and receiving of all faxes. Boilerplate documents were confined to locked file drawers. During the negotiations of the profit distribution between Chewco and Enron, Bill Brown, a Fastow hire from 1995, received a chilly warning from his boss. Brown was driving too hard a bargain on Enron's behalf, Fastow complained. Brown reminded Fastow that was his job—to get the best deal for Enron. Understood, Fastow replied, but the deal also had to close. Brown left the meeting with an uncomfortable feeling that Fastow was more involved in Chewco than he had initially assumed.

Fastow presented Chewco to Enron's board of directors in November via a telephone conference call. The board liked Andy. He was always well dressed and lively in his presentations, and he was by then an Enron star — and the board liked stars. This meeting, however, was a little rushed. Board member Pug Winokur announced that he was at an airport and his flight was boarding; he said he'd meet with Fastow further the next day and then hung up. Ken Lay arrived late from another engagement.

Jeff Skilling opened the presentation by recounting the history of JEDI and then turned the meeting over to Fastow, who explained the need for the SPE — to help CalPERS make an investment in Enron Energy Services by year's end. Next, Skilling went over what the minutes describe as "the financing, and the corporate structure of the acquiring company." The financing arrangement, Fastow said, involved a $250 million subordinated loan, guaranteed by Enron, to Chewco from a bank; a $132 million advance to Chewco from JEDI under a revolving credit agreement; and $11 million in "equity" contributed by Chewco's owners — the 3 percent at-risk money required by the accounting rules. No one present asked where this money would be coming from.

Fastow recommended approval of the deal and, in short order, the board gave it to him. Michael Kopper was present for the phone call, but at no point do the minutes show that his involvement was discussed — though according to Enron's code of conduct, it should have been.

Soon after, with great haste, Chewco was formed as a Delaware Corporation, with Michael Kopper in charge. V&E's lawyers prepared the legal documents in less than forty-eight hours. An Enron guaranteed bridge loan was arranged so Chewco could quickly borrow the $383 million needed to pay off CalPERS and the up-front fees and expenses needed to close the deal. The deal toy — a gift that commemorated the deal — was that huge, stuffed Chewbacca head commissioned by Fastow.

There was some bad feeling about Chewco within Fastow's organization when Kopper's colleagues discovered that he, in fact, was the third-party investor. People wanted to know why he had been so favored. He was getting the opportunity to get very rich — why weren't they? And people also wondered, privately, quietly, whether Kopper's involvement in the deal — as managing partner and as investor — threatened Chewco's status as a special-purpose entity.

But no one spoke up. Fastow and Kopper saved the day, even if the ultimate results—Wall Street's clear lack of enthusiasm for the sale of seven percent of Enron Energy Services—were disappointing. That situation was not Kopper and Fastow's concern.

The Chewco bridge loan was paid off on December 30, 1997. Arthur Andersen reviewed and signed off on the deal, collecting a fee of $80,000. Kopper received an annual management fee of $500,000 as general partner, even though there wasn't really much to manage. The few duties, clerical in nature, sometimes fell to Lea Fastow, who by late 1997 had left her job at Enron for full-time motherhood. Unbeknownst to most at the company, she was paid $54,000 to be a Chewco administrative assistant. Fastow, meanwhile, was promoted to CFO in 1998. It was typical of Enron that he was required to perform few of the duties normally associated with the title, like supervising accounting, projecting cash flow, and budgeting—those responsibilities remained with Chief Accounting Officer Rick Causey. Fastow pushed for the title because, he said, it would help him sell Enron's deals better on Wall Street.

Other Enron executives were routinely storming Skilling's office at the time, demanding higher compensation and bigger perks. Enron wasn't competitive with Wall Street, they claimed (*"Give me a raise!"*). Enron wasn't competitive with Silicon Valley (*"Give me more stock options!"*). Skilling didn't want to squabble; he just directed the complainer to the director of Human Resources to work out the details. When Fastow made his demands, Skilling shrugged. If Andy wanted that title, fine, give it to him. And so they did.

Fastow was now determined to become a star not just at Enron but on Wall Street. He set his sights on achieving a goal he had set for the company long before: improving Enron's credit rating. Doing so was the corporate equivalent of moving to a better neighborhood. Enron would pay less for the money it borrowed, but more important, it would give Enron access to bigger, better trading partners like Texaco and Exxon, which traded only with companies that had A ratings or better. (Enron's status had risen over time from just above investment grade, BBB– to three notches above investment grade, BBB+. Good but not great.)

The world of high-stakes "off-exchange" trading is based on perception and mutual trust, with the roles of buyers and sellers, switching thousands of times in a given hour to complete myriad trades that happen almost simultaneously. Most companies set up a credit line for their customers to complete these transactions, saving them the cash cost of margin deposits required by exchanges like the NYMEX. Depending on the price movements in gas or electricity or crude oil, counterparties might owe each other hundreds of millions one week and next to nothing the next. Accounts are typically settled on the dates the underlying contracts expire, months if not years in the future. Companies with the best ratings have the largest credit lines, because their customers know they are good for the money. Companies with poor credit ratings usually have to put up cash deposits or have much smaller credit lines, limiting the size of trades they can do. Enron's goal, then, was to improve its credit rating so that it could increase its trading business.

Fastow was ready to hit the road—to talk up Enron's investments and business plans, and lobby the rating agencies to consider an upgrade. Before moving forward, he quickly banished an old hand named Bill Gathmann, who believed in full disclosure with the agencies—he'd confessed in early 1998 that Enron might not make its operating cash flow targets. Fastow was livid; to him, the numbers could always be met. By late March, Gathmann was exiled to India for his honesty and Fastow replaced him with Jeff McMahon, the rising star who made such a name for himself in London.

Lobbying the rating agencies, Fastow and McMahon extracted one lesson: Enron had to issue more equity—sell more of its common stock—before they would consider improving Enron's credit status. Selling more common shares would give the company an infusion of cash that would lower its debt load, something the rating agencies wanted to see. With the huge capital spending spree that Skilling unleashed in the last half of 1998—$1.3 billion in Brazil, more than $2 billion for Mark's water company, and numerous smaller deals like the $250 million SK deal in Korea—Fastow and McMahon became even more insistent that an equity offering was essential if the rating agencies were ever going to consider improving Enron's status.

Senior management balked at first—no one wanted to dilute the value of their stock, a side effect of issuing more equity. But Fastow and McMahon persisted, and won. In February 1999, Enron issued 17.2 million shares of stock—at $62^{11}⁄16 per share—raising more than $800 million in the company's first significant public offering of common stock in five years. Fastow spread the underwriting business around to all the major players, Credit Suisse First Boston, Donaldson Lufkin & Jenrette (DLJ), Lehman Brothers, Merrill Lynch, Morgan Stanley, Prudential, and Salomon Smith Barney. Not surprisingly, many of their analysts had recently issued favorable reports: Morgan Stanley issued a January 1999 rating of Outperform, declaring "We are also increasing our 12 month price target to $72 from $60 to reflect our new 2000 [Earnings] estimate and recent business activities in EES"; Prudential's January 1999 research was even more bullish, rating Enron a Strong Buy and "raising our 12-month price target to $82 from $70 per share on a sum-of-parts valuation of the company's individual business units."

It was no surprise, then, when Enron's stock price took off. At the end of 1998, Enron was selling for around $50 a share. By March, it rose to $66. By April, it hit $72. In June and July, it soared into the eighties, so high that the board agreed to a split to make the stock cheap enough for average investors again.

But then the stock stopped moving at its post-split price of around $39—August, September, October, November—it didn't budge. Top management looked at the numbers and saw trouble ahead. How was Enron going to maintain its astronomical growth rate? There had been no summer heat wave for the traders to exploit. Worse, some of those "fair-valued" equity investments were going public, and Enron would have to mark its investment to a publicly traded and often volatile stock price instead of its own theoretical model. It was time for more out-of-the-box thinking.

In general, tech investments had not appealed to Jeff Skilling because of their volatility. But in 1998, the head of the company's fledgling broadband division pushed him to look at one particular deal, a small Internet company called Rhythms NetConnections, Inc. In 1998, Enron invested $10 million in Rhythms Net. In April 1999, Rhythms Net went public—and Enron hit the jackpot. Enron's investment in the company shot up in value, to $300 million. Most companies would have waited to book a gain when they actually sold their interest. But because Enron's 1999 earnings picture was looking dicey, Enron marked the *entire* $290 million gain as profit—almost one-third of the company's earnings that year. Then, because the risk was so high, Skilling was determined to lock in the value with a third party—in other words, he wanted to find a way to hedge the investment to retain the $300 million value on the books, no matter what happened to Rhythms Net's actual stock price.

It was yet another attempt by Skilling to protect the value of Enron's equity investment portfolio. He'd spent four years and pressured three different groups to come up with some kind of hedging plan, and his efforts came to nothing. But then Andy Fastow stepped in.

By this point, he was Skilling's go-to guy. Whatever Skilling wanted, Fastow seemed magically able to provide. In turn, he was lavishly rewarded. Fastow was a very rich man. As CFO, Fastow's salary was over $350,000 and didn't include bonuses that could wander into seven figures. He owned a summer house in Vermont and the requisite Porsche convertible. He occupied one of the plush two-story offices on the fiftieth floor, one with the expansive western view that best revealed Houston's oil boom growth and its near-psychedelic, chemically enhanced sunsets. He was, within Enron, a part of the social and political core: When Skilling was honored with the National Humanitarian Award at a Houston benefit for the National Jewish Medical and Research Center, Fastow chaired the dinner committee alongside Ken Lay's sister, Sharon.

Better yet, Fastow was famous outside the company. In October 1999, *CFO* magazine rated him "The Finest in Finance," one of the best CFOs in the country. He "transformed finance into a capital-raising machine"; according to the magazine, he was a genius at creating off-balance-sheet investment vehicles. In an interview in the same issue of *CFO*, Fastow claimed to be flattered that some of the instruments he created were imitated by banks, which, in turn, tried to sell them back to Enron. "We like to see our ideas get marketed back to us every once in a while," he cracked.

He seemed to have everything he wanted: wealth, respect, fame. But there was still one thing Andy Fastow lacked, and no one who knew him believed he would ever stop until he got that, too.

In June of 1999, Vince Kaminski, Enron's head of research, had a baffling experience in regard to Fastow. It was the job of the research department to develop all the complex option modeling and pricing for the traders, and to come up with the formulas that automatically updated the commodity price curves and the company's value at risk, or VAR, measurement. On an ad hoc basis, Kaminski's group was also used for just about anything mathematically challenging at Enron. On this particular summer day, Kaminski got a call from Rick Buy, Enron's chief risk officer. Solemn and unsmiling, Buy reminded people of a burnt-out beat cop—one who could spot trouble, but who had given up trying to improve the neighborhood. There were those at Enron who assumed he'd been put in charge of risk management specifically because he was malleable.

Buy asked Kaminski to price some put options for a new Enron-owned internet company called Rhythms NetConnections at the current stock price for a six-month period. Someone wanted to be sure that Enron would be protected against a decline in Rhythms Net's stock price. Buy presented his request as a theoretical exercise. The Rhythms stock, as a tech stock, was inherently volatile, and no one in the real world would actually try to do such a thing—but what if they did? What would the put cost? Kaminski listened and then hung up the phone slowly. What Buy was asking him to do made no sense at all—such an option would be prohibitively expensive.

Vince Kaminski was part of Enron's brain trust. He was a pale, sharp-featured, slightly built man whose credentials were beyond reproach, even in the intellectually competitive hothouse of Enron. Kaminski had a doctorate in economics from what is now, in Poland, the Warsaw Business School, and an MBA in finance from Fordham University, and had completed most of the work for a masters in mathematics as well. He taught economics at a university in Nigeria, programmed computers, worked as an "econometrician" with AT&T, and was a vice president of Salomon Brothers's Fixed Income Group. Kaminski joined Enron in 1992 and observed the corporate jockeying and creative accounting with the wry detachment of an Eastern European émigré. "Every era gets the clowns it deserves," he liked to crack.

He possessed a mathematician's passion for absolutes—in his mind, numbers never lied. And unlike many people at Enron, Kaminski was modest and helpful, maybe because he was a teacher. In his thick Polish accent, he would explain a particularly hairy calculation to an underling: "Just in case I am to be hit by the truck."

Now the truck appeared to be bearing down on him in the form of the Rhythms NetConnections project. He knew there were serious obstacles to hedging the investment. In the first place, Enron was subject to a six-month lockup period during which it could not sell its stock in the company. The stock price could decline during that time—given the tech sector's volatility, a decline seemed likely, in fact. The certainty of that decline would make a put very expensive, if not impossible. It was a little like trying to buy car insurance for a teenaged boy with a bad driving record—the risks were obvious. Then, too, Enron owned close to 30 percent of Rhythms Net. This was an enormous amount of stock to try to unload on the market. Whoever provided the hedge for such a gambit would risk enormous exposure—and would charge accordingly.

As Kaminski was ruminating on this problem with one of his senior researchers, Jeff Skilling appeared at his door and asked to go to a conference room—a pointed way of asking to see Kaminski alone. Suddenly, it became clear to Kaminski that for whatever reason, Skilling was behind this request for the pricing of the put. This kind of appearance by the COO was rare; the two men had spoken only a few times in person.

Kaminski got up and motioned for his subordinate to come along. Once in the conference room, Skilling tried to explain why he needed to hedge the $300 million, but his reasons were vague. It was important to Enron. It was good for the company. He needed Kaminski to get behind him on this one. Listening to him, Kaminski became even more confused. Why was an intellectual exercise so important?

After Skilling left, Kaminski called Rick Causey, the chief accounting officer, to try to get a better explanation of what he was supposed to do. Like everyone else, Causey told him that Enron wanted to buy a put on Rhythms NetConnections stock to hedge its exposure, but then Causey complicated matters even more. He told Kaminski to price the put in a manner to "make it as expensive to Enron as possible." Why? Kaminski wondered.

He placed a call to one of Causey's deputies, a man named Bob Butts, who finally offered some enlightenment. He directed Kaminski to the Enron Annual Report and something called "UBS forwards," which were forward contracts to buy Enron stock at a set price. Butts said that a portion of these contracts were "in the money." In theory, Enron stock had risen so much that if Enron exercised the contracts with UBS, they could buy and flip their own stock and make $250 million. The only problem was that accounting rules did not permit companies to profit from transactions in their own stock. The rules did permit companies to post such profitable deals as collateral, however.

Hence the deal before Kaminski: a special-purpose vehicle containing the $250 million in value from the UBS forward contracts that might be used to hedge the Rhythms NetConnections transaction. But the valuable forward position was not there to pay off Enron's exposure under the hedging transaction. It was designated instead as protection for the special-purpose entity should *it* begin to lose money on the Rhythms Net hedge.

This jerry-built financial contraption would allow for the fulfillment of Skilling's goal: Enron could now avoid a loss on its income statement, even if the Rhythms Net position, now valued and recorded at $300 million, lost value. (The difference between the $250 million value in the UBS forwards and the $300 million Rhythms Net position explained why Causey had asked Kaminski to price the put as high as possible. He was trying to narrow the gap.)

This idea struck Kaminski as crazy, but he had seen a lot of crazy deals at Enron. In fact, there were deals the research group called "Jasons," after the main character in the *Halloween* slasher movies. No matter how hard the researchers tried to kill the proposals, they always came back, sometimes stronger than before. This deal looked like another Jason: When Kaminski held a brainstorming session with his group to discuss the pricing of the put, everyone in the room cracked up. Even so, they worked on the whiteboard in the conference room and came up with a number.

The next morning, Kaminski took his work to Causey and then to Buy, where he again expressed his discomfort with the project. The whole idea, he said, "was so stupid that only Andy Fastow could have come up with it."

Startled, Buy admitted that, in fact, the idea *was* Fastow's. Not only that, Fastow would own and operate the newly formed SPE, an investment partnership that would enter into deals with Enron. How could Kaminski not have known who was behind this ludicrous arrangement? Fastow had long been an object of derision in the Risk Assessment and Control group; one of Buy's deputies had even worried aloud that Fastow would eventually ruin Enron with his financial ideas. Now Kaminski pointed out the obvious to Buy: This deal presented a clear conflict of interest. The CFO of the company would be running a partnership with interests that could run counter to Enron's. Buy listened, then asked Kaminski to look at the transaction again. He agreed.

Kaminski took the materials home over the weekend, made some calculations, and felt even worse about the plan. The following Monday morning, he went back to Buy's office and advised against it again.

First, he explained, there was the obvious conflict of interest, since Fastow was serving both as Enron's CFO and the owner of the outside investment partnership. Second, the Rhythms NetConnections hedging structure was skewed against Enron shareholders. "Heads Fastow's partnership wins, tails Enron loses" was the way Kaminski explained it to Buy. And that was if Enron ever got a payout, which Kaminski doubted would ever occur. (Fastow's partnership, meanwhile, would get its money very early from the put fee Enron intended to pay to the SPE.) Third, the structure was inherently unstable, because the partnership was effectively funded with contracts associated with Enron stock. If Enron and Rhythms Net stock declined at the same time, the partnership would not be able to meet its obligations to Enron. Kaminski did not stress this last point to Buy, because he thought the other two reasons would be strong enough to change his mind. Two years later, he would deeply regret this failure.

Buy listened with growing surprise. "Next time Fastow is going to run a racket," he said to Kaminski, "I want to be part of it." Both men chuckled, and Buy promised Kaminski he would try to stop the transaction at the board meeting scheduled to approve it. Kaminski offered to put his concerns in writing, but Buy waved him off. He would handle it, he said.

Assuming the deal was dead, Kaminski went out of town for a few days. When he got back to the office, he ran into Buy and asked what had happened to the proposed partnership. The board voted to approve the transaction, Buy told him. There was just too much momentum behind the deal for him to stop it.

What happened sounded very complex but was really very simple: Andy Fastow finally found a way to turn himself into a Friend of Enron. With his accounting deputy, Ben Glisan, he had come up with a partnership that would provide a hedge on the Rhythms NetConnections investment. Skilling wouldn't allow Fastow to enter into a conflict of interest when the stakes for Enron were small. The Chewco deal, in which Fastow wanted to invest, was just another off–balance sheet transaction, designed to keep debt off the books. But when it looked as if Enron might suffer an actual dip in earnings without the Rhythms Net hedge in place—and be humiliated on Wall Street—Skilling was willing to make a much bigger concession.

Fastow named his partnership LJM, after the first initials of his wife and two children. At the time, no one much cared how byzantine the structure was or whether it presented a conflict of interest. Fastow even told some colleagues that Skilling guaranteed that LJM would never lose money. If it ever got underwater, Enron would just pump more stock into it.

The deal could not be cemented, however, without the approval of Arthur Andersen. Andersen had almost as many objections as Vince Kaminski. A partner named Benjamin Neuhausen sent David Duncan, the head of Andersen's Enron audit team, a cautionary e-mail: "Setting aside the accounting, the idea of a venture entity managed by the CFO is terrible from a business point of view. Conflicts galore. Why would any director in his or her right mind ever approve such a scheme?"

"I couldn't agree more," Duncan answered. But he also said that if the Enron board approved the arrangement, he would go along.

And on June 28, 1999, they did. The Enron board waived its own conflict-of-interest requirements and gave birth to LJM, a partnership designed "to invest in energy and communications and related businesses and assets, including businesses and assets of the company."

Because most of LJM's funds were used for the RhythmsNet's hedge, Fastow began devising, in the fall of 1999, a bigger venture, LJM2. The first LJM raised limited-partner funds from two major banking clients of Enron's, NatWest and Credit Suisse First Boston. For LJM2, Fastow wanted clients of his own, and after a kickoff fund-raising dinner with Merrill Lynch, he hit the road, beating the drums for his venture. "I know where the value is at Enron," he would brag, pumping up his potential investors on the promise of LJM2. His behavior was startling to people in the investment community. Why was the CFO of a $35 billion company, whose traditional responsibilities usually included maximizing the value to shareholders, telling potential investors to contribute to another fund that could, essentially, raid the parent company? Even stranger was the actual makeup of LJM2—anyone who looked carefully at the fund would see that it didn't hold assets, exactly, but entities within entities that held assets.

Soon after, calls began to flow among Fastow's colleagues at Enron. Just what the hell, they wondered, was Andy trying to do?

But the board wasn't asking those questions. In fact, in October of 1999, they waived their conflict-of-interest rules again, allowing for the creation of LJM2.

And Vince Kaminski was reassigned. Skilling didn't like his attitude. He was killing too many deals.

10

Smoke and Mirrors

IN retrospect, it's surprising the Internet boom wasn't a siren song to futurists like Jeff Skilling and Ken Lay. It was hot, it was new, it moved at lightning speed, it valued intellectual capital over bricks and mortar, and it promised instant wealth. But to Skilling it seemed too risky, too far from Enron's core businesses. Unlike many people, for instance, he wasn't swayed by Netscape's initial public offering in 1995, the legendary IPO that touched off the new gold rush. On that day in August, the price of a share was offered at $28, opened at $71, rose as high as $75, and settled down, at the end of the day, to $58⅛. Nearly 14 million Netscape shares were traded in twenty-four hours, making it the most confounding debut in Wall Street history. What was even more miraculous was that the company was nowhere close to profitability at the time—and wasn't offering any guarantee that it would be soon. Investors were asked to bet on the future, and until then, no one realized how desperate they were to do so.

Netscape, the first Web browser for the general public, was a very good idea. It was followed, however, over the next few years by a lot of very dumb Internet ideas, all of which seemed to go public and all of which seemed irresistible to investors. People tried to sell pet food and groceries online. There was female-garden.com, designed to sell only female plants (the male plants, they claimed, released allergens), and cybergold.com, which paid viewers to read ads on their site. Every twenty-year-old with a business plan on a Starbucks napkin, it seemed, was out hunting for start-up money. Some had good ideas: Mark Cuban, for instance, was a forty-one-year old impatient to watch Indiana basketball online; he created a company, Broadcast.com, to do just that, and the day it went public, it was valued at more than $1 billion. Soon after, Cuban sold his company to Yahoo.com for $5.7 billion. This was, needless to say, a very inspiring story at the time.

The real darlings of this heady period were the companies trying to unite the world through Internet access or similar networks. The telecom companies like Worldcom and Level 3 had astonishing years; WorldCom stock shot from $17.50 a share in 1997 to more than $60 a share in 1999, and Level 3's share price rose from $31 past $80 a share in roughly the same period. The equipment and service companies like Cisco Systems became stars as well—thanks to its routers, the company's market cap grew from $9 billion in early 1995 to $102 billion by late 1998, and by 2000 hit a staggering $425 billion.

The big goal was to connect average consumers to the high-tech world: to provide cell phones that enabled their owners to be reached anywhere at any time, phone lines that would connect buyers to Web surfing and shopping, to movies that could be downloaded directly to their TV screens—to the enormous, seemingly infinite world of instant gratification (*Electronic tee times to golf courses around the country!*). Who cared if business was rickety or the management team didn't seem particularly seasoned? From 1995 to 2000, the Dow Jones Industrial Average jumped more than 7,000 points. The NASDAQ stock exchange, home to almost every tech stock that mattered, quadrupled in size. The tech boom and the Internet era had begun, and only a fool ignored the market.

That fool was not Joe Hirko. He was the CFO of Portland General when Enron purchased the company in 1997. At the time, PGE owned a small company called First Point Communications that owned a fiber-optic cable loop that circled Portland. Hirko wanted to run First Point, expand its fiber-optic network, and eventually spin the company off as a tech start-up. That's when he started pestering Skilling to get into telecom venture capital, the move that resulted in the Rhythms NetConnections purchase. The rest quickly became a glowing chapter in the Enron success story.

At around the same time, a trader in Enron's London office named Louise Kitchen was charged with putting Enron's trading business online. (As the overheated annual report explained, "In late April 1999 Enron's head traders sense the time is right to advance to the next level of wholesale energy transactions.") At that time, Enron traded like everybody else—over the phone, with people yelling at each other. Kitchen, being thirty-one and a stereotypical Enron VP, knew that the Internet could increase both the volume and the speed at which trades were completed, thus bringing in more business and, ostensibly, higher profits (and a bigger bonus for her, of course).

What happened next became one of the most frequently repeated tales in Enron's extensive marketing mythology: Kitchen, who had the same kind of aggressive, up-from-nothing background that so many Enronians had (except that she was British), proceeded to build the platform herself—without the approval of Enron's higher-ups. (Why she felt she needed to work around Enron higher-ups was touted but never explained.) Even so, Kitchen managed to commandeer 380 programmers, traders, and managers who, the official story goes, gave their time and effort selflessly in the service of Enron and the new world it was building.

The site launched in November 1999, and by February 2000 of the following year was processing a thousand transactions a day, valued by the company at almost $450 million. Enron Online would soon become the largest e-commerce site in the world, and it won, for Enron, another year on *Fortune*'s coveted "Most Innovative" list. And, of course, it proved invaluable to Skilling's goal of making Enron one of the leading companies in the world by turbocharging Enron's gross revenues with every click-trade. In fact, Enron's revenues more than doubled—from $40 billion in 1999 to over $100 billion by the end of 2000. By then, Enron had shot from thirty-fifth place on the Fortune 500 to seventh, and shared the top of the list with household names like ExxonMobil, General Motors, and Wal-Mart. The now impossibly rich Kitchen was promoted to managing director and trans-ferred to the Houston office headquarters. (In the future, she would prove herself a master of Enron's politics.)

It was during this time that Skilling had his change of heart about tech. Suddenly, tech was it—instead of being peripheral to the company's busi-ness, he made it core, repositioning Enron as a New Economy company. The word *pipeline* seemed like an embarassment in the 1999 Annual Report: "Enron is moving so fast that sometimes others have trouble defin-ing us. But we know who we are. We are clearly a knowledge-based compa-ny, and the skills and resources we use to transform the energy business are proving to be equally valuable in other businesses. Yes, we will remain the world's leading energy company, but we also will use our skills and talent to gain leadership in fields where the right opportunities beckon. . . ." The report continued solemnly: "We are participants in a New Economy, and the rules have changed dramatically. What you own is not as important as what you know. Hardwired businesses, such as energy and communica-tions, have turned into knowledge-based industries that place a premium on creativity."

Enron was nothing if not nimble: Integrated pipeline stocks were then trading at 18 to 25 times earnings, while tech stocks were valued at more than 40 to 60 times earnings (that is, if they had earnings at all). That was reason enough for Enron to throw over the past for a(nother) new begin-ning. As a result, First Point in Portland was shortly reborn as Enron Broad-band Services, and the company began furiously expanding its fiber-optic cable network, so that soon it stretched from Seattle to San Francisco, down through Salt Lake City and Las Vegas, and on to Los Angeles. The link between San Francisco and Los Angeles was particularly valuable; many telecom companies offered to swap space on other important routes around the country in exchange for space on Enron Broadband's California loop. In a matter of months, Enron had swapped its way into a nationwide network.

But that was just the beginning of the company's next great scheme. Enron was busy doing what it did best: buying its way into a new market by acquiring software companies (Modulus) and forming expensive alliances (Level 3 and Real Networks).

The boldest step into this new era took place on January 20, 2000, in the grand ballroom of Houston's Four Seasons Hotel, at Enron's annual presentation to the Wall Street analysts. For many people at Enron in finance and M&A units, real work had come to an end weeks before; instead, they threw all their efforts into getting ready for a grand unveiling, featuring slick interactive PowerPoint presentations, zippy videos, glossy flip books, and lofty customer testimonials ("ePower: a whole new internet experience," one DVD handout promised). "Mama's got her blue dress on," the underlings joked to one another—they were taking the company out and showing her off. But the problem was that no one knew exactly what could be put on display. Enron had been an energy company; now it was an Internet company. Because Jeff Skilling said so? Who was going to believe them? What, exactly, did Skilling plan to unveil?

Never mind that Enron had successfully charmed or bullied analysts in the past. In fact, the company had been buying them off with investment banking business for years. Goldman Sachs, Morgan Stanley, and DLJ were routinely slavish in their praise—the main holdout was John Olson, a tall, thin, mordant Houstonian ("Giacometti in pinstripes," in the words of a *New York Times* reporter) who, as an analyst for Merrill Lynch, seemed to take particular pleasure in needling Ken Lay. (It was Olson who suggested that Enron had an image problem after false reports of a trading scandal in 1995.) Olson was forever hearing from Lay and Skilling that he just didn't get it; in 1998, they finally drove him out of his job at Merrill. (Merrill executive Schuyler Tilney, husband of Enron Vision and Values queen Beth, helped to ease his exit, noting in a memo that Olson "often makes snide and potentially embarrassing remarks about the company in meetings with analysts while Skilling and Lay were present.") By then, analysts at the big investment banks had gone the way of accountants at the Big 8 firms—there was too much money at stake for honest opinions.

But on that January day, more than a few analysts were restive. Enron was trying harder, and that made them suspicious. The jazz playing over the PA system seemed a little more percussive than usual. The multimedia presentations depicting Enron's continued success seemed just a little bit frenetic. Skilling ticked off Enron's successes for the year—but everyone seemed to be waiting for something more. The usual energy analysts spied telecom analysts in the crowd. Why were they here? they wondered.

Soon enough, they got their answer. Skilling, spotlit at the podium, explained that Enron was launching something totally new. It was going to build a better, faster Internet, the Enron Intelligent Network. It was going to create a new market, one in which companies could trade space on the high-speed fiber-optic networks that coursed the Internet. Broadband technology, bandwidth trading—*five levels of service quality!*—Enron was going to do it all, bigger and better than ever. "So if you look at it, this software layer, is this a pipe dream?" Joe Hirko asked the crowd rhetorically. "Is this something that we're going to get done in the next five years? No, this is something that exists *today.*" Even if it really didn't, the stock price was jumping as he spoke.

Ken Rice, the new CEO, estimated that Enron Broadband Services was worth $29 billion to Enron. In 2000, he said, the company would have closed deals worth $54 billion. In 2001, $280 billion!

Then, as if on cue, there was a commotion in the back of the room. The buzz became a roar and rolled toward the podium. People craned their necks and squinted hard, as if they couldn't quite believe their eyes. It was a vision to make any techie swoon: Scott McNealy, the buck-toothed, irrepressible CEO of Sun Microsystems—the workstation dynamo that was eating everyone's lunch—had entered the room with his T-shirted, blue jeaned entourage and was headed for the podium. It was as if the star quarterback arrived to take a cute new freshman to the prom. The room erupted in hysterical applause.

Once order was restored, McNealy gave the analysts something to be really excited about: Sun and Enron were going to be partners. Sun was going to help Enron build its fiber-optic network, and it wouldn't be just any fiber-optic network, McNealy told the crowd. Ken Lay and Jeff Skilling just bought 18,000 of Sun's biggest, newest, most powerful servers. The stunned expressions on the analysts' faces showed they were doing the math in their heads—Enron had dropped $350 million in Sun's lap. All the Enron hype suddenly looked very real.

"Enron is a natural partner for us," McNealy explained, "because together we have the technology and expertise to transform the way that next-generation applications are developed and delivered on the Internet." He sounded as snowed as everyone else: "We also think that Enron does have some secret sauce here. That this isn't just a strict trading play and first-mover advantage."

Skilling chimed in, displaying his mastery of techspeak: "What this will mean for corporations is a new generation of mission-critical broadband applications that can be delivered to Internet customers in a secure, guaranteed, quality-of-service manner." Then he made a direct plea to the analysts: "If you in your wisdom decide to give us credit in the Enron stock for the full value of what we think is reasonable value, we're going to try to keep the companies together," Skilling said, a reference to the long-term marriage proposed between Enron Broadband Services and Enron Corporation. "If you don't, then we'll have to split them apart."

Split them apart? Was he kidding? The analysts were way ahead of Skilling at that point. Enron transformed the gas business. Enron changed the electricity business. And now it was going to change technology itself! How different, really, were phone lines from gas pipes and electric wires? And besides, Scott McNealy said Enron was okay.

The analysts could barely keep from crushing each other to get out of the room to spread the news. That day, Enron's stock moved up almost $14 a share—*25 percent*—from $53.20 to $67.25. The analysts created about $20 billion more value for the company overnight. Said Edward Tirello, Jr., an analyst with Deutsche Bank Alex Brown: "All we can say is WOW! Just when we began to ponder the potential with a very healthy skepticism, Enron brilliantly anticipated the reaction and thrust Sun Microsystems's billionaire CEO Scott McNealy into the mix." Raymond Niles of Salomon Smith Barney, said, "Trading bandwidth is a home run for the companies that traded energy commodities." Merrill Lynch's Donato Eassey added, "They said the natural gas market would not open up in the 1980s, and it has in a big way. It was the same with electricity. All the naysayers out there for broadband will be wrong too."

The hysteria over Enron's transformation taking place outside the company was also present inside the company. In January 2000, for instance, Sherron Watkins was ready for a change. When she had returned to work from maternity leave in September of 1999, she had followed her M&A

boss, Frank Stabler, and moved to the Caribbean operations. To better care for her daughter, Marion, she had also moved from commercial work to commercial support work. That meant she helped the people who did the deals instead of making deals herself; her hours were shorter, there was less travel, but there was also less opportunity. There had been cash flow in the Caribbean, and her bonus had been generous—she'd got $100,000 after her maternity leave, after expecting only $75,000—but the work wasn't really sexy or fun. Counterparties were slow to pay, and there was no real trading. Worse, Skilling was, in effect, dismantling Enron International by setting up harsh financial goals for each of the regions. Budgeted earnings were more than a stretch, new deals had to clear a 20 percent return target, and, if the regions' overall return on invested capital was not in the upper teens or better, Skilling threatened to close them down. Assets would be sold, jobs lost. It was obvious to Sherron that her job would disappear soon.

In the last four months of 1999, in fact, Sherron's Caribbean tasks were increasingly focused on window-dressing Enron's financial statements. She sold Promigas, the Colombian natural gas pipeline, to a new off-balance-sheet vehicle, Whitewing. The "sale" was in name only. Enron recorded the $136 million in cash from Whitewing as cash flow from operations, not as cash flow from money it borrowed, which in reality was more like it. One could argue—and people did argue—that one questionably designated $136 million deal didn't matter very much when Enron had more than $1 billion in cash flow from operations in 1999. But Sherron began to wonder just how many $100 million deals were designed to enhance the balance sheet in just that way.

Moreover, Whitewing's off-balance-sheet status seemed shaky. Whitewing (also known as Condor, its project name) featured an ownership chart involving more than twenty entities, most of them named after birds: Egret, Peregrine, Osprey Trust, Blue Heron, and Pelican Bidder. (The deal toy for this enterprise was a series of antique bird prints—birds of prey, of course.) But the overall entity, Whitewing Associates LP, listed Enron as both the general and limited partner. It was close to impossible to tell whether enough outside ownership existed in Whitewing to legitimately qualify it as an off-balance-sheet SPE.

The main issue was one of control—to qualify as an off-balance-sheet

SPE, control had to reside with the third-party investors. Arthur Andersen, dubious from the start, signed off on the deal only after they were shown a clause in the agreement that stipulated that the limited partners could remove Enron as managing general partner at will. That Enron was both the limited and general partner gave Andersen enough concern, however, to prohibit the company from booking any gains on asset sales to Whitewing. (Losses were fine.) Surprisingly—or not—nearly all the assets sold to Whitewing, which should have sold at market prices, were actually sold at Enron's exact book value.

Often, that value was inflated. The company had Promigas on its books at $136 million, but its publicly traded value was just over $105 million. Enron's accountants threw in a $50,000 consulting appraisal that somehow justified Promigas's worth at $134–$139 million. Whitewing was holding almost $1 billion in Enron assets. How many of its deals were as inflated as Promigas?

With the increased pressure from Skilling and his chief accountant, Rick Causey, Sherron soon found herself researching three more assets for possible sale to Whitewing. Insulated at Enron International for nearly three years, she didn't realize just how aggressive the parent company had become.

At the same time Sherron was arranging these deals, she learned that her group wanted to buy back Promigas from Whitewing at some point in the future. The company was crucial to Enron Caribbean's overall business strategy. A Colombia-to-Panama gas pipeline was planned to fuel growth along the Panama Canal Zone, and Promigas was central to those plans. At the behest of Frank Stabler, Sherron drafted buyback agreements with contract conditions that would allow Enron Caribbean to repurchase Promigas from Whitewing. Causey quickly shot them down: "No paper trail can exist with any buyback rights," he told everyone in her region.

A buyback agreement, he said, would "queer the sale treatment Enron is getting now." In other words, if they pushed Andersen any further, Whitewing would probably collapse.

The thought occurred to Sherron that it might be time to look for a job outside Enron. Her only hesitation was her desire to have a second child. Who would hire an executive who wanted an instant maternity leave?

Sherron decided to try and find something else to do at Enron for just a little longer.

Another reason she decided to stay is that Sherron's expenses were growing exponentially, just like Enron's. Her husband Rick loved his job in Canada, but it didn't help much with the bills. She'd bought herself some jewelry, they'd taken trips to Switzerland and Italy, and they'd relandscaped their backyard. She'd shelled out for some expensive portraits of her daugher Marion, bought a pricey oil painting in Santa Fe, and arranged for personalized Christmas cards. With the new baby, the new nanny, and the new house, Sherron needed to gross almost $250,000 each year, just to get by. And that was without taking high-end vacations or putting anything in savings.

So when word went out at the beginning of February that people who were ranked as 1's or 2's in the Performance Review System could go to a special recruiting meeting for Enron's new Broadband unit, Sherron started thinking. Broadband, like Enron Energy Services, was one of Skilling's pets. She heard the money was flowing there; and if she moved, she could retool her résumé for the tech business. No Internet company would hire her with her current experience, but thanks to Enron, she suddenly had the opportunity to work for one. Skilling said he'd rather teach Enron people telecom than teach telecom people Enron. She was ready and willing to be reeducated.

Around that time, Sherron got a call from a man named John Bloomer, who was already working at Enron Broadband Services. He asked whether Sherron would like to work for him in his product development group, a unit that would be working on new offerings for the Internet, like better streaming video and videoconferencing. Before moving to Enron, he bragged, he was the creator of MSNBC. Sherron figured Bloomer knew what he was doing; he wore a pager, a cell phone, and a Blackberry just to prove his connectivity. She met with him and signed on.

Then she went to the Broadband job fair—"The Quick Hire Process," as it was called around Enron—to meet her new colleagues. The fair was held in the banquet hall of the Doubletree Hotel, a building conveniently connected to Enron via walkways from the company parking garage. Sherron found herself packed into the ballroom, shoulder-to-shoulder with many of Enron's best and brightest. It felt a little like the NBA draft, only more tense.

First Jeff Skilling spoke, urging everyone to come on board. We've built a first-class luxury liner, he said. Don't worry about your seat—just get aboard! Things were going to get a little mixed up—vice presidents might wind up working for lower-ranked directors—but no one should worry. They'd sort it all out later. This was a new world.

Joe Hirko and Ken Rice, Broadband's co-CEOs, followed Skilling on stage with a repeat of the January analysts' presentation, the one that caused such a stir in the investment community. With excitement building, each business unit head from Broadband came up to sell his group. Around the perimeter of the ballroom, the Broadband executives had set up booths for the same purpose. There was a table for Broadband's new venture capital business, a table for Broadband's new finance business. David Cox, the former head of Enron's paper and pulp business, donned designer sunglasses and pushed Broadband's content group. "If you want to go to Hollywood," he crooned, "just sign up with me!" Enron, he claimed, was going to stream matches for the World Wrestling Federation and maybe even Major League Baseball. They'd already signed up AtomFilms, a Web site that streamed short films; its most famous work was about a frog in a blender, a favorite of teenage boys.

There was free wine and cheese, but everyone seemed too anxious to have a good time. One of Sherron's friends was having a small moral crisis in the lobby: She'd come to Enron because she'd believed bringing power to Third World countries was making a contribution to society. But now the CEO of the company was telling her to abandon proposals and deals she had been working on for months, to scrap them all and get to Broadband. Broadband was better for her career, but what about her foreign customers and, maybe more important, her values? Around 7 P.M., Sherron wandered back into the ballroom; another presentation had started. Kevin Hannon, the COO, was calling out the names of various employees. Who wants so-and-so? Who'll take so-and-so? It looked like an employee auction—but no one was buying. "I don't need anybody," one guy whined. "We don't have any business," complained another. "Why do we need more people?"

Just then, Hannon caught sight of Sherron and spoke to her sharply.

"Hey, Sherron. This meeting is just for EBS people."

"I've been hired," she answered. "Bloomer hired me last week."

"Just wait outside, please," he told her.

A few days later, Sherron's phone rang. It was Hannon. He didn't think she should stay in product development. Given her experience, she should be in sales with David Cox. But, she argued, she'd already committed to Bloomer, and she thought things were going well. Bloomer was from the industry. He knew the ropes. "Can't I stick with him for a while?" she asked Hannon. To herself she thought, What did David Cox know about high tech? Wasn't it better to get up to speed on the technical side before she had to sell?

In the next two to three months, Broadband grew from 300 to 900 people. Everyone was pumped. The new offices weren't to Sherron's taste, exactly—it was awfully industrial—but clearly they were cutting edge. The elevator doors to the executive floor opened to reveal a huge, glistening motorcycle called the Bandwidth Hog. Custom made by a company in Louisiana, it cost $50,000. The trading-floor lobby was nearly pitch black, with a floor-to-ceiling Lucite column illuminated with changing colors— like optical fiber color bands!—brightly announcing Enron Broadband. A fashionable Boston firm named Perry Dean Rogers designed the two floors (soon to be three) of the Enron tower occupied by Broadband. Instead of Enron Corp.'s august charcoal carpet, its black granite tabletops, and its darkly stained woods, there were knee-high file cabinets on wheels with cushioned tops (the portable cubes doubled as guest chairs) and concrete floors that evoked an e-company warehouse. Whiteboards stretched from floor to ceiling. The place was dim, the better to highlight the myriad, glowing computer screens. It resembled the interior of a 1930s insurance company or a Soviet submarine, except for the proliferation of whiteboards and the big-screen plasma TVs.

Despite the flashy offices, within a few weeks Sherron realized she had made a big mistake. John Bloomer wasn't giving her any airtime; he was missing in action for the most part, as was Ken Rice, who was always off at some car race. Bloomer had hired a second in command who passed himself off as a vice president, but he turned out to be just a director. Sherron Watkins, who had slaved her way to VP status, was working for an impostor.

Worse, no one seemed to know what they were supposed to be doing.

Associates flew off to promotional meetings and contracted for services Enron Broadband could not yet perform. Techies hired satellite companies and film crews to stream events for customers that never signed contracts with Enron. Need a dedicated line tacked up? No problem. Stream the Wimbledon tennis matches without cable over the pond? Tough, but doable. It seemed to Sherron that nobody was minding the sandbox. Shouldn't someone have signed a contract and collected a fee before a one-time event was streamed? And wasn't Enron's sales team just a little bit ahead of its technology? What good was having Wimbledon streamed to you over the Internet when all you got was the audio with still pictures?

But no one was complaining inside Broadband. Sherron felt as if she were surrounded by kids at a soccer match who were all running toward the ball; the Broadband recruits were chasing after the newest thing, with no concept of or interest in creating a sustainable business.

In late March of 2000, Enron announced within the company that it was working on a partnership with Blockbuster, the company that pioneered video rentals. The two companies would develop the technology to deliver movies into private homes via the Internet. Enron Broadband was looking at a twenty-year exclusive deal to deliver Blockbuster's movies; all Enron had to do was figure out a way to stream a movie over the Internet with VHS quality for under $1. Within days, most of Sherron's colleagues told her they were moving to the Blockbuster group. We want to be on the *winning* team, they told her. Enron was a deal shop and there was nothing bigger at Broadband than the Blockbuster deal. Sherron had been too slow to get it— Bloomer was a loser, he was on the way out, and if she didn't find something to do, she would be too.

Before she could start looking, Hannon sent a minion to say that she was being transferred to work as a business unit coordinator for David Cox, the salesman with the sunglasses. Cox wasn't good with numbers, he explained—Hannon wanted Sherron to help Cox with his business plan for content and distribution. Forget Hollywood—this would be number crunching for distribution costs, and calculating revenue on Internet wrestling events and live gospel weekends. Hannon wanted her to take an accounting role, but he didn't really need a VP in the job. Not a lot of bonus potential there, either.

But Sherron didn't have much choice: She'd already bucked the COO once, and she wasn't about to do it again. Meanwhile, she was growing more and more unhappy in her job. Broadband was filling up with young Enron Capital & Trade transfers with no institutional memory. They got priority in the unit, and they had her pegged as an Enron International loser, not realizing she'd been at Capital & Trade before they were born—or, for that matter, that Jeff Skilling had approved every one of Rebecca Mark's deals (deals they scorned) since 1997. Sherron spent a few months trying to pull together numbers for Cox's content group: How many new customers did they need to watch AtomFilms's *Frog Bender* clip before Enron earned more than pennies per month? How much revenue was needed to cover an exploding burn rate of expenses? Someone from Enron's investor relations department came to call, excited about the new business. "Where do we stand?" she wanted to know.

Sherron thought carefully before answering. "Well," she said, "we haven't signed any new customers, but we do have more distribution partners, and more Sun servers in the field." The woman seemed satisfied with Sherron's answer: *Enron was continuing to expand its network.* Investor Relations could report that thousands of additional servers were now deployed. This was, Sherron knew, essentially true. There were Enron servers all over the country. The problem was, no one knew exactly where they were, and for that reason most were not yet in service. Enron had spent hundreds of millions on equipment, and now no one could find it. Meanwhile, competing service providers were starting up every minute. How was Enron going to catch up? But Enron executives didn't seem worried. The top executives took five company jets to Hollywood for the Blockbuster Entertainment Awards.

In late September, Hannon moved Sherron again, this time to set up controls in the Network Group, which was building the Enron Intelligent Network, installing equipment, monitoring software, and streaming videos. There the technical gurus, accustomed to Enron's open checkbook, were buying equipment like crazy: Cisco routers weren't good enough; Avici made a better one. Sycamore had a great switch, but someone else liked Ciena's better. Before long, Enron's Intelligent Network, built with incompatible parts, could no longer communicate with itself.

Sherron's new job—putting in controls and saying no to people—made her very unpopular. Only Hannon, whose lack of telecom knowledge was matched only by his unpleasant demeanor, was less popular. He'd been brought in by Ken Rice, who had no experience with broadband either. Neither did Frank Bay, the man in charge of the Blockbuster deal; he was a lawyer for the pipeline company before joining Broadband.

Soon, everyone within the new division was at war: Those charged with building the network hated the Enron managers who supervised them, and vice versa. The employees in Portland who had been part of First Point Communications wanted to build a well-rounded services business centered around fiber in the ground; they hated the Enron managers in Houston, who were more interested in building a bandwidth-trading business with other companies' networks. The Houston traders kept threatening to sell the entire network, which would kill the business the Portland people had started. As revenge, Portland started throwing away contracts to keep deals from moving forward. Or they would sign a contract and not tell anyone in Houston, including the lawyers. That act of defiance would be followed by massive firings in Portland, which would be followed by more sabotage. Most of the services in place somehow stopped working.

By the end of 2000, Sherron Watkins was pretty discouraged. There was no money coming in to Broadband, but plenty was flying out the door.

Thank God, she thought, the rest of the company was doing so well.

11

Dancing on the Edge

To outsiders, Enron was doing incredibly well. The stock price split in July 1999, only to double in value by March of 2000. Its stellar performance was not an isolated incident. The entire market was berserk, with the Dow Jones climbing toward 11,000 and the NASDAQ briefly breaking 5,000 in early spring. The new wealth was creating a new society, or, rather, the celebrity culture that came of age in the 1980s went into a brief remission after the stock market crash of 1987, then came roaring back with the bull market of the 1990s. As all kinds of people made more money than they'd ever imagined—retirees, dot-comers, bartenders, dentists with good brokers—they came to desire the kind of luxuries and expect the kind of deference once reserved for movie stars, heads of state, and old money. Freshly minted Ivy League MBAs, in particular, told for years that they were members of a new privileged class, acted accordingly and demanded salaries and perks that would once have made a CEO blush.

So many people began to think that they were entitled to great wealth and its trappings that a psychiatry professor at Cornell Medical School, Robert B. Milman, gave the resultant behavior a name: acquired situational narcissism. The symptoms of classical narcissism, according to Milman, included a lack of empathy, grandiosity, and an almost insatiable need for approval. Its by-products were an inexplicable rage (when, say, you got raspberry instead of blueberry sorbet) and a peculiar social isolation (because you couldn't leave your Bel Air mansion without being set upon by paparazzi, for instance). In the past, few ordinary people fell prey to the syndrome—they weren't exposed to great wealth and so didn't crave it (there weren't magazines and television shows incessantly touting the lifestyles of stars and other insanely rich people), and the attendant pressures were unappealing.

But at Enron, being ordinary was the kiss of death, and being a star—rich, smart, and free—was everything. Ken Lay and Jeff Skilling believed that to attract the best, they had to create the kind of company that would make the best and the brightest want to leave the hippest investment banks in New York or the coolest tech companies in Silicon Valley or Seattle. In comparison, Houston and Enron were a tougher sell. To compete, Enron had to become even more generous than its most generous competitors, which, given the robust economy and the intensely competitive job market, had already converted themselves into corporate Xanadus of lavish stock options, massive bonuses, and free medical care. Enron had to go farther. Consciously or unconsciously, the decision was made to treat its most valued employees like Hollywood royalty.

At Enron, for instance, the connection between fantasy and reality grew increasingly tenuous. No one was expected to make a financial sacrifice to pursue a dream, as they might have in the real world. Salaries were high, bonuses were usually higher, and the stock options beneficent, particularly as the stock price continued to rise. But that was just the beginning. By 2000, all employees got PCs at home, high-end computers with expanded memory and Pentium chips, large monitors, speakers, CD/ROM drives, along with subsidized high-speed cable or DSL connections. (By June 2001, PCs had been ordered for 66 percent of U.S. employees—almost 8,200 machines in all.)

Domestic partners received health benefits. Family members enjoyed long-term nursing home and hospice care coverage. Enron donated $100 toward the textbooks of employees' college-age children. If your child was sick or the sitter didn't show up, you could park him at the Knowledge Beginnings Childcare Center or Kids on the Mend, or, in summertime, at Camp Enron. You could nurse your newborn in the company's lactation room.

Enron employees had their own on-site gym, with aerobics, yoga, kickboxing, and top-of-the-line weight-training machines. Cashless badges allowed workers to buy coffee at the Enron Starbucks or gourmet food at the Enron Energizer. (The Big E Café held special Friday lunches that celebrated diversity, featuring food and live entertainment from different cultures, including Asia, Africa, China, and Latin America.) Didn't have time to pick up your dry cleaning or take your dog to the vet? No problem—the Enron Concierge could do it. If you were smart enough and tough enough to work at Enron, you deserved to live like last year's Oscar winner.

Nirvana was not limited to the Houston office. Enron Europe moved its London headquarters from Millbank near the Houses of Parliament to a new office building that overlooked the gardens of Buckingham Palace. Enron christened this new base Enron House, and pointed out with uncharacteristic nostalgia that the site had once been home to the British Coal Building, England's old energy giant. England's newest energy giant occupied a six-story glass building, its impressive atrium visible from every floor, as well as from the glass-walled elevators.

In such a cushy atmosphere, Ken Lay—and, by extension, Enron—became increasingly indulgent, eerily evocative of many affluent, late-nineties parents who refused to discipline their children because it crushed their creativity and spontaneity. And like those parents, Lay and Enron would eventually discover that their progeny were not grateful but were, instead, growing ever more grasping and insatiable. The Chosen spent a lot of time and energy splitting hairs over who was the *very* best of the best, as the competition for money and power became not just brutal but baroquely brutal. The wailing at bonus time could be heard down the halls of the fiftieth floor, as one executive or another bawled about being "dishonored" by a paltry $400,000 bonus. (The caterwauling got so intense that Jeff Skilling routinely disappeared the week bonuses were distributed.)

Taking "no" for an answer was a sign of weakness. Whether it was bullying the young zombies in the Risk Assessment and Control group to sign off
on a deal—or if RAC refused, going over their heads—or arguing, as young
associates did, that their company-issued London apartment should be
walking distance to Enron House, life at Enron became a constant test of
smarts and status. As he rose up the ranks, trader Greg Whalley sometimes
switched sides in the middle of an argument, just to see if his opponent
could keep up. Another trader demanded that interviewees calculate square
roots on the spot to see if they could think on their feet like he could. There
was so much infighting over who got financial credit for a deal in the Performance Review Committee that the total amount credited to individuals
far exceeded the *total* company income for the year. Even so, everyone felt
obliged to quibble over the smallest points, because if you didn't, you got a
reputation as a chump.

The point of it all—the debating, the jockeying, the murderous politick-
ing—was to prove that you were out there, dancing on the edge, where it
was more exciting, more innovative, more *real*. Traders got big bonuses
because their jobs were, in the language of the times, "High Risk/High
Reward." In theory, executives in charge of major business units were compensated for the enormous responsibilities weighing on their shoulders—
even if their projects failed miserably. Eventually, High Risk/High Reward
came to define the Enron lifestyle around the clock: You deserved the best
laptop and hotel room because you were traveling around the world booking million-dollar deals. You deserved to cheat on your spouse because you
were so stressed traveling around the world—or holed up in front of your
LCD screen—booking million-dollar deals. On the edge, there were no
rules to constrain your thinking at the office and, as it happened, no rules to
constrain your behavior outside it. The youngest traders bought themselves
silver Porsche Boxsters and submitted $10,000 expense reports for nights at
Rick's or other Houston gentlemen's clubs. They deserved it.

It was as if they had all seen *Wall Street*, Oliver Stone's classic film about
the 1980s stock market boom, and felt compelled to replicate it for their
time. So working around the clock on a deal was not draining but glamorous. No cell phone ever went unanswered, even in the most important
meetings. ("They did all the things people do to convey that they're impor-

tant and you're not," observed someone who did business with Enron frequently.) The Porsche, the Blackberry, the Dockers, and the McMansion, the interior decorator, the art, the private schools for the kids, the trips to Bali—were more than accoutrements, they were symbols. (*Understated but flashy, rich but in touch!*) The language had to be impenetrable to outsiders, bonding to those in the know: No one at Enron would ever "build consensus," they would "come to shore," as in "We have to come to shore on this," or "Are you ready to come to shore on this?" One week somebody used the word "metrics" to mean the numbers in a deal, as in "We've got to massage the metrics!" Pretty soon, everyone was using the term "metrics" and anyone who used the term "numbers" or "calculations" was a "loser," the most popular Enron label of all.

The role models for such cultlike behavior were the people at the top, of course. As various Enron executives made more and more money, the precise definition and exact location of The Edge became ever more competitive and customized. Lots of senior executives used the company planes for personal business—Ken Rice flew to auto races and Nebraska basketball games, Rebecca Mark took weekend jaunts to her ranch in Taos, Ken Lay shipped his daughter's bed to the South of France. But there were so many more perks to demand, and each executive seemed determined to have his or her extravagance match his or her personality perfectly, like the best French couture or Saville Row suit.

The priapic Lou Pai, for instance, became The Marlboro Man. He bought one of Colorado's largest and most historic ranches, a 77,500-acre property on the West Side of the Sangre de Cristo Mountains that included the 14,047-foot Culebra Peak, jokingly referred to by the locals as Mt. Pai. (When Pai wanted to visit his Colorado ranch, he had an Enron jet fly from Houston's Bush-Intercontinental Airport to his home in Sugar Land, twenty miles away, to pick him up.) No run-of-the-mill horses were permitted on the farm he bought for his second wife, a former stripper: One equine named Gucci, after the trendy fashion house, performed at the funeral of Paul McCartney's wife Linda.

The once-homey Fastows evolved into aesthetes. They dressed in black and abandoned Houston's gallery owners for personal visits to artists' studios in Los Angeles and SoHo. They checked out the Venice Biennale, overpaid for art at auction ("They were big-dealing it," in the words of one Houston gallery owner), and subsequently loaned their pieces to the Menil Museum, long a bastion of the city's most rarefied tastes. (The loans also inflated the value of the Fastows' art, of course; Andy never missed a trick.) Subsequently, the Fastows invited the director of the Menil to serve on an Enron committee to make the corporation's collection World Class—a move that allowed the couple to meet still more artists who were likely to grant private discounts for the promise of corporate commissions.

Ken Rice, the quintessential midwestern farm boy, became the Lothario of Le Mans. He drove in Ferrari Challenge Races—"Guys who could afford not only to buy Ferraris but to wreck them," as one racing aficionado noted—and once hired the Skip Barber Racing School and rented the Texas World Speedway to teach twenty-four clients what it was like to, well, feel like him. ("I could go on a golfing or hunting outing every weekend," he told the *Houston Chronicle* at the time. "I just don't want to.") But Rice's most dangerous pastime was his affair with Enron executive Amanda Martin.

Maybe it was because the two were so glamorous—Martin was blond, Rice was seductively dimpled; they became the Enron equivalent of the head cheerleader and the star quarterback. Maybe it was because they were so flagrant in their affection for each other (Martin was divorcing at the time; Rice was not). For whatever reasons, the Rice/Martin affair captivated the company like a long-running soap opera. It was discussed, analyzed, evaluated, and used as a major distraction from real work for years. Were they really traveling together on a *business* trip? Did they really have separate hotel rooms? Was that Rice's wife and children paying a visit to his office while he was ensconced in Martin's? Would he ever really get a divorce? Coworkers could recite verbatim the angry voice mails from Martin's ex-husband; executives gleefully recounted spats aboard a company plane.

Finally, the inevitable occurred. A longtime subordinate of Rice's complained to him about Martin and soon found himself ousted from the company. He sued, allowing even more information about the couple to become part of the public record. (Drinking with the employee at the Peninsula Hotel in New York, Rice admired the large breasts of a woman passing by, bemoaning the fact that Martin's weren't that size. Once he realized what he had said, Rice then threatened to fire the employee if he repeated the remarks. Martin had previously told the same employee that Rice was very jealous—she had stopped at her ex-husband's house to discuss their two children, and after a few too many glasses of wine, decided to sleep on the sofa. Rice showed up at six in the morning on his motorcycle, revving the engine until the neighbors came out into the street.)

That this behavior might be bad for company morale, or bad for business—that it might interfere with making money—never seemed to occur to anyone in upper management. Or it did occur to people at the top, but they were compromised. With an extramarital past of his own, Ken Lay didn't have much clout in this department, and the same was true of several other high-ranking Enron executives. On the other hand, fidelity may have been a part of the old world that Enron held in such contempt.

The person who seamlessly combined Enron's passion for the future with personal excess was, in fact, Ken Lay himself. He had evolved from humble beginnings into an insatiable connoisseur. He owned houses in Galveston and Aspen. Enron paid $7.1 million for an entire floor at the Huntington, a River Oaks high-rise, which Lay and his wife then converted into a Venetian palace with dark woods, deep velvets, period statuary, and vaulted brick ceilings in the kitchen. On one European trip, several passengers were ejected from the corporate jet and sent home on a commercial airliner to accommodate Linda Lay's purchases.

But Lay's biggest extravagance was Houston itself. Here his role model was George Brown, the LBJ confidante and the creator, with his brother, of the construction behemoth Brown & Root. An incomparable philanthropist, Brown ran Houston with an iron fist from the fabled suite 8F at the Lamar Hotel, where he met with his cronies in business and politics to decide what was best for the town. Following in that tradition, it was Enron that underwrote the *Star Wars* show at Houston's Museum of Fine Arts. (The space Enron occupied as underwriter took up almost as much space as the show). It was Enron that secured the right to name the magnificent, new baseball field in the center of town. Lay was a major donor to the Holocaust Museum, and even though Enron had only one black member on its board and one black managing director (from commercial support, no less), Lay became a hero to the African American community, a friend to the leading black ministers in town, a godfather to local black businessmen. When the once-brilliant Congressman Craig Washington stumbled in office, it was Lay who, with powerful allies, handpicked his replacement, City Council member and master of the photo op Sheila Jackson Lee. (The black community retained a House seat, and Enron got another loyalist.)

What Lay bought with his largesse was something far more important than a fast car or a cutting-edge painting, he bought silence. The local news media only reported on Enron's good news. Ken Lay was a good guy and Enron was a great corporate citizen, and Houston was all the richer for both.

And so the excesses grew. Cliff Baxter, promoted to Senior VP of Enron North America, treated himself to mogul-sized yachts. Jeff Skilling went ice climbing in Patagonia. Only those who went to extremes were really worthy of the Enron name.

For people so enthralled with the cutting edge, they were surprisingly disinterested in social change, with the possible exception of Lay. In their private lives they weren't interested in new ways of thinking, new ways of being, new approaches to life or society. They spent, and they consumed.

Life was a game, the goal of which was to see how much could be extracted without ever paying up. They came of age in a time of much affluence and little peril, and they were now starring in their own action adventures, romantic comedies, or financial thrillers. And when and if the bills came due, well, hey, they could just stick the audience with the tab.

Jeff Skilling had only one problem during this heady time. Enron was growing exponentially, but so was its overhead—the gargantuan salaries, the bountiful benefits, the start-up costs of Enron Energy Services, Enron Broadband, and Enron Online. Meanwhile, very few business units other than the West Coast trading outfit and the dependable pipelines were actually bringing in cash.

Particularly problematic was Azurix, Rebecca Mark's water company, which she continued to run while Skilling busied himself dismantling the remnants of Enron International. He had tried to drive her off for years by making it crystal clear that he had no use for her business philosophy; her hard assets, he complained incessantly, were a terrible drain on Enron's bottom line. He pounded on her in meetings: "The organization has no confidence in you"; "Your deals don't make any sense"; "You can't get your skirt high enough to get out of this one." But Lay remained loyal to Mark, and Enron, which worked hard on its image as the most progressive company in America, was not about to invite a media disaster by firing its highest-ranking female executive.

So the opportunity to buy Wessex, the British water company, seemed a win-win deal for everyone back in 1998. Mark got the mother of all severance packages with the $2 billion acquisition, and Skilling assumed he would soon be free of his nemesis. Members of the Enron board opposed such a huge investment, but Skilling, uncharacteristically, pushed hard for the deal. His support should have been a warning to Mark, but she never seemed to notice that whenever Skilling was at his most helpful, he was also at his most dangerous.

She was still trying to figure him out. Mark, who retained her seat on the board, questioned his numbers in front of other members—"Explain to me how these sectors of the business will grow," she'd say, pointing an impeccably manicured finger at a set of figures she'd compiled with the help of a friendly Enron accountant. "Tell me how and why." But the board wasn't interested in what she had to say. Enron was trading near $80 a share, Wall Street loved the company and Jeff Skilling, and so, in turn, did they.

Azurix was formed in July 1998. Ken Lay made glorious pronouncements: "Currently, there are only a handful of large private-sector companies operating in the U.S. $300 billion worldwide water market, and there are tremendous opportunities for future growth as the water industry moves toward privatization and consolidation," he declared. Mark claimed that water was the commodity of the next century; she enticed hordes of Enron employees to join her crusade with promises of generous compensation and stock options. Azurix developed a flashy water-trading Web site, Water2water.com, to give the company a techie gloss. Around the clock,

Mark extolled the potential of her new company, making grand entrances at water conferences in miniskirts and mink coats, insisting, in front of the old-timers, that Azurix could and would save an antiquated business from itself.

Consciously or unconsciously, she was experimenting with Skilling's business model. Azurix would take over the water business, then create a trading organization that would make it the (very profitable and powerful) middleman between the parched and the inundated parts of the world. Once a believer in long-term growth, Mark now sold investors on a strategy of speed—she promised Enronlike returns within one year. To deliver, she embarked on a massive buying spree, one that would show the kind of expansion that would satisfy the high price-to-earnings multiples required of Wall Street stars. In addition to the Wessex purchase, she spent hundreds of millions on water companies in Argentina, Mexico, and Brazil. She met with Florida governor Jeb Bush to try to cut a deal to buy the excess water pumped from a refurbishment project in the Everglades. Her strategy appeared to pay off: In June 1999, with the stock market soaring, the Azurix IPO raised almost $700 million. Mark, already a rich woman, looked as though she would become even richer: Her salary alone was $710,000 a year, and she had also been granted half a million shares of Azurix stock, along with numerous options.

But Mark had walked blithely into a trap: Skilling structured the deal so that Azurix was required to pay back Enron's initial investment immediately after the IPO. Mark, wanting her freedom, agreed to the terms. In order to get the stock to open at $19 a share, Mark had promised steady growth; and to show it, she needed to spend all the money she'd raised buying new water companies. Now she was legally bound to return more than half of what she'd raised in the IPO to Enron. In other words, she was launching her new business the Enron way: starved for cash. Jeff Skilling repeatedly insisted that Mark could not run a business—now he was going to prove it to the market. He had promised her exactly one year of Enron's support, and no more. Now he sat back and waited.

By the fall of 1999, the company was already on the ropes. Every time Mark tried to buy something, her two major competitors, the French giants

Vivendi Environment and Suez Lyonnaise des Eaux, stepped in to drive up the price. (She had overpaid by $150 million for a water business in Argentina, just to ensure that she got it.) Meanwhile, as Enron was privately pushing Mark to grow to maintain Wall Street's interest, the company was publicly distancing itself from Azurix; its press and public relations efforts were much more focused on Broadband, giving the impression to potential investors that Azurix was an afterthought.

Mark exacerbated the problem. She was incapable of behaving like the penny-pinching CEO of a start-up: Azurix's downtown offices were outfitted with stately limestone floors, fine woods stained a regal red, sprawling oriental rugs, and Asian art. A spiral staircase connected two floors. Mark had four secretaries poised outside her office. Before long, she was being derided on Yahoo message boards as "Ms. Galore," a reference to the extravagant Bond girl in *Goldfinger* with the racy first name.

Then the problems really started: Azurix's collection system didn't work in Argentina. Wessex was accused of price gouging. The *Miami Herald* lambasted Enron's proposed involvement in the Everglades. (The Florida legislature's Everglades committee called it "the most sinister business proposition the state has ever had.") Worse, Mark soon ran out of things to buy: Small municipalities in the United States, in particular, weren't ready to give up their water to a private sector company, especially one with Enron's aggressive, customer-be-damned reputation. In Wall Street parlance, Mark's growth story had stalled, and worse, she was short on cash to operate the companies she owned. Skilling was routinely apprised of the problems but did nothing to help. As one Azurix executive explained: "Once he knew what he had to do to make Azurix succeed, he made sure it would never happen."

Mark retreated, ignoring the advice of the experts she'd brought in, berating them for not being smart enough to find solutions to the company's problems. As 1999 drew to a close, Azurix was forced to warn investors that it would not make its earnings for the fourth quarter. The result: Azurix stock fell 40 percent in one day. The analysts turned on her soon after. By the spring of 2000, most of Mark's trusted staff members moved on, including her CFO. A last-boat-out mentality set in, as Enron refused to take back any of the employees who had left for Azurix. The water company became, in the words of one former employee, "a bunch of kids fighting among them-selves for the right answers." Mark lost heart—she had married in October of 1999, and, shocking executives who were still trying to save the company, now interrupted strategy meetings with ideas for cookie bakeoffs and other morale boosters. By August 2000, she was ready to surrender.

In her final meeting with Lay in his fiftieth-floor aerie, he treated Mark like a stranger. This was not the kind of meeting he enjoyed, and now he had bigger things on his mind. Lay had spent much of the past year building another power base for himself—driving his own executives to donate ever more money to Texas governor George W. Bush's presidential campaign. By the summer of 1999—the same period that Bush deregulated electricity in Texas—Enron executives had contributed more than half a million dollars to Bush's campaign, and Lay had been named a "Pioneer," one of the sup-porters who personally raised at least $100,000 for the candidate. (On open-ing day at Enron Field, Lay hosted both former president George Bush and current governor George W.) Clearly, Lay was angling for a big job in the new administration, should Bush win. Rebecca Mark and Azurix were threatening not just his company but his future.

Because of that, there would be no last, leisurely tea in fine china cups, no gratitude expressed for Mark's eighteen years with the company. She was no longer the fresh young executive Lay put through Harvard, the glam-orous international CEO who finessed his meetings with prime ministers and other heads of state; today, she was a loser. She had moved too slowly and, in his eyes, cost Enron a fortune. She had betrayed him.

Lay was just as chilly toward his old protégé in public as in private: "A lot of capital has been chewed up," he told the *Wall Street Journal*. "I think it's best for Rebecca to start afresh." Mark cut one last deal for herself: She con-vinced Enron to release her from her noncompete clause and promptly started a water company of her own. Then she sold all her Enron stock, worth $80 million. It would prove to be one of the smartest business deci-sions she ever made.

The same *Journal* story that announced Mark's departure touted Skilling's brilliant rise at Enron. There was Broadband to look forward to; bandwidth trading, the article asserted, was generating $150 million in rev-enue. There was Enron's great new deal with Blockbuster to deliver movies on demand. Skilling was triumphant in print, eager to move full-bore into the future he was devising. "We will tie up capital only where there are high rates of return," he told the *Journal*. Enron's multifaceted trading business, he said, gave Enron "a once-in-a-lifetime opportunity to establish a position to last for the next 100 years."

But, with Mark gone, Azurix became his problem. As the water company's stock price continued to fall, investors grew restive with Enron—it was on Enron's reputation that they had poured money into Azurix. If it continued to founder, how long would it be before the press and the investor community—and the banks—started asking whether Enron's winning streak was coming to an end? Or, worse, what if investors started asking whether Enron had hyped a venture simply to unload it?

Skilling tried to keep all the Enron plates spinning: the rocketing stock price, the innovative reputation, the generous lenders, and the rosy press clippings. Azurix's rocky future threatened all of that. So in October, he did what he had to do—he bought silence by buying Azurix back for $275 million, or $7 a share.

The Azurix buyback intensified Skilling's constant search for cash. He had ordered the sale of all the South American assets in late 1999 under the code name Project California, but the market was saturated with just such assets and no buyer could be found. Next, nearly all the operating foreign assets were thrown together in a project known within the company as "Project Summer" and "Desert Lightning." The deal looked great. It involved a group of senior Enron International executives who would manage the new acquisitions for investors from the Middle East, headed by an advisor to the president of the United Arab Emirates. But the transaction became enveloped in a financial fog: The sheik in charge became deathly ill, and his partners wouldn't move without him. Then Skilling and Baxter began to suspect that the group didn't really have the $7 billion they'd initially promised, and called off the deal. Again no replacement buyers could be found. Another rush effort to sell some Brazilian assets collapsed when Joe Sutton, who had been involved in most of the foreign asset sales, resigned.

Then an agreement to sell Portland General, the Oregon power company, for more than $2 billion—a deal that had been signed in November 1999—faltered. Meanwhile, expenses at Enron Broadband Services kept rising, though few people seemed to mind. Once the unit was up and running, Skilling expected it to start throwing off millions, if not billions.

Tech's big skeptic was evolving into its biggest cheerleader. Months before the analysts' meeting in January 2000, McKinsey had warned Skilling against putting Enron on the broadband bandwagon. Gas pipelines were different from fiber-optic cable, they argued; in this arena, Enron wasn't first into the market. Moreover, the Internet was a service-oriented business, which Enron didn't seem terribly interested in or particularly good at. Further, McKinsey calculated the cost of streaming a movie into a private home at $70 per film. Where was the market for that? Finally, success was predicated on a partnership with the major phone companies, whose desire to form an alliance with Enron was, as yet, unproven.

But Skilling was suddenly determined, and so were his loyalists. "You just don't get it," Ken Rice, Broadband's CEO, insisted to one McKinsey analyst. The tired old telephone companies like SBC, Atlantic Bell, and AT&T didn't get it either, he said. They were just as dim-witted and self-satisfied as the old gas and electric utilities. And at the January analysts' meeting, McKinsey's doubts were drowned out by the analysts' hurrahs.

Over the next several months, Enron signed more and more deals, and Enron's PR department released a veritable blizzard of press releases. "Roadshow.com chooses Enron to deliver financial Web content," ran a February release. In March they announced, "Enron to broadcast international cricket tournament." A month later, they crowed, "Enron teams with Compaq to provide capacity for one million simultaneous broadband streams of Windows Media Player." And in July, the multimillion-dollar deal with Blockbuster to provide online movies was rolled out to much ado. Ken Lay called the deal "the killer app for the entertainment industry." John Antioco, CEO of Blockbuster, called it the "ultimate bricks-chicks-and-flicks strategy." Enron's Web site had a Blockbuster portal through which visitors could watch a preview of a movie as if it were being streamed to them. Meanwhile, back in Houston, an actor in a Darth Vader costume patrolled the lobby touting the deal.

By then, Enron's broadband venture was already in trouble. For months, the company had been able to generate income by swapping portions of its dark fiber network (dark, because the system was not yet operating, or lit) with those of other companies. These transactions were sometimes called "Barney deals," after the popular children's character who, at the end of each show, sang "I love you, you love me."

The going swap rate was $1,500 per route mile, though most companies, Enron Broadband included, actually built their networks at a cost of closer to $300. With broadband companies swapping route miles that cost them a fifth of the price, these deals provided both parties with fabulous revenues and profit (even if they had no effect on cash flow). But then the market became saturated, and Enron Broadband ran out of partners. It faced the threat of missing its earnings targets. The burn rate for Broadband alone was almost $500 million annually. Wall Street was not expecting it to show a profit, but it was expecting the unit to meet its loss targets of $100 million. Now Enron Broadband had to find $400 million just to hit that number.

In June, stuck with excess product and no possible buyer, Enron turned to the only person who could offer financial salvation: Andy Fastow. But with the close of the quarter rapidly approaching, Fastow was balking at spending $50 million on dark fiber as an investment for LJM2. Enron Broadband's accountants made frantic calls begging for the cash, but he refused to budge. Finally, they made one last call and reached Fastow on the golf course. He demanded a 10 percent up-front fee from Enron to sign off on the deal. Told that wasn't possible, Fastow had a message for the company's accounting chief: "You tell Rick Causey to get his fifty million somewhere else."

Eventually, however, Enron Broadband Services did sell the dark fiber to LJM2 at $100 million, enabling Enron to beat its earnings targets by two cents for the second quarter of 2000. After a great deal of internal debate, this transaction was disclosed in the second-quarter 10-Q, filed with the SEC on August 14, 2000. According to a related-party footnote, "In June 2000 Enron sold a portion of its excess dark fiber inventory to the Related Party in exchange for $30 million cash and a $70 million note receivable that matures in seven years and bears a market rate of interest. Enron recognized gross margin of $53 million on the sale." The admission was unusual for Enron, accustomed as it was to keeping as much financial information to itself as possible. No one thought it might be a red flag to Enron's critics, and in fact, nine months would pass before anyone noticed.

The Blockbuster deal, arguably Enron's most glamorous, was quickly sullied in the close-of-quarter grubstakes, too. Within months of the public announcement, it was sold to a special-purpose entity set up by Fastow's minions. The investment banking branch of the Toronto-based Canadian Imperial Bank of Commerce paid $115.2 million to, in essence, buy Enron's future earnings from the deal for the next ten years, allowing Enron Broadband to book $110.9 million in profit for the last quarter of 2000 and the first of 2001. Yet the Blockbuster partnership was going nowhere. The major phone companies, as McKinsey predicted, were not at all interested in helping Enron with its plans. By December 2000, Enron Broadband had two buildings in two cities that were actually streaming movies—to a total of 300 customers.

Worse, Enron Broadband had picked the wrong partner for movie "content." Hollywood hated Blockbuster. Blockbuster rentals provided Hollywood with substantial revenues—on most movies, nearly two-thirds of a film's total profits. (Only the real blockbusters generate lots of cash; most movies recoup their costs and make money on video rentals.) Blockbuster used its advantage over the years to negotiate hard for its share of the rental profits. If a studio didn't cooperate, it would soon find that new shipments of recently released films weren't showing up on Blockbuster's shelves. "Must still be in transit" or "We're busy unloading shipments" would be Blockbuster's reply to their complaints.

As a result, the studios had no intention of giving Blockbuster the digital rights to its movies. They'd whisper to the Enron Broadband team that they wanted EBS for distribution, but Blockbuster added nothing to the package. Blockbuster, on the other hand, felt Enron was pushing too hard and too fast—Blockbuster had made the deal, essentially, to keep *its* competition out of the movies-on-demand market.

Quietly, Enron Broadband started looking around for a new partner— without informing Blockbuster, of course. They set up camp at the Beverly

Hills Four Seasons and eventually struck up a relationship with Michael Ovitz. Once king of the Hollywood agents, the former Disney number two was now struggling to start a new business—sort of a combination studio/agency—and was suffering revenge at the hands of the very people he had exploited on his way up. Enron saw opportunity with Ovitz—maybe he could be the Hollywood partner they so desperately needed.

Several meetings followed. Ovitz got along well with Lay; the Enron CEO was folksy and self-effacing, a perfect counterpoint to Ovitz's samurai stance. But Skilling was another matter. The men were practically psychic twins—both were spectacular marketers and world-class narcissists. The power struggle between them began almost immediately. Skilling challenged Ovitz on his financials, and Ovitz challenged Enron on its business plan: Didn't they get it? Making movies was an even bigger gamble than trading energy. Soon after, Enron abandoned Ovitz and continued its search for Blockbuster's replacement.

Then, in November 2000, Skilling got some more bad news. He claimed that an anonymous letter from an employee in India informed him that Rebecca Mark's showpiece—the phase II expansion of her power plant in Dabhol—was collapsing. This venture was supposed to have been history-making, on the order of the Suez canal; it was to link a Middle Eastern liquefied natural gas operation with one of the largest power plants in the world, certainly the largest on the subcontinent. The only problem was—as the World Bank had warned and as the letter now stated—the project had gotten so large that the Indian government could no longer afford the payments and was on the verge of defaulting. Lay thought Enron should renegotiate. Skilling refused: The Indians didn't have the money to pay. Two of his executives, he insisted, had hidden the real costs from him. He wanted to stop construction and walk out on the deal in which Enron had invested, by then, close to $1 billion.

At around the same time, Enron faced yet another crisis with its foreign investments—a cost overrun on a project called Cuiaba came to $300 million. Skilling went to the board and got permission to spend the money that had already been spent.

It was about this time that he walked into an executive committee meeting and told the assembled that Mark's investments had cost Enron four years of income—close to $2 billion. (This wasn't entirely true. Skilling was a master of histrionics. Mark's roughly $6 billion of international assets would likely fetch only $4 billion in a fire sale, a $2 billion loss that would be incurred by Enron only if it chose the fire-sale route.)

When Skilling made a tally later that year, combining the project debt from international with the project debt from Dabhol and the project debt from Azurix, he came up with $11 billion. Skilling did not stress that this amount was non-recourse and therefore not a problem for Enron's shareholders. He just kept complaining about Mark while he continued to ignore the growing, multi-billion-dollar debt created off the balance sheet by his CFO Andy Fastow.

Knowing all that he knew, Jeff Skilling went to the November management meeting and promised his executives that the stock price would jump from $84 to $126. He claimed that the meltdown of telecom, which had started slowly in the spring of 2000 and was gathering momentum, was actually good for Enron. It meant the company could grow faster by buying failing companies cheaply. In addition, West Coast trading was still bringing in billions.

He waited, while Lay retired from media interviews and weathered the election crisis of 2000. Finally, the long-anticipated announcement was made: "The best time for the succession to occur is when the company is doing well," Lay told the press. "Enron is doing extremely well now." He intended to step down: In February 2001, Jeff Skilling would take over as CEO.

Enron made its annual earnings targets at the end of 2000, thanks largely to Enron Online and power trading in California. Among the accountants at Arthur Andersen and at Enron, the company's continued success became an ongoing joke. It was like auditing Sybil, one Andersen accountant liked to say, referring to the movie character with multiple-personality disorder. The traders were making so much money, they were stuffing it in drawers and under mattresses—even in reserve accounts—in order to lower revenues, so that Enron didn't look like Bandits, Inc. Meanwhile, the accountant continued, everyone else in the company was pulling lint from their pockets and trying to say it was worth something.

12

No Harm, No Foul

WHILE Jeff Skilling was trying to transform Enron into an Internet company, dispatch Azurix, Dabhol, and Rebecca Mark, and keep Wall Street happy, Andy Fastow was solidifying his long-coveted power base. This work started in earnest in June 1999, immediately following the Enron board's waiver of its conflict-of-interest rules on Fastow's behalf. In September of that year, Fastow hit the road, touting his much heftier LJM2 fund at a meeting with Merrill Lynch in the North Tower of the World Trade Center. He carried with him a chart titled "Why LJM2 Is Unique," which listed the following attributes:

1. Preferred access to proprietary deal flow
2. Enron and its investments have significantly outperformed the market
3. Investments analyzed/operated/structured by Enron
4. Ability for LJM2 to evaluate investments with full knowledge

5. LJM2 speed and knowledge advantage
6. Financial expertise of principals

Merrill was the perfect choice for Fastow. In the world of investment banking, its close-a-deal-at-all costs mentality nearly matched Enron's, and, like Arthur Andersen, its association with the company was so close as to be incestuous. Relations had been improving since 1998, when Ken Lay successfully bullied Merrill into eliminating the cantankarous analyst John Olson. The Enron relationship manager and head of Merrill's energy investment banking unit, Managing Director Schuyler Tilney, was good friends with Fastow, while Tilney's wife, Beth, remained at Enron and was a particular favorite of Ken Lay's. In general, Enron got what it wanted from Merrill, and vice versa.

The Wall Street bankers gathered around a conference table while Fastow made his pitch. He wore an Italian suit with very broad shoulders; despite a five-o'clock shadow, he looked like a little boy wearing his big brother's clothes. Fastow folded and unfolded his arms as he spoke, paced, and grimaced. When he became particularly anxious, or when he stressed a point, he whistled when he pronounced his "s"s. Michael Kopper rode shotgun at the presentation: Seated at the conference table in crisp white shirtsleeves, he was calmer and more confident, breaking in ("What Andy means is . . ."; "I think what Andy is saying is . . .") when his colleague seemed to falter.

Fastow explained that being CFO of Enron was "as good a CFO position as anyone in America could have," but that it was, for him, really just a stepping-stone. He wanted his own investment business, "and this is a unique opportunity to set it up with unique access to deals and to develop that track record I need to develop. . . . Let me say I can do twice better than anyone else since I will have better information than anyone else."

There was light laughter in the room, the kind you hear when people can't quite believe what they're hearing. "The business units own their assets at Enron, manage their portfolios, manage their risks in their portfolios," he continued. "Do I know everything that's going on? Do I sign off on every deal that goes on there? Yes. So I'm in the unique position of not having the ownership or the responsibility or obligation to sell assets, but I know everything about them and I've been involved in their approval and maybe in their structuring."

That last statement raised a question from a Merrill banker who spoke in a British accent. "Isn't your privileged position of having better information than any other bidder going to deter other bidders?" he asked.

Fastow shook his head definitively. "Really, it isn't," he said, unfolding his arms and beginning to pace. "It is in Enron's best interest because Enron needs the capital, number one, okay? They want to expand their businesses. . . . Number two, I'm not going to buy a deal and pay a lower price than someone else would pay in the market. It's that simple. So think about it as no harm, no foul. Even if someone three years from now comes back and says LJM2 . . . LJM2 earned a 300 percent internal rate of return, [then] Enron must have sold those deals at the wrong price. It was the best price in the market that they could get. We have competing quotes to validate it. So, again, if I didn't earn 300 percent, someone else would have earned 310 percent."

Anyone troubled by potential conflicts was not voicing them. "Do other bidders that are out there know that there's an insider there that can . . . have this opportunity?" another Merrill banker asked. "Are they aware that you're there? Or is this sort of like going to an auction?"

"It's like an auction," Fastow explained. "It's . . ."

"Where there is a house bid on the inside and you don't know what that house bid is?" a Merrill banker added helpfully.

"That's right," Fastow replied.

LJM2 offered a perfect opportunity to get inside information on Enron's best investments was what Fastow was saying, even if he didn't put it exactly that way. "The principals have all been involved in virtually all aspects of the fund business. That's a little hard to read," he said, "but I think you get the idea."

"We've been doing this for a while. We've been together as a team for a while. And I think we understand the issues that our investors will have, and the philosophy is generally to address those issues before they become issues."

In fact, Fastow was addressing "issues before they became issues" long before his LJM2 presentation to Merrill Lynch. It was true, as he claimed, that he knew about every deal at Enron: As CFO, no deal could be closed without his approval. At the same time, many Enron executives believed that Fastow was using the Performance Review Committee process (and its accompanying bonuses) to pressure people into dealing with LJM2 and to punish those who held up deals with his fund.

By early 2000, it was the most direct path to success inside the company. Even if you didn't like Andy—and by now a great many people didn't like him, because he was bullying Enron executives along with the bankers—you still had to make your earnings targets to survive at the company. If you couldn't find a buyer for an asset sale (and selling assets was the name of the game under Skilling), or you couldn't close a finance deal before the end of a quarter, well, now LJM2 was an option. It would buy what needed buying, or finance what needed financing—in other words, LJM2 would help you close the deal, hit the targets, and, of course, win the bonus.

Over time, this strategy applied outside Enron as well as inside Enron: There was a growing assumption among the bankers that the quickest way to get Enron's business was to invest in LJM2. Like many of the investment structures Fastow created, this one was byzantine but enormously benefi-cial—all roads, no matter how bumpy or circuitous, led to him.

LJM's gloss was even slicker than Enron's. With his promotion to CFO, Fastow begrudgingly ascended to the fiftieth floor (he hated to leave his team on twenty-eight), but he adapted quickly to the trappings of power. He installed video art in his office. He created the Fastow Family Foundation, which by 2000 had $4 million in the bank. He was active in causes like the Interfaith Ministries for Greater Houston. He bought a lot on one of the best streets in River Oaks. And he upgraded his Italian suits. Michael Kopper took on similar coloration: He bought property in Avalon Place, adjacent to River Oaks, in the shadow of Ken Lay's high-rise condominium. He met reg-ularly with his personal trainer. His decorator worked magic on the bland Enron office appointments, using his myriad deal toys—the antiqued globes, the kaleidoscopes with semiprecious stones—as focal points.

Even the administrative assistants in Fastow's world seemed better and sleeker than the ones at Enron: Kopper's secretary was as glamorous as a soap star, with long legs, glistening white teeth, and a flawless, Amazonian physique. He rewarded her hard work with Prada bags and gift certificates to local spas and, as a bonus, a long weekend to the locale of her choice, all expenses paid.

But the secrecy that had always surrounded LJM increased along with its glamour. This was so because Fastow and Kopper's ever-growing wealth had less and less to do with their talents as salesmen. By 2000, Andy Fastow was an expert at gaming Enron's system, with Michael Kopper his willing accomplice.

Their work started with the RADR deal in 1997. In that transaction, Fastow loaned money to Michael Kopper, who in turn loaned the same money to friends—those Friends of Enron that included Fastow's realtor and also Kopper's domestic partner, Bill Dodson, who then "bought" the wind company from Enron. RADR generated about $2.7 million in distributions to its investors, and when Enron eventually bought the company back in July 2000—as Fastow knew it would—the investors received about $1.8 million, portions of which went back to Fastow and Kopper. RADR was a small deal by Enron standards, but it served the purposes of the company's CFO: It was a trial run for bigger scams.

In December 1997, Kopper routinely passed on a portion of the management fees he received from the Chewco deal to Fastow and his family. A year later, Fastow demanded that Enron pay a $400,000 "nuisance fee" to Chewco for amending the JEDI partnership agreement in *Chewco's* favor. In turn, Kopper wrote personal checks for about $67,224 to Fastow and his family as part of that transaction. Everyone was having a good time: As early as 1998, Kopper's domestic partner, Bill Dodson, was e-mailing Lea Fastow, the $54,000 a year "assistant," with the message "Send lots of $$$$$$$!"

Then, in June 1999, Fastow found a much bigger opportunity, when Skilling became determined to hedge the Rhythms NetConnections windfall and the CFO became his enabler. In creating his first LJM fund, Fastow took on two limited partners, Credit Suisse First Boston (CSFB) and National Westminster Bank (NatWest). Each invested $7.5 million in the deal. Then he created a subsidiary of LJM, called Swap Sub, to issue the put on Rhythms Net stock that had so confused Vince Kaminski. Swap Sub was backed with Enron shares. (Again, this was a problem that concerned Kaminski and virtually no one else.)

By the first quarter of 2000, Enron stock and Rhythms Net stock were soaring, and so was LJM and Swap Sub, the entity supporting the put. This happy situation coincided with a problem facing three British bankers who represented one of the limited partners. The trio, Gary Steven Mulgrew, Giles Robert Hugh Darby, and David John Bermingham, were legendary in both England and the United States, at least partly because their exploits were chronicled by author Robert Kelsey in the British best-seller *The Pursuit of Happiness* ("Overpaid, Oversexed, and Over There"). Like his colleagues at Enron, Mulgrew, head of structured finance at NatWest, had a reputation as a visionary. "He kicked out the go-home-at-five gang and turned us into a forward-thinking department," Kelsey later wrote in Mulgrew's defense. Darby, a specialist in energy transactions, was, according to Kelsey, the "hatchet man. Mulgrew would see we'd need to get through a door and Darby would find a truck and rev hard." Bermingham, head of the structuring group, was the smoothie. In Kelsey's words: "Just as the door was about to be flattened Bermingham would say, hold on, I can pick the lock." All three enjoyed honorary good-ol'-boy status in Houston—they mastered golf course and topless bar etiquette, skills that mattered when it came time to do business. But in the fall of 1999, the cheery trio learned that NatWest was facing a takeover and they were facing unemployment. Their mood turned uncharacteristically somber.

There was some coinciding good news: NatWest netted over $20 million in profit on its $7.5 million investment in LJM. NatWest also had an interest in LJM's Swap Sub, but the bank considered that worthless. The bankers thought it was a good time to liquidate Swap Sub. In January 2000, Bermingham noted to Darby that, with Enron selling at $60 a share, the bank's interest in Swap Sub was "very valuable." According to e-mails later retrieved by the U.S. Department of Justice, the trick would be "in capturing it"—for themselves. "I have a couple of ideas," Bermingham wrote, "but it may be good if I don't share them with anyone until we know our fate!!"

By February 19, the men came up with at least one way to snare that value—they scheduled a meeting with Andy Fastow about restructuring Swap Sub. "The story looks compelling, and even Andy would have trouble arguing that the benefit split is anything other than equitable," Bermingham wrote. "For your info, our minimum profit per these slides"—a reference to his PowerPoint presentation—"would be $8 m, rising to $17 m for the middle bit, and then finally up around $30 m. Everybody wins."

One day later, Bermingham and Mulgrew were busily e-mailing again, this time about Fastow's take. "If I knew there was a realistic way to 'lock in' the $40 m and give him $25 m, we would also jump all over it I guess, since it would give us $15 m. . . . I will be the first to be delighted if he has found a way to lock it in and steal a large portion himself." Knowing his quarry, Bermingham added, "We should be able to appeal to his greed." In the meantime, they were busy writing phony e-mails to throw curious NatWest colleagues off the track. "Large numbers of people are asking what we are up to," the prolific Bermingham wrote. "I hate lies." They told one colleague that they were flying to Houston for a secret deal, but that he should not tell anyone and "just act dumb, please" if inquiries were made.

Three days later, Mulgrew, Darby, and Bermingham did in fact travel to Houston to make a presentation to Fastow and Kopper. The group experimented with several ideas, including one that involved selling Enron stock held by Swap Sub and then buying it back a few days later; this process would convert that stock from partnership property, which Fastow could not access, to so-called substitute property, which he could. According to the presentation shorthand, those present deemed this scheme "too obvious (to both Enron and LPs) [about] what is happening, i.e., robbery of LPs, so probably not attractive." Worse, there was "no certainty of making money." At a partnership dinner in the Cayman Islands on March 4, Fastow pulled Bermingham aside and said that he had to "move quickly." At around the same time, Kopper wrote in his work notebook, "Gary Mulgrew—spoke to AF, everything moving as planned."

Mulgrew then went back to his employer, NatWest, and spun his tale: Enron wanted to unwind the Swap Sub transaction and buy out NatWest's interest; NatWest should take the deal, he urged, because it was worth $1 million. This sounded like free money to NatWest. Along with the $27 million, they were going to get $1 million more? *Great!* They would probably have been less cheerful had they known their interest was really worth around $20 million.

On March 7, Kopper sent a letter to Darby formalizing the deal—Enron would buy NatWest's interest in Swap Sub for $1 million. Creating a nice paper trail, Darby then forwarded the agreement to Mulgrew, urging him to sign on. They even waited three days before formally agreeing to the deal.

In mid-March, Kopper created a new entity, the Southampton K. Co., which borrowed $750,000 from Kopper-controlled Chewco. On March 20, Mulgrew, Darby, and Bermingham signed an agreement with Kopper and Fastow that allowed them to buy a piece of the new company for $250,000. Southampton K. Co. now had $1 million to buy NatWest's interest in Swap Sub. A few days after that, Bermingham went to Mulgrew, his boss, and gave notice.

Soon after, Darby resigned from NatWest. (*Oh, you know, I just want to take time off, relax in the sun . . .*)

Near the end of April, the three men wired $250,000 to Kopper in Houston to buy into Southampton K. Co.

On April 28, Mulgrew was in Toronto when he got a call from Andy Fastow. Congratulations, he said, you just made $7 million! Mulgrew waited two more months before following his colleagues out the door. (*Oh, you know, take time off, relax in the sun . . .*)

Meanwhile, in Houston, parallel transactions took place as the spoils were divided among Fastow loyalists. Michael Kopper, who contributed $25,000 of his own money, received, for his labors, $4.5 million. Another investor, the Fastow Family Foundation, put in $25,000 and received $4.5 million. Two other Enron employees—attorney Kristina Mourdaunt and the team's head accountant and rising star Ben Glisan—each contributed $5,800 and walked away with $1 million. Two others contributed a couple thousand dollars each and got in return a couple hundred thousand. The whole deal took only a few short months, as winter turned to spring.

Such easy money might have raised questions among the recipients, and sometimes it did. "Andy says it's okay" was Kopper's routine reply to one worrier.

But most of the time, no one worried. "Did you ever believe you'd be so rich so young?" Kopper asked Ben Glisan, who could only shake his head, amazed at his luck.

In the spring of 2000, Jeff McMahon, then the treasurer of Enron, was not a happy man. This was not his normal state. McMahon was Irish to the bone—wide-eyed, broad-nosed, with wispy blond hair, ruddy cheeks, and an impish air. Regardless of his exalted status within Enron, he was the kind of guy everyone wanted to have a beer with after work at Keneally's Irish Pub, a dark, homey dive between downtown and River Oaks that seemed to be on every Enron executive's drive home.

McMahon was an Arthur Andersen alumnus—back in late 1987, he was one of those dispatched to investigate irregularities in Enron's trading operations in Valhalla, New York. Once at Enron, McMahon worked his way up through the ranks. Hired as a business unit coordinator in the accounting department, he supported Fastow's team early on, helping Michael Kopper monetize trading contracts in 1995. He was then dispatched to the company's London office, where he made a name for himself with the famous FAS 125 structure (the one that allowed Enron to book future profits on hard assets like power plants immediately, instead of booking them over time). McMahon left Houston as an accountant and came back less than three years later as a sort of überbanker, having made a lot of money for Enron and himself. In Europe, downtime included relaxing aboard bankers' yachts in the Mediterranean. Upon his triumphant return stateside, he installed a floor-to-ceiling glass cabinet in his Houston office, just to show off all his deal toys.

As treasurer, McMahon displayed a talent for cheerleading, his gift of gab winning over the skeptics. In January 2000, for instance, he successfully lobbied Standard & Poor's to upgrade Enron's credit rating from BBB to BBB+. In his PowerPoint presentation, he made light of Enron's lack of transparency, a growing issue on Wall Street. McMahon displayed a cartoon that parodied Enron's obtuse annual reports by showing a man trying to read one, with the caption: "Hmmm . . . Off-balance-sheet debt, structured finance, nonrecourse debt, guarantees . . . Can they make a more confusing annual report?" His next slides included what he called a "Kitchen Sink Analysis of Enron," though that, too, was accompanied by a humorous disclaimer. "Enron does not recommend using this analysis for anything other than illustrative purposes and for the purpose of concluding that the off-balance-sheet obligations are not material to Enron's consolidated credit analysis." The slide ended with the phrase "Cigarette smoking may be harmful to your health."

He could joke about Enron because, as the rest of his presentation showed, Enron was a thriving, robust company with a 39 percent growth rate in North America, a 50 percent growth rate in Europe, fantastic opportunities in a deregulating market in Japan, and so on. Enron was the number-one energy company in North America, was among the top three in Europe, and, in company-speak, was "The Energy Franchise." Enron, according to McMahon's presentation, could boast "credit-conscious management" and a "stellar reputation in bank markets," along with a $50 billion market capitalization.

Contrary to rumors, Enron did not have massive amounts of debt hidden from its credit profile, he continued, and its cash flows were stable and predictable. Management, he claimed, was extremely accessible. Communication with analysts, investors, and credit officers, he asserted, was direct and candid. Enron, he said, had a No Secrets policy.

More than anything, the presentation revealed McMahon's ability to play the good soldier. When Enron's trading shop faced its 1999 earnings crisis, for instance, McMahon came up with a novel solution. He approached Merrill Lynch and suggested that they purchase three Enron barges containing electricity generators that were floating off the coast of Nigeria. Enron was trying to sell the barges to a third party to generate cash, but the deal was dragging on, endangering the sale and increasing the likelihood that Enron Wholesale—the successor to Enron Capital & Trade—would not make its end-of-year earnings targets. Hence, the McMahon solution: Merrill could buy the barges from Enron until the deal with a *real* outside third party was ready to close; then Enron would buy them back from Merrill. It would allow Enron to make earnings in 1999 and generate a tidy fee for Merrill to boot.

Merrill, in this instance, did not jump at the chance to help Enron. The deal wasn't exactly a loan, but then, it wasn't exactly a sale, either. There followed much discussion within the investment bank about the deal—Enron was an important client, but the chairman of the company, James A. Brown, hated the transaction, and there were particularly expensive risks associated with going along. As one employee described the problem, in notes that would eventually wind up in the hands of a Senate investigative committee, "reputational risk i.e., aid/abet Enron income stmt manipulation . . ."

But Enron was a good customer, and that mattered at Merrill. Argued investment banker Robert Furst, in an interoffice memo: "Enron is a top client to Merrill Lynch. Enron views the ability to participate in transactions like this as a way to differentiate ML from the pack and add significant value. I completed several financings like this at CSFB and they all worked to CSFB's advantage. I strongly recommend we complete this transaction." (In fact, Furst and Tilney initially worried over the Fastow LJM conflict but calmed down after a reassuring meeting with Skilling in 1999. Then, too, Merrill's fees from Enron since 1997 were approaching $40 million.) So, when Merrill asked for Fastow's guarantee along with McMahon's that the barges would be bought back within six months, they got it. And Merrill would make $250,000 on the deal, a small fee by their standards, but a fee nevertheless, along with a 15 percent rate of return. (Eventually, another $725,000 or so would come their way.)

So, in late December, Merrill created a company called Ebarge and bought the three barges for $28 million. Enron booked $12 million in profit from the deal immediately, money that helped the company hit its earnings targets at year's end. And McMahon, along with Fastow, were heroes, a standing that was presumably reflected in their subsequent bonuses.

But for all his hard work on Enron's behalf—his cheerleading and his rescue efforts—McMahon was uneasy. He thought of creating an investment fund within Enron for Enron, but Fastow beat him to the punch with LJM, followed closely by LJM2. As time passed and Fastow's power grew, McMahon complained to several people about Fastow's conflict of interest. More and more, the two men seemed set on a collision course. Enron employees began complaining to McMahon about their negotiations with LJM2; Andy, they said, would punish them in the PRC if they pushed too hard on a deal for Enron that ran counter to the interests of LJM2.

McMahon also heard from bankers, who were getting the distinct message that they needed to provide debt financing to LJM2 in order to keep Enron's business. Someone from Merrill Lynch called to ask whether McMahon thought it was a conflict to invest in LJM2. When McMahon said that it was, he subsequently got a call from Fastow, who complained, in a torrent of obscenities, that McMahon was jeopardizing his business. In a short period of time Merrill Lynch invested $5 million, and 97 of its executives invested $16 million with the fund. A banker from First Union called McMahon to be sure that investing in LJM2 guaranteed him a place in the next Enron bond deal; that's what Andy told him. It occurred to McMahon that had he known that LJM2 was going to grow so big and influential, he would have opposed it at the finance committee meeting when it was pro- posed. Instead, he kept his mouth shut and lived to regret it.

Since 1999, Fastow had been running a bifurcated division—there was finance, under McMahon, and there was LJM, under Kopper. When the two came into conflict, it was no longer a mystery who would win. For instance, McMahon proposed closing out Chewco in early 2000, and sug- gested $1 million as the price Enron would be willing to pay Michael Kop- per for his general-partnership interest in Chewco. The need to keep JEDI/ Chewco off balance sheet was not as great then and the administrative costs of running the separate entities could be eliminated with a buyout of Kop- per's interests. Fastow came back with a number that was much higher— $10 million—and said that he personally would handle the negotiations with Kopper. He did. Kopper got $10 million.

In early March, a dispirited McMahon ran into Cliff Baxter at a party. Bax- ter was then vice chairman of Enron, and it was well known, as Skilling would later testify before Congress, that Baxter and Fastow detested each other. Talk to Jeff about your Andy problem, Baxter urged McMahon. Noth- ing would change unless he did. A week or so later, McMahon had a meet- ing with Greg Whalley, then in charge of Enron Wholesale. Whalley had heard that McMahon was unhappy working for Fastow, and he suggested McMahon move into a group he was starting, Enron Networks. McMahon turned him down. The job, helping to start a group related to e-commerce, didn't appeal to him. He didn't see much room for another tech business at Enron given the existence of Enron Online and Enron Broadband.

McMahon continued to stew. He talked things over with his wife, men- tioning the obvious consequences of going to Skilling with his complaints about his boss: If Fastow found out, McMahon knew, Fastow would try to get him fired.

Even so, McMahon finally made an appointment with Skilling, and he started making notes in preparation. On a legal pad he scrawled a list: "Untenable situation, LJM situation where AF [Andy Fastow] wears two hats." "I find myself negotiating with Andy on Enron matters and am pressured to do a deal that I do not believe is in the best interest of the shareholders. . . . My integrity forces me to continue to negotiate the way I believe is correct. In order to continue to do this, I must know I have support from you."

Two days later, at 11:30 A.M. on March 16, McMahon ascended to the fiftieth floor for his meeting with Skilling. He made his pitch: Enron employees were negotiating against LJM2 representatives, and yet they all reported to Fastow. To him, that seemed a major conflict.

Skilling sat quietly during his presentation, almost preternaturally still. At the end of the meeting, he simply said that he understood McMahon's concerns and would remedy the situation. Then it was over. McMahon had no idea where he stood.

A short time later, however, he got a call from Joe Sutton, who shared the vice chairman's job with Cliff Baxter. (The Ejection Seat was becoming an Ejection Sofa.) Sutton told McMahon that Skilling had asked him to look into the matter. McMahon met with Sutton and repeated his concerns. Sutton tried to dismiss McMahon, assuring him that Fastow stood to make more as Enron CFO than he would from some small private investment partnership. "Are you sure?" McMahon asked. Had Sutton seen Fastow's take home pay from LJM? Once Sutton understood that Andy might make as much as $20 million, maybe more, from LJM, he was dumbfounded. "That's more than I make, that's more than Lay makes, that's more than the two of us make combined!" He assured McMahon that he would pursue the matter further, but Sutton was gone before that happened.

Two weeks after the Sutton meeting, McMahon got a call summoning him to Fastow's office. When he arrived, McMahon found his boss pacing the office, red-faced, furious. He didn't know whether the two of them could work together anymore, Fastow told McMahon coldly. He knew that McMahon had gone to Skilling. Didn't he realize, Fastow said, that everything McMahon had said to Skilling got back to *him*?

McMahon trudged back to his office, demoralized. A few hours later, Skilling called him. There was a job at Enron Networks McMahon should really consider taking, he said. It would make better use of his skills. Jeff

McMahon, whose future at Enron had once seemed so promising, agreed without argument. (Asked about the encounter at a Congressional hearing, Skilling would recall that McMahon was solely concerned about his compensation. It was reflective of the Enron mind-set that many at the company agreed.)

Three months later, in McMahon's wake, Merrill anxiously reminded Enron of its commitment to find a buyer for the Nigerian barges. Enron did so; the buyer, they said, would be LJM2.

There was a superficial meekness to Jordan Mintz that belied his dogged nature. Mintz had been a tax lawyer for many years, and the precision required by that role clung to him—he wore his dark hair slicked neatly off his pale, scholarly face, he wore a T-shirt under his natty silk sport shirts, and he had a wit that was drier than a 1040 form. But the combative cadences of Brooklyn were audible even when Mintz spoke in his usual soft tones, and when he encountered something nonsensical, he puzzled and pushed and probed until he could get an answer that satisfied him.

The entire twenty-eighth floor of Enron, in fact, did not make sense to Mintz, which was a shame, because he had worked very hard and sacrificed much to get there. He left a big Houston law firm called Bracewell and Patterson to join Enron, and once there he labored in Enron's tax department under Robert Hermann, whose flamboyant eccentricities clashed with Mintz's natural reserve. Offered a job in Fastow's Global Finance— the latest name for Andy's fund-raising unit—Mintz jumped at the chance. He had met Andy Fastow socially several times, and liked him. And, of course, Fastow was going places, which meant more opportunities for Mintz.

He joined Global Finance in October 2000, his introduction to the job a brief and largely uninformative meeting with his predecessor, who never bothered to mention LJM. Mintz started inspecting his files and found a substantial amount of documentation regarding this unit. That discovery inspired him to begin performing what he liked to think of as his "due diligence."

Mintz had barely begun the new job when a senior attorney in the unit told him that a member of his legal staff was about to be fired. In short order, Michael Kopper and Ben Glisan appeared in his office and told Mintz to get rid of a particular attorney. They felt he was unresponsive to a deal involving LJM2. "You just hired me," Mintz told them. "Let me do my job and do my own assessment."

Mintz met with the lawyer, who told him he'd received an expletive-laced voice mail from Fastow about the deal he was working on. ("You motherfucking, goddamned son of a bitch, why are you trying to change the deal?" or words to that effect.) Ultimately, Mintz shuttled between Fastow and the attorney and made peace. But the obvious conflict between the needs of Enron and those of LJM2 bothered Mintz, and he subsequently met with Rick Causey, the chief accounting officer, and Rick Buy, the chief risk officer, to share some of his concerns about what he had begun to think of as the "dysfunctionality" on the twenty-eighth floor. Mintz was finding it next to impossible to tell the Enron employees from the LJM2 employees. The two groups, which were supposed to operate as separate entities, were openly negotiating with each other—sometimes a husband and wife sat on opposite sides of the table—often with inside information. Fastow was supervising employees as CFO while those same employees were negotiating against LJM2 on behalf of Enron. It was not sensible. What did Causey and Buy think, Mintz wondered, about going to Skilling with his concerns?

"I wouldn't stick my neck out" was Causey's reply. Jeff is very fond of Andy, they told him. "Don't go there."

Still, the situation nagged at Mintz.

In December, he sent a memo to Causey and Buy, noting clear conflicts of interest in a document being prepared for new investors in Fastow's next venture, LJM3. In carefully worded language, on Enron stationery bordered with the words "Respect," "Integrity," "Communication," and "Excellence," Mintz noted that Fastow was touting his dual role at Enron, stressing his insider status and knowledge of proprietary deal flows. "Due to their active involvement in the investment activities at Enron, the principals will be in an advantageous position to analyze potential investments," Fastow had written in promotional materials for LJM.

Then, too, Mintz was concerned that Skilling had not yet signed the

LJM2 approval sheets, as had every other officer at Enron. Again, Mintz went to Causey and Buy, who suggested he send Skilling a memo as a reminder. Skilling never responded. Mintz called Skilling's secretary to get on the schedule, but she never responded. Leave it at that, Causey and Buy told him. But he couldn't.

13

Coming Undone

I T was not exactly a secret that Jeff Skilling was miserable as the CEO of Enron—he made few attempts, in fact, to hide his growing frustration with the job. But few people chose to acknowledge that situation within the company. Maybe they knew how damaging it would be to Enron if word got out. Maybe they hoped he would rein in his increasingly erratic behavior after a period of adjustment.

He didn't like the ceremonial aspects of the job. He didn't like meeting with every single charity in town. He didn't understand why Enron had to be involved in so many good works that did nothing to make money. In his off hours, the CEO of the country's seventh-largest corporation was hanging out in the college bars around Rice University, drinking heavily, making passes at coeds half his age. Or he was taking long lunches with his girlfriend, Rebecca Carter, the board's new $600,000-a-year Corporate Secretary, at La Griglia, the Italian restaurant that was the midday canteen for

Houston's business and political elite. Skilling seemed to be doing anything he could to avoid the downtown tower at 1400 Smith.

The problems started almost as soon as Ken Lay began to talk about a succession plan in the late summer and early fall of 2000. From then on, Skilling's ambivalence grew. He had wanted the COO's job partly because he couldn't stand the thought of working for anyone else at Enron. Now he caught himself wishing that Lay might decide to stay on, leaving Skilling to collect the $25 million "Kinder clause" written into his contract.

But this time Lay seemed serious about leaving, and Skilling was left with a To-Do list that was, in a word, harrowing. The work included:

1. Fixing the billion-dollar bad-press problem that was India.
2. Fixing Enron Energy Services, which looked to have at least half a billion dollars of "mark to the model" gains on the books that might or might not materialize.
3. Revamping Broadband, which was foundering badly and might wind up a $2 billion disaster instead of the company savior Skilling was banking on.
4. Preventing a growing energy crisis in California from turning every man, woman, and child against energy deregulation and stanching Enron's enormous cash flow from that state—as well as Enron's growth plans for the rest of the country.
5. Getting Enron's stock price up, because if the price fell below a certain level, debt acceleration triggers in various Fastow-generated off-balance-sheet vehicles would be dangerously close to activation. If the triggers activated, $2–$3 billion would become due immediately, resulting in almost certain bankruptcy. A very bad way to start as CEO.

With such vexing problems looming, Enron's first real order of business, as 2001 dawned, was a public one: to keep the face it turned to the world—and to its employees—rosy and forward-looking. That meant perpetuating the momentum established at the November management conference—the one that included those car races through the streets of San Antonio, and the high-stakes gambling; the one at which Jeff Skilling promised that the stock, now at $67 per share, would go to $126.

In the self-involved psyche of Enron, it was time for a new mission statement. Once, Enron strived to be The Premier Natural Gas Pipeline in North America. It accomplished that goal in a blink of an eye. Then Enron wanted to be The World's First Natural Gas Major. That was accomplished too. Then Enron set its sights on becoming The World's Leading Energy Company, and aced that. "Our vision is clear," stated a press release announcing Enron's next step in February 2001. Enron was ranked sixth in revenues among the S&P 500, tenth in revenues among the top fifteen global companies, number one in compounded five-year revenue growth, and first in revenues per employee. There wasn't any discussion of the difference between revenues and profits, or asset size, of course. In any ranking by assets or earnings, Enron would never land anywhere near the top. But it didn't matter: Enron's new goal was going to be, as its new mission promised, The World's Leading Company.

The executives had, in fact, considered many other phrases before settling on that one. Skilling and Lay liked The World's Coolest Company (Lay joked about topping the Enron building with a pair of giant sunglasses), but the phrase didn't translate internationally. And so "Leading" it was. At a floor meeting, Skilling said he was glad he wouldn't have to change his license plate, WLEC, which once stood for World's Leading Energy Company. It could now stand for "We Love Enron Corp."

To anyone who wasn't inclined to probe very deeply—and few people inside or outside Enron were so inclined—things did look pretty good. First, a former Texas oilman was in the White House. Even if in the new Republican shorthand Lay wasn't as close to "43" as he had been to "41," he was there on George W. Bush's inauguration day, beaming in the rainy chill from his seat in the Pioneers' Box, the one reserved for those who raised $100,000 for Bush's campaign. (The total for the entire corporation amounted to several hundred thousand dollars, thanks to Lay's constant memos urging management to contribute.) Lay also provided an Enron jet to get George and Barbara Bush to the event on time. Enron donated $300,000 for the inauguration alone, and anted up $50,000 to be sure that the Texas State Society's 2001 Black Tie and Boots Inaugural Ball was everything it should be. There was a private luncheon at the White House to attend, an Enron-hosted dinner for several loyal congressmen. At every company function, Lay put in an appearance—radiant, pressing the flesh, puncturing the air with his sharp, affectionate bark. "Having a Republican administration is good for Enron. I'm glad to have gone to Washington to make sure that it went off without a hitch," Skilling told his employees subsequently.

From the inauguration, Lay flew to the World Economic Forum in Davos, where he hobnobbed with the likes of Michael Dell, the CEO of Dell Computer, and Carly Fiorina, the CEO of Hewlett-Packard. He lunched with Vicente Fox, Mexico's new president, and with the chairman of Korea's SK corporation, Tony Chey. He attended roundtables on "World Economic Brainstorming" and "The Shape of the Twenty-first Century Corporation." Davos was like a great college seminar, but with more powerful people, and Lay was a BMOC.

Over the next few weeks, in fact, about half a dozen graduates of his institution started packing for Washington, most notably Tom White, the vice chairman of Enron Energy Services, nominated to be secretary of the army. Lay was on the President's transition team; everyone from Dick Cheney to Don Evans returned his phone calls promptly. People thought it was only a matter of time before Lay himself headed for the capital, and he did nothing to dissuade them from that notion. When he didn't get treasury secretary, employees were sure he'd be appointed ambassador to the Court of St. James.

There was more good news from California—at least, if you worked for Enron. For residents of that state, life was getting perilously similar to that of Maharashtra, the Indian state in which Enron's Dabhol plant was situated. There were power blackouts and soaring prices—wholesale electricity rates were rising astronomically. California Edison defaulted on over half a billion dollars' worth of payments. In other words, the state faced economic and social chaos.

But in Texas, inside the halls of the great new energy trading companies—El Paso, Reliant, Dynegy, as well as Enron—the story was much more cheerful. Energy company profits were up 100 percent to 400 percent over the year before—the result of good business, energy companies claimed. In Texans' eyes, those selfish, spoiled Californians were getting what they deserved. As Ken Lay told the head of the Los Angeles Department of Water and Power, who at the time was begging the federal government for price controls while Enron was forcefully opposing them: "Well, Dave, in the final analysis, it doesn't matter what you crazy people in California do, because I got smart guys out there who can always figure out how to make money."

Enron had done its homework in Washington. Help came largely from the husband-and-wife team of economists Senator Phil Gramm and his wife, Wendy. Before joining the Enron board, Wendy Gramm had exempted energy futures contracts from government oversight in 1992; her husband now pushed for the Commodity Futures Modernization Act in December 2000, which would deregulate energy trading. There was strong opposition to Phil Gramm's bill in the House, mainly from the President's Working Group on Financial Markets, who included Secretary of the Treasury Lawrence Summers; Alan Greenspan, the chairman of the Federal Reserve; and Arthur Levitt, chairman of the SEC. But Enron spent close to $2 million lobbying to combat that opposition, while Gramm kept the bill from floor debate in the waning days of the Clinton administration. He reintroduced it under a new name immediately after Bush assumed office and got his bill passed. Enron, in turn, got the opportunity to trade with abandon. No one needed to know—or could find out—how much power Enron owned and how or why the company moved it from place to place.

Business at Enron was good all around, especially if you were an executive. In 1997, upper management had introduced something called the Performance Unit Plan, which promised managing directors and above enormous bonuses if Enron's return to shareholders by 2001 ranked in the top six companies on the Standard & Poor's Index. Enron did it—tech stocks failed in 2000, but Enron soared, from $22 to $72 a share in the last three years of the decade. (A stockholder who invested $1,000 in Enron in the three-year period from 1995 to 1997 would have seen only a 9 percent return, while someone who invested from 1998 to 2000 would have received 55 percent.) If, as some would later claim, the bonus plan served as incentive to shave a few corners or push beyond the boundaries of acceptable business practices, no one was looking inward just then.

The rewards from the Performance Unit Plan were mind-boggling, even by Enron standards. Andy Fastow added $1.7 million to his annual take-home pay. Skilling's bonus check was close to $2 million, and Ken Lay's was

$3.6 million. Michael Kopper's PUP check approached $600,000. The people who could have put the brakes on Enron's runaway financials got their fair share of the bonus pool too: Chief Accounting Officer Rick Causey and Chief Risk Officer Rick Buy added $350,000 and $760,000 respectively to their take-home pay. The general counsel of Enron Corp., the man minding the store, Jim Derrick, took home a Performance Unit Plan bonus of nearly half a million dollars.

Even in these good times, however, Vince Kaminksi was not an optimist by nature or experience. The head of research had a brief but frank conversation about Fastow's LJM2 partnership with Rick Buy in June 2000, after Buy had groused about buying a new fax machine for his summer home in New Hampshire because he had to sign so many DASHs—deal approval sheets—for Fastow's partnerships. LJM2 was ginning deals at a spectacular rate, and it destroyed the serenity of his downtime. Kaminski didn't have much of a reply, except to remind Buy that he believed the conflict inherent in LJM could destroy them both. To Kaminski, LJM's implosion was only a matter of time, but no one in high places listened to him anymore; since he had refused to help create Fastow's partnership, he remained in exile.

Then, in January of 2001, Kaminski was called back into service when Buy asked him to analyze some cross-guarantees—promises from one entity to pay the obligations of a sister entity—among some LJM2 entities called Raptors, named after the predatory birds. (This was a rare occasion when popular culture and Mother Nature coincided; a bird-loving attorney, not Fastow, chose the name of the fund.) The Raptors were conceived in 1999, coinciding with Skilling's desire to hedge the value of Enron's equity merchant portfolio—those investments in oil and gas companies, power companies, tech stocks, etc., whose value soared and was marked accordingly. Ben Glisan, a former accountant, devised the hedge structures with the approval of Arthur Andersen and the attorneys at Vinson & Elkins. They took flight in April 2000. Talon, as this first Raptor partnership was called, was (true to Enron form) mind-numbingly complex. In the first step, a subsidiary called Harrier was created, through which Enron contributed $1,000 in cash, a $50 million promissory note, and stock and stock contracts worth $537 million. LJM2 put in $30 million cash and was the manager of the deal and the sole equity owner.

The deal was, on its face, more advantageous to LJM2 than Enron—"remarkably favorable" in the words of an investigative report that would appear the following year. Enron paid all of LJM2's legal fees, accounting fees, and a management fee of $250,000 a year. More important, LJM2 had the only real cash in the deal, and Fastow demanded that he get his cash and return *first*—about $41 million. No real hedging could be done on Enron's merchant portfolio until that happened, he insisted.

To pay off Fastow, Glisan came up with the idea of a put option that, through another convoluted series of deals, funneled the $41 million to LJM2. LJM2 subsequently reported a return to its investors of 193 percent. But there was a problem no one seemed to notice at the time: Once LJM2 got out, there was no outside equity in the deal and Talon/Harrier no longer qualified as legitimate SPEs. Contrary to generally accepted accounting principles, Enron was hedging with itself. Even more potentially perilous, the portfolio was hedged completely with Enron stock. As long as that stock continued to rise, there was no problem (from an investment standpoint, at least)—there was plenty of money to protect the value of the portfolio. But what if Enron stock went down?

The Enron board did not know all the details of this transaction. Ben Glisan made one presentation on Project Raptor to the board in May of 2000, noting that the project did not "transfer economic risk but transfers P&L volatility." No one probed further. At the same meeting, Rick Causey assured the finance committee that Andersen was comfortable with the proposed transaction. Glisan also presented a chart that showed the three principal risks of Raptor:

1. accounting scrutiny
2. a substantial decline in Enron stock price
3. counterparty credit

He had solutions for every problem. In the first case, Causey and Andersen approved the transaction. Second, if the stock price declined, Enron could negotiate an early termination of Talon with LJM2. As for credit, the assets of Talon were subject to a "master netting agreement"—meaning that amounts owed Enron for hedges on poorly performing assets could be offset by gains on hedges on the stellar assets. (No one knew that only poorly performing assets were hedged with Talon/Raptor/LJM.) The finance committee approved the deal that day, and the full board signed off the next, May 20, 2000.

The board authorized two more Raptors in late June. In one meeting, Andy Fastow told a board committee that a second Raptor was needed because "there had been tremendous utilization by the business units of Raptor 1." At the time, however, there had actually been none (the fund was just generating cash for Fastow). Skilling was supportive; minutes showed that he spoke in favor of a subsequent Raptor transaction because it would "provide additional mechanisms to hedge the profit and loss volatility of the company's investments."

Raptor III was born in September of 2000. Unlike its predecessors, it was created to hedge a single new venture: Lou Pai's retail electricity spin-off, The New Power Company. Pai had belatedly realized sometime in 1998 that Enron was not cut out for the residential business, as it required inordinate attention to customer service. Since then, he'd been working on this new venture, and in November 1999 formed The New Power Company by folding in Enron Energy Services' retail efforts to date. Then he added a new team that included retail experts from AT&T and Visa/MasterCard, and impressive equity sponsors, IBM and AOL, along with Enron itself. There was such enthusiasm for this venture at Enron that employees were offered the chance to buy into the IPO at $10.75 per share, even though the estimated public stock price was $18–$20.

Naturally, Enron anticipated the value in The New Power Company and did a small private equity offering in late 1999, with DLJ Merchant Bank, GE Capital Corp., CalPERS, and the Ontario Teachers' Pension Fund. The latter two groups appeared to swap their ownership interests in Enron Energy Services, acquired in January 1998, for ownership stakes in The New Power Company. The transaction was further complicated by an SPE called Cortez that included LJM2 as an investor.

These steps appeared to have been taken so that Enron could recognize earnings in 1999—the company reported that Enron Energy Services brought in nearly $42 million on its New Power investment that year. Another private offering in mid-2000 generated more earnings, but not enough to satisfy Enron. The monetizing magic of FAS 125 was drafted into service to bring more cash and earnings into Enron Energy Services. Still more of Enron's ownership in The New Power Company was carved out and put into a series of SPEs under the project code name of Hawaii 125-0. All of these maneuvers provided Enron with gigantic profits in New Power Company while the latter was still, basically, a subsidiary with a few minority interest owners. In addition, these gains were booked long before New Power's IPO and well in advance of Enron's ability to actually sell its interest to true outside buyers. The whole enterprise flew in the face of established accounting principles, too.

New Power's IPO in October 2000 was promising. It opened at $21 a share and closed at $27 on the first day of trading. Enron owned approximately 40 percent of the New Power company with a cash investment of next to nothing. Of course, Enron immediately marked that investment to market—between the private stock offerings, the FAS 125s, and the fair value accounting, Enron booked over $250 million, all of which went to the struggling Enron Energy Services. Naturally, this led many investors to read the financial filings and believe that EES's facility-management business had finally turned the corner.

As he had with other gains, Skilling wanted to lock up the New Power increase. Once again, he called on LJM. It donated the necessary funding, $30 million, to create yet another Raptor (Raptor III). Then, in what had become standard operating procedure, LJM2 got its profit out—$39 million within one week—and promptly vanished from the scene, leaving New Power and Enron alone with their "hedges."

Then the trouble really started. After just a week of trading, New Power's stock value fell below $10 a share. This was a problem because the Raptor III contracts specified that if the stock price of New Power fell below a certain level, "triggers" in the contract would require Enron to start making up the shortfall. This was the difference between Raptor hedges and conventional hedges. Normally, as New Power's stock price declined, Enron would book a loss on its New Power investment but an offsetting gain from its hedges. But the ingeniousness of the Raptor structure required Enron to support the gains on the New Power hedges too. There was no hedging going on because Enron was on the hook on both sides. This was, to say the least, unusual.

This situation particularly bothered a young Enron attorney named Stuart Zisman. In the late summer and early fall of 2000, when the Raptors were being created, Zisman was almost as worried as Vince Kaminski. Among the problems he listed in a memo to his superior were these: "overall book manipulation, breach of confidentiality obligations, insider trading and liability . . ." He worried, too, about the quality of the investments in the partnerships: "Our original understanding of this transaction was that all types of assets/securities would be introduced into this structure (including those that are viewed favorably and those that are viewed as being poor investments). As it turns out, we have discovered that a majority of the investments being introduced into the Raptor structure are bad ones. This is disconcerting [because] . . . it might lead one to believe that the financial books at Enron are being 'cooked' in order to eliminate a drag on earnings that would otherwise occur under fair value accounting . . ."

The trouble was, the Raptors, like the rest of LJM2, had become something of a dumping ground for bad properties. In an effort to make quarterly earnings (and, of course, annual bonuses), Enron originators were hooked on making deals with Fastow instead of outside third parties—who would have asked a lot of questions, slowed down the process, and, in many cases, killed deals. Again, none of this mattered to most people at Enron, as long as the stock kept rising.

Zisman, however, sent his memo to an Enron lawyer who had requested his opinion. She then directed him to the general counsel of Enron North America, a man named Mark Haedicke. Zisman and Haedicke had a brief conversation—ten to fifteen minutes—during which Haedicke scolded Zisman for using inflammatory language in his memo. Then, nothing. (Only later would Haedicke's lack of interest in Zisman's concerns make sense: Haedicke received almost $1 million under Enron's Performance Unit Plan in early 2001; an investigation into Zisman's concerns during the summer of 2000 just might have resulted in a stock price decline, for which neither man would have been rewarded.)

By the end of 2000, Zisman was looking awfully prescient. Raptors I and III developed credit problems—the Raptor portfolio was heavily weighted in tech stocks, and the tech bubble began to burst, causing the value of the Raptors to fall. Raptor III contained nothing but New Power hedges, which were moving in only one direction, down. At the same time, Enron's stock price began to slip—not seriously at first, but seriously enough for people at the company to see that if Enron stock declined at the same time as the Raptor hedges, Enron was going to have a hard time covering the Raptor losses.

So, under intense pressure at year's end, Enron and Andersen accountants modified the Raptors ever so slightly, "cross-collateralizing" all four with each other, so that the weaknesses of Raptors I and III were obscured behind the health of Raptors II and IV. No one mentioned this Herculean task to the board. There were, after all, no losses to report.

But in the first quarter of 2001—Skilling's first in the CEO job—Enron's stock stopped its flirtation with decline and went into a full-scale slide. It opened the year at $84, then soon fell to $72, then to $67. It finally ended the quarter at $58. Enron was then owed more than half a billion dollars by the Raptors. Unfortunately, they couldn't pay. The only good news was that the hedges weren't due to expire anytime soon, so the Raptors didn't have to pay up immediately. But Enron knew they weren't credit worthy—to the tune of almost $200 million. The credit department followed strict internal control policies; Rick Buy would have to write down the company's receivables from Raptor, incurring a big loss in Skilling's first quarter at bat. This may be why Rick Causey, along with a few others, would recall that Jeff Skilling was "intensely interested" in a restructuring of the Raptors in early 2001. In fact, several people who worked closely with Skilling at the time felt that fixing the Raptors was one of his highest priorities.

His concern may also explain why the Raptor returned to roost on Vince Kaminksi's desk in January of 2001. Shifting the finances of the four Raptors around didn't work: Kaminski started working on a mathematical model to save the hedges, and determined fairly quickly that the Raptors were not drowning but drowned—nothing could revive them. Each vehicle had the same exposure risk, he reasoned, because each was backed by (now falling) Enron stock. When Kaminski reported his findings, he met with the typical response: silence.

It would be March before he would discover that he was not the only person assigned to a Raptor resuscitation plan.

In another corner of the company, a young man named Ryan Siurek, a senior director in Enron's transaction accounting group, found a way—albeit a very rickety way—to succeed where Kaminski had not. He completed his restructuring around 4 P.M. on March 26, 2001. Almost immediately, Siurek's phone rang. It was Jeff Skilling, calling to thank him for all his hard work. Andy Fastow called him too, and told him that saving the Raptors was a good deal for Enron and a good deal for LJM2.

One group that was not so pleased with Enron's work on the Raptors and other SPEs were the accountants at Arthur Andersen. In fact, the firm was growing more and more anxious about its most lucrative client.

As early as February 1999, David Duncan, the head of Andersen's Enron Team, flew to London for a meeting at the Four Seasons Hotel with the Enron board's audit committee. In general, he was bothered by what he called Enron's "risky accounting," and he noted to the board members that there was a "high probability" it would be questioned. "Obviously we are on board with all of these," he noted in the margins of his pad, "but may push limits and . . . others could have a different view."

Being an obstructionist was not in Duncan's nature. He was sharply handsome in a patrician sort of way, but his personality was soft. He thrived in the cushy, cozy Republican suburbs of West Houston, happiest when playing golf with Rick Causey, the firm's most important client.

As such, Duncan was the near polar opposite of another Andersen partner named Carl Bass. Bass was an early star at Andersen—twenty years before, when Anderson's comers competed on technical prowess alone, Bass was a standout. A manager working with both Bass and Sherron Watkins once tried to motivate her by claiming she "wasn't fit to hold Carl Bass's jockstrap." He had added that Sherron was more like the chicken, dedicated to working with the pig to make a ham and egg sandwich, but not quite like Bass, who was as fully committed as the pig.

Bass was more than committed to the technical side of the business; he was in love with it. He served as an Andersen advisor to the Financial Accounting Standards Board for a number of years, then had returned to Houston from Washington as part of Andersen's prestigious Professional Standards Group. Pudgy with wiry red hair and a pasty complexion, raised in Bartlesville, Oklahoma, Bass was also a stereotypical, by-the-book, resolutely cheerless accountant. His nickname, in fact, from his very first year at Andersen, was Partner Basshole, because his social skills were inversely proportional to his technical skills. Colleagues wished he would spend more time on his golf game.

Bass took up Enron instead—the relationship of LJM to Enron in particular. After his promotion to the Professional Standards Group in December 1999, Bass was asked by Duncan to devote "500 to 700" hours a year to Enron. He didn't like what he saw: Concerned over the sale of some options within LJM, he voiced his objections. Even so, within a few weeks, Duncan sent a memo to the Professional Standards Group in Chicago claiming that Bass "concurred with our conclusions." In fact, Bass continued to object to LJM2, virtually in its entirety. "This whole deal looks like there is no substance," he wrote his colleagues in a February 2000 memo. "The only money at risk here is $1.8 million in a bankrupt proof SPE. All of the money here appears to be provided by Enron. . . ."

Throughout the winter and early spring, Bass remained recalcitrant, griping in interoffice e-mails: "I am still bothered with the transaction we discussed yesterday . . . I have to ask myself, why not do a straight deal with Goldman? [Enron] said so themselves, it would be too expensive . . . Why is the SPE not capitalized with 97% debt? Because no bank is dumb enough to loan money whose repayment is dependent on changes in value of an internet stock. . . ."

Over the next year, as LJM2 grew from a minor distraction to a major player, more Andersen partners began, quietly, to share Bass's concerns, so much so that in February 2001, a group of partners met with David Duncan and another partner, Tom Bauer, to consider whether they should keep Enron as a client.

In a conference room in Andersen's downtown headquarters, they tossed the idea around. They worried about how much debt Enron was stashing off the balance sheet. They talked about Fastow's conflicts of interest. They expressed concern over the disclosure—or lack thereof—in the company's financial footnotes of SEC filings, and they wondered about the views of the Enron board in general.

The accountants asked themselves whether they really understood Enron's most byzantine transactions. Enron had converted mark-to-market accounting into nothing more than "intelligent gambling," they agreed. Maybe Enron was too dependent on closing deals to meet its financial objectives; maybe it was too aggressive in its financial structures.

Maybe. But in the end, the Andersen team put their worries aside. They had the right people in place, after all. And besides, fees from Enron could reach $100 million per year.

Caution dictated, however, that they advise their client of their concerns, so they made up a to-do list to present to the board at an upcoming meeting. Topics included going over the Fastow relationship from an SEC perspective, and adding a board oversight committee to review the fairness of LJM transactions. Enron, they suggested, should "Focus on . . . preparing their own documentation and conclusions to issues and transactions." Yet when the board met a week or so later, on February 12, Duncan and Bauer were inexplicably mute—perhaps because it was the day the board approved Jeff Skilling's promotion to CEO.

But Carl Bass kept carping. In late February, Enron Chief Accounting Officer Rick Causey met with Andersen's CEO, Joseph Berardino, where, it was subsequently alleged, Causey angled to have Bass removed. At the time, David Duncan made some notes: "Carl. Too technical . . . Client satisfaction involved." As March began and the pressure on him increased, Bass, like a dogged detective, tried to remain on the case by writing an impassioned defense to his boss, a man named John Stewart. "I know you did not ask for this, but I believe you should at least have a version of what I know about this Enron 'thing' from me."

Bass denied, as had been asserted, that he had a problem with Causey "that results in me having some caustic and inappropriate slant in dealing with their questions." In fact, he noted, he took Causey as his guest to a Financial Accounting Standards Board task force meeting where the topic was important to Enron. Yes, he was worried about certain transactions, like the Blockbuster-Enron joint venture, but his caution, he said, was in Andersen's best interest. "At that time I was told that they were going to have some $50 million gain on the sale of this venture interest immediately after the contract was signed and the venture was entered into. Furthermore, the other venture partner was not contributing anything." Bass went on to call the Blockbuster deal "a very risky transaction" where certain procedures were "nowhere to be found in the accounting literature." The debt-concealing cross-collateralization of the Raptors that so concerned Vince Kaminski worried him too. These year-end issues, he warned, "represent about $150 million plus of income or avoided losses at year end."

In general, Bass thought that Enron knew too much about Andersen's business. "Apparently part of the process issue stems from the client knowing all that goes on within our walls on our discussions with respect to their issues. I believe that when we are either having discussions or have reached a decision, the FIRM has done so. . . . I have first hand experience on this because at a recent EITF meeting some lower level Enron employee who was with someone else from Enron introduced herself to me by saying she had heard my name a lot—'So you are the one that will not let us do something.'"

For three single-spaced pages Bass went on in this vein, to no avail. On March 12, Andersen took him off the Enron account.

Without Bass to hold the line, Duncan was an easy mark. When Andersen's Professional Standards Group objected to some of Enron's actions, Duncan overrode them, and moved on. Doing so was acceptable policy at Andersen, but no one ever did it.

14

Flakes vs. Cowboys

I N the sea of peril that was about to engulf Enron, the co-opting of
Arthur Andersen was a very small ripple. That was especially true when
compared to the energy crisis in California, which was deepening
simultaneously.

In the mid-nineties, California was the first state to deregulate electricity. It happened as companies were leaving the state in droves, creating a
devastating recession. Along with the exorbitant state taxes, businesses complained about the high costs of energy. Deregulation was supposed to break
the back of the old-fashioned, entrenched greedy utilities and, by 1998, give
rate payers a 10 percent reduction in their bills. There didn't seem to be any
downside.

But the solution turned out to be worse than the problem. California
deregulated the wholesale side of its energy market, while keeping price
caps on the retail side. Simultaneously, the state barred its utilities from
signing long-term fixed-price (i.e., cheaper) deals for power, forcing them

into an increasingly volatile spot market. The stage was set for disaster. Soon the utilities were paying a fortune to power producers but couldn't pass their costs on to their customers.

Enron joined the deregulation fight early and poured millions into on-the-side-of-angels public relations campaigns, styling themselves as the good guys against the antediluvian utility owners. Skilling promised the state's regulators in June of 1994: "Under deregulation, California would save about $8.9 billion per year. . . . If you had $8.9 billion . . . you could triple the number of police officers in Los Angeles, San Francisco, Oakland and San Diego . . . you could double the state of California's construction for hospitals . . . you could double the number of teachers in Los Angeles, San Francisco, Oakland and San Diego . . . and you'd have enough pin money left over to cover the CPUC's budget." Enron promised to deliver power more efficiently, and to build better plants that ran on cleaner, cheaper fuels.

There were just a few signs that Enron might not have been playing straight with the market. One occurred in May 1999—a difficult year in Enron's earnings department—the so-called Silver Peak Incident.

Timothy Belden was another Enron star. When he graduated from college in 1990, he joined the Lawrence Berkeley National Laboratory, a research institution supported by the Department of Energy. He was a wonk who wrote policy reports on topics like "Theory and Practice of Decoupling." From Berkeley he moved to Portland General, where he continued to ponder the state of the electricity market: "It is doubtful that state PUCs will have time and expertise to reconstruct and dissect hedging decisions made by distribution utilities," he noted presciently in one report. He also stated that PUCs should act to "guard against speculation on the part of distribution utilities, even though it can be difficult to establish simple rules that can prevent speculative transactions."

But then, in 1999, Belden went to work on Enron's trading desk, where he came to run the western electricity-trading operations. Whatever contemplative life he may have envisioned for himself fell away under the pressures and rewards of his new employer. Before long, the committed environmentalist became a company man, swaggering across the trading floor, making millions for himself and the company.

Hence the events of May 24, 1999: Belden tried to send an enormous amount of power over some aged transmission lines—2,900 megawatts of power over a 15-megawatt path. Such a plan was destined to cause congestion on the line. California had an automated response to overloaded lines. Immediate electronic requests went to all the state's suppliers—*Do you have power coming across this line? Can you remove it? We will pay you to take it away!* But on this day, there also happened to be a human watching the wires for California's Independent System Operator, who couldn't imagine why someone would send so much power over such a small line. "That's what you wanted to do?" the dubious operator from the ISO asked when she called to check to be sure that the transaction had not been requested in error.

When Belden replied in the affirmative—"Yeah. That's what we did."—she became even more incredulous. "Can I ask why?"

"Um," Belden replied, "there's a—there—we just, um—we did it because we wanted to do it. And I don't—I don't mean to be coy."

The operator suggested it was a pretty "interesting schedule."

Belden agreed. "It—it's how we—it makes the eyes pop, doesn't it?"

The operator conceded that it did, and for that reason she would have to report the transaction to the power grid regulators because it was, in her words, "kind of pointless."

"Right," Mr. Belden answered.

From Enron's perspective, the trade wasn't pointless. Belden's move caused congestion that, in turn, drove the price of electricity up 70 percent that afternoon. The compliance unit of the state's power exchange investigated the trade and a year later fined Belden $25,000, but that was a small price to pay—Enron cleared $10 million that day, while California's electricity customers overpaid by around $5.5 million.

California's human-free automated system was completely dependent on the honesty of the power suppliers. But they weren't honest. Abusers like Belden found novel ways to game the system, converting it into a slot machine perpetually set on "jackpot." Belden was only too happy to pay meaningless fines when and if he was apprehended by plodding state regulators. And he was not alone.

By June of 2000, the people of California, who had expected lower rates and better service from deregulation, found they had neither. Wholesale electricity rates in the state jumped 300 percent, an amount that made Texas energy trading companies who supplied the power—Reliant, El Paso, Dynegy, as well as Enron—delirious.

Whatever Enron and its competitors promised about deregulation—lower prices, freedom of choice, et cetera—they found out that they needed volatility, not stability, to make money. In a stable market, no one worried about their power supply, because the lights always came on and the air conditioner always worked. But if the supply was questionable, customers got anxious, and if the supply dwindled, they became willing to pay any price to keep their homes and businesses running smoothly. As Belden would write in an e-mail to Houston in the spring of 2000, as power prices soared, "We long. Prices keep going up. So far so good."

By the fall of 2000, California's major electricity generators had a big problem: They were facing power shortages but realized that they could not afford to buy power from the companies selling it on the spot market, as deregulation required them to do. The utilities began pushing for rate increases they could pass on to their customers. When the legislature refused, the power companies had no choice but to institute cutbacks.

Consumers were furious when denied power. The state then petitioned the Federal Energy Regulatory Commission to install price caps on the suppliers so it could afford to buy what little power was available. When the FERC did so, out-of-state suppliers immediately vacated the scene.

By December 2000, the situation was perilous: That month, the state experienced its first Stage Three "rolling blackout"—meaning that the state was close to exhausting its electricity reserves. Literally, California's lights were going out, and with it the health and well being of the state's economy. The California official charged with keeping power flowing throughout the state panicked and then asked the FERC to lift price caps so that power sellers would return to the state. They did—charging even higher prices than before.

Meanwhile, in Houston, an Enron attorney named Stephen Hall started to worry. He was asked in October to research the company's electricity-trading practices because of an investigation conducted by the California Public Utility Commission. The more he researched, the more concerned he became. With a team of attorneys, he wrote an eight-page memo that detailed the tactics Enron's traders were using to take advantage of the state's energy crisis. With names like "Fat Boy," "Death Star" and "Get Shorty," Hall revealed how Enron created false congestion on power lines, transferred energy in and out of state to avoid price caps, and charged for services the company never actually provided.

Hall later met personally with various Enron executives, including Mark Haedicke, the general counsel for Enron's Wholesale Trading Group, and Richard Sanders, a vice president and assistant general counsel, and warned them that the practices could violate ISO tariffs and, more important, criminal laws. Sanders would later claim that after he got the memo in December he demanded that the practices be stopped. (He would brief Skilling on the subject in June 2001.) Internally, executives argued about repaying the California ISO for money made on improper trades, but decided against it. "If we send money back," traders told Sanders, "they'll know what we're doing." Whatever did or did not happen next, the subject became the hottest of hot potatoes. Haedicke's name subsequently disappeared from the distribution lists of Hall's anxious memos.

The situation in California did not improve, however, with the end of California state price caps and Enron's promises to behave. In fact, things got worse.

By mid-January 2001, California Edison defaulted on $596 million worth of payments to power companies and bondholders, and the rolling blackouts spread to northern California—that is, Silicon Valley and its environs. Governor Gray Davis drafted emergency legislation allowing the state to buy power, a situation that only made things better for the Texas companies— now they could negotiate long-term contracts at inflated rates with hapless state employees. Residential rate hikes were imposed in January and March, increasing rates by 40 percent. In April, Pacific Gas and Electric filed for Chapter 11 bankruptcy protection. It was at this time that Texas Senator Phil Gramm chose to weigh in, in an interview with the Los Angeles *Times*: "As [Californians] suffer the consequences of their own feckless policies, political leaders in California blame the power companies, deregulation and everyone but themselves, and the inevitable call is now being heard for a federal bailout. I intend to do everything in my power to require those who valued environmental extremism and interstate protectionism more than common sense and market freedom to solve their electricity crisis without short circuiting taxpayers in other states."

That statement sounded good if you lived in Texas: Those flakey, self-absorbed Californians plunged themselves into the energy shortage because they wouldn't despoil their paradise with enough plants to power their laptops, air conditioners, and juice bars. California, they charged, built no new plants in a decade, so what did they expect?

Enron rolled out a cadre of academics to back them up, people like economist Paul Joskow, the director of MIT's Center for Energy and Environmental Policy Research, whose funding came from Enron and Reliant, among others. In a *New York Times* Op-Ed piece, Joskow chided California for failing to build enough power plants for its population: "The lesson to be learned from California's [electricity crisis] . . . is not, as some have suggested, that deregulation is a bad idea."

The new U.S. president turned his back on California too. In early 2001, Bush adamantly refused to reinstate price caps in a state that, coincidentally or not, had supported his opponent.

Investigators from various governmental bodies began working on the crisis in the late winter and early spring, and made some interesting discoveries: They found that Californians, already ranked as the second-most-efficient energy consumers in the nation, actually used *less* energy in July of 2000 than the same month of the previous year. Then, too, California's energy usage during the current energy crisis never approached the all-time peak that had occurred in July 1999. Even more interesting, the actual demand for electricity never exceeded the generation capacity of the state's plants. Demand in January 2001 — the month Senator Gramm chastised the state — was nearly 10 percent *lower* than in previous years, when there had been no blackouts. Power usage on blackout days was also lower than in previous years.

And contrary to popular opinion outside California, 170 new generation and cogeneration facilities had been built in the state in the 1990s, plenty to meet the energy needs of the populace.

It began to dawn on some California public officials that maybe some plants being shut down for maintenance—as their owners claimed—didn't really need it. Maybe drought conditions—also blamed by power generators for the crisis—weren't to blame either.

Maybe there was another explanation entirely for California's problems.

15

Suspicious Minds

ROM January through March of 2001, Enron's stock price, which had been on a steep, upward trajectory for almost three years, began to teeter, and then began to fall. It was in the $80 range when the year began, but dropped to $55 by the end of the first quarter. At first, the slump merely vexed Jeff Skilling, and then, as the stock remained in the doldrums, it began to haunt him like an angry ghost, and he began to look a little like a haunted man himself. In contrast to earlier days, when Skilling quoted the stock price frequently and with enormous pride, he started telling people to change their priorities.

Of course, focusing on the stock price of any company was by then a national pastime. People at Enron were just more enthusiastic because the stock had been a steady source of good news since 1990. At the same time the stock started falling, Ken Lay stopped doing press interviews. Whether it was because he wanted a job with the Bush administration (rumor had him turning down the energy secretary job, hoping to land treasury), or because he wanted to enjoy life more, the job of being Enron's public face in good and bad times now fell to Skilling, who, initially at least, appeared to handle the spotlight very well. The company had started retooling his image when he took over from Kinder in 1997. Many people at Enron had feared his ascension, and had hoped instead for Mark's touchy-feely management style. "Jeff was not warm and fuzzy—we had to put some fur on him," said one marketing executive. Following GE's lead—Enron even hired a PR person from GE—Enron pitched Skilling as a younger, cooler Jack Welch, the embodiment of the new Enron brand. (There would be an almost immediate shift away from branding CEOs in 2002.)

Skilling turned out to be a very good pitchman, both inside and outside the company: Lay hated Enron floor meetings and depended on prepared text to get through them; Skilling showed up in shirtsleeves, Diet Coke in hand, with no index cards in sight. He spoke off the cuff, appearing candid, thoughtful, and, most important, sincere in his love for the company. If he still had trouble winning over the old-timers—who never forgot his seething contempt—younger members of the company were snowed, and put their faith, otherwise known as their stock, in his hands.

For business reporters constantly on the prowl for something new, Skilling also filled the bill. Lay was so nineties—true, like most of the people they liked to write about at the top of the corporate ladder, he lived lavishly, hobnobbed with world leaders, and donated to good causes. But he was also balding and folksy. In contrast, Skilling was hip. He posed in front of his Land Rover, dressed to trek. (Lay had done virtually the same thing four years back, but now his jogging shorts looked outdated.) Skilling had stubble, like those dot-com kids. And where Lay was a plodding speaker—almost Elmer Fudd–like at times—Skilling was sharp, made eye contact, and knew how to use all the right buzzwords. He didn't need handlers; he spoke his mind: "Those big companies will topple over from their own weight," he declared in a speech condemning Old Economy dinosaurs like Exxon. Jeff Skilling was, in a word, millennial.

In February, *Business Week* celebrated his promotion by putting him on their cover holding a glowing orb next to the words "Power Broker." Inside, they portrayed Skilling as a New Age corporate swashbuckler—a risk-management guru who took wild, 1,000-mile dirt bike trips through Mexico. Said the story: "Enron executives insist that CEO-elect Skilling, 47, combines an odd mixture of tight risk-management controls with a free-wheeling entrepreneurial style that has helped boost Enron from $4 billion to more than $100 billion in revenues since he joined in 1990." Rick Causey told the magazine that Skilling was "the most innovative guy I've ever been around." Skilling offered a self-evaluation, "I've never not been successful in business or work, ever."

That same month, he gave a speech in Houston before the Cambridge Energy Research Associates' annual conference, one of the world's most prestigious gatherings of energy executives. The other men on the panel, which included the Pulitzer-winning author of *The Prize*, Daniel Yergin, wore gray suits, white shirts, and conservative ties in burgundy or navy; their hair was gray, and they sat hunched over their seats on the dais. Skilling bounded to the podium in a sports jacket, golf shirt, and khakis, and the tables that had been emptying out during the day started to fill up again, until the ballroom was SRO. Skilling started by proposing radical change in the energy business. He bashed Exxon. He bashed Shell. He bashed Ford for holding on to a horizontal business model for too long. Enron, he said, was revolutionizing the energy business. It knew how to strip out and pass on the risks. It had *reintegrated*—shifted the business hierarchy from the traditional pyramid to a flat organization. It had *decapitalized*: Hold on to the assets your company needs, Skilling advised, but sell the rest and then focus solely on what you do best.

That model was working great for Enron, he insisted. "Preliminary reports tell us we'll be number six on the Fortune 500 behind ExxonMobil, GE, Wal-Mart, and GM." Enron's market cap had gone from $2.2 billion in 1985 to $74 billion as of 2001—"just by getting more efficient." And there was more good news to come: "This is a time when we should be proud of our industry," Skilling declared, "and we've got a tremendous future ahead of us."

When he finished, most of the people in the audience rewarded him with thundering applause. Trade reporters tripped over themselves just to shake his hand. But they couldn't catch him. Skilling had to leave immediately—*warm and fuzzy!*—for his son's soccer game.

There were just a few people in the room who weren't convinced. The CEO of a small Canadian oil company wasn't buying, for instance. He leaned back in his chair and turned to the executive seated next to him. "That," he said, indicating Skilling and by extension his company, "is a short."

In fact, there were other people whose doubts about Enron had been growing, perhaps as the California energy crisis deepened (and Texas companies looked more and more like profiteers) and maybe since the filing of the 2000 second-quarter report. That document contained one small, clear paragraph in its rather long and undecipherable related-party footnote. It referred to some dark-fiber sales to LJM2 that provided $53 million of gross margin to Enron Broadband, allowing Enron Corp. to make its earnings targets by two cents. That note caught the attention of a reporter for a special Texas edition of *The Wall Street Journal*, Jonathan Weil. Weil, a laconic, dark-haired thirty-one-year-old, had received a tip from a private investment manager to look into Enron.

Weil spent the next few months researching the company, then wrote what amounted to the first critical piece on Enron since *Forbes* had raised questions back in 1993. In fact, Weil asked many of the same questions. "Volatile prices for natural gas and electricity are creating high-voltage earnings growth at some companies with large energy-trading units," he warned. "But investors counting on those gains could be in for a jolt down the road." He was bothered by Enron's extensive use of mark-to-market accounting: "What many investors may not realize is that much of these companies' recent profits constitute unrealized, noncash gains. Frequently, these profits depend on assumptions and estimates about future market factors, the details of which the companies do not provide, and which time may prove wrong."

And Weil had concerns about "quality of earnings"—a buzz phrase among the financial cognoscenti that distinguished between money made from profits and money made from moving things on and off the balance sheet. "The heart of the situation is an accounting technique that allows companies to include as current earnings those profits they expect to realize from energy-related contracts and other derivative instruments in future periods, sometimes stretching over more than 20 years." In other words, Weil suggested that Enron's reported earnings were, at best, optimistic.

Enron's response was immediate. Actually, it was preemptive. The company's PR department swiftly solicited responses from various analysts to discredit Weil. They obliged: Curt Launer, for instance, an analyst with Donaldson, Lufkin & Jenrette and a longtime Enron loyalist, published an impassioned if somewhat exasperated defense of mark-to-market accounting ("a superior analytical tool for understanding, assessing, and projecting the business performance of our companies") and kept Enron rated as a top stock pick.

Maybe Enron shouldn't have bothered. Few readers outside Texas see the Texas *Journal*, so Weil's story remained relatively obscure.

But one person did take note of the piece, a short seller in New York by the name of James Chanos. Chanos was something of a Wall Street eccentric, a man who made his name by predicting the savings-and-loan crisis of the eighties, but then lost heavily for his clients when he guessed wrong (in the short term, at least) on the tech boom. Chanos' interest was in companies whose profits seemed heavily based on future projections. After reading Weil's story, he started focusing on Enron. He analyzed the quarterly statements and annual reports, and he came up with numbers very different from those touted by Enron. Chanos calculated that Enron was churning out a 7 percent return on its capital, while its cost of capital was over 10 percent. In other words, Enron was like a credit-card abuser whose monthly take-home pay was less than the minimum monthly payments on his credit cards. That's a doomed scenario, particularly when the offender, as Chanos observed of Enron, kept borrowing more and more (at 10 percent) only to produce returns that were lower. And then there were all those related-party footnotes—they made no sense to Chanos at all. Then energy traders started telling him that Enron's trading wasn't all it was made out to be. So why, Chanos wondered, would anyone pay six times Enron's book value to own it?

Chanos took his question to a group of short sellers he hosted every year in Miami—his "Bears in Hibernation" gang. At the end of the confab, they picked Enron as one of two stocks to short. Several other short sellers followed suit, as did some oil and gas analysts who weren't as enthralled with or as beholden to Enron as some of the more successful analysts—the ones tied to the investment banks. Then, from the perspective of a large, Fortune 500 corporation, Chanos did something far worse: He shared his hunch with a reporter for a national business magazine.

As *Fortune's* Bethany McLean began her reporting, Enron—realizing that the days of the magazine's slavish fandom had come to an abrupt end—went into crisis mode. Skilling listened to a few of McLean's questions, called her unethical and hung up on her. Lay called *Fortune's* managing editor and suggested McLean had her facts wrong. When bullying failed, the company dispatched the head of public relations, the head of investor relations, and Andy Fastow (acting as CFO) to *Fortune's* office to answer all questions "completely and accurately." *Fortune's* "Is Enron Overpriced?" was not complimentary. McLean focused on the company's lack of transparency ("Just how does Enron make its money?").

At around the same time, John S. Herold, Inc., a respected, old-line energy research firm from Connecticut, published a six-page report titled *The New, New Valuation Metrics: Is Enron really worth $126 per share?* The report acknowledged Enron's dominance in the world of energy and power trading but asked somewhat rhetorically, "Is Enron worth today's market valuation of $55 billion, much less $111 billion, the value recently cited by Mr. Skilling as his company's internal valuation?" The authors didn't think so. Using their own proprietary valuation model, Herold arrived at a value of $53 a share—not quite two thirds of the current share price. Herold's analysis sparked the by-now familiar barrage of damning phone calls from Enron's Investor Relations department.

Next up was a *Frontline* report on the California energy crisis. It painted Enron as a company of New Age robber barons.

In the face of such criticism, Skilling held firm. Had the California PUC been gamed by power generators, as they claimed? No, Skilling insisted—people were just looking for scapegoats. Had there been an abuse of market power in the summer of 2000? Absolutely not, Skilling insisted. Was there any evidence of gaming from the traders or from the people at Enron? "No, I think quite the opposite," Skilling said. "When this thing was hitting, not only did everybody have incentive to, but I think everybody was working extremely hard to get every possible electron into the California market."

After the interview, someone asked him what his chief goal would be as Enron's new CEO. His answer came swiftly, as if the topic were already weighing on his mind."To get the stock price up," he said.

By then, of course, it had made that precipitous drop from $84 to $55.

Jordan Mintz, the attorney for Fastow's group, waited for Jeff Skilling to respond to his memo about his missing signature on the LJM2 documents for about a week. When he didn't hear from Skilling, he decided to give him five more days. Meanwhile, the checklist that would satisfy Mintz—and that would fulfill the board's obligations to maintain the Chinese Wall between Enron and LJM—sat incomplete on his desk. "Has the audit committee of Enron Corp.'s Board of Directors reviewed all Enron LJM transactions within the past twelve months?" Mintz checked the word "No." "Have all the recommendations of the audit committee relative to Enron LJM transactions been taken to account in this transaction?" Again, Mintz checked "No."

Meanwhile, the dysfunctionality continued unabated on the twentieth floor. In February 2001, Mintz asked Rick Causey to take the issue of Fastow's compensation to the board, but he didn't. He became more alarmed by news of Fastow's latest project: He intended to buy a wind company from Enron for $600 million. This was a much larger than normal cash outlay, even for LJM2, whose purchases were usually in the $10 million range. This expenditure would, naturally, be accompanied by large bonuses for Fastow and his team. That is, if the deal went through: Michael Kopper had recently appeared in Mintz's office to try to extract information about LJM's competition—he'd heard that Enron was working hard to sell the wind company to a private equity fund controlled by an outside firm, UBS. Mintz referred Kopper to the Enron attorney involved in the sale, his way of saying "Bug off, Michael."

Where was Jim Derrick in all this? Mintz wanted to know. The diminutive, prim Derrick was Enron's chief counsel, but suffered, like Ken Lay, from an overabundance of optimism. Mintz had spoken with Derrick several times about the conflicts between Enron and LJM and felt he was getting nowhere. After a March meeting, for instance, Derrick took no action that Mintz could see.

So Mintz had an idea. Breaking the chain of command, he set out to find a first-rate law firm that could shed some light on the problems he saw with the LJM/Enron relationship. As it turned out, this was not easy—many firms nationwide had done work for or against Enron. Then a headline on a newspaper at a Starbucks caught his eye: Harvey Pitt was the new head of the Securities and Exchange Commission. The law firm Pitt was leaving, Fried, Frank, Harris, Shriver & Jacobson, had never been involved in any Enron business. Even better, the managing partner in the Washington, D.C., office was a friend of Mintz's. So, without speaking with Rick Buy, Rick Causey, or Jim Derrick—or any other executive at Enron, for that matter—Jordan Mintz made a call to Fried, Frank.

When they responded positively, he felt liberated. "I want to thank you for taking time out from your hectic schedule to visit with me over the telephone yesterday in connection with the above referenced item," he wrote to Richard A. Steinwurtzel in May, enclosing eighteen attachments that served as a briefing book on the history of LJM and Enron. Then, over the next month or so, Fried, Frank got as worried as Mintz—and so, too, did the investment community.

There was the California crisis, there were more negative stories like the one that appeared in *Fortune*, there were eerie missives like the one that appeared on Yahoo's message board on April 12: "The Enron executives have been operating an elaborate con scheme that has fooled even the most sophisticated analysts. The first sign of trouble will be an earnings shortfall followed by more warnings. Criminal charges will be brought against ENE executives for their misdeeds. Class action lawsuits will complete the demise of ENE." When the stock price started slipping further— below $50 a share—Skilling decided to act. He told Fastow to let go of LJM.

Fastow agreed, but not without a fight. He threw a tantrum in a meeting with Causey, Mintz, and Kopper after Causey told him that Arthur Andersen would require a letter stating that Fastow had given up all interest in the fund. Why don't they trust me? Fastow demanded. Causey did not respond, but let the melodramatic moment pass. In time, Fastow apologized: He had created this partnership, he explained, and selling it was very emotional for him.

With Fastow on the way out, Mintz thought the task ahead would be much simpler. LJM would die a quick death with Kopper in charge—no one at Enron would have the incentive to deal with him, Mintz reasoned; he wasn't CFO, for one thing—and the conflict would disappear. Mintz thought that all he had to do was follow Fried, Frank's latest advice: take this opportunity to clean up LJM's involvement with Enron on the balance sheet. It was an issue of "optics."

It was around this time that Mintz had a long lunch with Cliff Baxter. The two men were friends and colleagues, but now Baxter was leaving the company for good. His progress through Enron, over ten years, had been lucrative if erratic. Baxter was a deal guy—he loved being in the throes of a transaction, staying up around the clock, bragging about his skills, letting the rest of the world fall away—but once it was over, he deflated. He became sharp and abusive with underlings—his voice louder, his language coarser—and his complaints that he was ignored and undervalued more frequent. He was a lost, angry child until the next deal came his way.

His relationship with Skilling changed over time too. Baxter remained one of the few people who could speak his mind to the CEO, but as Skilling moved up, he both cared for and marginalized Baxter. At one time, Baxter wanted to run his own business unit like Broadband or Enron Energy Services, but once Skilling advanced him to the company's trading jewel, Enron Wholesale Services, Baxter couldn't take the pressure of making earnings targets. He especially didn't like meeting the targets by selling assets to LJM2—because he couldn't stand Fastow. In June 2000, Skilling and Baxter fell out over Baxter's powers. Baxter didn't like reporting to Joe Sutton, who was now vice chairman and whom he didn't respect. When Skilling questioned Baxter's authority in a meeting, in front of about twenty-five people, Baxter resigned, as he had done so many times before.

Eventually, Skilling lured him back with a fancy title—this time it was chief strategy officer. Baxter returned to a large pay cut and no direct reports. Finally, it became clear to everyone that it was time to go. Baxter told friends that he had made enough money and the pressure was no longer worth it to him. "Over the past ten years, Cliff has made a tremendous contribution to Enron's evolution, particularly as a member of the team that built Enron's wholesale business," Skilling wrote in the press release announcing his departure. "His creativity, intelligence, sense of humor and straightforward manner have been assets to the company throughout his career. While we will miss him, we are happy that his primary reason for resigning is to spend additional time with his family and we wish him the very best."

Now, leaving in just a few days, Baxter was in a mellow, contemplative mood. He and Mintz touched briefly on LJM, and Mintz joked once more about the crazy behavior the two of them had witnessed. Listening, Baxter looked thoughtful. He never understood why the board waived Enron's conflict of interest policy to allow Fastow to create LJM. Mintz agreed.

In the following weeks, however, Mintz realized that his new, nostalgic attitude was premature. Fastow was dragging his feet over the disclosures Andersen required to close out LJM in the quarterly report and in the proxy filing. Finally, after Mintz was particularly persistent on this point, Fastow told him why he didn't want to reveal any information about his finances. If Skilling ever knew how much money he'd made, Fastow told Mintz, Skilling would have no choice but to shut down LJM entirely. In other words, he'd made so much money that Skilling would have to tell the board, and the board would put an end to the operation. Who knew how damaging that might be?

In fact, Skilling had been concerned about Fastow. Rick Causey would tell investigators that Skilling offhandedly asked him to make sure that "too much money wasn't made" in LJM, but maybe "too much money" was too vague a term at Enron. A year later, before Congress, Skilling would "absolutely, unequivocally deny that there was any agreement, any agreement, period, that would have provided a riskless rate of return to anyone that we dealt with as Enron Corporation." But if Fastow's situation was not win/win for him, then why the concern for how much money he was making?

In contrast to the blazing stars of Enron, Keith Power was a bit player, a nearly invisible man. That was despite his considerable height, which was well over six feet; but then he had a habit of stooping, like many tall people who want to be accommodating. Power wore his short hair parted unfashionably down the middle, his clothes were baggy, not Enron crisp, and his skin was ruddy and a bit pocked. Though he was not a doleful person, something about his countenance suggested he was. He looked older than a man in his forties. What he was, really, was formal and deeply respectful of people he considered his betters: When Power spoke to people he didn't know well, he used their names often, like a person practicing a memory trick or a person who wanted to be exceedingly polite to make a good impression.

The fact was, Keith Power felt lucky to be at Enron. His was a story similar to that of many people up and down the ladder at the company: Power's father owned a small gas station and convenience store in a small town in Nebraska called Holdredge; Keith's plan to follow in the family business was thwarted in the 1980s, when a chain came to town and drove his father, who expanded to compete, into bankruptcy. Since there was no money for college, Power "outsourced himself" and went looking for a job.

At around the same time, he met a young woman through mutual friends, and before long the two married. She was the opposite of Keith, which meant she was outgoing and vivacious. She was an administrative assistant to a vice president at Internorth, in Omaha, and, being a southern girl from Mobile, she jumped at the chance to move to Houston after Internorth and Houston Natural Gas merged in 1986. The couple abandoned the Midwest for the new promise of Houston.

That promise was not immediately apparent. Houston had not yet recovered from the oil bust when they arrived, so there weren't many opportunities for a quiet guy with no college degree. The couple found an apartment near the Galleria, Houston's fanciest shopping mall, and while his wife continued as a secretary at Enron, Keith took a job selling shirts at Macy's.

In March of 1987, Power's wife convinced him to apply for a temporary job as a payroll clerk at Enron. Keith found he liked the work—the people were nice (most of them were from Omaha) and the task was fairly challenging. Soon, they had enough money to put a down payment on a foreclosed condominium on the west side of town. And, like so many other people in Houston, Power's situation began to improve. Enron hired him full-time in November of 1987 as a benefits clerk, where he spent a lot of time on the phone trying to help older employees and retirees with various forms. He'd try to talk them into changing their investment habits, as too many plowed all their savings into Enron stock. Guys who worked on the pipelines for thirty years, and who made $3,500 a month, now had around three quarters of a million dollars in their Enron retirement accounts. "If you're sixty," he'd say, "I'm gonna introduce the word *diversification* to you." Power wasn't supposed to give advice like that—company rules prohibited giving investment advice, but he figured there was no sin in introducing options.

There was another advantage to being a benefits clerk. Before the advent of computerized funds management, the executives called in their investment changes and Keith mimicked their moves. The Powers had a little nest egg of Enron stock courtesy of the Employee Stock Ownership Plan the company had instituted back in the eighties, the one devised to thwart takeovers by putting more stock in friendly hands. By watching and learning, Power built himself a healthy portfolio.

By 1992, in fact, he and his wife had saved enough money to buy Berkshire Hathaway stock—the class B shares, that is. So Power started going to the annual meetings back in the Omaha Civic Auditorium, and listening to Warren Buffett. The man was unassuming and steady, two things Power could relate to.

Then, in July 1992, Power went for an interview with Andy Fastow. Although he was more than ten years older, Power saw Fastow as a role model. Andy hired him to create a filing system, but in the small office—just Power, Fastow, and a new Harvard MBA—Power felt part of the team.

Fastow was mercurial, but he treated Power well. He invited Keith to his house for a Christmas party—it was a formal place with high-backed wing chairs that reminded Power of a banker's waiting room—and he also encouraged Power to grow, to stop thinking of himself as an hourly employee. "You gotta figure out what you want," Fastow told him.

He worked harder and got promoted to a staff-level job, where he started monitoring the Enron stock held in JEDI. Sometime after the formation of Chewco and the buyout of CalPERS's interest in JEDI—the end of 1997—

Power noticed a change around the office. He was supposed to supervise the day-to-day debt administration for JEDI—Enron had to send certain reports along with interest payments on its debt every thirty days—but with Chewco that duty went to a female superior. Suddenly she did all the calculations and supervised the faxing of documents; she even stood over the fax machine until all the paperwork went through and then stored these and all the other Chewco filings in a locked drawer in her office. "It's just something Michael wants me to handle, so I told him I'd do it," she said to Power when he asked what was going on.

In 2000, Power was promoted again, this time to help with presentations to banks and third parties about JEDI's assets. As part of his duties, he read everything published about the fund's investments. Interested in the topic, he threw himself into what he called "public equity commentary." For eighteen months he sent out memos comparing JEDI's assets to others in the marketplace. He couldn't help noticing—and forwarding—his perception that Enron had overvalued the assets in JEDI. Using fair value accounting, he noted, Enron assessed an oil company, Mariner, at maybe 13 times its actual cash flow, while the real market would value it at only 6 to 8 times cash flow. Power described this discrepancy in his memos. Eventually, Rick Buy told him that assessing the value of the assets was the responsibility of Buy's Risk Assessment and Control Group. Power should knock it off.

But Power was bothered by the RAC group's numbers. It seemed to him that they started with the number they wanted as the final outcome, and backfilled to get to the proper starting point. As he read more and more about how to value public companies, his faith in Enron's mathematical modeling—the one that promised investment outcomes with a 95 percent confidence level—began to waiver.

In May 2001, an executive came into Power's office and told him about a negative Enron story that appeared on TheStreet.com's Web site; it referenced a longer report by someone named Mark Roberts, who ran a firm called Off Wall Street. Have you seen this thing? the executive asked. Can you get a copy? Power did a little research and discovered that Mark Roberts was a highly regarded Boston-based stock analyst. His reports were proprietary and very expensive—around $25,000 a copy.

Power first phoned Investor Relations, because he heard they had a copy of Roberts's report. But the managing director in charge of the group, Mark Koenig, never returned his call. A week later, Power decided to call Mark Roberts himself. He phoned around 6:30 P.M. A man answered who didn't identify himself. Power described what he was looking for—a negative report about Enron written by Mark Roberts.

I'm Mark Roberts, the guy on the other line told him.

Roberts agreed to send Power the thirty-page report and told him he was welcome to distribute it around the company. Then he faxed Power the pages.

It was interesting, if dense, reading. The news—not surprising to Power—wasn't good. "We think Enron is currently overvalued" was the way Roberts' opus began. He believed that "street analysts," as he referred to them some-what contemptuously, couldn't correctly evaluate Enron because they hadn't noticed that the company was now a trading company instead of an asset-based pipeline company. That transformation caused Roberts consid-erable concern: Enron now needed a huge trading volume to meet earnings targets, and he further noted that to keep volume high, Enron needed volatility in the energy markets, and he saw none in sight. He wasn't impressed with Enron's risk management, either, pointing out that problems with India and Azurix "are just two examples from Enron's 'risk free' investment portfolio." He also questioned the quality of earnings. Finally, there was Enron's incomprehensible balance sheet: "There are indications that Enron may be utilizing certain types of transactions and accounting techniques to manage and to boost earnings." There simply wasn't enough cash flow—by his calculations, Enron should have been operating in the red for the last three years. Meanwhile, Roberts noted, senior executives were selling stock like crazy. Like Jim Chanos, Mark Roberts thought Enron was flunking the smell test.

Power was a manager now, and Enron managers were supposed to be self-starters. He copied the report and distributed it to six or so vice presi-dents in Rick Buy's group.

At the same time Power was hunched over the copy machine, the finance guys—Skilling, Fastow, and Buy, among others—were in Florida trying to raise capital. One of the people who got the report from Power called Buy. Two days later, Power's boss came in to see him—the same man

Left: Rebecca Mark, the head of Enron International, successfully pushing through a billion-dollar power project in India. (© *AFP Photo/Raveendran*)

Below: Ken Lay as Enron's ambassador to the world, the role he loved best. Here he shakes hands with Mikhail Gorbachev at an Enron event at Rice University's Baker Institute. Former Secretary of State James Baker stands to his right. (© *Houston Chronicle*)

Above: Jeffrey Skilling's mansion in Houston's exclusive River Oaks neighborhood.

Right: Vice Chairman Cliff Baxter, the tough negotiator from Long Island, was affectionately referred to as the Big Dog. Baxter committed suicide in the aftermath of Enron's filing for bankruptcy.
(© *AFP Photo*)

The new Enron tower, nearly completed, with the original Enron tower on the right. A circular skyway connects the two buildings.

Above: Sherron Watkins (left), Jeff Skilling (center), and Jeff McMahon (right) being sworn in before the Senate hearing on February 26, 2002. (© *AFP Photo, Stephen Jaffe*)

Below: The Senate hearing room chairs intended for Jeff McMahon, Jeff Skilling, and Sherron Watkins for the hearing held on February 26, 2002. The Senate staffers supplied 3-inch foam cushions for all but Skilling, the Senate's subtle way of making him appear even smaller than he already was. None of his high-priced defense counsel noticed Skilling's predicament that day as he sank lower and lower into the worn chair seat.

Left: Michael Kopper in Houston, after pleading guilty. (© *AFP Photo/ James Nielsen*)

Below: Andy Fastow being sworn in before Congress. He, too, pled the Fifth. (© *AFP Photo/Stephen Jaffe*)

Above: The two Ricks—Tweedle-dee and Tweedle-dum. Rick Buy, Enron's chief risk officer, on the left, and Rick Causey, Enron's chief accounting officer, on the right, being sworn in. Both pled the Fifth. (© *AFP Photo/Stephen Jaffe*)

Below: Sherron Watkins, with her attorney Philip Hilder, testifies to members of the House of Representatives on the financial collapse of Enron on February 14, 2002. © *Shawn Thew/AFP/Getty Images*

Above: The house that Andy Fastow continued to build in River Oaks even as thousands of Enron's employees were joining the unemployment line. In 2002, Fastow sold the house for more than $3 million, reportedly to search for a much bigger house in Florida, where he could shelter more of his fortune. Texas and Florida are the only two states that protect individual residences in the case of a bankruptcy.

Below: The Enron sign being dismantled at what had been called Enron Field. (© *Houston Chronicle*)

Jeffrey Skilling scowling at his detractors. This is the side of Skilling—arrogant and intimidating—that the media rarely saw. (© *AP/Wide World Photos*)

who had asked him to hunt down the Roberts report. "Hey," he said, indicating the report, "this is really bad news."

Power agreed.

"You shouldn't have distributed it," he said. Then he told him not to distribute it to anyone else. In fact, he told Power, he should forget that he ever saw that report. Later in the day, he returned to Power's office and reiterated his message. Under no circumstances should Power give the report to anybody else. Power had probably made a career-terminating move by stepping so far out of bounds, he said.

Three days later, Power got the news that he was being transferred to the Trade Credit Group, which for a RAC manager was like being sent to Siberia. Long hours, little reward. Power was angry. When Kinder was at Enron, he told his boss, people thrived on being challenged; they loved to duke it out. Now, he said, he was working at a company that couldn't confront bad news. What did that tell you? Power figured he'd be out by Christmas.

Over the next few days, people who read the report stopped in to talk about it. Where had it come from? Did he believe it? And, Power knew, they started selling their stock because of what they'd read.

16

Trapped

As it had for Jeff Skilling, 2001 started out relatively well for Sherron Watkins, though she, too, was ambivalent about her job. Trying to instill cost controls at Broadband was not much fun—she felt like a hall monitor in a school full of disorderly kindergartners. Broadband still had too many people with too little to do—every time she tried to move ahead with a new cost-control plan, someone else would scream that it was their job, not hers. Why someone wanted to fight over such tedious work—internal control development? Who cared?—was beyond her.

If the work was boring, at least the pay was good. Sherron had been shocked to discover that her February bonus amounted to $125,000—only $50,000 less than the one she got when she worked so hard on the Korea deal. She was now making almost as much as her best "deal year," and she was getting home by six every day.

But the world of Broadband was a troubled one. The fabled partnership with Blockbuster—the one that was going to save the company—had collapsed in January; Enron paid Blockbuster $5 million for the privilege of walking away. But without a content partner, Enron did not have a movies-on-demand product. The company threw around the names of a lot of potential partners—Sumner Redstone's came up along with Ovitz's—but nothing came of it. In a May 2001 board meeting, Ken Rice assured those present that the business was going well, and he was especially enthusiastic about the start of bandwidth trading. Skilling backed him up—despite the fact that the market for bandwidth was already glutted and there was no real need to trade spare capacity.

In truth, no one at Broadband was selling anything. EBS lost $102 million in the April-to-June quarter and generated only $16 million in revenues. The impending failure of the new division was crystal clear to the third in command, a former power trader by the name of Jim Fallon. Fallon, who, for good and for ill, could pass for an IRA sharpshooter, moved from Enron's wholesale-power-trading group to jump-start the trading in bandwidth. Fallon got to Broadband and realized, like many of his new colleagues, that the business wasn't going anywhere. There was no real leadership; chaos reigned. But unlike many who saw the problems at Broadband but kept silent, Fallon went to Skilling. Going around his boss, Kevin Hannon, wasn't a problem. Fallon was a seasoned corporate fighter. He made $60 million for the company in one day back in 1998, and he still had a lot of currency around the office.

His power play worked: After listening to what Fallon had to say—that Rice was MIA, and that Hannon may have been a great trader but did not have any mastery over this new technology—Skilling agreed to move the two men out and Fallon in. The official notice of their departure stated that Hannon was needed at International. No mention was made of Rice, whose retirement was imminent, along with Lou Pai's. (Rice left with more than $70 million, Pai with a staggering $353 million.)

But under Fallon, things at Broadband did not improve. What's the plan? subordinates asked, and he would only shake his head. "There is no plan," he answered, though he was trying to retrench and start over.

None of which was good news for Sherron Watkins. She had known Fallon when he was a young associate and she was a director. She didn't like him then—he never seemed to listen to her—and she was in no mood to take orders from him now. As it turned out, she wouldn't have to. One after-noon in early June, she got a call from Barry Pearce, who worked under Fal-lon. "I hate to tell you this," he said, "but Fallon wants to divide up your people and give some to me and some back to the accounting department." In other words, her job was being eliminated. *He doesn't even have the balls to tell me himself!* Sherron thought.

She didn't have time to be furious—she needed another job. Sherron contacted the head of Broadband's HR department, who told her Enron definitely wanted to keep her on—she was not being "redeployed." She wondered if she'd be better off in the redeployment pool, where she would have six months at full pay to look around for another job from the Enron offices in Three Allen Center nearby—nicknamed The Departure Lounge by those who found themselves there as Enron's stock price began crumbling in 2001. She calculated that with her tenure and salary, her sev-erance check would be equal to a whole year's pay. Two of Sherron's own directors actually asked to be redeployed in the last few months. Mulling it over, she also called a friend who worked at Reliant Energy, just down the block.

Paula Reicker, an Enron managing director in Investor Relations, had tried to recruit her earlier in the year. Sherron put in a call to her now, although she wasn't sure it was a good idea: The stock was selling for $45 because of the tech bust and what Sherron called The California Overhang, and she herself was suffering from an ethical overhang. Sherron wasn't sure she could hype Enron. It was one thing to work at a company that employed aggressive accounting; it was another thing altogether to push total strangers to buy in. Even so, she met with Mark Koenig, the head of Investor Rela-tions, who told her Skilling thought the move was a good idea.

Then, coming out of the elevator bank at lunch hour, Sherron ran into Andy Fastow. How was she doing? he asked. She told him her job was being eliminated and that she was looking for a change, and she watched the familiar, mischievous light come into his eyes. "Come talk to me," he said. "I think I've got something for you." So, four and a half years after escaping Fastow, Sherron Watkins was thinking about going back to work for him. She went home and poured herself a very large glass of wine.

Over the next few days, Sherron weighed her options. She met with Fastow, who told her he had inherited Baxter's duties; she could be his eyes and ears, and even better, she could put her name on any deal she found for herself. And by the way, Michael Kopper was buying him out of LJM. The partnership was too sticky for Enron.

Sherron left the Fastow meeting and made another call to Reliant. Nothing was even conceivably available for at least a month. She couldn't get an interview until late July.

She needed some good advice. So she did something she hadn't done in a very long time: She picked up the phone and called Jeff McMahon. McMahon was now the CEO of a newly formed unit called Enron Industrial Markets; she'd also heard he had left the treasurer's job because of trouble with Fastow. She and McMahon were close at one time—they were running and drinking buddies when they worked for Arthur Andersen in Houston. Sherron flew in from New York for his wedding; he and his wife came from London for hers. The two grew apart with his promotions, but he still returned her phone calls. This time, she left a message saying she needed some career advice; it was important, she said—she was thinking of going back to work for Andy.

McMahon called her back the next day. When she listed her options—Fastow or Investor Relations—McMahon told her to go to Investor Relations. Was that because McMahon never got along with Andy? she asked. No, he told her, he and Andy had buried the hatchet. Investor Relations, he said, was a better job.

But, she argued, she had a two-year-old, and her husband was working in Canada. There were long hours and hysteria before the quarterly meetings—two weeks of hell four times a year. On good days, you had to be at work by 7 A.M. to take calls from East Coast investors—which meant the nanny had to be at her house an hour before.

McMahon listened and considered. Maybe you're right, he said. Maybe the devil you know is better than the one you don't. But, he added, be careful.

The conversation turned to Enron's flagging stock price and the root causes. There was the decline in Enron's stock price-to-earnings multiple, dropping from a tech boom–induced high of 45 to a more rational 25. There was California and the litigation threat from a very angry Governor Davis. At the mention of California, McMahon's mood darkened.

"Have you been there lately?" he asked Sherron. "The traffic lights just go out—it's unbelievable. It's just not right; just because some moron leaves his keys in his Jaguar," McMahon added, "doesn't give you the right to steal it."

What did McMahon mean exactly? Sherron wondered. What did he know that she didn't?

Thanks to Ryan Siurek's restructuring genius, Enron reported $425 million in earnings at the end of the first quarter of 2001. The threat of losses from the Raptors passed; Enron could move forward—and gloat up and down Wall Street.

Jeff Skilling arrived for the analysts' call in a better mood than usual. Like a star giving himself a moment before entering the stage, he kept them on hold listening to Enron's taped rock-and-roll music while he prepared himself.

"Pretty good stuff," Skilling said when he finally came on the line. "We're all dancing here."

And for the next fifteen minutes, he went into his usual spiel about how it was going to be another great year, how things at Enron had never been better.

"So in conclusion, first-quarter results were great," he said. "We are very optimistic about our new businesses and are confident that our record of growth is sustainable for many years to come."

No one asked about India, or about Broadband. When someone asked about California—did Enron have exposure there—Skilling tensed, and a steely edge came into his voice. Enron had been in the business for ten years, he said; he knew the credit quality of every trading partner they had, and there were five thousand of them. Enron was not going to get left holding the bag in California.

He had just started to relax again when they told him a Richard Grubman was on the line. Grubman's company was called Highfields Capital Management, but to Skilling he was just another short seller, and he wasn't in the mood to take the abuse. Grubman started in almost immediately:

Why didn't Enron release its balance sheet, with assets and liabilities, at the same time it reported its profits?

"That's not our policy," Skilling said, his voice tight.

"You're the only financial institution that can't produce a balance sheet or a cash-flow statement with their earnings," Grubman retorted.

For just a moment, there was silence. *Who does this guy think he is?* "Well, thank you very much," he said through clenched teeth. "We appreciate it."

Then Skilling turned to the other people in the room, met their eyes, grinned, and turned back to the microphone. "Asshole," he added.

On another floor of the Enron building, the entire PR department let out a collective gasp.

Every time Skilling got one thing under control, it seemed something else gave way. First it was the Raptors, then it was India—Enron walked away from the deal, leaving $1 billion in equity to rust after the government refused to pay its bills. (Rebecca Mark offered to come back to renegotiate the deal for free—she didn't want to leave the Indians in the lurch—and Lay had considered the idea. "This is very interesting," he told Skilling about her proposal, after traveling to India himself and meeting with all the wrong government officials. But Skilling nixed Mark's return.)

Now, as winter turned to spring, it was California that threatened to spin out of control. In April, the Federal Energy Regulatory Commission ordered a set of price controls reinstated, and threatened to add more. The effect on Enron's cash flow would be devastating. Then, in May, California filed lawsuits against Enron and several other power merchants, alleging conspiracy and price fixing. The effect on the stock price was predictable: It dropped into the low $50s. It had not gone up since Skilling became CEO.

Skilling's drinking increased. His temper was short; he even shot the finger at Enron employees who dared to honk at him as he cut them off to get his car into the garage ahead of them. He wasn't sleeping. One morning, at a fiftieth-floor meeting, Lay sent him home to get himself cleaned up, as if he were a high school senior who showed up for first period after spending the night on the town. Skilling said that he was dressed sloppily because he was working on his new house.

L ay had problems of his own. Clinging to his unshakable faith in PR,
Enron launched a campaign to fight increasing regulation in California
and to spruce up its reputation. Steve Kean, Enron's head of government
affairs, hit the road to educate the masses with a presentation called "The California Electricity Debacle and the Lessons to Be Learned." The presentation
described the "myths" the state of California was creating, which included
"California is the victim of out-of-state power suppliers"; "California has sufficient power generation and transmission capacity to meet its needs"; and
"Enron played a leading role in the California debacle and should pay
refunds." Enron "facts" included these points: "California is the victim of bad
decisions by state officials, despite warnings that its unique regulatory structure
was flawed"; "California completed no new electricity-generating facilities in
over ten years, despite recent blackouts"; and "Enron is owed substantial sums
by California utilities that *far exceed* the state's de minimus refund claims
against Enron." The presentation concluded with an appeal: "Based on myths,
Gov. Davis says, 'Where do we go to get our money back?' Enron says, based
on these facts, 'Where do we go to get our good name back?'"

Lay followed Kean on the hustings, hosting an ill-conceived meeting in
Los Angeles with Richard Riordan, Arnold Schwarzenegger, and Michael
Milken. But the tide was turning against the energy companies, as rates and
blackouts increased. If this was deregulation, California's citizens wanted no
part of it. Enron's press grew darker: California Attorney General Bill Lock-
yer told *The Wall Street Journal* that he would love "to personally escort Lay
to an 8 × 10 cell that he could share with a tattooed dude who says, 'Hi, my
name is Spike, honey.'"

But Lay remained largely above the fray, because he had retired to the
chairman of the board spot. Skilling had to take the pressure now, and his
usually acute inner radar seemed to go totally dark. On June 12, Skilling
spoke to the Strategic Directions technology conference in Las Vegas. From
the dais, he was introduced as the leader of "America's most innovative
company," and he was described as "the number-one CEO in the entire
country." He bounded on stage, his shirt collar open, his jacket flying. His
topic was the Internet and all the as-yet-undiscovered applications to come.
"We couldn't do what we're doing now without the technology of the Internet," he told the crowd, which was with him.

Then he asked for questions from the audience.

What did he think about the power crisis in California, someone asked. What could the state have done differently to avoid its problems?

"Oh, I can't help myself," Skilling said, and those who knew him tensed in their seats. "I know I'm going to regret this," he added.

He gave himself another beat, one in which he could have stopped himself, but he didn't. "What's the difference between California and the *Titanic*? At least when the *Titanic* went down," he said, "the lights were on."

The next day, June 13, the California Attorney General announced an investigation into energy price increases. On June 18, the FERC bowed to pressure from state officials and the U.S. Senate and expanded the price caps instituted in April to all the western states. Prices across the West were frozen; power sellers could no longer go next door and force higher prices on California from across the border. The crisis ended.

Skilling was unrepentant. He kept his date with members of the Commonwealth Club in San Francisco, one of the oldest speakers' forums in the country. He was not exactly a local hero. From 2000 to 2001, California experienced 265 power emergencies, thirty-nine of which were Stage Three with authorized blackouts. But Skilling wanted to tell his side of the story. Enron's lawyers told him not to go. He was a subpoena risk, and the possibility of service was likely.

Warning him only made Skilling more determined to go. Enron could step up security and give him a Kevlar vest; he was going. No one could tell him what he could and couldn't do. He took a briefing on the handling of hecklers and started packing. A few days earlier, meeting with a group of associates, someone had asked him how he was doing. "This," he said, "has been the worst day of the worst week of the worst month of the worst year of my life." But he was going to keep fighting.

When the Enron team arrived at the club, Skilling had the limousine driver circle the block twice. He couldn't believe the size of the crowds out front, and he couldn't believe how angry they were. Some of them were wearing homemade masks of his face, and they were chanting "Jeffrey Skilling, stop the killing." (No one, in fact, had died from the energy crisis, but the rhyme was slick.)

Inside, the San Francisco Police Department had set up metal detectors and was checking bags. The room—deeply paneled and softly sunlit in a nineteenth-century way—was packed. The crowd hushed as Skilling walked in, having entered the building through a service door. The audience was surly. The hecklers were heckled by members of the audience, who insisted Skilling be allowed to speak.

He was midway through his PowerPoint presentation—telling the crowd that the Midwest built peaker power plants almost overnight to solve their crisis in 1998—when she came at him, a young woman in baggy clothes with stringy blond hair, rushing the stage. The next thing he knew, something warm was dripping down the side of his face—blood mixed with blueberry pie. He wiped his face with a few proffered paper towels—and kept talking.

In mid-June 2001, Sherron Watkins began working for Andy Fastow again. It was a fact she preferred not to dwell on, because it made her feel as though somewhere, somehow, in her careful advancement within the company, she had taken a wrong turn. Everyone seemed glad to see her: Running into Sherron in the lobby one day, Lea Fastow hugged her and said how happy she was that Sherron had returned to the fold. She was busy being Enron's art buyer now, spending around $4 million to ensure that the company had a collection worthy of its cutting edge reputation. Andy was nice enough, too. He'd told Michael Kopper, "Hey, we need to get Sherron into one of these LJM deals."

Sherron's job was to review all the assets that Enron was considering for sale and determine the likely economic impact.

The work was dull, but she went home at five, which was her goal. In her opinion, Fastow had really hired a spy. He didn't know what to do with his new M&A responsibilities, and he'd inherited Baxter's M&A personnel who did. In the world of Enron, they were lying in wait for Fastow to slip up. He wanted Sherron to be his eyes and ears.

She had stepped from one political mine field into another. The head of Enron's M&A group tried to move her out of Fastow's cost center into his; he didn't see why Fastow should have a private M&A executive. Fastow fought the man off, but that didn't stop the M&A head from telling Sherron that he was going to treat her as if she worked for him anyway. Now she had two bosses. If she didn't toe the line, she'd probably suffer in the PRC, made worse by Skilling's reinstatement of the dreaded forced ranking system. The only good news was that Jim Fallon's purge of Broadband had continued and her friend Kristina Mordaunt was the new general counsel of Fastow's M&A division.

Sherron worked with an Excel spreadsheet that was not very sophisticated—probably, she thought, because it had originated in Rick Causey's accounting office. The work was hellish—she pored over a worksheet filled with microscopic print listing more than 250 international and domestic assets. The goal was to determine which assets Enron should sell in 2001 and 2002 for the best deal. In other words, Sherron was hunting for cash.

First she took an inventory, trying to figure out the nature of each asset— which ones were hedged, which ones were off balance sheet, which ones were on balance sheet, which ones were generating earnings, and which ones were a cash drain. Elektro, the big utility in Brazil, for instance, could be sold at a loss compared to its Enron book value, but that loss would still generate close to $1 billion that could be used to lower the company's debt. Really, Sherron thought to herself impatiently, this was not work worthy of a VP.

But then a series of assets attracted her attention. Avici, New Power, Hanover Compressor—they were all part of a group of assets hedged with an entity called Raptor. The Raptors, unlike other entities on the spreadsheet, were distinguished by very large losses—losses in the hundreds of millions of dollars.

Sherron called someone in Causey's office to talk this over. She was then directed to Enron Energy Services and a pair of jolly employees, Jimmie Williams and Javier Li, who were more than happy to explain the relationship between an asset called New Power and something called Raptor III. Sherron met with them in an office with an extra-large whiteboard, which was needed as they drew multiple boxes connected with multiple arrows to show just why Enron expected losses on assets that were supposedly hedged with Raptor. If the two men had reservations about the Raptors and about the accounting, they didn't have the time to pursue them; they were too busy working on real business, and after all, Andersen had signed off on the deals. Who were they to question the accounting gurus? What Sherron could discern from the mind-numbing lecture was not complicated at all: The Raptors, devised to hedge Enron's equity investments in other companies, owed Enron hundreds of millions of dollars. They were capitalized with contingent (that is, promised) Enron stock, which was declining in value. By July, the stock dropped into the high $40s, a number inconceivable just a year before. As the value of the Raptors continued to fall, Enron had to keep adding more and more stock to keep them afloat—hundreds of millions of dollars.

Sherron said nothing after the demonstration, but she assumed the Raptors were a way to allow Enron to hedge risks in its left pocket with money from its right. While at Broadband, Sherron had heard that the unit had hedged its investment in the router company Avici with LJM2, and she'd marveled that Andy had raised such high-risk capital in his fund. Now she understood: He risked only the 3 percent equity slice in each Raptor vehicle; Enron was on the hook for the rest. She subsequently reviewed a related-party footnote in the financial statement for 2000 that indicated Enron had avoided booking a $500 million loss in 2000 with these Raptor structures.

She decided to start looking for another job right away. Enron was a disaster waiting to happen.

On August 14, she had lunch with Kathy Lynn, a former Enron VP now working at LJM and a friend with whom she shared Rockets basketball season tickets. Mostly they rehashed office gossip from earlier in the day—a major executive was resigning. Picking through their salads, neither woman could come up with a likely candidate.

Sherron changed the subject. She'd heard Michael Kopper had bought out Andy's interest in LJM2. "Michael must not have paid him very much with all those Raptor losses," she remarked idly.

Kathy Lynn gave her that Enron look, the one that said, *You are even dumber than I thought you were.*

If the Raptors go bankrupt, she told Sherron, it's no skin off LJM's nose. Then she told Sherron what a handful of others already knew—that Fastow structured the deals so LJM2 got its money out first. Sure there was equity at risk on paper, but LJM was out of the game. It didn't matter to them whether the Raptors went bankrupt or not.

But, thought Sherron, it mattered a lot to Enron: If LJM2 had nothing left at risk in the Raptor vehicles, who was at risk? Surely not just Enron. If so, the Raptors weren't just an aggressive accounting treatment. They were part of a scheme of income statement manipulation. The Raptors had kept hundreds of millions of losses off Enron's income statement.

Sherron became even more convinced she had to leave. I've got to get out of here, she thought. This is the worst accounting fraud I've ever seen. She would find another job and, on her last day, work up the nerve to confront Skilling with what she knew.

But Skilling beat her to the punch.

With the coming of summer, Skilling became a wraith. Addressing one hundred Enron Energy Services employees in early August, he tried to rally the troops. But one employee asked him why he was selling so much Enron stock. Annoyed at the question, he said that his sales were programmed for estate planning and to raise money for his new $4.2 million house. He tried to change the subject: EES, he said, would be a half-billion-dollar company in the next few years. How could that happen? another employee asked. "You guys are the creative ones," he said. "That's what you guys have to figure out." A few hours later, EES announced massive layoffs.

Then, on August 8, Skilling got the news that three Enron workers were killed in an explosion at the Teesside plant. Before he had time to process the news, he was on the plane, flying over the Atlantic to comfort the bereaved. He arrived and was driven by limousine to the homes of the families who lost their loved ones; he sat on the edge of the furniture for as long as was required, tried to say and do the right things, and wondered, simply, why he was there. What did it matter? Who was he to them? Then he was back on the plane, flying again toward Houston. The whole thing took forty-eight hours.

He had made his decision to leave back in July, having considered it as early as February, shortly after becoming CEO. Now he caught up with Lay after Lay returned from another trip to India. They covered a list of topics, and then, at the end, Skilling sprang it on him: He was quitting.

Why? Lay asked, stunned, partly because he was considering another job offer himself at the time.

Skilling said he wanted to spend more time with his family. His teenagers were going to college, and there was another family-related issue. Soon, the kids would be gone for good.

Was that it? Lay pressed.

The pressure, Skilling told him. The pressure and the slide in the stock price that he could not stop. He wasn't sleeping, he had lost weight, and he was powerless.

The two men talked for another half hour, and Skilling agreed to reconsider over the weekend, though he knew his answer would be the same the following Monday. On that day Lay tried, once more, to get him to stay. But Skilling was adamant.

That night, Skilling met with the board. Tearing up, he asked them to announce only that he was leaving for personal reasons, so that his children would not feel responsible for his departure. He didn't want any mention of health reasons, either. When they asked him once more to reconsider, reminding him how much work was left to do, he refused. He was through. The board met the following day, Tuesday, August 14, to formally accept his resignation.

Within days, Skilling was gone, off on a rafting trip with his youngest son. He left $20 million on the table, the value of his severance package. He didn't want anyone to entertain the thought that he had been fired.

17

Aboard the *Titanic*

SHERRON Watkins felt as if the wind was knocked out of her when she heard that Jeff Skilling was gone. Yes, there had always been jokes about Enron being on the brink of disaster—Rick Buy once began a talk at Enron's credit conference with a slide of the *Titanic*. But people made those jokes because they knew that whatever happened, Jeff would save them. He was Enron's ultimate hedge. And now, suddenly, Jeff had removed himself from the scene. Late at night, or in the early-morning hours when sleep remained elusive, Sherron lay in bed, stared at the ceiling, and tried to predict the future. She couldn't get the image of a sinking ocean liner out of her mind, one that lurched and listed through rough seas. The frightened passengers were howling, and the captain had just commandeered a cigarette boat and was speeding safely toward shore.

Skilling had left Enron because of his family? No one was buying that line, including Sherron. "Jeffrey Skilling's Surprising Split from Enron" was the way *Forbes* headlined his resignation. "The abruptness of the departure left

many analysts questioning whether a series of setbacks the company has suffered played a part in the decision," said the *The New York Times*. "Enron
CEO's Departure Not Passing the Smell Test," Christopher Edmonds
wrote in TheStreet.com. Michael Lewis was skeptical in Bloomberg: "It's a
bad sign for any big company when its male executives all of a sudden begin
to care about their personal lives. Having long since abandoned any chance of
a rich inner life, having shunted aside wives and kids for the sake of commercial glory, they are unlikely to experience any sort of inner awakening, unless
they sense there is no more glory left to be had." Sherron felt the same way.
This was the smartest man she had ever known. In her mind, Enron just
ran out of ideas. Enron Energy Services wasn't working, the New Power Company was floundering, Broadband was hopeless, and for over two years, despite
several efforts, none of the international assets had sold. What was going to
come down the pike and restore the company to health? And Sherron figured
that if she could do the math on the Raptors, so could Jeff Skilling. Meanwhile, the stock price kept dropping. Before Skilling resigned, it was in the low
$40s; the following day, it fell to $36, and was still moving downward. The
trading volume in Enron shares was through the roof, with nearly 30 million
shares changing hands on August 15, the day he resigned, while the usual volume was in the 2 to 4 million range.

Sherron's colleagues at Enron knew one indisputable fact about her:
Once she made a decision, it was virtually impossible to get her to change
her mind. This characteristic was something of an "issue" in her performance evaluations—she was impatient with people and sometimes ran
roughshod over them. (What one supervisor told her was this: "When someone says something you think is nonsensical, you cut them off at the jugular; then later, when you realize you've embarrassed the person or that he
might have something to contribute, you try to stop the bleeding, but it's too
late. He's got blood gushing down his shirtfront.")

Sherron also had only moderate respect for authority, a quality that was
generally admired at Enron. She wasn't afraid to challenge anyone when
she thought they were wrong. This was true of her even as a child. In eighth
grade her teacher was also the principal of her small Lutheran school; when
the man didn't show up often enough for class, or left kids on the play-
ground far too long, Sherron knew she was being shortchanged. Her uncles

were church elders, and so she went to them and complained. Soon the principal decided to move on. When you saw something wrong, she figured, there was nothing wrong with going to the top.

The day after Jeff Skilling resigned, Sherron Watkins decided to make things right. She sat down in front of her computer and started composing a letter.

Dear Mr. Lay,

Has Enron become a risky place to work? For those of us who didn't get rich over the last few years, can we afford to stay?

She believed that good always prevailed. The Raptors should be unwound. Enron should restate its financial reports. If someone—someone like her—presented a rational solution to upper management, they would do the right thing.

Sherron was not a pessimist. She believed that the people in charge at Enron would be grateful to her for pointing out a problem and suggesting solutions. She wasn't going to the press. She wasn't going to the government. She was going to go through channels, and display her loyalty to the company.

And so she kept typing:

Skilling's departure, she wrote, would raise suspicions of accounting improprieties and valuation issues. "The spotlight will be on us, the market just can't accept that Skilling is leaving his dream job," she wrote. She noted the problems with Raptor and the problems with Condor and wrote that unless the market got a clearer explanation of what was happening inside Enron, the company was going to look as if it was hiding losses from shareholders who, in turn, would flee once the deception was revealed.

"I am incredibly nervous that we will implode in a wave of accounting scandals," Sherron wrote. "My 8 years of Enron work history"—*Read: I am not a newcomer*—"will be worth nothing on my resume, the business world will consider the past successes as nothing but an elaborate accounting hoax. Skilling is resigning now for 'personal reasons' but I think he wasn't having fun, looked down the road and knew this stuff was unfixable and would rather abandon ship now than resign in shame in 2 years."

A public flogging was probably unavoidable. "We are under too much scrutiny and there are probably one or two disgruntled 'redeployed' employees who know enough about the 'funny' accounting to get us in trouble."

So what was Enron supposed to do? Sherron wasn't sure that anything could be done about the present situation, but there was still time to avert major disaster down the road. Lay, for instance, could still save Enron. "Can you give some assurances that you and Causey will sit down and take a good hard objective look at what is going to happen to Condor and Raptor in 2002 and 2003?" Otherwise, she thought, we've all booked passage on the same sinking ship. Although Sherron felt brave enough to put her concerns on paper, she didn't feel brave enough to sign her name to this memo. This was Enron, after all.

She put her letter in an unmarked envelope and asked her assistant to walk it down to the drop box that had been set up for employee questions, the ones that would be answered at an emergency meeting scheduled the following day to allay employees' concerns about Skilling's departure. A year or so back, she'd sent an anonymous e-mail to Skilling and Lay about the sale of some South American assets. The company kept the potential deal a secret—it was code-named "Project California"—from most at Enron International, which struck Sherron as "bass-ackwards." Why have a stealth effort when people within the international division knew which assets would sell quickly and which ones wouldn't move if you paid someone to take them? McMahon, who was treasurer by then, blanched when she told him about her anonymous missive. The ex-CIA spooks Enron employed had ways of locating the author, he told her. Don't do that again.

Sherron put another copy of her memo in an interoffice envelope marked "Confidential" and sent it to McMahon, putting her name in the "From" box. She wanted his opinion about what she was doing. When she didn't hear back from him within a few hours, she called to tell him what she had done.

"That was you?" he asked.

His secretary either missed or ignored the large CONFIDENTIAL stamp on the front of the envelope. She left it on McMahon's desk in plain sight. McMahon never saw the envelope. He read the memo and then passed it on to a few of his friends, who were probably passing it on to others right now.

Thank God, Sherron thought, no one knew who had written it.

It was safe to say that Sherron Watkins was not the only person at Enron operating in something of a state of shock.

When Skilling returned from his Idaho rafting trip, he ventured back to the building with his brother-in-law in tow, but the chill he felt inside the lobby was unmistakable. The fury of the traders was equal to the blind loyalty they once showed him. He knew he was no longer welcome, and so he stayed away.

In the meantime, Ken Lay was back in charge. Just seven months after leaving the company in Skilling's hands, he called an All Employee Meeting, and at 9 A.M., everyone who could leave their desks hustled the two blocks north to the Hyatt Regency ballroom to hear what he had to say. They came in waves—thousands of people cramming into a bright, windowless room designed to hold boozy partygoers at upbeat conventions and charity balls.

Lay entered the room in shirtsleeves and tie, smiling and waving triumphantly, like a president returned to office, which, in a way, he was. The employees who managed to find seats stood to give him a standing ovation as he approached the stage. They kept clapping deliriously, until he motioned for them to stop. There was something contradictory in the scene—the company of the future ecstatically greeting its past.

The only people who didn't look quite so delirious, Sherron noted, were the managing directors and other high-ranking executives seated in the first three rows. Greg Whalley, the head of Wholesale Services, looked particularly sour. The head trader was already jockeying to replace Skilling. *Lay doesn't know what he's getting into,* Sherron thought.

She looked around the room and saw employees with kids to educate, with sick parents or ailing spouses, people with house payments and bills to pay. Enron made its billions on volatility, but now they wanted stability, and they wanted an end to the dog-eat-dog hierarchy Skilling had built. But they still wanted to be part of the world's leading energy company. Every once in a while, a managing director would check his Blackberry—the fancy palm organizers that were de rigueur at Enron—just to see where the stock was going. Even with the announcement of Lay's return, it was still hovering in the mid-30s. "I can honestly say that the company is in the strongest shape it's ever been in," Lay told his followers. He was reiterating an e-mail he had sent to employees earlier in the day, promising, "Our performance has never been stronger. Our business model has never been more robust; our growth has never been more certain."

In front of the crowd, Lay vowed that the stock price would go back up. He would replace the departed with people of equal talent. The company still had plenty of bench strength, he said. And he would preside over a kinder, gentler Enron. "Our vision and values have slipped, *but*," Lay added, "we're gonna work on that." This last remark engendered rousing applause.

Things were going to work out just fine, Lay continued. But if anyone still had concerns, he wanted to hear them. Anyone could contact him — they just had to call the head of Human Relations, Cindy Olson. Olson, a bubbly blonde with big hair who stood nearby, beamed at the crowd, just as she had in 1999, when she stood beside Skilling at another all-employee meeting and answered a resounding *Yes!* when asked by a worker whether all his 401(k) money should be in Enron stock.

Leaving, Sherron felt as if she had been at a rousing tent revival. She'd gone early, sat up close, and listened intently while Lay talked about the need to improve Enron's values. She took him at his word when he promised to be available to all employees. Make an appointment with me through Cindy Olson, the head of HR, he'd said. After the meeting, Sherron headed straight for Olson's office. She didn't want to hide behind her anonymous letter anymore; she wanted to explain the problems to Lay face-to-face.

Olson's secretary looked dubious when Sherron asked for a meeting. Cindy was busy, she explained, and then she was catching a plane out of town. Did Sherron need to see her right away?

Well, yes. Sherron trusted Ken Lay — but only so far. She was glad he was back in charge, but she'd begun to worry that Lay might make Fastow or Causey COO. This move, she was certain, would spell disaster for Enron, and it was this message she had to convey to Lay. And to get to Lay she had to go through Olson. She told Olson's secretary she'd wait, and settled into one of the plush chairs in the reception area.

As the minutes stretched into an hour or so, Sherron could not help but notice how frankly feminine the floor was. The color scheme was both brighter and more tasteful than on the other Enron floors—gay hues right out of the J. Crew catalog—and the green and blue walls were punctuated with shelves displaying myriad awards thanking Enron for its generosity: a bowl from the United Way, Steuben from the NAACP. Almost all the gifts were crystal.

If someone gave Enron a simple wooden plaque, it got stashed away. Sherron even spied the crystal bridge she'd used as the SK deal toy, this one revamped to celebrate something else.

Finally, Olson emerged, rushing down the hall and heading for her office, beaming at Sherron without losing her look of purposefulness. Not for nothing was Olson known as Enron's biggest cheerleader. She'd been with the company since the Omaha days. She worked in commercial support for Skilling at Enron Gas Services; Lay moved her to the community giving program. Later, he gave her Human Relations, too. Like Beth Tilney, Olson was known to be a Lay favorite, although they were both referred to, by various detractors, as members of his "harem." Olson's stock fell with Skilling's rise—he didn't like community relations—but rebounded with his departure, and she now wore the pleased, confident look of someone who was going to do her very best for you, whether she was or not.

Olson ushered Sherron into her office, which contained even more awards courtesy of Neiman-Marcus and one gigantic framed photograph of sunset over Enron Field. Sherron sat down at her conference table and pulled out her copy of the anonymous letter she'd sent to Lay. After reading it, Olson looked vexed. "I'll tell you what," she began, "Ken gravitates toward good news." It was one of his greatest strengths and one of his greatest weaknesses, she said. In fact, Olson was sure Lay showed Sherron's memo around, and everyone—including Jim Derrick, the chief counsel, Andy Fastow, and Rick Causey—probably told him there was nothing to worry about. Olson thought Sherron would get a better result if she met with Lay in person. Ken responds better to people that way, Olson continued. Would Sherron be willing to identify herself and meet with Lay?

Absolutely, Sherron replied. Olson stood up, indicating the end of the meeting, and told Sherron she'd put in a call to Lay. He had left immediately after the all-employee meeting for New York, to calm the analysts. Was Sherron in a hurry? Could she wait until next week?

Well, Sherron said, she was not in a hurry as long as Lay didn't appoint anyone to the COO job until she had spoken with him. Uh-oh, Olson said. She knew Lay intended to move quickly on that very thing.

Just prior to Skilling's departure, Andy Fastow finally relinquished control of LJM. But there was a last-minute snag: It had to do with Chewco, the mother of all special-purpose vehicles that Fastow created in 1997. When Chewco was unwound in 2000, Fastow lobbied hard and got Kopper $10 million as his payout.

But during the summer of 2001, Kopper needed more money. He was buying Fastow out of LJM and was a little short. He thought Enron should pay the taxes on his profits from Chewco—$2.6 million in taxes, to be exact. It had been part of the original Chewco agreement, he insisted. Jordan Mintz consulted with Vinson & Elkins on the claim, and the law firm agreed with him that there was no way the contract covered this sort of request. It made no sense.

Kopper listened to Mintz's explanation that the contract terms were meant to cover temporary differences between taxable income and cash flow, and then told him he'd be back in touch after he spoke with Fastow. Mintz then called Fastow and told him, as he had told Kopper, that he would not approve the $2.6 million tax payment.

Fastow listened, and then told Mintz he would talk to Skilling about it. Shortly thereafter, Enron cut a $2.6 million check to Michael Kopper.

The night of August 16, Sherron Watkins found that she still could not sleep. Was she the only person who sensed that financial disaster was just an iceberg away? By her definition, Enron was a trading company, and trading companies did not survive accounting scandals. Customers didn't care about Waste Management's accounting games—and they had been big, one of the biggest in the last decade. As long as their trash got picked up, they kept paying Waste Management's bill. But trading involved an intricate series of promises that stretched far into the future. If Enron was having financial problems, how would their customers know they could depend on the company to buy or sell the power they needed? Maybe they should simply take their business elsewhere.

Then, too, trading contracts contained clauses that referred to "material adverse changes," which meant that any misfortune allowed a customer to accelerate the terms of an agreement and close out positions immediately, instead of on future maturity dates. Enron's trading activities were also heavily dependent on credit; an anxious customer could demand cash up front, or insist that more money be placed in a reserve account as insurance against future losses. It occurred to Sherron that even if Enron came clean and announced that its balance sheet had problems, equity investors would not be forgiving. They would want to know why Enron lied, and why they should ever trust the company again.

Back at her desk the next morning, Sherron started drafting another memo to Ken Lay. She wanted to recommend a lawyer at Vinson & Elkins, but couldn't remember his name. She picked up the phone and placed a call to Fastow's in-house attorney, Kristina Mordaunt, her friend.

When Sherron asked Kristina the name of the lawyer at Vinson & Elkins, there was a pause on the other end of the line. Why do you want to know? Mordaunt asked.

Sherron told her she was meeting with Ken Lay on some issues and might want to recommend him for a project.

What issues? Mordaunt wanted to know.

Come to my office, Sherron told her. I'll talk to you about it.

Sherron valued Mordaunt's counsel. Rail thin, with long dark hair, she was an attractive careerist—the rumor around the company was that she wanted to be chief counsel one day. Sherron showed Mordaunt the letter she had written and discussed the one she was drafting. Mordaunt responded with a grimace. Why are you doing this? she wanted to know. Are you trying to bring down the company?

For a moment, Sherron was speechless. She wasn't the one who had steered the ship into an iceberg. Couldn't Kristina see that she was just trying to save the ship or at least get the captain of the ship to man the lifeboats?

Kristina looked unimpressed and unconvinced, and Sherron felt herself growing more and more flustered. If this was Kristina's reaction, what would happen if she were ever named in the press as the author of the letter? Would twenty thousand employees blame her for sinking the company?

After listening to Sherron's doomsday scenario for a little longer, Mordaunt proposed a compromise. Before she went to Lay, Sherron should first see Jim Derrick or another Enron attorney, Rex Rogers. That way, she'd be going through the proper channels. Besides, V&E would be the wrong firm to investigate any problems with Andy's deals. They'd worked on too many SPEs and clearly had a conflict.

Sherron never liked the smell on the forty-eighth floor. It had been home to Enron's legal department for too many years. She couldn't understand why a floor in an ultramodern skyscraper smelled like her grandmother's attic in Tomball. It was permeated with the odor of rotting paper—not quite mildew, but lots of must. Rex Rogers seemed in keeping with that image; pale, with thinning hair, he reminded her of someone who didn't get out much. Kristina put in a call after her meeting with Sherron and lined up the midafternoon appointment with Rogers that very day. Sherron had worked with Rogers on JEDI; his office didn't appear to have changed much since 1995. The floor and furniture were covered with stacks of paper. He moved several piles to give Sherron room to sit down.

"Oh, *you're* the one," he said when she identified herself as the author of the memo to Lay. Like too many others at Enron, he knew about the memo. He had also heard that Causey and Fastow didn't think it raised any issues of concern.

Listening, Sherron felt a tightening in her jaw. (*Listen before you see blood gushing from their throats!!* . . .) Deliberately, she explained her concerns about the Raptors, Fastow's conflict, and other potential land mines, and then showed Rogers a crisis plan she had drafted: Enron, she stated, should hire another accounting firm—not Andersen—to go over the numbers again. Enron should hire a law firm—not Vinson & Elkins—to reexamine the legality of the various off-balance-sheet deals. And no one should be appointed to chief operating officer until that was done, certainly not Fastow or Causey. As she wrote in her memo: "Best case—clean up quietly, if possible. Worst case, develop public relations and investor relations campaigns, customer assurance plans." Don't behave, in other words, like Salomon Brothers, which in 1990 was almost destroyed by its own secretiveness in a Treasury bond trading scandal.

Rogers listened indulgently, then asked Sherron a question: Did she *really* want to take these concerns to Ken Lay? Arthur Andersen and Vinson & Elkins had signed off on all these deals. Andy Fastow and Rick Causey knew their business. These were big, experienced firms and very smart people. Why would they risk everything to proceed with the flawed structures she was describing?

Sherron's face grew hot, and her eyes started to fill. She looked down at the carpet, which was covered with Rogers' papers. Well, she began again, she was very troubled by what she found. So troubled, in fact, that she intended to quit. But after Skilling resigned, she decided that coming forward was the right thing to do. Lay was promising to restore the company to its former glory, and she wanted him to know what he was getting into.

Whether it was the tears or the force of her argument, Rogers began to backpedal. Yes, Enron did push its accountants, he said. And he had been remiss himself. He was supposed to review all of Enron's stock-related matters, but he hadn't looked at Fastow's closely since 1999. Fastow was using so much contingent Enron equity in his SPE deals—backstopping weaker assets with the promise of future Enron shares if the assets were insufficient to repay lenders—that he had asked for and received permission to hire his own lawyers for his Global Finance unit. Fastow operated more or less independently of Enron Corp. from then on. The meeting ended with Rogers saying he'd talk with Derrick about Sherron's concerns and tell him she was determined to meet with Lay.

Then he got up and walked her to the door. It might be a while before she heard anything about the investigation, Rogers told her. These were sensitive matters, and she would have to be patient.

Sherron had always prided herself on her Enron network, staying in touch with buddies in other divisions that kept her in the loop. Now, in anticipation of an August meeting with Ken Lay, she employed her exten-sive Rolodex in the service of her personal investigation. She called friends in the RAC group, friends in Global Finance, and friends in Credit, who briefed her on the history of the Raptors. In this way, she found out about the restructuring that had occurred in March, and gathered, from her con-tacts, that no one thought the fix would last. Trouble was looming, they told her. In fact, secretive teams were meeting now to come up with another fix for the third quarter, because the Raptors were underwater again. Once more, Enron would have to come up with additional stock to restore them—at least another quarter billion dollars' worth.

On the following Monday, August 20, Sherron arrived at her office to find that Cindy Olson had forwarded a copy of a confidential e-mail from Rick Causey dated August 15. He had read her anonymous letter and writ-ten to Lay, disagreeing with her disaster scenario. He thought, in fact, that Lay should avoid making any comments about Raptor or Condor at the upcoming all-employee meeting. "I would not read this question," Causey wrote. "I would simply state that there was a question submitted regarding structured transactions and the use of contingent equity."

If Lay felt compelled to answer, he should say that "all transactions that use Enron equity currently or in the future are fully accounted for today." Lay could also add that Enron routinely used contingent equity in its struc-tured finance deals, and when the economics of a transaction indicated that new stock would actually have to be issued, the company properly ac-counted for the additional shares in its earnings per share calculations to shareholders.

Huh? Sherron wondered. This was like a bank robber claiming that he didn't speed on the way to a heist. What about the $500 million of hidden losses on the income statement? Where was that?

Olson also left Sherron a voice mail: Lay said that if Causey's response did not satisfy Sherron, he was still happy to meet with her.

Sherron was *not* satisfied. She called Cindy Olson back. Yes, she still wanted to meet with Mr. Lay. Fine, Cindy responded, she could see him the day after tomorrow, Wednesday at 1 P.M.

Later that day, Sherron started organizing her presentation. Worrying that she had not told Rick Buy of her plans, she called his office. He was on vacation, his secretary told her. Sherron left a message. He was, after all, the chief risk officer of the company. He should know what she was doing and why. She'd worked with him in the past and believed that he shared her concerns about Enron's aggressive accounting. When Buy called her back later in the day, Sherron asked whether he'd like to see her materials. No, he told her, he'd rather not. He sounded deflated, exhausted by the thought of one more office battle.

It was also on this day that Sherron put in a call to Jim Hecker at Arthur Andersen, to ask for guidance. Hecker had been her mentor—he always urged her to push for what she thought was right—and he had an irreverent way of dispensing advice that Sherron was receptive to. If anyone could help her find her way through this thicket, Hecker could.

For about forty-five minutes, he listened carefully to Sherron's now familiar monologue on the dangers of the Raptors and Fastow's inherent conflict. His answer was not what she expected. "I hope you're not right, because this firm can't handle another scandal," he told her.

When Hecker got off the phone, he wrote a memo to the file at Andersen. "Based on our discussion, I told [Watkins] she appeared to have some good questions. I emphasized that I was uninvolved in the issues or client and therefore unable to give her any definitive advice or conclusions on these matters, especially [without] knowing all the facts, which she understood. However, I encouraged her to discuss these issues with anyone in the company who could satisfy her about the accounting and disclosures related to these transactions." He forwarded the memo to David Duncan and another Enron audit partner, Debra Cash, with a note that said: "Here is my draft memo, for your review, for 'smoking guns' that you can't extinguish."

Sherron also told Jeff McMahon that she intended to meet with Lay, and asked to show him her materials. When Sherron put the Raptor memos she intended to show Lay in front of McMahon, he winced at a headline, "Summary of Raptor Irregularities," and suggested she change it. The title was too inflammatory for Lay. Sherron toned it down to "Summary of Raptor Oddities." Then, after reading a few more paragraphs, he called his secretary to clear his calendar for the next few hours.

McMahon saw two problems with going to Lay: First, he told Sherron, she had a credibility issue, because it was her opinion against those of Causey, Fastow, Andersen, and V&E. Second, Sherron would have to be clear and credible in a very short time. Lay had a short attention span, so she would have to distill her very complicated discoveries into a half-hour monologue that was free of any accounting jargon. If she couldn't do that, she would be lost. Her goal, he advised, should be to make Lay just nervous enough to open an investigation.

Even then, he told Sherron, he wasn't sure she'd accomplish much. He'd gone to Skilling with his complaints about Fastow, McMahon told her, only to be turfed to another job within days. McMahon felt he was set up to be fired down the road, but luckily, the new company had made money. Sherron could tell Lay that story, he said. In the meantime, he would call Cindy Olson and ask her to tell Lay that he should hear her out.

That night, Sherron distilled her talking points down to a page and a half. The accounting treatment on Raptor looked "questionable." Enron booked a $500 million gain from equity hedges with a related party in 2000. That related party, she wrote, was thinly capitalized, with no party at risk except Enron. Further, she said, it appeared that Enron boosted its income statement primarily with its own stock.

The question she wanted to ask Lay was this: The related-party entity, a.k.a. the Raptors, had lost $500 million in deals with Enron. Who would bear that loss? Sherron could find no third-party debt or equity investors that would be responsible. If Enron was responsible for the loss, then Enron had been doing deals with itself. That was not a generally accepted accounting principle. Or, as Sherron put it, "I think we do not have a fact pattern that would look good to the SEC or investors."

In addition, the hedges on New Power and various tech investments were made at the peak of the market. It was unlikely that any other company (read: anyone in their right mind) would enter into such risky hedges in the first place. "This fact pattern," Sherron continued, "is once again very negative for Enron."

Then she added a few points from her conversation with McMahon. There was the "veil of secrecy around LJM and Raptor. Employees question our accounting propriety consistently and constantly. This alone is cause for concern." McMahon, she wrote, was "highly vexed over the conflicts of LJM." Cliff Baxter had complained to Skilling "and all who would listen about the inappropriateness of our transactions with LJM. I have heard one manager level employee from the principle investments group say, 'I know it would be devastating to all of us, but I wish we would get caught. We're such a crooked company.'"

If that didn't get Ken Lay to open an investigation, nothing would.

S herron didn't think of herself as a nervous person, but when she climbed the interior staircase to Ken Lay's fiftieth-floor office on August 22, she knew she wasn't completely in control of herself. For one thing, she hadn't slept in days. Every night, she found herself waking up at 2 A.M., revisiting her worries and rehearsing her description of them to Lay. She typed, cut, pasted, and inserted shorter, simpler words until it seemed to her that her two-year-old daughter could understand the problems. She was going to be earnest and respectful but a little pushy: Enron would have to come clean and restate its earnings.

When Sherron arrived, Lay was finishing a private lunch with Greg Whalley, the man most likely to succeed Skilling. Sitting in Lay's reception area, right outside his door, Sherron felt like a patient in a psychiatrist's waiting room—exposed to anyone who happened to pass by. The last thing she wanted was for Whalley to spot her and peg her for a troublemaker. With copies of her anonymous memo floating around the building, it wouldn't take long for him to discern the purpose of her visit.

"Is there someplace more private I could wait?" she finally asked Rosie, Lay's older but elegant assistant, who promptly escorted her into a small private conference room. This place was stocked with good coffee and shimmering crystal, along with the Spode china cups Lay favored. No plastic stir straws here, Sherron noted, figuring there were probably none to be had on the entire fiftieth floor.

Just then, Lay walked in. He wore the same wide, confident grin he offered George W. Bush and Mikhail Gorbachev, the grin that said he was a man of the world, and just this minute, he was happy to meet . . . *you.* He had been Sherron's boss for eight years, he'd sent her personalized Christmas cards, and he had signed off on every one of her bonus checks. Sherron figured his company had about a million dollars invested in her development.

"Hi," he said, extending his hand and locking his eyes on hers, "I'm Ken Lay."

She couldn't tell what Lay was feeling or thinking as she launched into her pitch. Maybe he was exhausted. He was traveling almost constantly since Skilling's resignation, meeting with investors, telling Paine Webber "there were no other shoes to drop," trying to fight rumors that Enron's credit rating was endangered. Unbeknownst to Sherron and virtually everyone around him, he was also selling stock. Over fifteen days in late August, he sold shares worth $20 million. By then, with the value of Enron's stock falling (stock he used as collateral for other investments), Lay was in a cash crisis of his own. He had sold shares in June, for about $19 million, just around the time Enron stock dipped below the trigger price specified in various SPE debt contracts and around the time of the India crisis and a contempt citation by a California Senate investigating committee. Some were sold as part of a series of automatic, or "programmed," sales, which he ceased as the stock price continued to fall. Proceeds from these sales were used to "repay" loans he had received from Enron. (Lay had used a $7.5 million revolving line of credit with Enron as his own personal ATM, disclosing in February 2002 that he'd "borrowed" $81 million from Enron in 2001 and repaid the company with its own stock—neatly avoiding the SEC disclosure rules that require CEOs to report their stock sales in the public market at the time they occur.)

Lay wasn't meeting her gaze, and he didn't ask many questions, but Sherron didn't think he was bored, either. "Andy's a good CFO, right?" he interrupted to ask her at one point. "He's doing a good job, right?"

"Well, uh, sure," Sherron answered, though she wondered how he could ask that question while she was giving him this particular presentation.

She continued, and he interrupted her once more. "You haven't gone outside the company with this, have you?" No, she said. She wanted him to make things right at the company.

When she finished, he asked a very familiar question: Was she sure something could be wrong? The board and Arthur Andersen went over the Raptor deals in detail, Lay noted. Well, Sherron explained, going into her deliberate voice again, it was never appropriate for a company to use its stock to directly affect its income statement, whether it was to hide a loss or boost revenues. To her mind, that is just what happened with Raptor.

Also, she warned, Andersen had been wrong in the past—remember their involvement in the Waste Management scandal? Skilling's departure was sure to raise questions in the marketplace. Enron had to be ready.

Lay listened for another moment, nodded studiously, and then, suddenly, became animated again. What could he do for *her*? he asked.

She told him she'd like to move to Cindy Olson's group until another job could be found. She couldn't stay with Fastow. Lay nodded in agreement. Sherron told him she was going to Mexico for a short vacation; Lay said he'd speak with Olson and have an answer for her when she returned.

That night, she packed gleefully for San Miguel. She spoke out, and Lay stepped up. Andy called just before she left the office, and the conversation was cordial. He had no idea.

Everything was going to work out fine.

18

The Spin Cycle

THE first sign that all was not well was the number of urgent messages in Sherron's voice mailbox the day she got back from San Miguel de Allende. There were at least two voice mails from Jeff McMahon, one angrier than the one before. He said that somehow his support of Sherron led Ken Lay to the conclusion that he—McMahon—agreed with everything she said in her memos. McMahon was not happy about this. He reminded Sherron that he hadn't been an accountant for almost a decade, hadn't been treasurer for eighteen months, and didn't know anything about the Raptors. She shouldn't have spoken for him.

Flustered, Sherron called him back right away. She didn't mislead Lay about McMahon's opinions. Lay heard what he wanted to hear, she said. All Sherron did was tell the story of McMahon's transfer after complaining about Fastow to Skilling; Lay drew his own conclusions from that.

McMahon was only slightly mollified. He had also spent what he called "a very uncomfortable hour" with Fastow, who now knew Sherron was the author of the anonymous letter. Fastow accused McMahon of being her ghostwriter, or, at least, her instigator. McMahon's last words to Sherron were unequivocal: This was her deal with Ken Lay. "Leave me out of it," he said, and hung up the phone.

The next morning, Sherron went to an ethics seminar required for maintaining her CPA license, so she got into the office late. It was August 30. She found that in her absence, Ken Lay had ordered an investigation of LJM and the Raptors, and that Fastow was screaming for her head. Sherron's secretary didn't tell her about the message she received from Andy's secretary. It was Sherron's birthday, and she didn't want to spoil it by telling her that Fastow wanted both of them out of the building by the end of the day. Another message summoned Sherron to Cindy Olson's office. Steeling herself, Sherron headed for the sixteenth floor. "Andy is not behaving appropriately," Olson told her, raising her eyebrows for emphasis. He wanted Sherron fired immediately, and he wanted her computer. The good news was that his behavior was so suspicious that it had made Ken Lay mad. He told Fastow he wasn't going to make him COO, and that he, Lay, was launching an investigation into LJM.

What Sherron didn't know was that Enron had launched another kind of investigation simultaneously. A lawyer at Vinson & Elkins sent a memo to Sharon Butcher, an Enron attorney in charge of employee relations. The first half of the memo was devoted to helping the company help Sherron make a transition to a new job. Her new position, he advised, should be comparable to her old one. "I suggest that . . . she not be treated adversely or differently because she made the report," the attorney advised.

Then there was the second half of the memo: "You also asked that I include in this communication a summary of the possible risks associated with discharging employees that report allegations of improper accounting practices," he continued. The attorney noted that Texas law did not protect whistleblowers; however, in any lawsuit that resulted from the firing of a whistleblower, "the company's accounting practices and books and records are fair game during discovery—the opposition typically will request production of volumes of sensitive material." Juries, the memo continued, were easily confused by technical material, and cases such as these were expensive and time-consuming to litigate. There was also the risk that "the discharged employee will seek to convince some government oversight agency (e.g., IRS, SEC, etc.) that the corporation has engaged in materially misleading reporting or is otherwise non compliant."

In other words, firing Sherron Watkins was worth considering, but it probably wasn't a good idea.

Ken Lay's response to Enron's problems—the declining stock price, the expanding spread on bond debt, the departure of major executives—was rooted in his unshakable faith in the power of appearances. Once again, he would present a concerned, calming, competent face to the world, and once again, he would, at the urging of Cindy Olson and Beth Tilney, commission a marketing survey of his employees. As was always the case at Enron, much time and effort went into the project, which was christened, with steely earnestness, The Lay It On The Line survey. Employees arrived in the lobby the last week of August to find smiling HR staff surrounded by boxes and boxes of Lay's potato chips. They passed out a bag to each employee along with a small card that imitated the bag's color scheme but offered Enron's Nutritional Facts: "Honest Feedback 100%, Confidential 100%, Responsive action steps 100%, Two-way communication 100%, Ingredients: Stuff to make us the world's leading company."

The card and the staff urged employees to go to Enron's Web site and click on "Lay It On The Line" to complete their survey right away. The nutritional fact card included a beaming Lay, who looked as if he might just reach out from the card and pat you on the back. Even though the survey was upbeat, the subtext was that, somehow, Enron had lost itself and didn't have much time to find itself again. Would you recommend this company to a friend? the survey asked. What are the biggest obstacles to achieving our goals?

People sat at their keyboards, clicked away, and sent messages to headquarters: They hated the Performance Review Committee, the "rank and yank" system Enron had for evaluating employees. They hated the way they were treated by traders like Greg Whalley. A few even expressed some concern about Andy Fastow, LJM, and Enron's accounting methods.

The HR department summarized the results for employees: They suggested improvements in the PRC, and they forwarded comments about specific executives to the subjects themselves. Some traders received a stack of etiquette tips nearly an inch high. No mention was made of any accounting concerns, maybe because HR valued quantity over quality. More than 3,000 people described their hatred of the PRC, while only a dozen people were worried about the accounting. The survey that should have provided Lay with *100% honest feedback* turned out to be less than that. It was as if Lay had been told the proverbial inmates were unhappy with the color of the asylum carpet and not about the homicidal maniac loose in the building.

By accident or design, no constructive action was taken. Maybe it was because people at the top were already too busy putting out other brushfires, and maybe it was because the real solution was untenable. Many employees wanted to get back to the old days, when people were nice to each other, but what no one seemed to recall, or wanted to admit, was that those were the days when Enron was just another $10 stock.

Lay left the navel-gazing to subordinates and hit the road, meeting with analysts and investors to preach the gospel of a kinder, gentler (read: much more open and transparent) Enron. Skilling launched a small simultaneous PR blitz, granting an interview to *The Wall Street Journal* on August 16, just a few days after resigning. Celebrities go to Barbara Walters or Dianne Sawyer to spruce up their reputations; businessmen go to the *Journal* for the same reason. Skilling confessed that the personal reasons he cited as the impetus for his resignation included his inability to get the stock price up. ("Mr. Skilling noted that Enron's share price had fallen by some 50% this year.") That move angered Lay and the board, who thought they'd made a deal: Publicly, the troubles were supposed to be Skilling's alone, not his former employer's.

Now, shuttling from Wall Street to big Boston banks, Lay had to work even harder to prove that Enron was in good shape. Countering, he confessed to a *Journal* reporter that Skilling had not responded well to the pressure of being CEO since he'd taken over in February.

Then, on August 28, which happened to be the day the *Journal* reported something fishy about Enron in its "Heard on the Street" column, Lay sat down for his own profile with the paper. The stock price was $38 a share. He talked about restoring Enron's lost credibility and mentioned that Fastow was out of LJM. He promised more detailed financial information to "give a better idea of the profitability of various businesses." The next day, Lay publicly announced his promotion to the Office of the Chair, a.k.a. the COO's job. The position would be divided between Greg Whalley, from trading, and Mark Frevert, a seasoned veteran from the pipeline world who'd successfully run the London trading operations. Whalley was the front-runner for the COO and eventually the CEO title. Within the company everyone assumed Frevert was along for the ride, to keep an eye on Whalley so Lay could return to semiretirement. The day after that, Lay announced the departure of two of Skilling's top loyalists, Ken Rice and Kevin Hannon, who once reigned as the emperors of Enron Broadband Services.

As far as Enron's rank and file was concerned, they might as well have stayed on. The appointment of Whalley signaled the final ascension of the traders. No matter what Lay promised, he was showing his loyalty to the asset-lite Enron that Jeff Skilling created.

As August eased into September, with day-to-day leadership of the company reinstated, Lay settled back into his comfortable role as head cheerleader. The falling stock price, he told employees, made Enron a great buy. "Our third quarter is looking great," he told them in an online meeting. "We will hit our numbers. We are continuing to have strong growth in our businesses, and at this time I think we are very well positioned for a very strong fourth quarter." Now was the time to recommend the stock to friends and family: "My personal belief," he said, "is that Enron stock is an incredible bargain at current prices."

But in some of Houston's wealthiest circles, like the lunch crowd at the Coronado Club, where investment advisor Fayez Sarofim dined each day, and where Amanda Martin and Rebecca Mark once stopped conversation with their abbreviated hemlines, people thought otherwise.

Part of the problem had to do with the rumors swirling about the Raptors. In August, accountants at Arthur Andersen realized that they had made a big accounting mistake. A supersized mistake. Despite the intense care given the vehicles, Andersen erroneously approved an accounting entry when the Raptors were restructured in the first quarter of 2001. Enron con-tributed $1.2 billion of contingent common shares to Raptor in exchange for a $1.2 billion note. Andersen booked the amount wrong: as a note receivable (an asset) instead of a charge against equity (something like a debit).

No one caught the mistake for two quarters. By then, Enron was faced with reversing—that is, reducing—shareholders' equity by $1.2 billion in the third quarter, the one that was already being closely watched because of suspicions surrounding Skilling's resignation. How was Enron going to finesse this problem? Especially when the stock price was sliding from $36 a share to around $30.

Just as the stock looked as though it might rebound thanks to Lay's relentless sales pitches, two hijacked commercial jets, piloted by disciples of Osama Bin Laden, crashed into the World Trade Center on the morning of September 11. The towers collapsed less than an hour and a half later, resulting in a death toll in the thousands. Another struck the Pentagon, killing hundreds more. A fourth hijacked jet heading for Washington crashed in a fireball in a field in Pennsylvania. Most Americans thought they were witnessing the beginning of World War III, a threat to the very existence of the United States. The nation came to a standstill, as people huddled close, attended prayer vigils, and wondered what additional acts of terrorism tomorrow would bring. The New York Stock Exchange closed Tuesday morning in the wake of the attacks and did not open again until the following Monday. When it did, all stocks fell precipitously, including Enron's, which dropped to $25 a share. More important to financiers, how-ever, was the overall tightening of capital. It would become increasingly dif-ficult, in the months following 9/11, as the day of infamy became known, for large corporations to borrow money.

Within Enron, few people had time to notice the tightening credit lines because yet another, more pressing problem arose. In late September, while investigating problems with the Raptors, Carl Bass came across David Dun-can's notes from September 2000—the memos Duncan prepared in sup-port of the vehicles' creation. Bass was stunned to discover that Duncan had omitted Bass's strong objections; in fact, judging from Duncan's comments, it sounded as if Bass had been a big Raptor booster. Bass drafted a point-by-point retort to Duncan. "The conclusion implies that I was consulted with and concurred with all issues discussed in this memo. That is not accurate." He insisted on the restoration of his initial objections.

Around this time, Vince Kaminski was having Raptor issues of his own. No one had told him that the vehicles were restructured in March 2001. Now he looked at the structure again and was troubled by how much the deals benefited Fastow at the expense of Enron. He also saw that there was no effective transfer of risk from Enron to LJM. In other words, the Raptors were not true SPEs and should be consolidated with Enron. That action would erase all the gains Enron had booked on the Raptor hedges.

By this time, Kaminski was an Enron cynic. He believed that the Raptors were never supposed to be real hedges, but vehicles to hide losses to engage in earnings management—what he would refer to, in his darkest, driest tones, as "an act of economic self-gratification." What really infuriated him was that Causey's group was asking him to do calculations and adjustments on vaguely defined transactions that he suspected were actually the Raptors in disguise. In other words, Enron management was still trying to use him to endorse deals he publicly opposed. He was Enron's Carl Bass. Kaminski subsequently refused to sign off on anything having remotely to do with the Raptors in specific or LJM in general. Causey was shocked at his refusal, but there was no danger to Kaminski's job anymore, he said. This was the new, open Enron. "We'll be honest," Causey said.

A few days later, there was another attempt to get Kaminski involved in the Raptors, and again he refused. This time Buy called him and, referring to a memo containing warnings about the Raptors that Kaminski had recently sent to an Andersen employee, told him to stop communicating with the accounting firm. On that day, October 4, Kaminski told his group they would no longer work on Raptor issues under any circumstances.

Other people in the company were anxious and distrustful, too. In an online chat, one worker asked Lay what would happen to the company in ten years, when Enron's "accounting tricks come home to roost". Lay refused to take the bait. "I would guess ten years from now our net income will be four to sixfold what it is today, and our market cap will be eight to ten times what it is today." The markets overreacted in crises, he said. But they would correct for Enron, and the stock would continue to perform well.

If Lay was optimistic in public, in private he made a momentous decision. Fastow and Causey wanted to restructure the Raptors, to put the problem and any potential bad news off for another quarter. But Lay, with Whalley concurring, decided to "unwind"—dispose of—the Raptors now. (Enron's accomplished cynics assumed that Whalley, who had long lusted after a CEO job, wanted to dump all the bad news in the first quarter after Skilling's departure, so that he could blame the problems on his predecessor.)

Enron would start fresh, admit that it had made a mistake on its balance sheet, and move on. The stock was going up. Merrill Lynch was saying it would be back to $40 by the end of the year. And there was still the Sherron Watkins issue to contend with. She was a loose cannon. No one knew whether she might decide to take her concerns to the SEC.

On October 4, while Ken Lay touted deregulation in a speech in Washington, Enron's treasurer, Ben Glisan, started calling the analysts to prepare them for the bad news. Enron was about to report significant losses for the third quarter. The stock was then selling for $33.

The question for Enron, as always, was how to present the news. Not surprisingly, executives at Enron wanted to say as little as possible. Andersen had just been down this path with Waste Management and Sunbeam, clients accused of cooking their books. Andersen, still smarting from those two revelations, urged Enron to come clean. In particular, David Duncan strongly objected to Enron's choice of the word "non-recurring" to describe the upcoming losses. The term could be misleading to investors, he thought. Also, Enron's application of the term was not in accordance with generally accepted accounting principles. In other words, Enron was trying to say that these losses were the result of something unusual on the company's part, when Duncan saw them as a result of the normal course of business.

For once, Duncan was adamant. He didn't want the phrase to appear in any public filings that included Andersen—Enron's 10-Q and 10-K, for instance. "Our advice was that the company should consider changing the presentation or should otherwise undertake whatever procedures they might deem necessary, including the involvement of counsel," Duncan wrote in a memo to an associate. The response from Enron was typical: "Causey," Duncan continued, "acknowledged my advice."

On Monday, the night before the press release announcing the losses, Duncan was agitated enough to check in with Causey again. He got nowhere. Causey told him that he raised the issue internally and that the press release went through "normal legal review." Andersen was along for the ride.

The next day, before Duncan forwarded his press release critique on to Enron. Nancy Temple, an Andersen attorney, suggested a few revisions to his draft. She wanted him to delete his advice that Enron get a legal opinion about its actions, and she specifically wanted her name removed from the memo. "Reference to the legal group consultation arguably is a waiver of attorney client advice and if my name is mentioned it increases the chances I might be a witness, which I prefer to avoid."

Temple also suggested deleting language that suggested Andersen knew that the press release was misleading and was a violation of SEC rules. "In light of the non-recurring characterization, the lack of any suggestion that this characterization is not in accordance with GAAP [generally accepted accounting principles], and the lack of income statements in accordance with GAAP, I will consult further within the legal group as to whether we should do anything more to protect ourselves. . . ."

Enron Reports Recurring Third-Quarter Earnings of $0.43 per Diluted Share; Reports Non-Recurring Charges of $1.01 Billion After Tax; Reaffirms Recurring Earnings Estimates of $1.80 for 2001 and $2.15 for 2002 and Expands Financial Reporting," read the headline of Enron's October 16 press release. The non-recurring charges, totaling $1.01 billion after-tax, or a $(1.11) loss per diluted share, were recognized for the third quarter of 2001. "After a thorough review of our businesses, we have decided to take these charges to clear away issues that have clouded the performance and earnings potential of our core energy [trading] business," Lay declared in the press release.

The next day, he hosted a conference call with several other executives, including Whalley, Causey, and Fastow. Most of the news was good, Lay said. "For the third quarter of 2001, Enron reported strong recurring operating performance, which included a 35 percent increase in recurring net income to $393 million versus $292 million a year ago, and a 26 percent increase in diluted earnings per share compared to 24 cents a share a year ago," Lay said, sounding relentlessly upbeat. "As these numbers show, Enron's core energy business fundamentals are excellent."

Then, in almost the same breath, he downshifted to the bad news: "We are recording non-recurring charges of slightly over $1 billion this quarter. The recognition of these charges is the result of a thorough review of each of our businesses. We are committed to making the results of our core energy business more transparent to investors. . . ." He promised to provide more detail later in the call.

He did, to some extent. The non-recurring charges of $1.01 billion, he said, consisted of $287 million related to Azurix and a few other assets. Another $180 million was associated with the restructuring of Broadband. He rattled off a few more numbers—$44 million related to an early termination during the third quarter of certain "structured finance arrangements with a previously disclosed entity" as well as losses in tech stocks. All told, the third category of losses came in at around $600 million.

Then Lay went on to say this: "In connection with the early termination, shareholders' equity will be reduced approximately $1.2 billion, with a corresponding significant reduction in the number of diluted shares outstanding."

Then, before anyone could ask any more questions, Lay was back to the good news: the large cash flow from operations, the company's closeness with the rating agencies—there would be no change there. Enron was comfortable with its liquidity position, he added, and was actively issuing commercial paper for its current short-term needs. "Our $3 billion committed revolver remains undrawn," he said, referring to the money Enron kept in reserve for emergencies.

So there was no problem. Or was there? Once the call ended, a small, nagging worry remained in the minds of the analysts. Lay had mentioned a $1.2 billion "shareholder equity reduction." Was that the same billion as the "non-recurring charges"? Or was there some other problem? It didn't sound like it. Lay ended the call on a reassuring note: "If we thought we had any other impaired assets," he'd said, "it would be in this list today."

The analysts were on the team. The stock opened at $33 that day, and closed at nearly the same amount.

Enron would weather the storm.

In September, Sherron Watkins moved from the forty-ninth floor to the sixteenth, from the glamour of Global Finance to the succor of Human Relations. She left behind her mahogany credenza, her granite-topped table, and her glorious view of Houston. On sixteen, she faced other Houston skyscrapers, and the furniture in her office seemed to come from one of those places that bought and resold damaged or flooded office equipment. Everything was made of metal, and it was nicked and pocked; one file drawer refused to close no matter how hard Sherron tried.

If it wasn't beautiful, it was safe. Sherron could buzz along with everyone else about the plans for the upcoming Christmas party—estimated cost $5 million—which would be held at Enron Field and was supposed to climax with a giant fireworks display. The logic of holding the party at the ball field was partly to celebrate the company's continued success—Enron Field was Enron's field, after all—but it also made it easier on the executives. Instead of dropping in on several parties scattered around town, they could now just glide from the grand concourse (Enron Wholesale), to the boxes (Enron Corp), to the nosebleed section (Enron Pipelines), without wasting a lot of time.

Sherron, in fact, had only one gripe with her new situation—she didn't really have a job. Lay took her advice and launched an inquiry into her concerns, but while that was going on, she was operating in suspended animation. She tried to get work with Rick Buy. He told her he wanted to wait until the investigation was complete before making any decisions. Cindy Olson confided in her that Rex Rogers and Jim Derrick thought she, Sherron, was trying to shake the company down, that she wanted money to go away. But, Olson told her, she and Ken knew that Sherron had the company's best interests at heart.

In fact, Sherron was obsessed with the company. She was spending her free time—and there was now a lot of it—strategizing and stewing and trying to get someone to pay attention to her ideas. She surfed the Internet, researching what happened to companies that restated their financial statements, which meant that they admitted earlier financial reports were wrong. She studied Andersen's recent woes and, more important, the SEC's 2000 efforts, under then chief Arthur Levitt, to revamp the public accounting system. As she saw it, Levitt's efforts were stymied in Congress because the politicians could claim there were no significant audit failures. Levitt lacked a smoking gun. Well, Sherron thought to herself, he was about to get a smoking cannon. The only thing that worried her was that, despite her advice, Lay hired Vinson & Elkins to conduct the investigation of his company.

On one level, this made sense. As Houston law firms went, V&E was one of the best and biggest in town—in the world, for that matter. It boasted hundreds of lawyers, and offices in New York, London, Moscow, Singapore, and Beijing, along with Austin and Dallas. It was perennially listed in *The Best Lawyers in America* guide, and it was known for innovation, particularly in the field of oil and gas. It was that reason—along with the firm's historic passion for political influence—that made Vinson & Elkins Enron's firm of choice.

Houston's grandest law practices had distinct personalities: The stuffy, patrician Baker & Botts was James Baker's family firm, and locked up the business with most of the oil majors; Andrews Kurth was Howard Hughes' law firm, as well as that of Humble Oil, which became Exxon. Vinson & Elkins, in contrast, represented the wildcatters; its founding partner, Judge James Elkins, used his position as head of First City Bank to carry the oilmen through the dry spells. V&E was also former Texas governor John Connally's firm, and for many years he embodied the firm's wealth, glamour, and influence.

Like Enron, Vinson & Elkins was also known for being aggressive, arrogant, and edgy. The innovations and raw power that souped up the firm's reputation also made for novel behavior in the off hours. During the oil-boom years of the late seventies and early eighties, a story circulated around town that an amorous couple fell through the ceiling during the firm's annual Christmas party; another revel ended badly when two summer recruits from Brigham Young University reported the presence of "The Salad Sisters" at a bachelor party for a V&E attorney that was held, naturally, in one of the city's finest restaurants. Like Enron, V&E didn't have to follow the rules because they made them.

The oil bust humbled the firm somewhat—Connally went broke, and so did First City. V&E recovered, reemerging as experts in project finance. In a financially troubled city, they specialized in back-on-your-feet deals. For pipeline mergers and FERC approvals, V&E was the place to go.

Finally, like Enron, V&E was a political institution. The firm gave generously to political candidates ($208,000 to Bush's gubernatorial campaign, more than any other law firm) and hired those with easy access to legislators and lobbyists.

With all these similarities, it wasn't long before many V&E lawyers were moving to more financially promising quarters down the street, at Enron. Amanda Martin, Jim Derrick, and another member of the legal department, Rob Walls, just to name a few. Like Arthur Andersen accountants, these attorneys didn't have to be schooled in Enron's ways, because they helped create them.

That Enron and V&E were joined at the hip might have been reason enough to assign the investigation of Enron's off-balance-sheet vehicles to someone else, but not to Ken Lay. This was, after all, the man who steered Enron's business to his sister's travel agency and who kept his son on the payroll. Now, he invited V&E in and gave them their marching orders: There was to be no "second-guessing" of Arthur Andersen's accounting treatments and no transaction analyses, no "discovery-style investigation."

The job went to two senior V&E partners, Joe Dilg, the soon to be managing partner of the firm, and Max Hendrick III, the head of the litigation department, who spent the final, torrid weeks of late August and early September in Enron's offices asking the kinds of questions that had never really been asked before.

They met with Jeff McMahon, who mentioned the inherent conflict of interest between Fastow as CFO of Enron and Fastow as general partner of LJM, but also stated that his concerns were "not with the fairness or valuation of transactions that were placed in LJM." V&E reported, "McMahon pointed out that the anonymous letter addressed accounting issues, and that accounting issues have never been the subject of his concern. He was not involved with and is not competent in those areas of accounting issues and is further confident that Causey and Arthur Andersen & Co. make sure that things are done properly." Jordan Mintz "observed the awkwardness and disfunctionality that was brought about by the LJM structure," but did not mention that he had once hired an outside law firm to investigate Enron's dealings with LJM or that firm's damning conclusions.

Rick Causey told them that any problems with the Raptors were not insurmountable. Besides, Ken Lay and Jeff Skilling knew all about them. "At the end of the day," he'd told the lawyers, "this structure will do its job, but it may be in a more noisy fashion." David Duncan told the lawyers that all the information on the Raptors was properly disclosed. "The accounting treatment might look facially questionable," he said, "but it satisfied all the technical requirements." Rick Buy wasn't concerned about the Raptors, either. Enron's accounting, he said, was "aggressive but not over the line."

Fastow was incensed by the investigation. Enron had the necessary controls, he insisted. The office of the chairman, V&E, and Arthur Andersen reviewed all transactions. "On the one hand, he applauded the employee who wrote the letter because it takes fortitude to stand up and complain, even on an anonymous basis," the lawyers wrote in their interview notes. "He questions the employee's motives, however, because the person is smart enough to know that the structure and all transactions within the structure were reviewed by Arthur Andersen and found to be appropriate." Then Fastow gave them a tip: He "also stated his belief that this employee is acting in conjunction with a person who wants his job." That is, Sherron Watkins conspired with Jeff McMahon to take out Andy Fastow.

Then the lawyers met with Sherron Watkins for over three hours. She repeated her concerns and showed them the same research she had shown Ken Lay. The men took extensive notes and said very little. They later wrote, "The interview was somewhat disjointed because it felt better to let Watkins discuss issues she wanted to address initially before questioning in particular areas." Sherron tried to support her opinion that Enron was facing certain peril. She brought up Waste Management's recent problems—the removal of its board, the return of bonuses, the payment of tremendous fines. "She viewed Enron's actions as being much more horrific."

The interview notes were sprinkled with doubts about her veracity. Watkins repeated information she had "overheard at cocktail parties" or that was "known to her through casual conversations." Watkins "admitted that she had not seen the legal documents on the Raptor transaction," nor did she "know how LJM got its money out of the Raptor transactions." The attorneys never met with a few people she said could substantiate her impressions, including Vince Kaminski.

By the time the lawyers submitted their final report, on October 15, they were convinced there was no real problem at Enron. "The facts disclosed through our preliminary investigation do not, in our judgment, warrant a further widespread investigation by independent counsel and auditors," concluded Dilg and Hendrick. The conflict created by Fastow's ownership of LJM vanished when he divested himself of the fund; Sherron Watkins had no new information about Raptor and Condor. The attorneys acknowledged "that the accounting treatment on the Condor/Whitewing and Raptor transactions is creative and aggressive, but no one has reason to believe that it is inappropriate from a technical standpoint."

What did concern V&E were what the attorneys labeled "potential bad cosmetics." "Concern was frequently expressed that the transactions involving Condor/Whitewing and Raptor could be portrayed very poorly if subjected to a *Wall Street Journal* expose or class action lawsuit," they noted. They then added just one small caveat to their report: "The bad cosmetics involving the LJM entities and Raptor transactions, coupled with the poor performance of the merchant investment assets placed in those vehicles and the decline in the value of Enron stock, made for a serious risk of adverse publicity and litigation."

"Finally," the report continued, "we believe that some response should be provided to Ms. Watkins to assure her that her concerns were thoroughly reviewed, analyzed, and although found not to raise new or undisclosed information, were given serious consideration."

The attorneys met with Watkins on October 16 to do just that. See, they said, indicating the stable stock price of $33 the day the company announced quarterly earnings and the overall loss of $681 million. Everything was going to be fine. The market had responded, and the news was all good.

Listening, Sherron could not contain her intolerance for the illogical. She stood up and put her hands on her hips. If the accounting was correct, she snapped, "Why did the company take a $1.2 billion hit to shareholders, equity and a $700 million loss?" Those were big numbers to book just to "avoid a distraction," as Lay claimed. The men shifted in their chairs and looked uncomfortable. Restatement was the only course, she said. Otherwise, Enron was taking a huge risk. Yes, the stock price was holding for the moment, but the company's luck wouldn't.

Any company can survive one negative story in *The Wall Street Journal.* That one ran on October 17, with a front-page headline that read "Enron Posts Surprise 3rd Quarter Loss After Investment, Asset Write Downs." The story focused particularly on Andy Fastow and the "unusual arrangement" he had with his employer. The reporters were the first to expose LJM to the light of day. Worse for Enron, the two reporters, Rebecca Smith and John Emshwiller, clearly had the partnership documents. "While the company says that this arrangement was proper, some corporate governance watchdogs have questioned whether a chief financial officer, who is responsible for overseeing the financial interest of the company, should have been involved in such a partnership that was, among other things, looking to purchase assets from Enron," they wrote.

Suddenly, all the concerns about bad cosmetics were no longer theoretical. Under the microscope of the country's most influential business daily, Enron's flaws were obvious. Enron had a $618 million loss because of a $1.01 billion write-off; but closing down some related-party transactions— the Raptors—also required Enron to repurchase 55 million shares that had been part of the deals, resulting in a $1.2 billion loss to shareholder equity. If few readers really understood the details of the story, they sensed one thing clearly: Enron did something bad.

Worse, Enron reverted to type when it was time to respond: The company executives would not submit to an interview. Fastow, in particular, was MIA. Thus, the *Journal* was free to paint the partnerships in the most mysterious, and therefore most damaging, light possible.

In addition, the story reiterated all the problems Enron had experienced in the last few months; the shrinking value of retail power, the crash of Broadband, the buyback of Azurix, and the departure of many top-level executives. The only Enron person who spoke up was board member Charles LeMaistre, an outside director who was president of MD Anderson Cancer Center at the University of Texas. He confessed that the partnership arrangement was just a way to keep an invaluable employee—Fastow—at Enron. "We try to make sure that all executives at Enron are sufficiently well-paid to meet what the market would offer," he said.

That might have been bad enough, but the next morning, the *Journal* ran another story. "Enron Says Its Links to a Partnership Led to a $1.2 Billion Equity Reduction." Walking readers through the problem, the reporters explained that the loss of shareholder equity was not disclosed as part of the $1.01 billion charge to earnings—Enron's situation was much worse than the company initially advertised. Then Smith and Emshwiller said that Moody's had put Enron's long-term debt on review for a possible downgrade.

Lay was in Boston that day, trying to assure analysts that Enron was moving past its problems. "This is a one-time thing," he said. "There is nothing else out there." That day, Enron's stock price dropped below $30 a share.

The next day, October 19, Emshwiller and Smith had yet *another* story. "Enron's CFO's Partnership Had Millions in Profit," that day's headlines read. This story revealed still more about the money Fastow made and the conflicts Enron tolerated. The stock dropped to $25 a share.

By this time, Ken Lay was in a panic. He and Greg Whalley were frantically meeting with officials in Washington to raise cash or find more credit, maybe even land a federal bailout. He met with White House Budget Director Mitch Daniels, while Whalley frantically phoned Treasury Undersecretary Peter Fisher. Commerce Secretary Don Evans wasn't taking Lay's calls.

Lay was furious with his public-relations staff, and when he returned to town, he descended from the fiftieth floor, his jaw set, his eyes hard, to berate them for being unable to stop the stories. "This is a public-relations problem," he snarled. "Why can't you solve it?"

Shortly thereafter, he hired a crisis-management team to advise him.

In fact, Lay was mulling over another public-relations plan at the time. The management committee ignored The Lay It On The Line survey. So Beth Tilney and Cindy Olson brought in a bigger gun: pollster Frank Luntz, whose Arlington, Virginia–based Luntz Research Companies were used by both Democrats and Republicans to fine-tune major political campaigns. Though Luntz seemed much more interested in networking with Lay— he wanted personal meetings, he wanted to fly with Lay on the company jet—he set up several focus groups at different levels within the company. His conclusion that the company was in total chaos and most valuable workers were already looking for new jobs could have surprised only the most distracted executive. Employees were fed up with the power-mad traders, the PRC, and the constant reorganizations (there had been six in eighteen months, some of which were used to hide problems at Broad-band and EES). What employees really wanted was a savior, and Luntz thought they should get one: "When it comes to all the key attributes in delivering a corporate message that your employees will believe and accept—credibility, confidence, and trust—Ken is your most powerful weapon," he wrote. "A personal commitment from Ken Lay will go further than the entire executive team combined." Lay should talk about positive change, Luntz advised. He should talk about the future. He should talk about innovation. "When these words come from Ken," Luntz claimed, "employees will listen."

"But whatever you do, be very careful with where and how he focuses his message," Luntz continued. The PRC is a classic example of the type of policy Lay should avoid. "Employees associate the PRC with Jeff Skilling, and the last thing you want is for that negative association to shift to Ken. So pick your messages very carefully."

It was a directive Lay would be hard-pressed to keep over the ensuing weeks.

In late October, employees were locked out of withdrawing money from their 401(k) plans because of an earlier decision to switch plan administrators. No one thought better of postponing the switch. As the stock price dropped, all the employees could do was stand by helplessly for three weeks as their savings dwindled.

Keith Power, however, had been ready for disaster. He stuck it out with the Trade Credit Group, even though they made it clear that, as far as they were concerned, he was a dead man. They never invited him to important meetings, and they sent junior people to meet with clients on jobs he should have been undertaking. When it came time for his review, they knocked him down a level. "You're mediocre," his bosses said, even though his peers gave him high marks.

When he stepped into the lobby and saw the banners preaching "Respect" and "Integrity," he felt his throat tighten with anger. This wasn't the Enron he used to know.

He had sold his Enron stock—all of it—in spring 2001. It was not enough to make him a rich man, but it was enough to make a substantial nest egg, enough to buy a small house in Southampton if he'd been inclined, which he wasn't. But he still had investments in Enron through his wife, and she was refusing to part with her stock, even as the price dropped almost every day. He convinced her to sell some when the stock hit $50 a share, but from then on she held tight, even as it dropped below $40, and below $30.

"The stock's for sale every day of the year," he told her, weekly. "You can always sell it and buy it back." But she wouldn't. She had spent her life with Enron. Like so many employees, she just couldn't let go.

On October 22, Ken Lay hosted a meeting of all of the company's managing directors in a conference room at the Hyatt Regency Hotel. The stated purpose was to review the third-quarter earnings report, but everyone expected a more thorough examination of the company's finances. There were about a hundred people in the room, but one person was conspicuously absent: Andy Fastow.

His star had plummeted in recent days, since *The Wall Street Journal* reported on the nineteenth that he had made $7 million in management fees from LJM in one year. That this figure was substantially less than Ken Rice or Lou Pai or Rebecca Mark made was not a topic for discussion—they were gone, after all, and the board hadn't ever waived its code of ethics for them. Nor had they made the board look like chumps. Now they were going to get to the bottom of Fastow's betrayal.

Board member Charles LeMaistre had actually tried to investigate Fastow's compensation before. In May 2000, Fastow told the board that he was spending about three hours a week on LJM, and that he was earning an 18 percent rate of return for his trouble. Assured that Skilling, Buy, and Causey were reviewing every one of Fastow's transactions, the board didn't pry. Ken Lay had appointed the board members, and they trusted his word and the word of his people. Many members were older men, polite and deferential, in awe not just of Lay, but mavericks like Skilling and Fastow. Then, too, Lay paid his board members well, in accordance with the times—on average, over $300,000 a year. Finally, no one had really demanded much of them in the past, so they remained, for the most part, obedient, loyal, and incurious.

There was to have been a review of Fastow's compensation in October 2000—after the board waived their conflict-of-interest rules for the second time—but the members never quite got around to it. Then, after a short but somewhat critical mention of LJM appeared in *The Wall Street Journal* in August, the board tried to take another pass at Fastow. LeMaistre asked the Enron compensation officer to look into it. She told the board she did not have the information.

LeMaistre tried to get the information another way. Later that month, he asked the compensation officer for a list of the outside income of all officers of the company, including Fastow. Once again, he was rebuffed. Finally, LeMaistre had enough. He went to Jim Derrick for help. The trouble was, Fastow had that nasty temper and no one wanted to upset him. On the other hand, the SEC was making noise about looking into the partnerships.

With Derrick's help, LeMaistre worked on a script. "Andy, because of the current controversy surrounding LJM1 and LJM2, we believe it would be helpful for the Board to have a general understanding of the amount of your investment and of your return on investment in the LJM entities. We understand that a detailed accounting of these matters will soon be done in connection with the response to the SEC inquiry. We very much appreciate your willingness to visit with us."

On the phone, Fastow was cranky but eventually settled down. His aggregate income attributable to the first LJM, including salaries, consulting fees, management fees, and partnership distributions for his $1 million investment came to $23 million. His $3.9 investment in LJM2 had returned $22 million. The grand total was $58.9 million.

LeMaistre made one marginal note at the time. "Incredible."

But now, even with Fastow on ice, Lay faced a room packed with very surly people: Various executives remembered all too clearly a recent management committee meeting where Fastow said that the balance sheet "had never been better"—when they knew Enron's publicly traded bonds were moving closer and closer to junk status. They weren't happy about rumors over a potential SEC inquiry either. The managing directors had made millions at Enron, but being so successful meant that they knew the company well and knew how rapidly their fortunes could evaporate. Company loyalty was for stooges. Most of them made a year-by-year, bonus-to-bonus determination as to whether they would stay. Now they were thinking very hard.

They were angry. Skilling was gone, and their faith in Lay was tenuous. Whalley was a great trader, but everyone in the room had some experience with his management skills or lack thereof. For the most part, the guys in the room, who routinely prided themselves on their ability to read a deal, were trying to figure out how they had misread this one so badly.

Ken Lay didn't talk about the SEC. Instead, he said that he and the board were behind Fastow all the way, and he wanted the MDs to get behind him too.

When they challenged him on the company's finances, Lay waffled. "Well, we don't think we did anything wrong," he said, "but knowing what we do now, we would never do it again." Another MD piped up, "If you're promising a new and better Enron, does that mean the company can miss its earnings targets?" Whalley deflated the crowd with his answer: Targets were good motivators, he said. After too many questions, Lay's face hardened into an angry glare that matched many in the audience.

Finally, Vince Kaminski rose from his chair. He walked to the front of the room, a man about Lay's height and build, though slighter and sharper. "I am in the terrible position of having to disagree with you," Kaminski began, and then went on to condemn the creation of LJM. Enron should never have become involved in those deals, he said; he was against them from the start, in 1999. What Fastow did was not only improper, Kaminski said, "It was terminally stupid." Enron's only chance for survival now was to come clean and issue a restatement of its earnings.

Lay looked stunned.

"That's enough, Vince," Greg Whalley said. He put an arm around Kaminski's shoulders and led him away from the podium.

L ife got no better for Lay the next morning, when he faced an analysts' call at 9:30. Also present were Fastow, Causey, Whalley, and Ben Glisan, among others. The PR department had crafted a rational explanation for the creation of LJM in response to reporters' queries. But no one remembered why it seemed so crucial in 1999. Finally, V&E lawyer Ron Astin penciled in an edit identifying Fastow as the father of the fund. Reading the change, Fastow erupted. "It was Skilling!" he shouted. Then everyone sat down at the conference table and acted like the outburst never happened.

The purpose of the call, Lay said, was to address questions and concerns raised over the last few days. He said that he was disappointed with the company's low stock price, since things were going so well.

LJM, he said, was established to mitigate the volatility associated with some of Enron's merchant investments, including New Power and various tech deals. The termination of those vehicles caused the $1.2 billion reduction in shareholders' equity and a corresponding reduction in notes receivable. Then he started to turn the meeting over to Fastow, but not before he paused to add a final comment: "I might add that I and Enron's board of directors continue to have the highest faith and confidence in Andy, and believe he is doing an outstanding job as CFO."

Fastow was ready with the good news. As far as liquidity was concerned, everything was fine. The company had not drawn down their revolver, he said, implying that Enron still had $3 billion in liquidity. Enron had the continued support of its banks. Further, its BBB+ rating was holding at S&P and Fitch, though Moody's, he admitted, had placed Enron on review. The company was working diligently to satisfy them.

The mike went back to Lay, who boasted about the company's outstanding third-quarter results. Then he opened the forum up to questions.

One of the first callers was Curt Launer, of CSFB, a longtime Enron loyalist. Launer had a simple question. If not for the LJM partnerships, what would Enron's income statement have looked like in 2000? In 2001? Causey told him that there would have been minimal impact because Enron could have entered into similar transactions with other third parties. Lay parroted Causey's responses. Another analyst pointed out that Lay had promised to be more transparent with Enron's financial disclosure, yet the company had just issued a quarterly release without a balance sheet. Why?

Lay said the balance sheet would come when it usually did, within a week or two after earnings were released.

Could it be made available sooner? he asked.

Possibly, Lay answered, though no one in the room thought it could.

Another analyst asked what would happen if Enron's credit rating dropped below investment grade. No chance of that, Lay said. "We'd have to be downgraded three notches to go below investment grade. And there's—at least we don't think there's any chance of that," he said.

Then they asked about Fastow. How could Enron make sure this never happened again? "Let me first say from the standpoint of LJM and Andy's role that obviously the board and of course even the lawyers and the auditors and everybody else recognized that there would be an inherent conflict of interest there. And basically, the board developed and prescribed certain procedures and how in fact that could—that in fact would be dealt with, and primarily in a way that Enron's interest and Enron's shareholders' interest would never be compromised.

"And I will also say that having checked just in the last several days, these procedures have been rigorously followed. So we do not—we're very concerned the way Andy's character has been kind of loosely thrown about over the last few days in certain articles, as well as, of course, the integrity of the company. But we think in fact that all of the necessary protections and procedures were put in place on the front end to make sure that Enron's shareholders were in fact fully protected."

Then it was David Fleisher's turn. The analyst from Goldman Sachs was a longtime Enron fan, but now even he sounded dubious. "I guess what I'd like to do is make this partly a question but more of a comment, and just point out, with all due respect, that what you're hearing from some of these people and many others that you haven't heard from in this call is that the company's credibility is being severely questioned, and that there really is a need for much more disclosure. And I appreciate where it's real difficult for you to get into a lot of details on one specific issue with one questioner, but that's exactly what I think needs to happen over maybe a series of conference calls.

"There is an appearance that you're hiding something or that you just don't want to, that maybe there's something beneath the surface that's going on that is less than—that may be questionable. I guess you need to do everything in your power to explain to investors, to demonstrate to investors that your dealings are aboveboard. . . ." Lay should have daily conference calls until the crisis was past, he urged.

Well, there were limits to what he could say because of potential lawsuits and the probable SEC inquiry. "But again," Lay stressed, "we are trying to be as transparent as we can. We're trying to provide information. We're not trying to conceal anything. We're not hiding anything."

One of the last calls came from Richard Grubman, the short seller who had infuriated Skilling six months before. Lay had previously mentioned some upcoming asset sales involving an SPE called Marlin, which was created to keep Azurix debt off balance sheet. Grubman wanted to know whether Enron had recognized all the related losses associated with Azurix. He did some math on the third quarter write-down, and by his calculations, Enron should have taken more.

Causey jumped in to insist that Marlin was healthy, and Lay soon backed him up.

Grubman disagreed. He couldn't find any value in the vehicle at all.

Lay listened for a few more minutes, and then cut him off. "I know you want to drive the stock price down, and you've done a good job of doing that, but I think that's that. Let's move on to the next question."

From there, Lay went to another all-employee meeting at the Hyatt. This time, there were no standing ovations; the crowd was restive and angry. The stock price was at $19, and people were watching their savings and retirement evaporate. Lay was still taking his cues from the Luntz report. (*A personal commitment from Ken Lay will go further than the entire executive team combined!*) Enron, he reminded the crowd, started with nothing more than a $2 billion market cap. It weathered the collapse of gas prices in 1986. It survived the nationalization of the Peruvian oil and gas fields in 1985. It survived rogue traders, who cost the company $180 million in 1987, and ten years later, it triumphed over the $600 million loss from J-Block. Enron would be back, he told them.

"Let me say right up front, I am absolutely heartbroken about what's happened. Many of you who were a lot wealthier six to nine months ago are now concerned about the college education for your kids, maybe the mortgage on your house, maybe your retirement, and for that I am incredibly sorry," he said. "But we are going to get it back." Then he mentioned, briefly, against the advice of his PR team, that he had lost money himself. *What, down to your last $100 million?* people in the crowd wondered. He then hit them with a flurry of good news. Enron's market cap was $17 billion. *That's good news? Hadn't it been $70 billion in 2000?* Enron did 882 billion cubic feet equivalent in physical trading volumes in the third quarter of 2001. *What the hell was he talking about?*

Then Lay opened the meeting up for questions, some of which were solicited in advance. He opened the first and read aloud: "Are you on crack?" someone had asked. "If not, maybe you should be." Lay's smile was a rictus.

An executive got up to speak and began pelting Lay with questions. *Could* LJM lose money? He'd heard that it couldn't. Was there really risk capital in LJM? He'd heard that there wasn't. Who else was in LJM? He'd heard more Enron employees than just Andy Fastow. And so on.

Lay reminded the crowd that the LJM vehicles were terminated (which, in point of fact, they weren't—Fastow passed them on to Michael Kopper) and, as he had reminded the analysts earlier that morning, that Enron offered LJM assets for sale only when it was in the best interests of the company.

"Andy Fastow acted in the most ethical manner," Lay said.

The executive pressed again. "Well, is there anyone else in LJM?"

Lay looked a little confused.

"I think it's just Andy," he said.

At that point, Fastow popped up from the front row. "Well, there's Michael Kopper," he prodded.

"Oh," Lay said, "Michael Kopper."

Then, quickly, he moved on. "I think we've had enough airtime for that question," he said.

19

The Death Spiral

THE next morning, an Enron vice president named Bill Brown came to the office early. He couldn't sleep, and so, at around 7 A.M., found himself walking into Enron's new building, to the fourth floor where he'd recently moved with his boss, Jeff McMahon, along with the Industrial Markets group. McMahon was already there.

Why was McMahon in so early? he asked.

McMahon answered that Fastow called him in. Enron had barely rolled its commercial paper the night before, and Andy needed his help.

Commercial paper was one of those financial instruments set up for the good of all—until, not surprisingly, there was a financial crisis. Backstopped by undrawn credit lines, Enron routinely borrowed money for short-term needs from companies and investors that had it to lend, usually at rates cheaper than the banks. The money was unsecured but generally considered safe—largely because such loans weren't extended to risky companies. Unfortunately for Enron, it was now slipping into the risky company category, and the commercial paper markets knew it. They were losing enthusiasm when it came to loaning to Enron, and McMahon was calling in favors to get the cash in the door.

Later that morning, Enron's executive committee met at 1400 Smith. Fastow was present, as were Whalley, Lay, and McMahon. Whalley sat down and, while Lay remained mute, gave Fastow the news: He was out and McMahon was in as CFO.

Fastow was stunned. Why? he demanded.

The banks, Lay explained, had lost confidence in him.

One bank, Fastow countered. The night before, when the commercial paper had looked as if it wasn't going to roll, Fastow had made the mistake of telling Lay that one bank had expressed a loss of confidence. Now, he whined, he was being punished for doing so.

But no one was about to relent.

Soon after, Fastow threatened a $10 million suit for wrongful termination.

McMahon's first duty as CFO was to get out the good news. On October 25, he announced that the company was still the market maker of choice, that Enron Online had recorded more than 8,400 transactions for a gross notional value of approximately $4 billion. "We know we have our work cut out for us if we are to rebuild our credibility with the investment community, and we're working on that," Lay chimed in, "but in the meantime the best evidence of our strength is the willingness of customers to bring their business to Enron."

The third paragraph of the press release noted that Enron was working to dispel uncertainty in the financial markets. Specifically, that Enron drew down its committed lines of credit—in the amount of $3 billion. Despite Fastow's prior assurances that Enron had no liquidity issues, Enron had drawn down its revolver. But the company now claimed this was a good thing. "We are making it clear that Enron has the support of its banks and more than adequate liquidity to assure our customers that we can fulfill our commitments in the ordinary course of business," McMahon said. "This is an important step in our plan to restore investor confidence in Enron."

What he did not say, of course, was that because Enron could not roll its commercial paper, the company needed the cash to service its debts. The money was going out the door as quickly as it was coming in.

In signing off on the revolver, someone had to sign a boilerplate admission that there was no material adverse change in the fortunes of the company. Usually an underling signed off, but on this day no Enron executive, even CFO Jeff McMahon, would provide a signature. Finally Ken Lay was brought in. He didn't want to sign either, until a V&E partner told him it was okay.

Meanwhile, the SEC announced that it was shifting its Enron inquiry to a formal investigation. This pressure was finally enough to force Lay to do what Sherron Watkins had urged him to do in August. He hired a new law firm, Wilmer Cutler & Pickering, and created an internal investigating body headed by a newly appointed Enron board member, the dean of the University of Texas Law School, William Powers.

No one at the company worried much about his choice. Enron gave so much money to UT, they said, Powers couldn't possibly be objective.

It was almost impossible, at this point, to believe that things could get any worse for Enron, but, in fact, the bad news was just beginning. One of *The Wall Street Journal* stories mentioned that Michael Kopper was involved in Chewco, which inspired the board to request an update from the company's treasurer, Ben Glisan. Glisan had been Fastow's lead accountant, joining Enron after stints at two of the Big 5 firms. In fact, he left one to work for Andersen, just to get to Enron. Glisan wanted to go where the cutting-edge accounting theories were being tested, and with the creation of the Raptors, he had made some innovations himself. He was promoted to treasurer of Enron when McMahon vacated that post in the spring of 2000. McMahon had recommended several former bankers for the job, but Fastow chose Glisan. Somehow he knew that Glisan was his kind of guy.

But in the fall of 2001, Glisan was frantic. He spent long days and longer nights in the war room adjacent to Jeff McMahon's office, where the truth of Enron's situation became clearer by the minute. The company's finances, chaotic by design, were even more so because of Fastow's contempt for the CFO's conventional obligations. When someone asked Glisan for things like the schedule of debt maturities—something a typical treasurer would have at his fingertips—he could only respond with a stricken look. "I think I could pull that together," he said after a long pause.

In the past, Glisan bragged about his inside knowledge of Fastow's world: He had once told Rodney Faldyn, Causey's lead transaction accountant (the one who had played Fastow as a pimp in Enron International's 1997 skit), that the reason the Chewco documents were shrouded in secrecy was because an Enron employee was involved. Tom Bauer, an Andersen accountant, used to review the documents alone in a room and was never allowed to make copies, lest other Enron employees learn about the deal.

But now, in preparation for his Chewco board presentation, Glisan was serving as investigator himself. He started a cursory review of Chewco's documents and saw the problem right away. There was not enough real equity in the deal to make it a legitimate special-purpose entity. To provide 3 percent equity, Barclay's Bank gave Enron $11 million for Chewco, but asked that $6 million in cash be put in a reserve account for its benefit. The requirements for an SPE weren't that rigorous, but the 3 percent equity from outside third parties had to be money at risk—real money, as opposed to borrowed money. Studying the documents, Glisan saw that this was not true in Chewco's case.

In fact, when he studied the documents he said, "We're toast." Kristina Mordaunt, who was in the room at that moment, wore a different expression, one that some would later describe as vexation. Some insiders found it hard to believe he hadn't known about it all along.

It fell to Faldyn to take the information to Causey. From there, Faldyn and Ryan Siurek—the young accountant who had so pleased Skilling with his restructuring of the Raptors—headed for Arthur Andersen to see what could be done to keep Chewco from landing on Enron's balance sheet at the worst possible moment.

Unlike Carl Bass, Tom Bauer was not a natural skeptic; his inclination as an Arthur Andersen accountant was to help the client at all times, to build consensus. That may be why, on October 26, when he took a call from Rodney Faldyn and Ryan Siurek, he didn't immediately sense the devastation that was spinning toward him, like a tornado on the horizon.

Bauer met with Causey and Faldyn about Chewco the next day. Deborah Cash, the Andersen partner who worked with Bauer to oversee Enron's Wholesale group, was present, as was the lead partner on the account, David Duncan. The group pored over the documents and noted two items of interest right away. First, they saw that one of the investors was a man named Bill Dodson—Michael Kopper's domestic partner—and second, that the Barclay's contribution looked more like a loan than an investment.

These discoveries inspired a rash of complaints from Bauer. Andersen never got enough documentation on the Chewco transaction at the time of its creation, he said. He had asked for third-party documents, but Glisan told him they were unavailable, and he had let it go.

A week or so later, on November 2, Arthur Andersen received a set of documents gathered by the new special committee headed by UT's William Powers. Bauer took one look at the papers and blanched. There was a document he had never seen before, a two-page side agreement between JEDI and Chewco. The side agreement was dated December 30, 1997, the very same day that the loan between JEDI and Chewco was finalized.

Bauer had seen the loan agreement before, during the 1997 audit, but he had never seen—nor had anyone told him about—the side agreement, even though the signatures on both documents were the same. The problem with the side agreement was that it significantly altered Chewco's identity. Reading over it, Bauer came to the same conclusion about Chewco that Glisan had. In the agreement, JEDI was directed to deposit $6.58 million into reserve accounts for entities called Big River and Little River, created for the benefit of Barclay's Bank. Barclay's $11.4 million contribution to Chewco appeared to be conditional upon the receipt of the $6.58 million from JEDI. In other words, the equity at risk—the crucial requirement for an SPE—was not $11.4 million, as stated, but in fact much less. Much less than the 3 percent needed for the entity to qualify as a special-purpose vehicle. Chewco belonged on Enron's balance sheet—and should have been on it since 1997.

Bauer was mystified as to why the side agreement had been withheld from him four years back, but he felt that it was done on purpose, to mislead both Andersen and himself. If he had seen the document, he never would have allowed JEDI and Chewco to remain off the balance sheet. The next evening, Bauer met with several Enron employees, including Causey, Glisan, and Mordaunt, as well as attorneys from Vinson & Elkins, including Ron Astin. They were trying to find any way that Chewco could legitimately call itself an SPE.

Causey and Astin said that the equity situation was debatable in their minds; there just wasn't enough evidence to demand Chewco's immediate presence on Enron's balance sheet. As for Bill Dodson, Causey wondered whether he was a related third party or not. How close was he to Enron, after all? Gamely, Mordaunt suggested that Texas law didn't recognize same-sex relationships. Bauer countered that the legal definition of homosexuality might not matter for accounting purposes. In a nice way, he was telling her that Dodson lived with an Enron executive with whom he was in business— common sense made him a related party.

Then Bauer brought up the side agreement. No one seemed to recall it. Luckily, Bauer had a copy he could show the group—and then helped them search for it among the Enron papers assembled in the room. Once the group found Enron's copy, Causey, Glisan, Mordaunt, and Astin scanned the paper. All said they had never seen it before.

No one wanted to acknowledge the document unless they had to. As Bauer explained, the agreement reduced the 3 percent net equity to perilous levels. It killed any chances that Chewco could possibly remain off Enron's balance sheet.

Bauer warned the group that they—not he—should decide on a course of action. In the most delicate terms, he told them that Enron would have to restate its earnings, and if it did not, he was obligated to report what he had learned to the SEC.

Sherron Watkins took no comfort in the events that unfolded after she drafted her first memo. The scenario she envisioned—that the company would act on her suggestions, come clean, and avert disaster—was not going according to plan. She couldn't exactly put her finger on when her problems had begun, but she felt that certain people at Enron did not want much to do with her. She bumped into McMahon on the way out of the building one evening in September, and when he asked how she was, she told him she felt a little like a pariah. "Well, what did you expect?" he replied. A new addition to the HR staff was warned to stay away from Sherron after she'd stepped into Sherron's office to introduce herself. Whalley and Lay, engrossed in conversation praising George W. Bush, snubbed her in the parking garage. Worse, no one seemed to want to give her any work. Jeff McMahon had been appointed chief financial officer in Fastow's place. (As Lay put it in his press release, "Jeff has unparalleled qualifications and a deep and thorough understanding of Enron . . . Andy Fastow will be on a leave of absence from the company.") But Sherron wasn't sure whether he wanted her on his team or not.

She sent him a congratulatory note after the announcement and used the opportunity to stress her determination to be part of the crisis management team. In particular, she was worried about the trading franchise. "It can disappear overnight," she wrote, "and I believe there's more bad news coming re these Raptor deals (i.e. restatement)." But he never responded.

Worn out by Sherron's entreaties, Cindy Olson finally sent her to McMahon's office on the twenty-sixth of October. It was Sherron's first trip to the new building, and as she made her way through the halo of glass and steel that was the circular skyway between the old and the new Enron buildings, she felt hopeful for the first time in weeks. This new building, by Cesar Pelli, seemed both fresher and more fortresslike than its predecessor and made Enron seem somehow more invincible.

Upstairs, the trading floors appeared normal, but in the corner of the fourth floor near McMahon's office, Sherron found chaos. The adjacent conference room was now a war room for raising capital. Whalley and Louise Kitchen huddled there, while McMahon shuttled between this command center and the fiftieth-floor executive suite in the old building, looking drawn and harried.

Sherron didn't know how long she stood in the hall, staring, before another executive named Ray Bowen asked her into his office. He directed her back to the old building—she was to see Mark Haedicke, who had a job for her. "You should get off this floor," Bowen warned. Another executive had seen her talking to the man who had challenged Lay at the recent all-employee meeting, he said, and was convinced Sherron was a troublemaker.

Sherron hurried back through the halo and ascended to the thirty-third floor to meet with Haedicke. He was the Enron lawyer who, a year or so back, had criticized attorney Stuart Zisman for raising the same concerns Sherron subsequently brought up. But he promised Sherron he'd have a job for her by the following Monday. He would give her a call, he said.

"This is all Jim Derrick's fault," he told her. "He didn't handle this right." Sherron couldn't quite tell whether Haedicke was referring to her situation or Enron's. But it was typical of Enron that the second in command would be using her situation to attack the man above him. She wondered whether sailors on the *Titanic* had fought to get into the wheelhouse. She was on a sinking ship with no one lowering the lifeboats.

H ey, Sherron, I'm sorry I haven't gotten back to you all week," McMahon's message on her office voice mail began on October 28, a few days after Enron stock had closed at $15. "But it has been very, very crazy. It's one-twenty Saturday night. Just walking in the door, sat down, opened a beer to listen to my forty-seven voice mail messages, of which you are one. So I'm trying to tell you what life's been like since Wednesday—pretty crummy. Anyway, I don't know why you are getting the message that you are unwanted around the company, but it's just crazy right now. I mean, we are running a mile a minute, as you can imagine, to try and keep us afloat. We are just trying to get cash, and it's extremely, extremely busy. . . . What's happening is we're basically working with all our banks, we're going through bank credit due diligence, basically, to put a secured loan together to hopefully get there by Monday morning, for our press release. We'll see if we get there." He was not sure that Sherron could add much to the process, he said. Maybe they could talk next week, when things slowed down. "But I got to tell you right now it's just crazy. This is crazy."

With time on her hands, Sherron spent the weekend before Halloween drafting another memo for Ken Lay. This one was entitled "Disclosure Steps to Rebuild Investor Confidence."

Sherron's idea to rebuild investor confidence was very simple: Enron should restate its earnings. But how to get Lay to do it? She had long been in the Skilling camp where the current and former CEO was concerned. It was commonly accepted at Enron that Kinder, then Skilling, had actually run the company. As someone like Cindy Olson might put it, Lay was the *outside* face of the company, while Kinder and Skilling were the *inside* faces.

It was a shrewd management technique on Lay's part, Sherron now realized. On Sunday the twenty-eighth, in fact, she read a don't-throw-the-baby-out-with-the-bathwater piece about Lay in the *Houston Chronicle* that reminded readers of all the contributions to the city made by Lay and his company. Bob Eury, president of Central Houston, Inc., a downtown development group, said, "A loss of his [Lay's] and Enron's leadership would be profound, but most Houstonians expect Mr. Lay to weather the company's difficulties and continue his marvelous leadership out in the community." Another active civic leader, attorney David Berg, added, "In Houston, nobody's dancing on his grave, there's a lot of residual respect for Ken Lay, and it's not going to go away even if he goes bankrupt, but that isn't going to happen." While making Enron a demigod with everyone from the NAACP to the Juvenile Diabetes Research Foundation to the Harris County Republicans, Lay had managed to stay on just about everyone's good side. Sherron would have to make her pitch in a way he would understand. She resumed typing at her computer:

"1. Lay to be open about his involvement or more importantly, his lack thereof." In other words, he trusted the wrong people—not just Skilling and Fastow and Causey, but V&E and Arthur Andersen. "Ken Lay and his board were duped by a COO who wanted the targets met no matter what the consequences, a CFO motivated by personal greed and 2 of the most respected firms, AA & Co and V&E, who had both grown too wealthy off Enron's yearly business and no longer performed their roles as Ken Lay, the board, and just about anybody on the street would expect as a minimum standard for CPAs and attorneys." *How's that for going for the jugular?* she thought.

Lay, she said, should meet with the SEC. "This is a problem we must all address and fix for corporate America as a whole.

"My conclusions if Ken Lay takes these steps:

"1. The bad news: this is horrific. Plaintiff's attorneys will be celebrating. The trouble facing the company will be obvious to all.
"2. The good news. The wild speculations will slow down, if not
cease. Nobody wants Ken Lay's head. He's well respected in the
business and the community. . . .

"My conclusions if we don't come clean and restate:

"All these bad things will happen to us anyway, it's just that Ken Lay will be more implicated in this than is deserved and he won't get the chance to restore the company to its former stature."

That, Sherron thought, should scare him to death.

W hen she took her next memo to Lay, he thanked her and gave her some good news. He was getting rid of V&E and Andersen, he said, and was bringing in a special investigative committee that would work with new lawyers.

Maybe, Sherron thought, *he's finally going to do the right thing*.

Then Lay told Sherron he'd like her to share her ideas with Beth Tilney. "She's helping me on PR," he said.

So Sherron copied her e-mail and sent it to Cindy Olson and Beth Tilney, whose husband worked so closely with Andy Fastow. "Ken thinks it would be a good idea for me to work for you in our PR and IR efforts re: our current crisis. Beth, I think you know my involvement from Cindy, and that I haven't really had a job since my first meeting with Ken re: these matters in late August. I can jump on this ASAP. . . .

"I can effectively play devil's advocate on the accounting issues and be sure we anticipate the tough questions and have answers. My personal opinion is that it's very hard to know who in the organization is giving us good answers and who's covering their work."

M cMahon left Sherron Watkins another voice mail on that same day, October 29, when Enron's stock closed at $13.81. "Hey, Sherron, it's Jeff. Got your voice mail. Finally leaving the office before 4 A.M., 3 A.M. actually, finally! Anyway, I'm traveling now, we are hopefully getting progress on this loan. Hopefully. And I'm also seeing the rating agencies. So maybe you can leave me your ideas on my voice mail if you don't mind. . . .

"We've got lots to do to build investor confidence, let me tell you. . . . But any ideas you have, I would like to hear them."

That day, Moody's cut Enron's credit rating to two notches above junk.

The company said Enron was "suffering from deteriorating financial flexibility" since the write-downs and equity changes from the previously undisclosed partnership investment, "which triggered difficulties in rolling over commercial paper."

Enron was now trading at $13.75. In two weeks, as the value of its bonds fell as well, the company lost more than half of its market value. Keith Power's wife finally let go. In the last year, they had lost 23 percent of the money they'd saved since 1985.

It was around this time that Kristina Mordaunt had an attack of conscience and went to Jim Derrick to give him a piece of bad news about herself. Though she was an Enron lawyer who was supposed to be protecting Enron from LJM, she had made a small investment in Fastow's fund. Now she didn't want Derrick or Lay to be embarrassed if the information came out.

In March 2000, she explained, Michael Kopper had approached her, probably on Andy Fastow's behalf. He'd offered her the chance to invest in a new company called Southampton Place, LLC (named after the neighborhood where so many Enron employees made their home). The fund was being formed to buy out NatWest's interest in an LJM subsidiary.

Kopper told Mordaunt she could get in on the deal for less than $6,000. She obliged, along with five other Enron employees. As Mordaunt would explain to Derrick, she tried to make sure that Enron was not involved in the transaction.

Less than two months later, Mordaunt received a nice return on her $5,800 investment: $1 million.

Soon after confiding in Derrick, Kristina Mordaunt was fired.

So, too, was Ben Glisan, another investor in the fund.

Losing Glisan at this time was a blow to the company—he had star quality, and he was someone everyone had the highest of hopes for.

Jeff McMahon called Glisan at home that night. Why had he lied when asked whether he invested in the fund? McMahon asked. Hadn't he known better, as an Enron employee, than to invest in an LJM deal?

Glisan answered that he had only invested in a company that purchased a subsidiary of LJM, not LJM or Enron. So, he said, it wasn't technically a lie.

Tf there was anyone who could read the Enron tea leaves clearly, it was Jeff
ISkilling. He spent the fall trying to teach himself to relax, and planned a
trip to Florida with Cliff Baxter. But in Florida he could not relax—he knew
that Enron was slipping into a death spiral.

Instead of spending the night on the town, he locked himself in his hotel
room and brooded. The next morning he flew back to Houston. The cash
drain, he knew, was like a fire in the building. The company was dead if he
didn't do something about it.

He put in a call to Lay.

"Ken," he told him, "you've got to bring me back." He offered to return
as an interim CEO or as a consultant. We have to fire up the engines, he
told him. Tell Jimmy Lee, Chase's vice chairman, there's not a problem. *Tell
him we will pay him back!*

Lay listened. "Very interesting," he said, "very interesting."

Within a few hours, Lay called Skilling back. Whalley was coming over
to his house to talk to him. Lay wanted to be sure Whalley was on board with
the idea of a Skilling return.

When Whalley arrived, the two men compared numbers.

Skilling asked Whalley what he was thinking.

Liquidity of $3 billion to $4 billion, Whalley answered.

They had to get on a plane that night, Skilling urged. Were there people
in New York already? Every minute counted.

Whalley left, pledging his support.

We've got to go now, Skilling told Whalley as he walked out the door.

Then Skilling waited. Two days passed, and finally his phone rang. They
couldn't take him back, Lay said. What would the press say?

McMahon returned another call to Sherron Watkins on November 2 to
continue an earlier discussion. "I hear you loud and clear," he said
about her conviction that Enron should restate its earnings. "But I guess my
question is, any restatement of any magnitude, even though it's not related to
the core business, has major credibility issues with the investor community."
He felt that the equity community (the shareholders) could forgive and forget, but he wasn't sure about the debt community (the lenders). "A restate-

ment results in some nasty stuff," he continued. "I guess where I'm heading is—I think you might be able to come in as the new guy and fix it all. That's a possibility. Not so sure you can hang around as the old guy that was around when all this happened and say whoops. Right? I don't think that flies. . . ."

Sherron listened to the voice mail and realized, for the first time, that Jeff McMahon was talking about Ken Lay, but also about himself. A major restatement of prior financial reporting is an admission of guilt; a company confesses that it misled its investors, whether through avarice or ignorance. The management in place when the truth was stretched usually didn't get to stick around to rebuild the company and restore confidence. In other words, by calling for a restatement, Sherron was advocating that Enron's upper management resign en masse.

Not a good career move for her.

Two hours later, at 9 P.M., the Enron board's audit and compliance committee held a meeting. Enron's stock closed at $11.30 earlier that day. The cheery, confident gatherings in Palm Beach and the lazy social hours at various Four Seasons hotels had long since faded from memory. Night had fallen, and the lights shining in other offices in other Houston skyscrapers were painful reminders of other companies conducting business as usual.

At Enron, the faces were pale and drawn, especially those in this particular conference room. There was some good news: Citigroup and Chase agreed to provide $1 billion in additional loans; Enron had to pledge its pipeline assets as collateral, but at least it had more cash in the door. But Enron needed more; it was still hemorrhaging money to support its trading operations. The trading customers with leverage were busy using it, invoking material-adverse-change clauses, threatening to go to the press and claim that they'd lost confidence in Enron as a trading partner—anything they could use to force Enron to close out positions and pay them what they were owed. Hundreds of millions were flowing out the door, and still there were more bills to pay. These were the problems now facing board members such as Wendy Gramm, Bob Belfer, and Charles LeMaistre. Lay was there, too, stone-faced, with Causey, Derrick, and, eventually, David Duncan. Causey opened the meeting with an update on the SEC inquiry and then moved on to the really bad news: Arthur Andersen wanted the company to restate its earnings, to the tune of about $1.2 billion, from 1997 through year-end 2000.

At that point, Ken Lay broke in. He had spent the last week on calls to Alan Greenspan, to Commerce Secretary Don Evans, and to Treasury Secretary Paul O'Neill. They were all turning their backs on him, even when he claimed that Enron's collapse could put the entire country's volatile energy trading markets at risk.

O'Neill spoke in turn with Peter Fisher, the undersecretary for domestic finance, who told him that scenario was unlikely. Enron was not quite as important as it had always seemed to itself. All of Lay's money, the good works, the lavish contributions, were coming to nothing. He was a pariah. He took it out on Andersen: Enron should have restated long ago, he said, and Andersen should have told them to do it.

Then Causey moved on to explain the $1.2 billion restatement. Chewco had insufficient equity to qualify as an SPE and should be placed on the balance sheet. Andersen had also made an error in accounting judgment related to an LJM transaction in 1999; this transaction also lacked sufficient equity to meet *its* obligations and should be reviewed for restatement. The room filled with recriminations—maybe, Enron people said, none of this would have happened if Andersen had done its job in the first place. Maybe, Andersen said, this wouldn't have happened if Enron hadn't concealed documents from Andersen.

Of course, it was too late now. Causey told the committee what each and every member already knew: All this information would have to be filed in the company's third-quarter report. Enron, already enmeshed in the fight of its life, would have to restate its earnings.

Wearily, Lay tried to rally his troops once more over the next few days. In a memo to the staff, he listed the bad news—the investigation by the SEC and the declining credit rating. On the other hand, Enron Online had done almost six thousand transactions in one day, so trading looked solid.

"Serious issues have been raised in the media and investment community that have put our credibility and reputation as a company in question," he wrote. "We're taking an introspective look at our business dealings, our core values, and our organization as a whole. We're doing everything we can to deal with issues that are affecting our company.

"And that's where you come in. Look around you. Look at the excellence that you and your team represents. That's the reason we hired you—you're the best. Now, more than ever, work for Enron and especially for each other."

On November 8, Enron filed an 8K report with the SEC. "This restatement will have no negative impact on Enron's reported earnings for the nine-month period ending September 2001," the document said.

The financial press didn't buy it. "Enron Restatements Don't Go Far Enough" was the headline in a story on TheStreet.com, which noted that the restatements had factored in losses with LJM1 but not LJM2, particularly those pesky Raptor vehicles Sherron Watkins was still complaining about within Enron.

That day, Enron's stock fell to $8.41.

Lay was more concerned with a paragraph in the 8K that referred to Kopper and Dodson.

Domestic partner? Lay asked. What was that?

When someone defined the term for him, he was stunned.

"What the fuck is going on here?" he demanded.

Everyone around him froze. No one had ever heard Ken Lay talk that way before.

Enron now was perilously close to losing its investment-grade rating. If that happened, debt-acceleration clauses lurking in many off-balance-sheet vehicles would be triggered, as Enron upper management knew. But in the hallways, coffee break rooms, and work areas, employees were focused on another topic: How did the company expect the rating agencies—S&P, Moody's, and Fitch—to keep the company rated above junk when Enron's publicly traded bonds were already trading like junk? Bankruptcy seemed inevitable.

Enron needed cash and it needed it desperately. An equity investor was the preferred route, one that could offer a bailout similar to Warren Buffett's rescue of Salomon Brothers in 1991, when that firm faced a crisis over a Treasury bond trading scandal. In fact, Whalley, McMahon, and the head of the M&A group flew to Omaha to see if Buffett was interested in another save. He wasn't. He'd never understood how Enron made money and he, like Houston-based money manager, Fayez Sarofim, only invested in businesses he understood. Next, the group called on all the big private equity firms—KKR, Apollo, Blackstone, Chase Private Equity, and AIG. Some were interested, some were not. Nearly all of them wanted a gas pipeline or two in exchange for their equity investment in Enron. "Looks interesting," was the standard response, "We'll get back to you next week." Trouble was, Enron didn't have a week.

Hope appeared in the form of a man named Chuck Watson. Watson was a beefy, broad-faced man who looked like a lot of guys in the stands at UT football games—guys who played defense in college, their muscle now aged into a cinder-block solidity.

Watson had been around almost as long as Ken Lay. He had started a gas-trading business called Natural Gas Clearinghouse, which grew into Dynegy. Dynegy considered itself an Enron competitor—but to Enron, Watson's company was just another small, slow, uncool business that was always nipping at its heels. On the other hand, Dynegy never made the commitment to virtual commerce with the passion that Enron did. Though it had a trading division, its pipeline guys still mattered.

That turned out to be a plus for Enron the day Stan Horton had lunch with a Dynegy executive. Horton was the consummate pipeline guy—sturdy, straightforward, bankable in word and deed—and so when he floated the idea of saving Enron through a sale to Dynegy, it had a gravitas that captured Watson's attention when he got the news. It's safe to say that Watson could not have missed the irony, either; here was a chance to rub Enron's nose in its failure, to punish the company for more than a decade of arrogance. Lay took a break from his frantic calls to Washington on October 26 and welcomed Watson to his vaulted-ceiling kitchen to work out a tentative agreement. Lay would step down—again—and Dynegy would buy Enron, becoming a force to be reckoned with in the energy world. As they liked to say at Enron, it was a win-win deal. Jobs would be saved, and Lay could retire from the field with honor. He was thinking about running for mayor of Houston. Around Enron, there was a lot of joking about the deal: "We're gonna own *them* in three months," Enron people said.

On November 7, the two boards tentatively agreed to the merger. But Enron was still burning through cash—$2 billion in the week after it signed the merger agreement–and it had not told Dynegy about that problem. At the same time, Moody's was threatening another downgrade. If that happened, the merger would be doomed.

This time, maybe because of pressure from the New York banks, Moody's relented. But they wanted Dynegy to put more cash into the deal. Watson agreed and put in $1.5 billion. But he did it for a price: If the merger didn't go through, he could take the Northern Natural Gas pipeline, Enron's crown jewel.

On Friday November 9, with Enron at about $9, they waited for Chevron/Texaco, Dynegy's major shareholder, to agree to the deal. The minutes stretched into hours, and the shadows grew long. Chevron and Texaco were celebrating their recent merger and had better things to do than to worry about a couple of minor Texas energy trading companies.

At the end of that day, in time for the local news, Lay and Watson finally gave a press conference announcing the deal. While Watson hailed the merger, Lay sat quietly in a folding chair behind him. Then the head of Dynegy offered the head of Enron the podium.

Before getting out of his chair, Lay stooped to pull up his socks—an eerie bow of subservience. He was, suddenly, an old man at fifty-eight.

On the same day, Sherron received a call from Bob Williams, an in-house attorney and head of Enron's litigation team. She had offered her services to litigation support; she'd helped Andersen with lawsuit strategies more than a decade earlier and thought Enron might be able to use her in the same capacity. But there was a complication—she might be called as a witness in suits against Enron. "They did want me to remind you that all this should be kept confidential," he said. "I told them I was sure that you were aware of that, so . . . as much as your friends want to hear about Enron and everything, just like mine do, we need to keep all this in-house for now. So the plaintiffs and the lawyers don't start to smell even more blood in the water."

Williams was a little late. By then, twenty-two lawsuits—from share-holders, former employees, and others—had been filed against Enron.

That day, Standard & Poor's also downgraded Enron's debt from BBB to BBB–. Only the promise of the Dynegy merger, the agency said, kept it from going lower.

By mid-November, Ken Lay was refining his exit strategy. He would leave the company with tens of millions in stock sales and other savings plans. He also intended to exercise a clause in his contract that stated that in the event the company was sold, he would receive $20 million annually for every year left on his contract. Because he had three years left, the sale of Enron to Dynegy would give him the chance to walk away with another $60 million. But, on a bleak day in November, he faced an obstacle to his plan: An Enron trader named John Lavorato, who went to his office to tell Lay that he could not possibly cash out in that fashion.

Lavorato was not a popular man at Enron—with a tic that kept him obsessively plucking his shirt from his shoulder, he was almost a cliché of the boorish trader. But he was great at his job, and when Whalley ascended, so, too, had Lavorato.

Now Lavorato had the gall to tell Lay that there would be a revolt on the gas floor if he took the $60 million.

Without the traders, Lavorato explained, there would be no Enron and, in turn, no company to sell. Before he could leave with his bonus, Ken Lay would have to make provisions for his most valuable asset—the trading group. Truth be told, most traders had already demanded cash payments to stay. They shared $50 million in "stay put" bonuses paid in early November to those who would move down the street to Dynegy.

As a result of his meeting, Lay changed course and issued a memo. "As many of you know, I have a provision in my employment contract which provides for a payment of $20 million per year for the remaining term of my contract in the event of a change of control of Enron. . . . Given the current circumstances facing the company and our employees, I have been giving a lot of thought these last few days to what to do about this payment. Initially, I thought I would use part of the funds for a foundation for our employees and take the remainder in stock and cash. However, after talking to a number of employees this afternoon, I have decided that the best course of action would be for me to waive my right to any of this payment."

An Enron vice president of corporate systems by the name of Allan Sommer had been at Enron for several years, setting up computer systems for the payrolls of the various business units. He was like a CIO, keeping an eye on payment systems, banking interfaces, accounting systems, and the like. A Danish immigrant approaching forty, he had a broad, handsome face and Old World manners. Enron was an eye-opener for Sommer, but he went with the flow. The events of the last few weeks, however, made him increasingly uneasy. People in his office were jumpy and secretive. Sommer, known for his bluntness even around Enron, began asking questions no one could quite answer. Finally, his boss, Rick Causey, called him into his office, wanting to know whether Sommer was on board or not.

It was Sommer's experience that when such a question was put to him at Enron, there was, in his words, some unpleasantness ahead. He soon learned what that unpleasantness would be. People were going to be laid off, Causey told him, lots of people. But, Causey added reassuringly, Sommer was "a keeper."

Sommer went home, poured himself a glass of good red wine, and thought about what was coming. He had never really trusted Causey, and now he trusted him even less. He knew, for instance, that Causey, along with Rick Buy, had negotiated a very large raise for himself, retroactive to January, just before the October 16 write-down. What kind of people did that in a company mired in financial tribulation?

Over the next few days, the people working under Sommer started receiving strange phone calls. One person was asked to set up a new relationship with a bank Enron had never used before, and the deposits started rolling in; this was money that could be used, for instance, for the payment of emergency bonuses to keep people in times of crisis. Other people were charged with withdrawing money from companies that might be included in a potential bankruptcy filing and moving it to companies that would be immune. Hundreds of millions were shifted in a matter of hours.

"This is not the time to be worrying about your own ass," Causey chided. But when Sommer proved uncooperative, his days were numbered.

O n the evening of the day that Ken Lay left $60 million on the table, he went home to his high-rise condo, changed into a tuxedo, and headed to Rice University for an event that would once have been a source of enormous pride. The evening had been scheduled months before: It was the awarding of the Enron Prize for Distinguished Public Service from the James A. Baker III Institute for Public Policy of Rice University, yet another instance of Enron's seemingly boundless corporate largesse. On the orderly, oak-shaded campus, with building after building named after great Houstonians, it would have been almost possible for Lay to forget all the bad news; at the dinner held at the Baker Institute, the faces turned toward him were, if not quite reverent, at least sympathetic. Old Houston had embraced James Baker when he retired from public life; they chipped in, along with the Saudis, for his school of international studies, turning out for the high-minded events that brought such a nice international gloss to the campus and the city.

Ken Lay was one of them. These were nicely tanned, tastefully dressed, unfailingly polite Republicans, the men with faces weathered by golf, bourbon, and dove hunts, the women stylish enough in gowns that were appropriately but not insistently dowdy. This crowd mixed well with the campus academics and a smattering of visiting politicians, the people with higher purposes—the people Lay had always felt closest to.

Honorees since the award had been established in 1997 had included Colin Powell, Nelson Mandela, Mikhail Gorbachev, and Eduard Shevardnadze. That night's guest of honor was Alan Greenspan, the doleful chairman of the Federal Reserve, the one who had warned America against the kind of irrational exuberance that now threatened to destroy Enron. But for Lay, the night was just a little off-kilter, like the beginning of a very bad dream or, worse, a portent. Washington had nothing for him or his company. He was meeting with his church minister for solace, but solace escaped him.

Lay endured Greenspan's turgid speech with practiced attentiveness. "The long-term marginal cost of extraction presumably anchors the long-term equilibrium price," Greenspan droned. Lay himself could have written such lines on global energy policy. "Thus, it is critical to an evaluation of the magnitude and persistence of any current price disturbance."

An evaluation of the magnitude and persistence of any current price disturbance—who at Enron could have dreamed it? Lay had weathered all crises past. Was this one so different?

Greenspan sent Lay a signal that it might be. During the question-and-answer session, someone asked for advice about entering the job market. Greenspan, the man who had once been "Alan," who had taken Lay's calls and listened to him solicitously, gathered himself for an answer. "I do not deny that there are innumerable people who survived in business by being less than wholly ethical," Greenspan said, "but I will say to you that those are the rare examples. The best chance you have of making a big success in this world is to decide from square one that you're going to do it ethically."

When he headed back to Washington, Greenspan left behind his crystal award and his $50,000 Enron honorarium.

On November 19, with the stock at around $9, Greg Whalley and Jeff McMahon hosted a presentation at the Waldorf-Astoria, to calm Enron's biggest bankers. This was the new "open kimono" Enron. The team provided an extensive PowerPoint presentation explaining the company's decline. Points included "a complete loss of investor and creditor confidence," "the nervousness of the trade credit markets," the lack of short- and long-term capital, the bad investments from Azurix to Broadband, and the related-party transactions, as well as "the failure of management to respond quickly." But this was Enron, and so the men also had solutions. Management would change; they would rebuild investor confidence. And, of course, there was the Dynegy merger, which would bring in much-needed cash.

Enron could change, and they had a chart to prove it. The old Enron had a "deal shop mentality." The new Enron had a "liability management focus." The old Enron had "compartmentalized information." The new Enron would provide "open communication." The old Enron was a "black box." The new Enron offered "financial transparency," and so on. Enron would from now on be cash driven as opposed to earnings driven, fair value would be replaced by market value, the eternal search for new businesses would be replaced with a focus on core businesses, and related-party deals were a thing of the past. The focus was "on achieving a successful merger." This new incarnation of Enron, then, was going to be well behaved and conventional.

Unfortunately, the presentation occurred the same day that Enron filed its tardy third-quarter report with the SEC. This document contained enough bad news to sink a healthy company, much less one that depended on perception more than ever to save itself.

The first bit of bad news had to do with the amount of Enron's losses. They had been listed at $618 million in the October earnings release and reported as $635 million in the November 8 restatement, and now the company was claiming the loss was $664 million.

The second problem had to do with an off-balance-sheet entity called Marlin, the one that had so concerned analyst Richard Grubman, a.k.a. the man Skilling called "Asshole." The day Lay and Grubman had their tiff back in October, Lay assured the analyst that Marlin, created to keep Azurix debt off Enron's books, was healthy. Now, triggers in Marlin as well as Whitewing came back to haunt the company: If Enron's debt was downgraded and its stock price fell below a certain level—unfortunately, the stock-price trigger happened months before—the company would have to "repay, refinance or cash collateralize additional facilities totaling $3.9 billion." Enron had approximately $13 billion of debt on its books, and now the investment community discovered that $3.9 billion more had not been factored into the load. It was sitting there, off the balance sheet, waiting like a ticking time bomb for Enron to lose its investment-grade rating.

The third problem had to do with Enron's current credit rating. Standard & Poor's November 7 downgrade triggered the payment of a note on an SPE called Rawhide that would be due on November 27, 2001. The ineptness of Fastow's finance shop was now painfully obvious to anyone who had missed it before. No one had realized a trigger existed in the Rawhide loans until Enron got the default notice. Then, Enron had to come up with *another* $690 million.

Despite Enron's promises to be honest and straightforward, its executives had left a crucial person out of their loop: Dynegy CEO Chuck Watson. He was now furious, and wrote Ken Lay a letter to that effect: "We have not been consulted in a timely manner regarding developments since November 9. We were not briefed in advance on the issues in your 10-Q. Our team had to make repeated phone calls to your finance and accounting officials in an attempt to obtain information. Some of the most significant information in the Q was never shown to us at all."

Even so, Watson still wanted to go ahead with the deal. He could not resist the siren's song of owning Enron, of being a player on the world stage. So, with Chevron/Texaco's money, he handed over the $1.5 billion he had guaranteed in anticipation of the merger, figuring he'd get the Northern Natural Gas pipeline either way.

Citicorp and Chase had each loaned Enron $500 million just weeks before, and they'd taken Enron's Transwestern Pipeline Company as collateral. (The banks were forced to step in—Enron owed them so much that they had to find a way to keep it going if they were to have a prayer of seeing their money again.) Enron now took the Dynegy cash and headed back to business. All in all, the company borrowed a total of $5.5 billion, adding over $3.5 billion in debt to its balance sheet.

Even so, it wasn't enough. With a lower credit rating, Enron had to put up more and more collateral to keep trading. The trading customers were now refusing to do business with Enron without cash deposits. Where once Enron had demanded such reserves from other, weaker customers, it now had to make those up-front payments. By late November, with the stock hovering around $4, it owed about $18.7 billion to its trading customers. (The company had receivables on the other side that could have offset its trading liabilities, but it was caught in a squeeze. While customers screamed about material adverse changes at Enron, Enron could make no such demands on its customers, who paid when gas or power was delivered.) No one at Enron had ever imagined that the material-adverse-change clauses in the trading contracts could ever have applied to them. The company always negotiated hard for the clauses, thinking that Enron would be the one to invoke them. But the tables had turned, and the clauses were virtually impregnable.

From another perspective it hardly mattered. People were beginning to wonder whether there would be a business to hand over to Dynegy. The credit downgrade meant that fewer and fewer businesses were willing to trade with Enron in its current situation. Enron's traders, who used to roar into the office at 7 A.M. and didn't leave their desks until well after sundown, now headed home in the early afternoon. Enron was radioactive. Skilling had won his fight for deregulated transparent trading markets—now there were plenty of other trading houses for Enron's customers to patronize.

Worse, there was word on the street that Chuck Watson was getting cold feet. Standard & Poor's called McMahon to ask whether Enron had a deal or not. If not, they would have to downgrade the company's rating once more.

Do what you have to do, he told S&P.

At nearly the same time, Watson was asking where his $1.5 billion had gone. When he saw how much cash Enron was actually hemorrhaging, he finally threw in the towel and withdrew from the merger. He couldn't get a straight answer out of anyone at Enron, he complained.

With that, Enron's last chance at salvation was gone.

On November 27, Moody's downgraded Enron to B2. One day later, S&P followed suit to BB.

As a result, the $3.9 billion of off-balance-sheet debt triggered. It was due and payable thirty days after the lenders notified Enron of its covenant breach. The stock price fell to 27 cents.

On Saturday, December 1, the rain fell cold and hard in Houston; it had been raining that way, it seemed, since Thanksgiving. Inside the Enron building, the gloom was palpable; everyone knew it was over. "We've got to file now," Whalley said. Moody's wouldn't even take another phone call. Once more the Enron board gathered; they unanimously voted to declare bankruptcy.

But Enron could not resist one last lick. The headline of the *Houston Chronicle* the next day was a twofer: "Enron Declares Bankruptcy/Sues Dynegy for Breach of Contract." Enron would not hand over its pipeline without a fight.

The remaining executives at Enron shook their heads. No one could believe Watson had bothered with the merger in the first place, when all he'd really needed to do was invest in Enron's intellectual capital. After all, it was just a trading company, driven by traders. For the right price, he probably could have hired whomever he wanted. A company of mercenaries is not a company of loyalists.

They couldn't believe anyone could be so dumb.

20

Payback

THEY'RE still trying to hide the weenie. That's what Sherron Watkins thought as she read a newspaper clipping about Enron two weeks before Christmas, 2001. The term came from her Andersen days, and was a reference to recalcitrant clients who wouldn't come clean at audit time. Over the years, "hiding the weenie" came to refer to more generalized acts of corporate or political obfuscation. John Gutfreund tried to hide the weenie at Salomon Brothers. Michael Milken tried to hide the weenie at Drexel. Bill Clinton was the grand champion weenie hider of all time. Hiding the weenie, in Sherron's mind, never worked out. Even so, people kept trying.

She was lying in bed with Marion sleeping peacefully beside her, a glass of Chardonnay on her nightstand. Rick was working in Canada, but had faxed home an Enron story from *The Globe and Mail* that commanded her full attention. It quoted Jeff McMahon, addressing the company's creditors and cautioning them against a rash judgment. "It may well be that the final story is that 99 per cent of the losses suffered are due to a crisis of confidence on Wall Street," he said. "Don't assume that there is a smoking gun."

Sherron knew McMahon and Enron well enough to know that the company was in extreme spin mode. Enron's bankruptcy filing was being followed in Houston by a rash of rumors that became more grandiose and more hysterical every day: Skilling had fled to Brazil (he hadn't); Lay had hired bodyguards (he had); Fastow had fled to Israel (he hadn't, and to prove it he appeared at a televised press conference just long enough to display a deer-in-the-headlights stare and to wish reporters a happy holiday). Congressional, Justice Department, and SEC investigations loomed, but, meanwhile, the U.S. attorney's office in Houston recused itself from any prosecutions because of close ties—husbands, wives, former employers—to Enron.

Yet here was McMahon pooh-poohing it all. Even Andersen, in the same story, was trying to make amends: "The head of Enron Corp.'s long time auditing firm told Congress yesterday the company's collapse shows that the accounting firm and the entire profession will have to change." This from the soon to be disgraced and dismissed Joe Berardino, who, according to the same *Globe and Mail* article, "admitted for the first time that the Big Five accounting firm had erred in its treatment of one Enron financing vehicle used by the company to keep debt off the balance sheet. . . ."

One accounting vehicle? "We made a professional judgment about the appropriate accounting treatment that turned out to be wrong. . . ."

How, Sherron wondered, do you get the biggest bankruptcy in history from *one* off-balance-sheet vehicle?

She lay back on her pillow and considered her options. Christmas was fourteen days away. She estimated she had one, maybe two more paychecks coming, enough to cover one more house payment, and, if she was lucky, a couple of Christmas bills. Then, most likely, her salary and bonus would drop to exactly $.00. Four months from that moment, she calculated, she would either have to sell the house or raid her retirement fund. Good-bye to the damask tablecloths, the silk lampshades, the plantation shutters, the garden patio, the pretty tree-shaded street in the perfect neighborhood. Good-bye First Presbyterian preschool. Good-bye, for that matter, to the whole half-million Southampton starter package she was just getting used to. Sherron's stomach did backflips. She could give it all up, sure—move back to Tomball, put Marion in Lutheran day school—but after making an eight-year invest-ment in her Enron career, was this really how it was all supposed to turn out?

"But Mr. Berardino said Houston based Enron also withheld informa-tion from Andersen and that Andersen notified Enron's audit committee of 'Possible illegal acts within the company. . . .'" Right again. Could they have whispered any louder? Sherron figured she might as well be out on the street already, with the 4,300 other angry, broke, and betrayed Enron employees who had been laid off, for all the good Andersen did Enron.

The first few weeks of December were, true to Enron form, chaotic. Ken Lay's bankruptcy lawyers gave him the news that he would be letting his myriad employees go with a severance package of no more than $4,000 each. Over voice mail to Enron's employees, announcing the collapse on December 2, he kept up a good front: "While there will be a lot of changes over the next few days," he said, "we are continuing to operate and have a lot of information for you about what all this means, so we need you to come to work tomorrow." He sounded to Sherron as if he were describing a minor inconvenience, as if the lights were flickering or the air conditioner was on the blink. But what most employees found the next morning when they arrived at work was, simply, disaster.

When Sherron visited the new building's trading floor, she found her friend Andrea weeping as she packed up her desk. Her boss, Ray Bowen, gave a brief farewell to his employees: Friday's paycheck was their last, he said; they were to clean out all their personal items and go. He tried to be inspirational, telling them how much he enjoyed working at Enron Indus-trial Markets, but no one wanted to listen. They would have been even grim-mer if they had known that he received a $700,000 bonus to stay for ninety days. These outlandish bonuses were being given out in secret to chosen executives. In many cases, the amounts were two to five times—one as high as fourteen times—a year's salary. COO Greg Whalley met in a room with a few lieutenants, and, for the most part, gave the money to people he liked and valued. Louise Kitchen, the creator of Enron Online, got $2 million. John Lavorato, the head trader, got $5 million. Jim Fallon, the Broadband chief du jour, got $1.5 million, as did CFO Jeff McMahon.

Fifty-five million dollars had been parceled out the week before bankruptcy. Twenty executives received 75 percent of the outlay. This was on top of the $50 million paid to key traders in early November.

The same farewell ritual occurred on floor after floor: Managers with bonuses that sometimes reached into the millions dispatched people who did not know how they would pay their Christmas bills. *My wife's about to have a baby—what about my insurance?* Sherron heard someone ask. I don't know, was the answer. *What about severance?* Well, a check for $4,000 should be coming in the next few weeks. That was it.

Depending on the compassion level of the various managers—that is, how much time they gave their employees to clear out—some floors looked hit by smart bombs, the kind that vaporized people in their tracks. People left drawers open, apples half eaten, coffee cups half full. White boards held calculations that would never be completed. Laptops and Palm Pilots lay abandoned, their passwords canceled. The floors were littered with the deactivated cards that had once allowed employees to come and go from the building and to charge their double lattes. Outside, employees hugged one another and cried, while brigades of camera crews from the world's news organizations moved in for close-ups. People used their $800 Herman Miller office chairs as luggage carts, and then left them in the parking lot.

Sherron, however, was safe for the moment. One of Enron's attorneys told her she had at least another month of employment, because she might be needed as a witness in upcoming lawsuits. In the meantime, Sherron confided in a close friend about her memos and the company's response to them, forgetting the woman was married to a federal prosecutor. Soon, he was on the phone. Did she have a lawyer, he wanted to know? She told him she didn't need one, and he countered that she did and he had one for her.

Within a matter of days, she found herself sitting in the office of Philip Hilder, a criminal attorney who had also been a federal prosecutor. Hilder, tall, dark, and pugnacious, was interested, but he seemed dubious as she recounted for two hours the events of the last four months. Despite his skepticism—he couldn't believe Enron was *that* nutty—Hilder predicted SEC and DOJ investigations if Sherron was right. He mentioned legal costs. Great, Sherron thought. Just as her income was evaporating, her expenses were about to increase exponentially.

She started dragging her heels. People who committed crimes needed attorneys. What had she done wrong? Then she got a how-are-you-holding-up e-mail from a friend, a high-powered New York lawyer. When she called him for advice, he was more adamant than anyone else about her need for representation. "Sherron, if it's the last $10,000 you have, spend it on an attorney," he said. "I want you to find the biggest, meanest lawyer you can, and don't let him leave your side." Then he told her to be especially wary of any Enron attorneys who were acting like a friend. "If they're not on your payroll, don't trust them," he warned her.

The directive tipped her into an uncustomary depression. No one at Enron wanted to believe her story, she suspected, because it wasn't in their interest to do so. Her only hope of validation was a tidbit she received about the Wilmer, Cutler attorney running Enron's special investigation with William Powers. Her friend in New York told her that Bill McLukas had been an enforcement attorney with the SEC for nineteen years. He was a straight shooter. Maybe, she hoped, he would see things her way.

She hired Philip Hilder. True to her friend's prediction, Enron wanted her to use the same attorney as Rick Causey and Rick Buy, a conflict of interest if ever there was one. Even worse, the company intended to use her memos for defense purposes—to show that Enron thoroughly investigated an employee's complaints and found nothing wrong. The only ray of hope came from another Wilmer, Cutler attorney, Chuck Davidow, who, after investigating Enron's arcane SPE structures, told her he was impressed by how accurate she'd been in her assessment of Enron's problems. It was one of the first times Sherron felt that maybe, in struggling against the Enron current, she was no longer swimming alone.

She was relieved to have Hilder in her court when her SEC subpoena arrived the first week in January, demanding, within seven days, all Enron records, bank records back three years, and all stock records. They also wanted to interview her within the week. "Start preparing your warts list," Hilder told her, meaning she should chronicle any vulnerabilities—speeding tickets, felony convictions—anything that could possibly be used against her. She shook her head. She'd had none of those. But she'd disposed of some stock and options this year, did that count? she asked.

In August, she sold $31,000 worth of stock she'd been granted in January, and griped that she had paid taxes on the grant value then, $80,000. She sold her remaining stock options in late September and early October, when Enron's stock rebounded from the low $20s after the terrorist attacks to the mid-$30s. In the first case, she had been concerned about Skilling's resignation and opted to take a tax loss; in the second, she had been panicked about the possibility of another terrorist attack and wanted to maximize her cash. She'd netted, after taxes, about $17,000 from her option sales. Satisfied, Hilder sent her home to pull together all the records requested by the SEC. She spent the next few days in her garage, poring through files, assembling her papers, and trying not to think about how she was going to pay her bills or her growing unease about her situation at Enron. Her husband Rick stayed home from Canada that week, believing his family might be in danger.

Then, on the afternoon of January 14, Sherron abandoned her cataloging to run a few errands. Coming back into the house, she heard the phone ringing. For the next few weeks, it never stopped.

A congressional investigator for the House Committee on Energy and Commerce stumbled across her memos among thousands of subpoenaed documents. Within days, reporters got them, and the media onslaught began. The first call was from Peter Behr of the *Washington Post*. Then *The New York Times*. Then *The Wall Street Journal*. Then CNN, NBC's *Today Show*, the NBC *Nightly News*, ABC News, CBS's *60 Minutes*, CBS News' *Sunday Morning*, Fox News, Bloomberg News, the *Los Angeles Times*, *The Chicago Tribune*, *The Dallas Morning News*, *The Financial Times*, Dow Jones, the BBC, AP, *Business Week*, *Newsweek*, and producers for Connie Chung, Dan Rather, Dianne Sawyer, Barbara Walters, Matt Lauer, and Cokie Roberts. Was she the author of the memo? Why had she written the memo? What light could she shed on the situation at Enron? After sputtering a few responses to Behr, Sherron referred all calls to Hilder and tried to get control of herself.

The next morning, as she dressed for the office, Rick came in with news that there were camera crews on their front lawn and in the back alley. She could not remember a time when she had been so rattled. She could feel her heart pounding, and, as she reached for the doorknob, noticed her hands were shaking. Then she spied her Bible on a nearby table. Despite her salty language, Sherron's faith had always been important to her. She'd grown up a churchgoing Lutheran, and after 9/11, joined a Bible study group.

Now she grabbed her Bible and frantically flipped the pages in search of a comforting passage. She found Hebrews 12. "Therefore since we are surrounded by so great a cloud of witnesses, let us lay aside every weight that hinders . . . and let us run with perseverance the race that is set before us. . . ." Her eyes filled, and her throat tightened. She ran past the reporters and headed for her car, and the office, and whatever else lay ahead.

Her first call was to Cliff Baxter; she wanted to let him know she mentioned him in her memos to Lay, and that reporters and investigators would probably be trying to reach him. When Baxter answered, he didn't sound happy to hear from her. "Sherron," he said gruffly, "what is the nature of this call?"

She told him of the leak, and read him what she had written: "Cliff Baxter complained mightily to Skilling and to all who would listen about the inappropriateness of our transactions with LJM."

Baxter softened. She was correct, he said. He had complained to Skilling. It didn't look right for a company of Enron's stature to do business with its CFO's partnership.

"You did all you could do," Sherron told him. "You were one of the few good guys in all this mess."

Baxter sighed, and a defeated tone crept into his voice. "I don't think this will turn out 'good' for any of us," he said.

Over the next two months, from January through February 2002, the Enron story shifted from a reasonably contained accounting scandal to a full-blown, all-American morality play. Much like the O. J. Simpson prosecution, the Jon Benet Ramsey murder investigation, and the Bill Clinton/Monica Lewinsky scandal—more than adequate predictors of the way Enron would be treated in the press—this story, though complicated on its face, could be reduced to a few simple elements that anyone could understand, i.e., greedy executives live large while duping loyal employees and unwitting shareholders. It was a sign of the story's mass appeal that like the O. J., Jon Benet, and Monica stories, *The New York Times* and *The National Enquirer* covered it simultaneously, while TV news presented All Enron All the Time.

On January 16, the same day the press reported that David Duncan was fired by Arthur Andersen for supposedly shredding documents in violation of federal law, news of Sherron Watkins' memos broke on the front page of the *Times*. This turn of events gave the story a heroine. Sherron was immediately cast in the role of whistleblower. The narrative also provided a plethora of villains. At dinner tables around Houston, there were the kinds of discussions that would have been unthinkable just a year or so before: Was Ken Lay, the benevolent philanthropist, a fool or a crook? Was Jeff Skilling a messianic manipulator? Was Andy Fastow, family man, really nothing more than a common thief?

Other CEOs and corporate cheerleaders lost no time distancing themselves from Lay on the pundit circuit. "A CEO who receives a memo this important, this detailed, and also ignores it does so at his own peril," insisted one business commentator to huzzahs all around. The supporting roles— Andersen's David Duncan and Merrill Lynch's Schuyler Tilney, among others—offered even more opportunity for speculation. Who knew how many supposedly fine, upstanding members of Houston's business community were in on this vast conspiracy? No one could decide whether David Lynch or Oliver Stone should direct the movie. The cast of bad actors grew after Salon.com published the list of dozens of people who, just days before bankruptcy, secretly divided among themselves the $55 million in retention bonuses.

Then at 2:20 A.M., on January 25, Cliff Baxter's body was found in the driver's seat of his black Mercedes, which was parked near his home in "Sugarland's most exclusive neighborhood," as noted by the Houston *Chronicle*. He died from a gunshot wound to the head, and left a note apologizing to his wife, explaining that "where there was once great pride, now it's gone." Baxter had lashed his identity to Enron's in the best of times, and then could not separate himself from the company and the people he had loved there. He had been furious about the plaintiffs' lawyers, heartbroken about the bad press. The last time he saw Skilling, he was devastated. "They're calling us child molesters," he stated, ". . . and that will never wash off." Most of Baxter's close friends at Enron had worried over his mood swings for years (he was on medication to treat his mental state), and his movements in the last days of his life—dropping in for unscheduled visits, in particular—suggested he was saying good-bye to people closest to him.

In the hysteria that gripped Houston at this time, Baxter's death unleashed a maelstrom of conspiracy theories. While close friends gathered for a memorial service at the St. Regis Hotel, his autopsy report was posted on the Web at a hastily created site called whokilledcliffbaxter.com. A tabloid headline asked "V.P. Cliff Baxter: Murder Disguised as Suicide?" "He may have been the proverbial man who knew too much and needed to be kept quiet."

Then reporters abandoned Baxter for the Reverend Jesse Jackson, newly arrived in town. He came to meet with Ken Lay and demand "justice" for Enron employees. He organized a bus caravan from Houston to Washington in the coming weeks to protest the lack of protections for laid-off office workers. Jackson set up camp in one of the city's oldest African American churches, the Antioch Baptist Church in the shadow of the Enron building, and divided his time between posing for photos with ex-employees and praying with Lay, whom he compared to Job. ("Ken Lay built up an awful lot of credits" was the way Mr. Jackson explained his dual role as both defender and critic of Enron's CEO. The *Times* noted that Jackson would not say whether or how much Lay might have contributed to his charitable organization, PUSH.)

Jackson was pushed off the front pages by the appearance of Ken Lay's wife, Linda, on the *Today* show, a two-day media extravaganza that showed just how tone deaf Ken Lay had become to public sentiment. He had resigned as CEO under pressure from the board on January 23, though he held on to his board seat. Advised by other high-powered executives to speak out on his own behalf, Lay recalled a former Enron publicist from her job at Hill & Knowlton, and a media plan was created. Because Lay was forbidden by his lawyers to speak, he sent his wife as his emissary. Linda Lay appeared in a turtleneck sweater and leather pants, her hair expertly frosted. Tearfully, she told *Today*'s viewers that her husband had trusted the wrong people. "He didn't know what was going on." She claimed that they had "lost everything" and were selling everything they owned. She had barely gotten the words out before reporters started swarming over the Lays' real-estate holdings, determining that few of the multimillion dollar properties were, as yet, on the market. "Tears of a Clown" was just one of the headlines lobbed at Linda Lay over the next few days.

And then, on February 2, 2002, UT law school dean William Powers and Wilmer, Cutler released their report, a 200-page trip to the woodshed that contained enough hints of executive skulduggery ("Enron employees involved in the partnerships were enriched, in the aggregate, by tens of millions of dollars they should never have received"), balance-sheet manipulation ("Many of the most significant transactions apparently were designed to accomplish favorable financial statement results, not to achieve bona fide economic objectives or to transfer risk"), and falsified earnings ("Other transactions were implemented—improperly, we are informed by our accounting advisors—to offset losses. They allowed Enron to conceal from the market very large losses") to keep reporters busy for months.

Days later, Dean Powers testified in front of the House Energy Commerce Committee, expressing shock at what he had seen at Enron. His report named names: "While neither the Chief Accounting Officer, Causey, nor the Chief Risk Officer, Buy, ignored his responsibilities, they interpreted their roles very narrowly and did not give the transactions the degree of review the Board believed was occurring." The board promptly fired the two. Ken Lay was "the Chief Executive Officer of Enron and, in effect, the captain of the ship. As CEO, he had ultimate responsibility for taking reasonable steps to ensure that the officers reporting to him performed their oversight duties properly. He does not appear to have directed their attention, or his own, to the oversight of the LJM partnerships." That very day Lay resigned from the board and through his attorney announced that he would plead the Fifth in his Senate appearance scheduled for the following Tuesday. The Board of Directors "failed in our judgment, in its oversight duties. This had serious consequences for Enron, its employees, and its shareholders." Andersen "failed to meet its responsibilities." Vinson & Elkins should have "brought a stronger, more objective and more critical voice to the disclosure process," adding that "Management and the Board relied heavily on the perceived approval by Vinson & Elkins of the [LJM] structure and disclosure of the transactions."

It was at this point—"a nuclear detonation every day," in the words of one local energy-company executive—that the Enron story and Houston seemed to be spinning out of control. The latter became a city occupied by the press, by federal investigators, and by the plaintiffs' lawyers. It was a place judged harshly by the outside world for the "cowboy culture" that supposedly created the current mess. ("As I've written in this space before, Enron is the product of the Houston business culture, which at its worst is capable of an arrogance and hubris that guarantees disaster," Michael Thomas critiqued in the *New York Observer*, ignoring the fact that most of Enron's "cowboys" came from the Midwest.) Houston had come full circle: Enron, which was going to lead the city into the future, led it right back into its past. Only a town full of yahoos, the subtext of national stories suggested, could have produced a yahoo-sized bankruptcy like this one.

As the revelations continued, the only asset Enron had left was its notably fluid identity. In the hands of the media, this identity became a metaphor for all the ills of the last decade—the illusory tech bubble, the silly excesses ("Lifestyles of the Rich and *In*famous" was the title of one local news story on wealthy Enron executives), the corruption of the political process, and the (now believed to be) phony financial wizardry of the Clinton bull market. In short, Enron represented the whole sorry devolution of American capitalism at the end of the twentieth century. Soon, the number of Enron jokes traded on the Internet—and on Leno and Letterman, the late-night barometers of the culture—rivaled the number of SPEs created by Andy Fastow. One of the most popular was the following, which demonstrated the public's speedy mastery of the latest accounting methods:

ENRON CAPITALISM
Feudalism: You have two cows. Your lord takes some of the milk.
Fascism: You have two cows. The government takes both, hires you
to take care of them and sells you the milk.
Communism: You have two cows. You must take care of them, but
the government takes all the milk.
Capitalism: You have two cows. You sell one and buy a bull. Your
herd multiplies, and the economy grows. You sell them and retire
on the income.
Enron Capitalism: You have two cows. You sell three of them to your
publicly listed company, using letters of credit opened by your
brother-in-law at the bank, then execute a debt-equity swap with
an option so that you get all four cows back, with a tax exemption
for five cows. The milk rights of the six cows are transferred

through an intermediary to a Cayman Island company secretly owned by the majority shareholder who sells the rights to all seven cows back to your listed company. The Enron annual report says the company owns eight cows, with an option on one more.

On the Internet, WitCity offered a parody of Enron's voice mail system. A male voice answers a ringing telephone with the following instructions:

Thank you for calling Enron. Please listen closely to the following options, as our menu has changed.
If you wish to serve a subpoena on a current or former Enron executive . . . Press One.
If you are an Enron shareholder and would like to learn how to turn your Enron stock certificates into decorative origami . . . Press Two.
If your Enron 401(k) plan is worthless and you would like tips on how to survive your retirement eating nothing but Mac n' Cheese . . . Press 3
If you are an Enron executive and would like to find out which prison inmate will be making you his bitch . . . Press 4
If you would like to invoke your constitutional right against self incrimination . . . Press 5
If you're Dick Cheney . . . Press 6. . . . And thanks for nothing, Dick!
If your company is looking to hire someone to record your voice mail menu . . . Please Press 7
Or stay on the line and an operator will assist you.
Thank you for calling Enron, The World's Greatest Company.

In the late fall of 2001 and the early spring of 2002, the U.S. government, once perceived as just another Enron business unit, attempted to vindicate itself by going after the company with a vengeance. Vice President Dick Cheney was subpoenaed to reveal what transpired in his energy policy meetings with Lay and other Enron executives. Hearings convened by the House Energy and Commerce Committee and the Senate's Committee on Commerce Science and Transportation provided the opportunity for many legislators to humiliate publicly the very executives from whom they had once accepted generous campaign contributions. (In a historic—and certainly comedic—turn, hordes of politicians were suddenly desperate to return campaign contributions. The money went to the Ex–Enron Employees Fund. In less than a month, it collected nearly $1 million.)

Perhaps sensing that the events on the Hill were, in company parlance, a lose/lose deal, most Enron executives took the Fifth, so the public was treated to the spectacle of Kopper, Fastow, Causey, Buy, and Lay, all with arms raised, faces grim, opting out of self-incrimination. They still could not escape the wrath of Congress. As the nation watched on television, Senator Peter G. Fitzgerald told a mute, smoldering Ken Lay, "You're perhaps the most accomplished confidence man since Charles Ponzi. I'd say you were a carnival barker, except that wouldn't be fair to carnival barkers."

For those who had not tuned in earlier, the hearings also provided a recap of events so far. Here was Jeff Skilling, testifying alongside several graying board members, insisting in a deliberate, determined tone that "Enron's failure was due to a classic run on the bank, a liquidity crisis spurred by a lack of confidence in the company. At the time of Enron's collapse, the company was solvent, and the company was highly profitable, but apparently not liquid enough." He defended himself as well: "At the time I left the company, I fervently believed that Enron would continue to be successful in the future. I did not believe that the company was in any imminent financial peril."

But there were a few glitches. Asked whether he recalled a board meeting in Palm Beach in October 2000, in which Fastow stated that LJM deals needed Skilling's written approval, Skilling was fuzzy. (Fastow had actually demanded this bit of back-up.) Skilling could not recall what happened. The lights were out that day, he explained; people were in and out of the room. Skilling's then-fiancée, Rebecca Carter, was the author of the minutes recording his presence during the discussion.

Skilling was followed by Jeff McMahon, Jordan Mintz, and Andersen's Tom Bauer, who cast further aspersions on Skilling's testimony, in particular the problems—social, financial, and ethical—caused by the LJM partnerships.

Finally, on Valentine's Day, the cameras turned to Sherron Watkins, in her powder-blue suit, attorney Philip Hilder beside her and her pastor in the row behind. In the first few minutes, while the world watched along with the panel of more than two dozen House members, she looked wide-eyed and anxious. But soon enough, she gathered herself.

The committee, she realized, was leaving it to her to weave the story of corporate culture and corruption that brought the company down. "Ms. Watkins, you said when you met with Mr. Lay you felt like the child who warns the emperor that he has no clothes," one congressman stated. Skilling and Fastow were the villains, she said. Lay, in her opinion, had been duped. Andersen and Vinson & Elkins fell down on the job. In a voice that carried just a trace of a Texas accent, she held up for five hours of grueling questions. "The saying around Enron was tails Mr. Fastow wins, heads Enron loses. . . . I was highly concerned that not only had the *Titanic* already hit the iceberg, but that we were already tilting."

By the end of the day, Sherron had made the great American transition from anonymous American to national folk hero. It may have been one of the great ironies of the Enron story that the woman who never quite made it to the company's inner circle now aced the crucial test before the court of public opinion. Connie Chung sent her a handwritten note of congratulations. Dianne Sawyer sent a huge spray of pastel pink roses. Hundreds of cards and letters from friends and strangers poured into her home, wishing her well and thanking her for her courage. The ex-Enron employees who had developed a T-shirt line immediately added one decorated with "Sherron Watkins, Our Hero." It competed nicely with the one emblazoned with "I got Lay'd by Enron."

Just as theater was an important part of Enron's rise, it continued to be an important part of Enron's fall. The Senate, annoyed that it was upstaged by the House hearings a week before, rearranged its schedule to make *its* hearings more dramatic. After being told she would appear on a panel alone, Sherron was subsequently informed that she would be speaking on a panel with Jeff McMahon and Jeff Skilling. Skilling had requested the showdown. The Senate obliged.

So, on February 26, Sherron Watkins found herself seated next to the former boss she once idolized and just a short distance from an old friend she felt she hardly knew. By then, McMahon was president of the company, presiding over Enron's final days from Lay's old office. Her recent conversations with him had not been pleasant. McMahon was unsympathetic to the plight of those who had lost their life savings with the deferred compensation solely available to vice presidents and above. When Enron filed for bankruptcy, about $435 million was frozen in the account. But like the retention bonus scam, some employees were warned early to get their money out—about $32 million worth. "Hand Picked Group Cashed Out at Enron" was the way the *Houston Chronicle* described the massive withdrawal. Those who weren't so lucky included an employee named Steve Pearlman, whose wife had cancer. He lost $280,000 on top of the health insurance he lost with the bankruptcy. Dozens of retirees had similar experiences, some losing millions.

Those people didn't need the money, McMahon told Sherron, and neither did lots of employees who whined about the lack of severance. Most Enron vice presidents should have enough put away to live on for a year and still keep their kids in private school, he asserted. Really, Jeff? Sherron asked. I couldn't. Which vice presidents could do that? The people he named were all managing directors—executives who had made millions. Listening to him, Sherron realized he'd lost touch with the way normal people—even upper-middle-class people—lived their lives. *He's off my Christmas list*, she told herself.

Skilling came out swinging before the Senate. He apologized "to all of those people affected by what Enron has come to symbolize." Casting a quick, icy stare at Sherron, he stated that he would not "respond to all the outrageous things said about me in this process because some have been so silly that they merit no response." He insisted that he had not lied to Congress, nor had he, as Watkins had asserted, duped Ken Lay. "What has happened thus far, primarily in Houston, should be cause for concern of every American," he insisted. "The entire management and board of Enron has been labeled everything from hucksters to criminals, with a complete disregard for the facts and evidence assembled. These untruths shatter lives and they do nothing to advance the public understanding of what happened at Enron. The framers of the Bill of Rights are watching."

But the senators, particularly California's Barbara Boxer, were in no mood to be lectured. Infuriated by his lack of contrition and his inability to recall many key events, she treated him as if she were a junior high principal and he were a student caught lying about losing a hall pass. "This was your chance to tell us what went wrong in the company, how you might do something different. And you know what you said? It's those MAC clauses—that stands for material adverse changes—that allowed the banks, the federally insured banks, Mr. Chairman, to pull out of this company. And you said if you ran the world, you would change that.

"Well, you're a good, smart student of history, and we saw what happened in the Depression," Boxer continued. "That's when we decided it was important, our predecessors, to federally insure banks. And I want to say to you, if that's your answer, I hope no one on this committee takes your advice, because we'd have banks going broke, and we'd have this government going broke because we would force them to stick with a company that was essentially a shell game, which apparently you didn't get. But your vice president did. . . .

"If you look at Ms. Watkins' testimony, she says it in a sentence. 'My understanding, as an accountant,' she says, 'is that a company could never use its own stock to generate a gain or avoid a loss on its income statement.' Did you—is that true?"

Mr. Skilling: Um.

Senator Boxer: Were you aware of that?

Mr. Skilling: I am not an accountant.

Senator Boxer: I didn't ask you that. Is her statement true?

Mr. Skilling: I think I'd have to be an accountant to know if it's true. I don't—

Senator Boxer: Wait a minute. You have to be an accountant to know that a company could never use its own stock to generate a gain or avoid a loss in an income statement? What was your education, Mr. Skilling? I know I read—it was pretty good. What—

Mr. Skilling: I have a Master's in Business Administration.

Senator Boxer: A Master's in Business Administration. And yet you didn't know this simple fact. Is that correct? You're saying you were ignorant of that fact, that Ms. Watkins has told us.

When Skilling tried to explain, she cut him off. Where did he get his master's degree? she asked.

Mr. Skilling: Harvard Business School.

Senator Boxer: Okay. In Harvard Business School, you did not know this. Is that correct?

In the space of a few minutes, she demolished him.

Enron—and the Harvard Business School, which had educated so many of its star employees—was humiliated for all the world to see. During a break in the testimony, Skilling passed Sherron in the hallway. He was red-eyed and looked as if he had been crying.

The government, of course, was just getting started. On March 14, Arthur Andersen was indicted for obstruction of justice in the Enron investigation, which resulted in partners leaving the accounting firm in droves. Andersen had already skated in accounting scandals with Waste Management and Sunbeam. There was no way the government was going to let them go a third time. Even so, the speedy indictments were a risky, hasty move, as was accusing the entire company for the actions of a few. During the trial, which began in April, it looked as though Houston attorney Rusty Hardin, fresh from representing a son of J. Howard Marshall in a will contest against stripper-turned-heiress Anna Nicole Smith, would win the case for Andersen and stop the Enron prosecution cold.

But, to the great disappointment of Houston's ambitious criminal bar, the government had convinced David Duncan to testify for their side, and if he wasn't entirely contrite, the rest of the evidence convinced the jury that someone had to pay for what had happened. ("You've been in the middle of a nightmare, haven't you?" Hardin asked. "This hasn't been my favorite year," Duncan replied.) The jury found Andersen guilty, and the government moved on. Within months Arthur Andersen, one of the biggest accounting firms in the world, had closed it doors, with most of its 85,000 workers moving on to the remaining Big Four accounting firms.

Next up were the NatWest bankers. At the end of June 2002, the three cheerful Brits—Darby, Bermingham, and Mulgrew—were facing charges of conspiring with Fastow and Kopper to defraud their respective companies. Two months later, Michael Kopper stood outside the Federal courthouse, wearing a funereal suit and a thousand-mile stare, as his attorney read his apology to a crush of reporters. He was the first major player in the saga to plead guilty and cut a deal with the government. He admitted to committing wire fraud and engaging in "monetary transactions in property derived from specific unlawful activity." Fastow was implicated every step of the way; Kopper even reported that he funneled money to Fastow by writing $10,000 checks to his children's trusts.

Fastow's turn came on a humid, cloudy morning in October. After months of speculation as to whether he would or would not cut a deal— even as it appeared that the government might prosecute his wife if he didn't—no compromise could be reached. After being booked at FBI headquarters northwest of town, Fastow emerged from a silver sedan near the entrance to the Federal courthouse in handcuffs ready to make the "perp walk," a street term by then familiar to executives from Tyco, Adelphia, and WorldCom as well. (Enron's most lasting innovation may be its ushering in of the Age of Corporate Accounting Scandals in 2002.)

In the courtroom upstairs, Fastow's jaw was so tight he seemed in danger of imploding as the judge informed him that he was being indicted on seventy-eight counts for creating schemes to defraud Enron and its shareholders. The fraudulent conduct involved "entering into undisclosed side deals, manufacturing of earnings through sham transactions, inflating the value of Enron's investments, backdating documents, and other illegal acts." His passports and property seized, the judge added one more indignity: Fastow's attorneys had failed earlier in the day to get the signature of his wife and parents on various property deeds that made up his $5 million bond. Now she demanded that they, too, come to court to sign for Fastow. Even on the day of his indictment, Andy Fastow was still treated like a bad little boy.

There was clearly more to come: The Senate's Permanent Subcommittee on Investigations held hearings on the role of the Board of Directors, the FERC, the credit-rating agencies and the financial institutions in Enron's collapse. The latter finally exposed the complicity of many of the nation's largest and most prestigious banks in Enron's rise and fall.

A California grand jury was investigating the trading operation. A Houston grand jury was looking into several angles, particularly Broadband. This would be another avenue for prosecuting Skilling, should Fastow fail to turn on his boss. There was a separate investigation of Lay pending, possibly on charges of insider trading. Plaintiff attorneys sued on behalf of shareholders and bondholders. They named twenty-nine insiders that had cashed in over $1 billion of Enron stock: In addition to Lou Pai's $353 million, and Ken Rice's $78 million, the list featured Lay at $101 million, Mark at close to $80 million, and Skilling with $75 million. Among Enron loyalists, the phrase "Financial McCarthyism" began to crop up routinely. There was growing infighting between government agencies—congressional investigators, Department of Justice investigators, FBI investigators, etc.—but the executives' shock at the government's perseverance went a long way toward explaining the actions of some of Enron's bad apples. No one ever believed they'd get their wrists slapped, much less humiliated in front of the whole world and buried under an avalanche of civil and criminal charges.

If official justice was slow in coming, the unofficial kind was swift. As 2002 drew to a close, it seemed as if everything Enron had tried to do—control the press, buy off the government, make itself look like the smartest, shrewdest corporation (*The World's Leading Company!*)—had all backfired. It had claimed its place in the culture forever, but as a joke—not just on the late-night talk shows, but around the world. Even the Houston Astros preferred the name of an orange juice company on their baseball field.

Someone thought they spied Ken Lay one day, walking alone, around the perimeter of his old field, but he could have been wrong. Ken Lay was spending a lot of time on the phone, lobbying local black leaders for support, calling in chits and spinning his story anew. "Don't believe everything you read about me in your paper," he cracked to the new editor of the Houston *Chronicle*, as he grasped his hand and pumped it warmly. Lay needed all the help he could get. Anyone who called the White House searching for a man or woman to speak up for Lay was sure to be disappointed. He had been disinvited to the White House Christmas party in December, and now they could barely remember him. Not around much, they said. Not really a factor. Meanwhile, Linda Lay and her daughter Robin opened an antique store, Jus' Stuff, to speed the disposal of their many possessions.

E ven with all its major executives gone—Greg Whalley moved with the trading operation when it was sold to UBS in February, McMahon resigned under a cloud in April because of his involvement with the Merrill

Lynch Nigerian barge deal—Enron's culture remained. There were more retention bonuses; lawyers for the various creditors picked over the carcass, spending money at breathtaking speed. As of December 2002, Enron was billed over $300 million, setting a record for legal billings to a bankrupt company in one year, even as, true to the company's identity, there was no reorganization plan in place. Meanwhile, Enron's bankruptcy experts crisscrossed the country on the company jet. When they worked in Houston, they preferred to stay at the Four Seasons Hotel.

There was an auction at which much of the company's furniture and equipment sold, fittingly, at ridiculously inflated prices. The big E that once graced the front of the building went for $44,000 to the owner of a small computer store in a strip mall on the Southwest Freeway. He thought buying the symbol was good publicity for the shop. Soon after, Enron put its remaining E's on the block. "After the last auction it became clear that the E's do have value," an Enron spokeswoman told the *Chronicle*. "This is part of our continuing efforts to maximize value for the creditors."

The selling off of other assets did not go quite as well. The esteemed trading operation, with Greg Whalley, John Lavaroto, and Louise Kitchen at the helm, sold for virtually nothing, which was logical since no one wanted to trade with the devils from Enron's evil empire. Within nine months of "buying" the unit, UBS announced that it was shutting it down and laying off the nearly eight hundred people it had absorbed from Enron. Meanwhile, Warren Buffett, once scoffed at by Skilling as a sorry midwestern fossil, picked up Enron's most valuable asset for a song. He bought the Northern Natural Gas pipeline from a now struggling Dynegy for $900 million, two-thirds its value.

Sherron Watkins left Enron in late November 2002. The day she walked out of the building for the last time, the lobby was quiet as a tomb. The multimedia screen that once blared the news of stock market surges and Enron's triumphs was black, and empty metal frames hung where brightly colored inspirational banners once danced from the ceiling. There were no anxious hordes charging across the lobby anymore, just the bankruptcy lawyers ambling from the elevators to the sleek black limos waiting to take them to the airport. The Enron parking lot was almost empty too. The Ferraris and the Boxsters seemed part of another lifetime. It wouldn't be long before a new company came in and made the building over in its own image, and every trace of Enron would disappear. Houston would forget Enron quickly, as was its way with sad stories.

Pulling out of the parking lot, Sherron realized her past was disappearing too. She had spent the last two decades working for three companies that were no more—Enron, Andersen, and MG, the remains of which Enron bought in 2000. She had put her faith in the hands of important men, and they had disappointed her.

She would not do it again. She had said her piece, and she had no more illusions.

Postscript

J ust as we were going to press with this paperback edition, the progress of the Enron prosecutions shifted from methodical to radical. On January 14, in a crowded Houston federal courtroom, Lea and Andy Fastow pleaded guilty, she to filing a false tax return, he to two counts of conspiracy to commit securities and wire fraud. They were sentenced, respectively, to five months in prison and five months of house arrest, and ten years in prison. Barely a week later, former Chief Accounting Officer Rick Causey was indicted as well, and the web the government was constructing around Jeff Skilling and Ken Lay was growing tighter every day. Enron watchers could finally glimpse some sort of resolution to the story, a few possible morals in what had long been billed as a morality tale.

Progress toward that end has not been as glacial as it sometimes seemed. Not counting the Fastows, there have been ten indictments, six guilty pleas, and one five-year prison term—former Enron treasurer Ben Glisan was marched off, in handcuffs, to a federal prison in the Hill Country near

Austin after refusing to cooperate with the government. The Fastows' case, however, evoked some of the tension and drama of the company's rise and fall, although, unlike typical Enron deals, it proceeded coldly and methodically (on the government's part, at least), with no pressure to close by any particular quarter. Andy stood indicted on ninety-nine counts of criminal behavior, including conspiracy to commit wire fraud and conspiracy to commit securities fraud, as well as obstruction of justice, money laundering, insider trading, and filing false income tax returns. But he proved as belligerent about cutting a deal with the government as he had about cutting deals with Enron's bankers, or his own colleagues for that matter. So the government indicted his wife, Lea, on charges of conspiracy to commit wire fraud, money laundering, and four counts of filing false tax returns. Those charges meant that the couple's two boys were facing the possibility of growing up without their parents, and the Fastows, once exemplars of the two-career marriage, stood to become poster children for the two-career prison term. It still took more than a year to get Andy to cave; with the children used as leverage—and a battalion of some of the best lawyers in Houston and beyond—he managed to get what was thought to be, at the very least, a twenty-year sentence reduced to ten.

Prosecutors also persuaded one more executive (in addition to the head of West Coast energy trading, Timothy Belden) to plead guilty to manipulating the California energy market, and another is under indictment; seven former Broadband division executives, including Jeff Skilling's golden boys, Ken Rice and Kevin Hannon, were indicted for engaging in a scheme to mislead the public about the value of Enron stock and profiting from insider sales of their own holdings. (At the time of Rice's indictment, in May 2003, Justice Department prosecutors were trying to seize as ill-gotten gains a necklace he purchased made of diamonds, sapphires, and platinum, as well as his $2.3 million thirty-seven-acre Telluride ranch off the portentously named Last Dollar Road. One associate, trying to put the best possible spin on his profligacy, told the *Houston Chronicle*, "I don't know what incompleteness, unhappiness in his life was driving him, but he was compensating with toys. Enron let the dark side come out.")

In October 2003, Wesley Colwell, a top accountant in Enron's wholesale trading division, agreed to become a key government witness against former executives. His plea agreement contained admissions that executives had hidden nearly $1 billion in losses at Enron Energy Services in the company's trading division; that traders had hid enormous profits from the California energy crisis by tinkering with the company's reserves; and that other groups had marked up the value of Enron's assets to meet budget demands. Since Colwell worked closely with Rick Causey, many saw his deal as a sign that indictments of bigger fish were coming. Indeed, at the end of October, David Delainey, another Skilling protégé, who headed EES in 2001 and who was also head of Enron North America, pled guilty to insider trading and agreed to forfeit around $8 million in ill-gotten profits from Enron stock sales. Like Colwell, Delainey agreed to testify against his colleagues at Enron; the government's fifteen-page indictment revealed a new strategy devised to terrify Enron executives who had been defending themselves by blaming Enron's lawyers and accountants. (That is, Arthur Andersen and Vinson & Elkins said it was okay, so Enron thought it was okay, too.) Instead of complicated financial charges, the Delainey indictment points to more than half a dozen fairly simple but intentional "wide ranging schemes" to artificially inflate the share price of Enron's stock from 1998 through 2001. In other words, the government does not want to try a complex (and stultifying) accounting case before a jury—instead they will probably try to prove how Enron executives made decisions to write up the value of assets, hide losses in profitable divisions, or change accounting classifications, all to snow Wall Street. The government is also going after the bankers who aided Enron over the years. Four Merrill Lynch bankers have been criminally charged in the "sale" of the Nigerian barges, and to avoid a firm-wide charge in its dealings with Enron, Merrill settled with the government for $80 million and the promise of reform. The money went to Enron's victim's fund, which was further supplemented, at the behest of the Securities and Exchange Commission, with $255 million from Enron cohorts Citigroup and J.P. Morgan Chase (so much for exploring the potential guilt of Enron's enablers). In a classic Enron move, the company is suing the banks for knowingly loaning Enron money that the bankers knew was being reported as revenue.

Corporate reforms proposed in the wake of Enron's fall have been hampered by President Bush and his administration. The Public Company

Accounting Reform and Investor Protection Act of 2002, better known as the Sarbanes-Oxley Act, makes CEOs legally responsible for the accuracy of their company's financial reports, and called for increased funding for the SEC to increase corporate oversight. But the SEC's expansion was delayed for nearly two years by President Bush, who signed the bill into law with much fanfare, then dragged his heels when it came to funding. (He finally bowed to public pressure and agreed to double the SEC's budget—instead of increasing it by 20 percent, as he preferred—but not until 2004.) He also tried to limit whistleblower protection contained in the Sarbanes-Oxley Act by extending protection only to employees of companies under Congressional investigation.

The administration's questionable commitment to containing corporate abuses was also apparent with its disastrous—if brief—appointment of Harvey Pitt to head the SEC. That his ties to the accounting industry were far too close was revealed most clearly in his choice of William Webster to head the new oversight committee—despite the fact that Webster had failed to oversee proper audits at U.S. Technologies, where he sat on the board. Pitt resigned in embarrassment, but not before telling the press, "It would be unthinkable to deprive the people of my expertise." So far, the new chairman, William Donaldson, appears to be more serious about reforms, proposing that shareholders be allowed to nominate their own board slates without proxy fights, for instance.

In addition to the SEC, the average investor has a relentless champion in New York Attorney General Eliot Spitzer, who has found and fined capitalist outlaws among the most prestigious investment banks and mutual fund managers. When it comes to limiting corporate abuse and protecting shareholders, however, the best news may be the departure of Senator Phil Gramm from the Senate, especially his exit from the Senate Finance Committee. In June 2002, Gramm told the press that the myriad revelations of corporate wrongdoing were drawing to a close—"The feeding frenzy is pretty much over," he said—and added that the marketplace had corrected its excesses, "relieving Congress of the need to enact comprehensive legislation." When continued corporate malfeasance gave the lie to that statement, Gramm declined to run for reelection—his ties to Enron may have been a factor—and accepted a position as Vice Chairman of UBS Warburg.

Faith in corporate America's leaders continues to decline. *Fortune* magazine ran a cover of a pig-headed business-suited CEO under the banner "Oink! CEO Pay Is Still out of Control." A Gallup poll conducted during the summer of 2002 showed that public trust in CEOs of large businesses ranked at its lowest point in decades, standing just above the two least-trusted groups in America, managers of HMOs and car salesmen. Little has occurred to change their minds in the last year—in August 2003 "corporate watchdog" Dick Grasso, head of the New York Stock Exchange, was forced to resign when it was revealed that he was taking home an aggregate pay package of close to $200 million. In October the CEO of Putnam, the nation's fifth largest mutual fund, was forced to step down in the wake of fraud charges at his company; so, too, was the head of the SEC's New England office when it was revealed that his office ignored a whistleblower with information about Putnam's irregularities. Equally disheartening but undeniably more entertaining were videos shown at the recent criminal trial of the former chairman of Tyco, L. Dennis Kozlowski, who celebrated the birthday of his second wife on the island of Sardinia at a lavish party that included an ice scupture of Michelangelo's *David* urinating Stolichnaya vodka into crystal glasses, along with a birthday cake honoring the female form complete with sparklers protruding from the breasts.

Enron, the company once revered as the poster child for the New Economy, barely exists anymore. The glamorous office buildings that housed the enterprise—the designer skyscrapers it leased but never, of course, owned—stand virtually empty, awaiting new tenants. The company that once had 7,500 Houston employees now has only 1,300, and will soon be moving to more modest headquarters in a more innocuous downtown high-rise. The company that had $67 billion in assets in 2001 now has $67 billion in debt—and only $12 billion in assets with which to meet its obligations. Creditors will be paid less than a fifth of their claims—on average, 14.4 cents on the dollar—with most of that money coming from sales of those hard assets that Jeff Skilling had deemed so worthless. (If anyone has been vindicated in this story, it is Rebecca Mark, who provided Enron with things it could actually sell, in the clutch. In contrast, Skilling's much-vaunted trading operation, it has been noted, sold for next to nothing and has since been virtually dismantled.) Then, of course, there are the Enron legal fees, which, at $27 million a month—they've exceeded $500 million—continue to break all records. (So far Enron's bankruptcy lawyers, Weil, Gotshal & Manges, have earned a total of $87 million for their work. The court-appointed examiners, led by Atlanta attorney Neil Batson, aren't far behind. Affixing blame—their responsibility—is proving to be very time-consuming and expensive; Enron has paid Batson's firm, Alston & Bird, $76 million.)

Of course, the biggest question is why the two men most responsible for Enron's fall are still free of criminal prosecution. The explanations for this situation vary. One is that investigations of this complexity can take years. Enron's situation isn't as simple as WorldCom's, for instance, which was a bigger bankruptcy but is also just a straightforward case of fraud—specifically, moving a very large expense number to the balance sheet and calling it an asset. Then, too, it is conceivable that Ken Lay did not technically commit a crime. Ignoring the day-to-day dealings of the company, or turning a blind eye to malfeasance, for instance, may have played a part (a large part) in the company's collapse, but the so-called Ken Lay Defense was only recently made illegal by the Sarbanes-Oxley Act, which now holds CEOs personally responsible for their company's financial reporting. Prosecuting Skilling will prove to be more difficult—that he was both wily and vague in his directives to subordinates gives him lots of wiggle room now—but as we write, the rumor mill is carrying tales of an imminent Skilling indictment. Colwell, Delainey, and Fastow's deals to cooperate with the government account for this shift in the gossip winds.

Indictments or not, neither executive is, as yet, living happily ever after in Switzerland or on a (tax-sheltered) Caribbean island. The men who demanded customized creature comforts now have customized punishments: Lay, who saw himself as a global player, has been relegated to the very small world of his family and the most loyal of friends. (On New Year's Eve 2002, he served snacks at his sister's condominium in Kemah, near Galveston.) Skilling, who wanted to be remembered as a corporate visionary, is now seen as someone who was, maybe, not so smart after all. Both men—as well as unindicted executives Lou Pai, Jeff McMahon, Greg Whalley, and members of the Enron board—face civil suits that promise to drain their remaining fortunes for years to come.

Sherron Watkins, their nemesis, speaks frequently on corporate ethics and has opened her own consulting firm. She leaves it to others to debate whether or not she was a true whistleblower, the current argument among Enron chroniclers. She was, however, deeply honored to have been chosen, along with the FBI's Coleen Rowley and WorldCom's Cynthia Cooper, as *Time* magazine's Person of the Year.

Appendix A

Sherron Watkins' Anonymous Memo
to Enron CEO Ken Lay

(reprinted from original document)

Dear Mr. Lay,

Has Enron become a risky place to work? For those of us who didn't get rich over the last few years, can we afford to stay?

Skilling's abrupt departure will raise suspicions of accounting improprieties and valuation issues. Enron has been very aggressive in its accounting—most notably the Raptor transactions and the Condor vehicle. We do have valuation issues with our international assets and possibly some of our EES MTM positions.

The spotlight will be on us, the market just can't accept that Skilling is leaving his dream job. I think that the valuation issues can be fixed and reported with other goodwill write-downs to occur in 2002. How do we fix the Raptor and Condor deals? They unwind in 2002 and 2003, we will have to pony up Enron stock and that won't go unnoticed.

To the layman on the street, it will look like we recognized funds flow of $800 mm from merchant asset sales in 1999 by selling to a vehicle (Condor) that we capitalized with a promise of Enron stock in later years. Is that really funds flow or is it cash from equity issuance?

We have recognized over $550 million of fair value gains on stocks via our swaps with Raptor, much of that stock has declined significantly—Avici by 98%, from $178 mm to $5 mm, The New Power Co by 70%, from $20/share to $6/share. The value in the swaps won't be there for Raptor, so once again Enron will issue stock to offset these losses. Raptor is an LJM entity. It sure looks to the layman on the street that we are hiding losses in a related company and will compensate that company with Enron stock in the future.

I am incredibly nervous that we will implode in a wave of accounting scandals. My 8 years of Enron work history will be worth nothing on my resume, the business world will consider the past successes as nothing but an elaborate accounting hoax. Skilling is resigning now for "personal reasons" but I think he wasn't having fun, looked down the road and knew this stuff was unfixable and would rather abandon ship now than resign in shame in 2 years.

Is there a way our accounting guru's can unwind these deals now? I have thought and thought about how to do this, but I keep bumping into one big problem—we booked the Condor and Raptor deals in 1999 and 2000, we enjoyed a wonderfully high stock price, many executives sold stock, we then try and reverse or fix the deals in 2001 and it's a bit like robbing the bank in one year and trying to pay it back 2 years later. Nice try, but investors were hurt, they bought at $70 and $80/share looking for $120/share and now they're at $38 or worse. We are under too much scrutiny and there are probably one or two disgruntled "redeployed" employees who know enough about the "funny" accounting to get us in trouble.

What do we do? I know this question cannot be addressed in the all employee meeting, but can you give some assurances that you and Causey will sit down and take a good hard objective look at what is going to happen to Condor and Raptor in 2002 and 2003?

Appendix B
Sherron Watkins' Follow-Up Memos
to Ken Lay and Others
(reprinted from original document)

Summary of accounting irregularities:

Raptor

The Raptor entities were capitalized with LJM equity. The contributed equity is technically at risk; however, the investment was completely offset by some sort of cash structuring fee paid to LJM. If the Raptor entities go bankrupt LJM is not affected, there is no commitment to contribute more equity.

The majority (i.e., 99%) of the capitalization of the Raptor entities is some form of Enron N/P, restricted stock and contingent stock rights.

Enron entered into several equity derivative transactions with the Raptor entities locking in our values for various equity investments we hold.

As disclosed, in 2000, we recognized $500 million of revenue from the equity derivatives offset by market value changes in the underlying securities.

This year, with the value of our stock declining, the underlying capitalization of the Raptor entities is declining and Credit is pushing for reserves against our MTM positions.

To avoid such a write-down or reserve in Q1 2001, we "enhanced" the capital structure of the Raptor vehicles, committing more ENE shares.

My understanding of the Q3 problem is that we must 'enhance' the vehicles by $250 million.

I realize that we have had a lot of smart people looking at this and a lot of accountants including AA&Co. have blessed the accounting treatment. None of that will protect Enron if these transactions are ever disclosed in the bright light of day. (Please review the late 90's problems of Waste Management—where AA paid $7 mm (sued for $130+ mm) in litigation re: questionable accounting practices.)

One of the overriding basic principles of accounting is that if you explain the "accounting treatment" to a man on the street, would you influence his investing decisions? Would he sell or buy the stock based on a thorough understanding of the facts? If so, you best present it correctly and/or change the accounting.

My concern is that the footnotes don't adequately explain the transactions. If adequately explained, the investor would know that the "Entities" described in our related party footnote are thinly capitalized, the equity holders have no skin in the game, and all the value in the entities comes from the underlying value of the derivatives (unfortunately in this case, a big loss) AND Enron stock and N/P. Looking at the stock we swapped, I also don't believe any other company would have entered into the equity derivative transactions with us at the same prices or without substantial premiums from Enron. In other words, the $500 million in revenue in 2000 would have been much lower. How much lower?

Raptor looks to be a big bet, if the underlying stocks did well, then no one would be the wiser. If Enron stock did well, the stock issuance to these entities would decline and the transactions would be less noticeable. All has gone against us. The stocks, most notably Hanover, The New Power Co., and Avici are underwater to great or lesser degrees.

I firmly believe that executive management of the company must have a clear and precise knowledge of these transactions and they must have the transactions reviewed by objective experts in the fields of securities law and accounting. I believe Ken Lay deserves the right to judge for himself what he believes the probabilities of discovery to be and the estimated damages to the company from those discoveries and decide one of two courses of action:

1. The probability of discovery is low enough and the estimated damage too great; therefore we find a way to quietly and quickly reverse, unwind, write down these positions/transactions.

2. The probability of discovery is too great, the estimated damage to the company too great; therefore, we must quantify, develop damage containment plans and disclose.

I firmly believe that the probability of discovery significantly increased with Skilling's shocking departure. Too many people are looking for a smoking gun.

To put the accounting treatment in perspective I offer the following:

1. We've contributed contingent Enron equity to the Raptor entities. Since it's contingent, we have the consideration given and received at zero. We do, as Causey points out, include the shares in our fully diluted computations of shares outstanding if the current economics of the deal imply that Enron will have to issue the shares in the future. This impacts 2002–2004 EPS projections only.
2. We lost value in several equity investments in 2000. $500 million of lost value. These were fair value investments, we wrote them down. However, we also booked gains from our price risk management transactions with Raptor, recording a corresponding PRM account receivable from the Raptor entities. That's a $500 million related party transaction—it's 20% of 2000 IBIT, 51% of NI pre tax, 33% of NI after tax.
3. Credit reviews the underlying capitalization of Raptor, reviews the contingent shares and determines whether the Raptor entities will have enough capital to pay Enron its $500 - $700 million when the equity derivatives expire.
4. The Raptor entities are technically bankrupt; the value of the contingent Enron shares equals or is just below the PRM account payable that Raptor owes Enron. Raptor's inception to date income statement is a $500 million loss.
5. Where are the equity and debt investors that lost out? LJM is whole on a cash on cash basis. Where did the $500 million in value come from? It came from Enron shares. Why haven't we booked the transaction as $500 million in a promise of shares to the Raptor enti-

ty and $500 million of value in our "Economic Interests" in these entities? Then we would have a write down of our value in the Raptor entities. We have not booked the latter, because we do not have to yet. Technically, we can wait and face the music in 2002–2004.

6. The related party footnote tries to explain these transactions. Don't you think that several interested companies, be they stock analysts, journalists, hedge fund managers, etc., are busy trying to discover the reason Skilling left? Don't you think their smartest people are pouring over that footnote disclosure right now? I can just hear the discussions—"It looks like they booked a $500 million gain from this related party company and I think, from all the undecipherable 1/2 page on Enron's contingent contributions to this related party entity, I think the related party entity is capitalized with Enron stock." . . . "No, no, no, you must have it all wrong, it can't be that, that's just too bad, too fraudulent, surely AA&Co wouldn't let them get away with that?" . . . "Go back to the drawing board, it's got to be something else. But find it!" . . . "Hey, just in case you might be right, try and find some insiders or 'redeployed' former employees to validate your theory."

Summary of Raptor oddities:

1. The accounting treatment looks questionable.
   a. Enron booked a $500 mm gain from equity derivatives from a related party.
   b. That related party is thinly capitalized, with no party at risk except Enron.
   c. It appears Enron has supported an income statement gain by a contribution of its own shares.

One basic question: The related party entity has lost $500 mm in its equity derivative transactions with Enron. Who bears that loss? I can't find an equity or debt holder that bears that loss. Find out who will lose this money. Who will pay for this loss at the related party entity?

If it's Enron, from our shares, then I think we do not have a fact pattern that would look good to the SEC or investors.

2. The equity derivative transactions do not appear to be at arms length.

    a. Enron hedged New Power, Hanover, and Avici with the related party at what now appears to be the peak of the market. New Power and Avici have fallen away significantly since. The related party was unable to lay off this risk. This fact pattern is once again very negative for Enron.

    b. I don't think any other unrelated company would have entered into these transactions at these prices. What else is going on here? What was the compensation to the related party to induce it to enter into such transactions?

3. There is a veil of secrecy around LJM and Raptor. Employees question our accounting propriety consistently and constantly. This alone is cause for concern.

    a. Jeff McMahon was highly vexed over the inherent conflicts of LJM. He complained mightily to Jeff Skilling and laid out 5 steps he thought should be taken if he was to remain as Treasurer. 3 days later, Skilling offered him the Chief Commercial Officer spot at a new venture, Enron Networks, and never addressed the 5 steps with him.

    b. Cliff Baxter complained mightily to Skilling and all who would listen about the inappropriateness of our transactions with LJM.

    c. I have heard one manager level employee from the principal investments group say "I know it would be devastating to all of us, but I wish we would get caught. We're such a crooked company." The principle investments group hedged a large number of their investments with Raptor. These people know and see a lot. Many similar comments are made when you ask about these deals. Employees quote our CFO as saying that he has a handshake deal with Skilling that LJM will never lose money.

4. Can the General Counsel of Enron audit the deal trail and the

money trail between Enron and LJM/Raptor and its principals? Can he look at LJM? At Raptor? If the CFO says no, isn't that a problem?

Condor and Raptor work:

1. Postpone decision on filling office of the chair, if the current decision includes CFO and/or CAO.
2. Involve Jim Derrick and Rex Rogers to hire a law firm to investigate the Condor and Raptor transactions to give Enron attorney client privilege on the work product. (Can't use V&E due to conflict— they provided some true sale opinions on some of the deals).
3. Law firm to hire one of the big 6, but not Arthur Andersen or PricewaterhouseCoopers due to their conflicts of interest: AA&Co (Enron); PWC (LJM).
4. Investigate the transactions, our accounting treatment and our future commitments to these vehicles in the form of stock, N/P, etc. For instance: In Q3 we have a $250 mm problem with Raptor 3 (NPW) if we don't "enhance" the capital structure of Raptor 3 to commit more ENE shares.
   By the way: in Q1 we enhanced the Raptor 3 deal, committing more ENE shares to avoid a write down.
5. Develop clean up plan:
   a. Best case: Clean up quietly if possible.
   b. Worst case: Quantify, develop PR and IR campaigns, customer assurance plans (don't want to go the way of Salomon's trading shop), legal actions, severance actions, disclosure.
6. Personnel to quiz confidentially to determine if I'm all wet:
   a. Jeff McMahon
   b. Mark Koenig
   c. Rick Buy
   d. Greg Whalley

Appendix C
Sherron Watkins' Memo from Her Last Meeting with Ken Lay

Disclosure steps to rebuild investor confidence:

1. Lay to be open about his involvement or more importantly, his lack thereof:
    a. As CEO, he relied on his COO, Skilling, as well as CFO, Fastow and CAO, Causey, to manage the details. Of note: CFO and CAO are Skilling's picks from his rise to the COO spot in late 1996.
        [It's fairly normal for a CEO to leave the accounting details and finance details to the COO, CFO and CAO]
    b. Lay to admit that he trusted the wrong people.
2. Lay to admit that as soon as Skilling resigned employees reported to him their opinions as to the inappropriate LJM transactions.
    a. Lay appropriately took the matter seriously and he began an investigation; however:
    b. Mistake #2: He relied on V&E and Arthur Andersen to opine on their own work. They advised him to unwind Raptor, but that the accounting was appropriate when recorded in 2000. Joe Dilg's Oct 16th comment to me when I said that Lay should probably come clean and admit problems and restate 2000, in order to preserve his legacy and possibly the company's was the following:

"Are you suggesting that Ken Lay should ignore the advice of his counsel and auditors concerning this matter?"

3. Lay to state that once the 3rd Quarter write downs and reversals were disclosed and investors raised concerns and it became apparent that Enron could not easily resolve the issues by making more detail disclosures, he realized that the advice from V&E and AA&Co was wrong, it was motivated by self preservation.

   a. First, the LJM Raptor transactions were highly irregular and Enron is restating 2000 financials.

   b. Second, he's firing Arthur Andersen & Co and V&E

   c. Third, he's committed to staying at Enron and returning the company to its former glory.

      NOTE: After restatement, the good news is that our core trading business is solid with strong numbers to report; the bad news: EBS was losing big money in 2000, the big losses didn't start in 2001, and EES did not start making a profit in 2000.

4. Lay to meet with top SEC officials. This is a problem we must all address and fix for corporate America as a whole. Ken Lay and his board were duped by a COO who wanted the targets met no matter what the consequences, a CFO motivated by personal greed and 2 of the most respected firms, AA&Co and V&E, who had both grown too wealthy off Enron's yearly business and no longer performed their roles as Ken Lay, the Board and just about anybody on the street would expect as a minimum standard for CPA's and attorneys.

   a. This is devastating to many—investors, the energy trading sector, the banking sector, the Houston economy—Enron could work with the SEC to develop a plan to address this calmly.

   b. Ken Lay and Enron need to support one of the SEC's long term objectives of requiring that the Big 5 accounting firms rotate off their large clients on a regular basis as short as 3 years.

My conclusions if Ken Lay takes these steps:

1. The bad news: This is horrific. Plaintiff attorneys will be celebrating. The trouble facing the company will be obvious to all.

2. The good news: the wild speculations will slow down, if not cease. Nobody wants Ken Lay's head. He's very well respected in business and the community. The culprits are Skilling, Fastow, Glisan and Causey as well as Arthur Andersen and V&E. The energy trading sector is scared to death that Enron won't make it—there will not be a cry for Enron's collective head.

Likely Enron outcome:
_____

The stock price will drop further

Hard to take over—it's people and trading business (ie, not contractual, not asset based)

Does Enron need to find a Warren Buffett type equity investor?

Can we build a ring around the trading business? How long will that take?

Will a restatement announcement hurt liquidity any more than our current situation?

My conclusions if we don't come clean and restate:
_____

All these bad things will happen to us anyway, it's just that Ken Lay will be more implicated in this than is deserved and he won't get the chance to restore the company to its former stature.

Appendix D
Example of Enron's Complex SPE Structures

The chart on the following page of the Whitewing partnership gives a sense of the incredible complexity of the off-balance-sheet entities Andy Fastow created that hid Enron's growing debt.

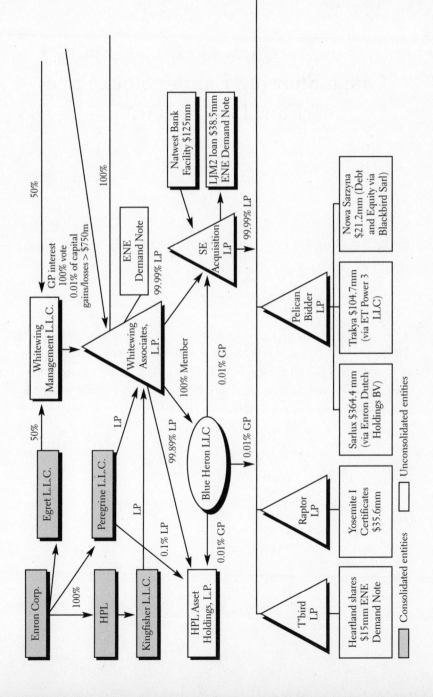

Appendix E
Graph Showing Enron's Stock Price
from 1993 to 2002

The chart on the facing page shows the rise, and precipitous fall, of the price of Enron's stock (adjusted for splits) from 1993 through 2002. Since Enron filed for bankruptcy in December of 2001 it has basically flatlined, and is now trading for mere cents on the dollar.

Enron's stock price, 1993–2002

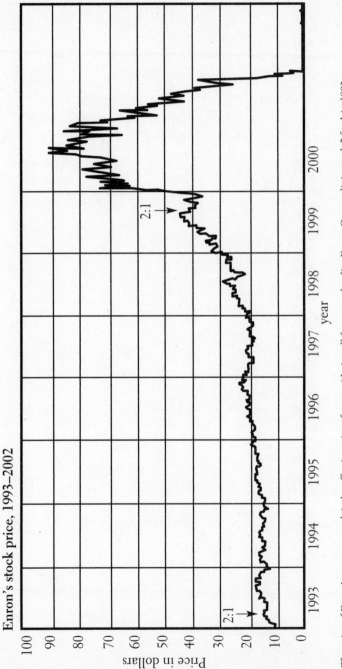

The price of Enron's common stock is the effective price after considering all future stock splits. Enron Corp. split its stock 2-for-1 in 1993 an- cated in the price graph above.

Note: The stock prices quoted throughout the text are actual prices at the time in question. For instance, at the start of 1993 a share; in the chart above, the early 1993 price is shown as $12.50, taking into account two 2-for-1 splits; in 1997, the stoc a share. In the chart above, the 1997 price is flat at $20, taking the 1999 split into account.

Acknowledgments

Many, many people helped create this book. That hundreds of them prefer to remain anonymous is testimony to the hold Enron retains on those associated with the company in the present and the past. At the same time, their concern that the truth be told impelled them to come forward, and their insights and their recollections, their intelligence, and their selflessness are all here. Enron was a company full of bright, smart, innovators, which made my job easier. They were a pleasure to talk to—inspiring, funny, and challenging, and I owe them a debt I can never repay.

A few on-the-record types deserve special mention, since I pestered them nearly to death: Philip Hilder, Robert McCullough, Brian Terp, Porter Farrell, Allan Sommer, Ms. Unger, MNBF, Jack Rains, Rusty Hardin, Rick Taylor, Christian Schreiber, Joe H. Allen, George Strong, Keith Power, Melissa Bauman, John Olson. Thanks also to Stephen Fox, whose knowledge of Houston is unsurpassed.

This book could also not have been done without the help, conscious and otherwise, of other reporters. The stories by Jonathan Weil, Rebecca Smith, and John Emshwiller of *The Wall Street Journal*, Bethany McLean and Peter Elkind at *Fortune*, Peter Behr at *The Washington Post*, Dan Fisher at *Forbes*, Kurt Eichenwald at *The New York Times*, and Sheila McNulty at *The Financial Times*, Mike Tolson, Alan Bernstein, Tom Fowler, and Mary Flood at *The Houston Chronicle* were a steady source of inspiration. To the *Times'* David Barboza and Jim Yardley, thanks are insufficient. This book could not have evolved as it did without their advice, acuity, encouragement, and friendship, which I will value always.

My research assistants were tireless: To Pokey Andersen, who can find anything on the Web, Johna Potter, who can find anything in any courthouse, and Lynn Cook, who can find anything or anyone, period, I am grateful for your enthusiasm and incredible doggedness. Jim Galasyn's chronology was invaluable.

At Random House, Sarah Rainone was resolutely sunny and kind and a great researcher; Kathy Trager was as gracious as she was circumspect. To Rebecca Holland, Chris Fortunato, Peter Grennen, Sue Warga, Tina Thompson, and Erin Matherne, thanks and thanks again for tremendous grace under pressure. Roger Scholl, our editor, was captivated by this idea from the moment he first heard Sherron's voice on the phone. His passion for this book and his determination to bring it to market kept us going through many late nights, early mornings, and lonely weekends. It would not have happened without his unflagging good humor, his drive, and his dedication.

Thanks, too, to the office of Collins-McCormick. To have my old friend and former editor serve as agent was a great gift. David McCormick's honesty, insights, and intelligence were an asset at every turn. Nina Collins was an incredible calming force, Leslie Falk a wonderful reader.

I'm grateful, too, to the staff of *Texas Monthly*, people who have stuck with me since 1986 and remain stalwart to this day in their affection and encouragement, particularly Mike Levy, Evan Smith, and the incomparable Paul Burka. Thank you for letting me leave, thank you for letting me come back, and thanks for always setting the bar so high.

To the unmatched Travis crowd, who drove carpool and did not complain when I dropped off the face of the earth, I promise now to pick up the slack— Hartzells, Mitchells, Kellys, Gianninis, Lunstroths, Smiths. To Emily Yoffe, Alison Cook, Tim Fleck, Lisa Belkin, Greg Curtis, Jan Jarboe Russell, Marie Brenner, and Sam and Lisa Verhovek, thanks for being there, always, with perceptions, advice, criticism, and constancy. Thanks also to Mary Nugent, who recommended just the right book at just the right time, and Bill Miller, who recommended just the right person at just the right time, Rob Jutson, who knew a few things about commercial paper, and to Katie Kitchen, Paul Kovach, Janet Landay, and Edward Hirsch, who lived for months with a journalist who had only one topic of conversation.

Sherron Watkins is a force of nature. No one could have asked for a better partner: funny, smart, indomitable, indefatigable, reflexively honest, and straightforward, with the patience of a saint. Even after explaining mark-to-market accounting five hundred times, she never cracked, nor did she lose her sense of humor under pressure almost as intense as those congressional hearings. To Rick Watkins, thanks for shuttling across town, sticking up for Tomball, and catching the difference between two states that begin with M.

I always wondered why other writers acknowledged their families last. Now I know. The toll a project of this magnitude took on the people closest to me is immense. Even so, my parents offered unflagging support and affection, as they have throughout my life. My mother taught me not to care what other people think, my father taught me to give everyone the benefit of the doubt; I could not have asked for a better combination of models. My brother Ed was, as always, a font of astounding knowledge and contacts, as was his wife, Nancy; my brother Jeff's sharp and witty advice about the book business was invaluable.

But mostly, I want to thank my husband, John, and my son, Sam. In marrying an editor, I got a twofer—a husband and critic who is wise and fair in life and work, a great example as well as a great support. He is also brave: "How do you know this is true?" is a question every editor has to ask every writer, but it's another thing to pose the query to a tired, grouchy writer wife, even when she's asked for a read. To Sam, I apologize for perpetual pizza and for being perpetually distracted. The love of both I treasure daily; I'm especially grateful to John for never complaining about my long hours and lost weekends, and to Sam for doing so routinely, reminding me that Enron was a part of life, but never all of it. Who knows, maybe such a sentiment could have saved the company.

—Mimi Swartz

I am grateful for the profound influence of my mother, Shirley Klein Harrington, who raised me in a wonderfully supportive and loving Christian home, equipping me with the tools and the inner strength to face life and its challenges. Her continuing example of how to live one's life is a source of inspiration to me.

I also want to thank my husband, Rick, for his unflagging support, and our darling daughter, Marion, for being a pressure-relieving distraction.

Last, I would like to thank Mimi Swartz, whose desire to tell the full story of Enron showed the delights of working there along with the now-infamous darker side of the company. Mimi has the rare ability to distill complex financial and accounting concepts into comprehensible, entertaining prose, and her witty insights on politics and society have helped to paint the Enron story onto the broader landscape of our times.

—Sherron Watkins

Index

389

ABOUT THE AUTHORS

MIMI SWARTZ is an executive editor at *Texas Monthly* and won a National Magazine Award in the public interest category in 1996. She has been a staff writer for *The New Yorker* and *Talk,* and has written for the *New York Times, Vanity Fair,* and *Esquire.* She lives in Houston with her husband and son.

SHERRON WATKINS is a former Arthur Andersen accountant who joined Enron in 1993, working for the man who later became CFO, Andy Fastow. She worked in Enron's finance group, its International company, and its Broadband division, before returning to work for Fastow as a vice president in corporate development. As as result of her memos to Ken Lay urging the company to change its accounting practices and restate its earnings, she has become known to the world as the Enron whistleblower. She testified before both the House and the Senate in hearings investigating Enron's business practices in February 2002, and was named along with two others as one of *Time* magazine's 2002 Persons of the Year.